海外道教典籍英文翻译方法论研究

何立芳　李丝贝　廖敏◎著

OVERSEAS ENGLISH TRANSLATIONS OF
DAOIST CLASSICS：
A METHODOLOGICAL STUDY

中国社会科学出版社

图书在版编目（CIP）数据

海外道教典籍英文翻译方法论研究 / 何立芳，李丝贝，廖敏著 . —北京：中国社会科学出版社，2024.3

ISBN 978-7-5227-2976-3

Ⅰ.①海…　Ⅱ.①何…②李…③廖…　Ⅲ.①道教—古籍—英文—翻译—方法论—研究　Ⅳ.①B95

中国国家版本馆 CIP 数据核字（2024）第 016890 号

出 版 人	赵剑英
策划编辑	周　佳
责任编辑	黄　丹
责任校对	胡新芳
责任印制	王　超

出　　版	中国社会科学出版社
社　　址	北京鼓楼西大街甲 158 号
邮　　编	100720
网　　址	http://www.csspw.cn
发 行 部	010-84083685
门 市 部	010-84029450
经　　销	新华书店及其他书店
印　　刷	北京明恒达印务有限公司
装　　订	廊坊市广阳区广增装订厂
版　　次	2024 年 3 月第 1 版
印　　次	2024 年 3 月第 1 次印刷
开　　本	710×1000　1/16
印　　张	22.5
插　　页	2
字　　数	358 千字
定　　价	118.00 元

凡购买中国社会科学出版社图书，如有质量问题请与本社营销中心联系调换
电话：010-84083683
版权所有　侵权必究

前　　言

本书是我完成的国家哲学社会科学基金西部项目"海外道教典籍翻译研究"（项目批准号：15XZJ012；结题证书号：20210350）的最终成果，是基于之前完成的教育部人文社会科学规划基金项目"道教术语英译研究"（项目批准号：10XJA730002；结题证书号：2014JXZ2772）的延伸性研究。这是首次系统性考察海外道教典籍的英文翻译问题，力图全面梳理海外道教典籍英文翻译中所涉及的问题，既有对普遍性方法论的探讨，也有针对具体译本的个案研究，对于认识海外道教典籍翻译的基本情况及其采用的方法策略具有重要的理论意义和实践价值。

围绕"海外道教典籍英文翻译方法论研究"这一主题，本书从经验总结到实践操作，从宏观解读到微观解析，对部分海外道教典籍英文翻译文本进行了评析与研究。在宏观层面上，基于道教典籍语言中类比思维这一典型特征的分析，重点阐述了道教典籍海外译介中的中国英语模式和民族中心主义倾向这两个突出问题，提炼了部分译者在译作序跋或具体译作中涉及的翻译原则与思考，以探讨道教典籍独特的英译机制；在微观层面上，将海外道教典籍英译成果分哲学、善书、戒律、仙传、炼养、综合六个专题进行归类解析，力图系统呈现海外道教学研究情况。

除了对海外道教典籍英文翻译的共性问题进行探讨，本书还深入考察了海外学者的道教典籍英译文本中对道教基本概念与主要思想的翻译及其相关问题。不仅积累了许多有价值的翻译文献材料，还为进一步把握海外道教典籍翻译的各种问题提供了良好的文本分析，其中涉及翻译问题的解析也为当今学界如何进行中国文化文学典籍的对外传播提供颇有价值的视角和方法。此外，本书在归纳总结他国学者英译道教典籍成败得失基础之上的道教典籍翻译实践是对道教文化如何进行跨文明传播的主动尝试，在当今推进中华优秀传统文化传承发展，实施中国文化"走出去"战略时代背景下，可为中国文化"走出去"提供有益的历史经验和现实参考。

道教文化是中国文化最早"走出去"的重要内容之一，对西方文明文化产生过重要影响。随着中国国际地位的日益提升，在中国文化"走出去"的当今时代，道教文化更是中国文化国际传播的应有之义，既是为中国和平发展创造良好外部环境、增强中国文化软实力的需要，也是实现中华民族伟大复兴中国梦的需要。本书将海外道教典籍翻译问题放在整个中外文化交流体系中加以系统梳理和理论分析，并揭示出一系列的方法论特性和规律，分析其中存在的普遍问题和不足，为人们更好地把握其中的规律，更好地传播道教文化和中国传统文化，更好地吸收外来文化，具有重要的方法论价值和思想文化价值，对于当今全球化（甚或包括逆全球化）中不同文化文明之间的交流、沟通、互鉴、互赏具有现实意义。对海外道教典籍英文翻译的研究，有助于中华文明海外传播，有助于中国故事、中国声音的海外讲述。从学术价值层面来看，本书除了可为国内道教学和中华传统宗教文化的研究提供一些借鉴，还可为国内学者从事道教典籍乃至中国传统宗教文化典籍的海外译介研究提供方法论上的启迪，对丰富和深化国内道教学、语言学和文化传播学研究均有促进作用。

项目研究开展五年之久，得到了全国哲学社会科学工作办公室的基金资助，得到了电子科技大学科学技术发展研究院、外国语学院领导和老师的关心和帮助，得到了学界前辈和朋友的大力支持，在此一并致谢。感谢我的导师潘显一先生，回想当年从四川大学道教与宗教文化研究所博士毕业之际，恩师曾教导我要利用自己的外语学科背景为我国道教学术文化的拓展做出自己的贡献，感恩老师的谆谆教诲让我步入了海外道教典籍翻译研究的殿堂；感谢四川大学道教与宗教文化研究所的张泽洪教授，感恩老师的传道解惑让我对本书涉及的一些道教思想的理解更为深入；感谢成都工业学院的李丝贝老师、电子科技大学的廖敏副教授在本书第二至第七章译文解析中所做的细致工作；感谢伦敦大学学院（UCL）学者大讲台项目访问学者陈先乐先生、电子科技大学特聘专家李慧辉博士在《畅玄》《微旨》两篇内容译文的修订完善阶段所提供的鼎力协助。本书得以完成还要感谢参考文献部分所列出的各位专家学者，得益于互联网时代的便利，我才得以获取许多海外学者研究翻译道教典籍作品的 PDF 版本，保障了所有研究对象均为第一手资料，感谢专家学者们为本研究所提供的灵感与启示。

  需要指出的是，尽管我努力从语言学、宗教学、文化传播学角度对海外道教典籍英译文本展开系统性研究，但受限于学力，书中的疏漏、不足和错误之处在所难免，敬请专家学者不吝指正。

何立芳

2024 年 2 月 26 日

目 录

绪 论 ·· (1)
    一 道教典籍海外译介概述 ·· (2)
    二 海外道教典籍英文翻译方法论研究的思路、价值与创新 ··· (6)

第一章 海外道教典籍英文翻译方法论 ······························· (12)
  第一节 道教典籍中的类比思维与翻译 ································ (12)
    一 道教典籍语言特征解析 ·· (13)
    二 道教典籍海外译介中的隐喻认知与中国英语模式 ········· (15)
  第二节 道教典籍海外译介中的民族中心主义 ···················· (18)
    一 道之本体"玄""道""一"的内涵与变异 ················· (19)
    二 道教"玄""道""一"与基督教"上帝"的文化等同 ··· (20)
  第三节 道教典籍海外译介中的译学思考 ···························· (23)
    一 马绛团队的翻译五原则 ·· (24)
    二 柏夷的翻译思考 ·· (26)

第二章 道教哲学文本翻译研究 ··· (32)
  引 语 ·· (32)
  第一节 《道德经》的英文翻译研究 ···································· (34)
    一 《道德经》在海外的译介简况 ·································· (34)
    二 安乐哲、郝大伟《道德经》译本特色 ······················· (37)
    三 安乐哲、郝大伟《道德经·第一章》译文解析 ········· (39)
  第二节 《庄子》的英文翻译研究 ·· (44)
    一 《庄子》在海外的译介简况 ······································ (45)

二　梅维恒《庄子》英译原则及译本主要特色 …………………（48）
　　三　梅维恒《庄子·知北游》译文解析 ……………………………（50）
　小　结 ……………………………………………………………………（59）

第三章　道教善书文本翻译研究 ……………………………………（61）
　引　语 ……………………………………………………………………（61）
　第一节　《太上感应篇》英文翻译研究 ………………………………（63）
　　一　《太上感应篇》的海外传播 …………………………………（63）
　　二　理雅各《太上感应篇》译本特色 ……………………………（65）
　　三　理雅各《太上感应篇》译文解析 ……………………………（66）
　第二节　《文昌帝君阴骘文》英文翻译研究 …………………………（90）
　　一　《文昌帝君阴骘文》的海外传播 ……………………………（91）
　　二　铃木大拙、凯拉斯《文昌帝君阴骘文》译本特色 …………（91）
　　三　铃木大拙、凯拉斯《文昌帝君阴骘文》译文解析 …………（93）
　小　结 …………………………………………………………………（105）

第四章　道教戒律文本翻译研究 ……………………………………（106）
　引　语 …………………………………………………………………（106）
　第一节　《赤松子中诫经》英文翻译研究 ……………………………（109）
　　一　孔丽维对道教戒律的认知和解读 …………………………（110）
　　二　孔丽维《赤松子中诫经》译本的篇章结构特点 …………（113）
　　三　孔丽维《赤松子中诫经》译文（节选）解析 ………………（114）
　第二节　《洞玄灵宝天尊说十戒经》英文翻译研究 …………………（125）
　　一　《洞玄灵宝天尊说十戒经》在海外的传播 …………………（126）
　　二　孔丽维《洞玄灵宝天尊说十戒经》译文解析 ………………（126）
　小　结 …………………………………………………………………（133）

第五章　道教仙传文本翻译研究 ……………………………………（135）
　引　语 …………………………………………………………………（135）
　第一节　康儒博《与天地同寿：葛洪〈神仙传〉翻译与
　　　　　研究》简介 ………………………………………………（138）

第二节　《神仙传·老子》英语翻译研究 …………………………（139）
　　一　康儒博《神仙传·老子》译文底本的说明 ……………………（141）
　　二　康儒博《神仙传·老子》译文解析 ……………………………（141）
第三节　《神仙传·张道陵》英文翻译研究 ……………………（168）
　　一　康儒博《神仙传·张道陵》译文底本的说明 …………………（169）
　　二　康儒博《神仙传·张道陵》译文解析 …………………………（170）
小　结 …………………………………………………………………（185）

第六章　道教炼养文本翻译研究 ……………………………（187）
引　语 …………………………………………………………………（187）
第一节　《周易参同契》英文翻译研究 …………………………（189）
　　一　《周易参同契》在海外的传播 ……………………………………（190）
　　二　玄英《周易参同契》译本特色 ……………………………………（192）
　　三　玄英《周易参同契·太阳流珠章》译文解析 …………………（194）
　　四　玄英《周易参同契·关关雎鸠章》译文解析 …………………（202）
第二节　《悟真篇》英文翻译研究 ………………………………（210）
　　一　《悟真篇》在海外的传播 …………………………………………（211）
　　二　玄英《悟真篇》译本特色 …………………………………………（213）
　　三　玄英《天仙金丹·五行情性第三》译文解析 …………………（214）
小　结 …………………………………………………………………（219）

第七章　道教综合类文本《抱朴子内篇》翻译研究 ………（223）
引　语 …………………………………………………………………（223）
第一节　《抱朴子内篇》在海外的传播与反响 …………………（224）
　　一　《抱朴子内篇》在海外的传播简况 ………………………………（224）
　　二　魏鲁男《抱朴子内篇》英译本在海外的接受与反响 …………（226）
第二节　基于魏鲁男《抱朴子内篇》英译本的翻译批评 ………（228）
　　一　魏鲁男《抱朴子内篇·畅玄》译文解析 ………………………（229）
　　二　魏鲁男《抱朴子内篇·微旨》译文解析 ………………………（258）
小　结 …………………………………………………………………（311）

结　语 …………………………………………………………（314）

参考文献 ………………………………………………………（319）

附录Ⅰ　《抱朴子内篇·畅玄》新译………………………（329）

附录Ⅱ　《抱朴子内篇·微旨》新译………………………（335）

绪　　论

　　道教是土生土长的中国传统宗教，关注人类生存、生活、生命的基本法则，浸透着中华文化的基因，其独特的思想和范畴体系，有关人与自然、人与人、人与社会的关系理论，不仅是中国传统文化贡献于世界的精神财富，也是当今世界所需要的文化资源。早在18世纪海外学界便开启了借助翻译道教典籍研究中国道教的学术活动。针对海外道教研究普遍重视翻译，不断推出道教典籍新译本这种现象，朱越利教授在其专著《理论·视角·方法——海外道教学研究》一书的前言中谈到要向海外道教学的方法论学习，指出：作为海外道教学研究，还有一个中国道教学者如何对待外国道教学者将中文古籍和研究成果翻译成外文的问题，特别是如何对待道经的外文译本问题（朱越利，2012：72）。研究外国学者的道教典籍译本是海外道教学研究的一项重要内容，这是因为"通过外国道教学者的译本，不仅可以看出译者的文字能力和道教学水平，看出该国道教学的进展，而且可以看出该国文化语境的微妙变化"（朱越利，2012：73）。很显然，研究海外学者的道教典籍译本有助于国人了解他们的研究立场，从而反省自己的缺失。此外，研究这些译本还有助于我们了解他们的翻译策略，从而反观国内学者从事典籍翻译所遇到的困境，以寻求有效的解决途径和方法。

　　相对于其他学科领域的译介研究而言，我国道教典籍的翻译研究尚处于起步阶段，还需研究者们做好以下两个方面的深入探讨：（1）对海外道教典籍翻译的借鉴性研究；（2）对从事道教典籍翻译实践新问题的探索性研究。只有深入研究好这两方面的内容，并将其有效结合起来，才有可能逐渐把经验和技巧升华为具有科学性的道教典籍翻译机制。作为国家社科基金西部项目"海外道教典籍翻译研究"的最终研究成果，本书关注的内容正是外国学者对中国道教典籍的翻译研究，重点关注其中的道教典籍英译成果，研究海外道教学者对道经的理解和翻译，归纳海外道教文化研究范式，以总结国内学者从中可获取的从事道教典籍翻译的启示。希望在借鉴他国学者译介道教典籍的成功经验基础之上的道教典籍的对外翻译实践能更好地服务于道教文化的国际交流，借此思考中国传统文化（道教范畴）如何进行跨文明传播，为中国文化走向世界助一臂之力。

一 道教典籍海外译介概述

作为中国传统文化构架中的重要组成部分，道教文化不仅契合于国人的日常生活，渗透于中国文学艺术，同时也随着东学西渐影响着西方世界。对中国道教进行学术研究一直都是海外汉学（Sinology）研究的一个重要分支，对道教经典的解读和翻译也一直是汉学家们研究了解中国传统文化的主要途径。

法国早在18世纪末就成立了法兰西学院、东方语言文化学院等一批汉学和教学科研机构（朱越利，2012：60）。法国学者对中国道教典籍的翻译研究最早可以追溯到19世纪汉学家雷慕沙（Jean-Pierre Abel-Remusat，1788—1832年）1816年出版的《太上感应篇译注》，在他1823年出版的《论老子的生平及其作品》一书中载有《道德经》四章内容（第一、二十五、四十一、四十二章）的法文译本。在雷慕沙担任法兰西学院汉学讲座首任讲席期间，他的一名德国学生尤利乌斯·海因里希·克拉普洛特（Julius Heinrich Klaproth，1783—1835年）于1828年出版了《太上感应篇》的法译本（*Chrestomathie mandchou ou recueil de textes mandchou*）。据此，上海社会科学院陈耀庭研究员认为，可以说克拉普鲁斯（克拉普洛特的另一种音译）是德国汉学家中研究道教的第一人（陈耀庭，2000：201）。但依据武汉大学张思齐教授的研究，早在1682年，德国医生安德烈·克雷耶（Andreas Cleyer）就曾把中国的《脉诀》（又称《崔真人脉诀》）一书翻译成拉丁文呈现给欧洲读者，是目前所知德国道教学的最初起源（张思齐，2007：87）。

英国不仅产生了几位西方道教学界的大师级人物，且有着道教学研究和道教典籍翻译的辉煌成果，在世界处于领先地位。如果把英国道教学分为成长时期（19世纪及其以前的整个时期）、成立时期（或称初创时期，指20世纪前半段）、当代及当前三个阶段进行研究，再把视角定位于道教典籍的翻译，其成长时期的主要成绩是"准备道教研究所需要的基本典籍之英文文本"（张思齐，2010a：205）。英国传教士湛约翰（John Chalmers，1825—1899年）1868年在伦敦出版的《对老子思辨哲学、国家说、道德论的考察》(*The Speculations on Metaphysics, Polity and Morality of the Old Philosopher, Lao-Tsze*)一书是一部融翻译、串讲和必要的历史背景介绍为一体的介绍道家学说的较早的专著，开启了英语世界《道德经》英译研究的历史。在此之后，来华经商的巴尔福（Frederic Henry Balfour，1846—1909年）1879—1881年在《中国评论》第8、第9、第10卷发表了译著《太上感应篇》《清静经》《阴符经》等。作为单行本在伦敦和上海出版的有《南华真经》（1881年）和《道教经典》（1884年）。此外，1889年伦敦出版的《世界的宗教体系》(*Religions Systems of the World*)一书中，收录了他写的《道教》一文（张思齐，2010b：27）。紧接其后，世界大师级人物汉学家理雅各（James Legge，1815—1897年）陆续推出一系列道教经典的英文翻译文本，收录在《东方圣书》(*The Sacred Books of the East*)第39、第40卷，具体有《道德经》(*The Tâo Teh King of Lâo Dze*)、《庄子》(*The Writings of Kwang-dze*)、《太上感应篇》(*The Thâi-shang Tractate of Actions and Their Retributions*)、《清静经》(*Classic of Purity*)、《阴符经》(*Classic of the Harmony of the Seen and Unseen*)、《玉枢经》(*Classic of the Pivot of Jade*)、《日用经》(*Classic of the Directory for the Day*)等。

　　成立时期的英国道教学的主要成绩是"基本的道经的英语文本大体齐备，并且开始对世界各国产生影响"（张思齐，2010b：26）。翟理斯（Herbert Allen Giles，1845—1935年）是这一阶段英国道教学领域的另一位世界大师级人物。作为一名具有重大国际影响的英国汉学家，翟理斯的学术贡献多体现在道教文学的翻译研究方面。比如，他选译了蒲松龄的《聊斋志异》(*Strange Stories from a Chinese Studio*)，并在研究仙话的基础上撰写了《中国仙话》(*Chinese Fairy Tales*)一书，率先向海外读者介绍道教神仙的故事；在评判前人（湛约翰、巴尔福、理雅各等）翻译的《道德经》和《庄子》的基础上推出自己的新译本，书名分别为《老子遗存》（The Remains of Lao Tzu）和《庄子：玄学家、道德家和社会改革家》（Chuang Tzu: Mystic, Moralist, and Social Reformer）。在这两部道教研究论著中翟理斯借用中国的传统评点法，糅合译文，将中国哲学的神秘魅力和智慧传播给了西方民众，向西方读者译介了《老子》《庄子》的哲学思想。尽管翟理斯关于道教的著述不是很多，但鉴于他在汉学界的影响力以及他在翻译道教文学方面的突出成果，翟理斯被视为英国道教学成立期可与理雅各齐名的汉学家。

相较而言，美国汉学研究起步比欧洲晚，道教研究也不如欧洲。1848 年汉学家卫三畏（Samuel Wells Williams，1812—1884 年）著《中国总论》（The Middle Kingdom）只是开启了美国的汉学研究，道教研究在美国取得稳步发展应是在第二次世界大战以后。美国道教研究专家孔丽维（Livia Kohn）曾撰文探讨北美道教研究趋势，用了较大的篇幅介绍美国道教学者及其研究成果。在她看来，美国第一批道教学者活跃在 20 世纪 80 年代。虽然他们没有经过道教专门的训练，但是他们本身的研究领域属于汉学。他们越来越意识到，为了更好地完成自己的研究必须涉猎道教文献。因此，他们研究道经，并深受裨益（朱越利，2013：196）。这批学者往往依据各自的研究领域选择不同的道教文献进行研究。孔丽维在该研究成果专门提到美国道教学者对道经的翻译，她认为，具有文学背景又从事道教研究的学者总体上倾向于对重要的著作进行翻译。他们往往关注文本分析。在内容方面，他们喜欢研究各种不同的宗教习俗，并对神话的主题和神仙感兴趣。他们运用的研究方法是带有浓厚的宗教研究意味的文献学（朱越利，2013：202）。除了道教学者，孔丽维还列举了三位专门从事中国文言经典翻译的美国学者：华兹生（Burton Watson，1925—2017 年），克利里（Thomas Cleary），王艺文（Eva Wong）。在她看来，华兹生将大量的历史、文学、诗歌、宗教的著作翻译成了优美、平易的英文，由他翻译的道教经典《庄子》（1968 年）非常出色，一直是这个领域的典范（朱越利，2013：211）。克利里主要完成了以下典籍的翻译：《易经》（The Taoist I Ching），《悟真篇》（Understanding Reality: A Taoist Alchemical Classic by Chang Po-tuan），《仙姑 女真 坤道 女丹》（Immortal Sisters: Secrets of Taoist Women），《太一金华宗旨》（The Secret of the Golden Flower: The Classic Chinese Book of Life），等等。孔丽维对克利里道教典籍翻译的整体评价，"倾向于遵照字面意思进行翻译，阅读他的译作需要背景知识，或需要深入研究，但它们大受欢迎，塑造越来越多的美国人对道教的印象"（朱越利，2013：211）。王艺文主要翻译了《道教七真》（Seven Taoist Masters: A Folk Novel of China）、《清静经》（Cultivating Stillness: A Taoist Manual for Transforming Body and Mind）、《道学大观》（Taoism: an Essential Guide）、《列子》（Lieh-Tzu: A Taoist Guide to Practical Living）、《太上感应篇》（Lao-Tzu's Treatise on the Response of the Tao: T'ai-shang Kan-ying P'ien）、《慧命经》（Cultivatng the Energy of Life: A Translation of the Hui-ming Ching and its Commentaries）等典籍作品。据孔丽维介绍，"她的翻译对象往往侧重于与全真道的修行者有关的、历史上较为晚近的文本。她的翻译往往受大家欢迎，并且包含了一定程度的自由创作"（朱越利，2013：212）。

无论过去还是现在，道家道教典籍都是西方汉学界译介中国典籍的重要内容。尤其是1923—1925年我国整理出版道教典籍《正统道藏》和《续道藏》之后，西方译者翻译的兴趣逐渐增大，道家道教经文典籍的西文研究与翻译越来越多，似有"道教在中国，道教翻译研究在国外"之势。海外学者通常融翻译与研究为一体，在理解和翻译道教典籍的基础上进行他们的道教学研究。例如，2002年美国印第安纳大学学者康儒博（Robert Ford Company）出版他译注与研究葛洪《神仙传》的成果《与天地同寿：葛洪〈神仙传〉翻译与研究》（To Live as Long as Heaven and Earth: A Translation and Study of Ge Hong's Traditions of Divine Transcendents），该书提供了他翻译的《神仙传》译本。前文提到的美国道教学者孔丽维译介的道教典籍也很丰硕，在她2004年出版的《宇宙与社区：道教的伦理维度》（Cosmos and Community: The Ethical Dimension of Daoism）附有11篇涉及道教戒律的英译文本，其2010年的译著《坐忘：道教存思之要》（Sitting in Oblivion: The Heart of Daoist Meditation）包含了《坐忘论》《坐忘碑文》《定观经》《存神炼气铭》《内观经》等八部道经的翻译，此外还翻译了《墉城集仙录》《西升经》《奉道科戒》等。以研究内外丹为特长的意大利汉学家玄英（Fabrizio Pregadio）2006年出版了《上清：中世纪初期中国的道教和炼丹术》（Great Clarity: Daoism and Alchemy in Early Medieval China），里面有他翻译的三部上清派丹经（《九转流珠神仙九丹经》（"Scripture of the Nine Elixirs"）、《太清金液神丹经》（"Scripture of the Golden Liquor"）和《太极真人九转还丹经要诀》（"Scripture of the Reverted Elixirs in Nine Cycles of the Perfected of the Great Ultimate"）的英译文本。此外，他还研究翻译了道教丹道学经典《周易参同契》（*The Seal of the Unity of the Three*）、《悟真篇》（*Awakening to Reality：The Regulated Verses of Wuzhen Pian, A Taoist Classic of Internal Alchemy*）、《入药镜》（*Mirror for Compounding the Medicine*）、《金丹四百字》（*Four Hundred Words on the Golden Elixir*）、《黄帝阴符经》（*The Book of the Hidden Agreement*）、《重阳立教十五论》（*Fifteen Essays to Establish the Teaching*）等多达16部道教丹道经典作品，当代道教学者王沐（1908—1992年）谈及《悟真篇》渊源、丹法要旨和全文校注的学术论文集《悟真篇浅解》（*Foundations of Internal Alchemy*）也在他的翻译之列。这些道教炼丹文献的翻译作品均为译研结合体，译者的主流方法乃西方译者广为采用的深度语境化翻译策略，借助学术型导言、阐释性注解、批判性评论等，力图重构源文本产生的历史语境，最终指向源文本文化价值和文化事实的忠实传译。总体来讲，海外学者对道教进行学术研究逐渐形成为一门学科，其研究成果和翻译几乎涵盖了道教文化的方方面面，在一定程度上与国内的道教学术研究形成互补态势。

当今国际汉学可大致分为三大板块：俄罗斯汉学、西方汉学和东方汉字文化圈汉学（阎国栋，2005）。前文简略提到的内容仅为西方汉学板块部分国家的道教研究与翻译的简况，其他涉及道教研究且有显著性成果的国家还有加拿大、澳大利亚、荷兰、俄罗斯、日本、韩国等，虽然这些国家开展道教研究的历史长短不一，但都取得了较为丰硕的研究成果，其中也不乏许多道教经典的译注成果，在此不一一赘述。

二 海外道教典籍英文翻译方法论研究的思路、价值与创新

海外学者研究中国道教必须基于对道教文献的研究，需借助道教文献的翻译，因此，正确理解道教文献，努力减少对原作的误解是每位研究者首先要考虑的问题。道教文献的翻译文本是海外学者从事道教学研究的敲门砖，在海外道教学研究中扮演着非常重要的角色。中国社会科学院陈开科研究员曾谈到研究海外道教典籍译本的重要性，他认为，"在

汉学领域，译作一样重要。因为作为外国人研究中国的学问，首先存在的还是一个语言学问题，也即是否能准确理解原作的问题。倘若其翻译作品词不达意，那么势必存在对原作的误解。而建立在这种误解性学术基础上的所谓研究也就靠不住。……判断汉学家的翻译功夫是否扎实，对判断他们汉学研究水准的高低有重要作用"（陈开科，2007：48—49）。因此，对这些文本展开语言层面的研究不仅有助于深层次了解海外学者的道教学研究成果，也有利于拓展翻译学研究领域。本书对海外学者翻译的道教典籍作品展开翻译批评，"就语言转换后的译品与原作在思想、形象、风格、手法诸方面的差距大小以及造成差距的原因加以探讨，……翻译批评的指归在研究译品、褒优斥劣、探讨译法"（王克非，1994：34），针对具体的译作或与译作有关的某种翻译现象发表评论，借分析某种翻译现象来说明某个翻译方法的问题，目的指向提炼出可供借鉴的道教典籍翻译方法。

（一）研究内容与思路

海外道教学者有着天然的语言优势，能将"字字珠玑，语义繁复"的道教典籍翻译成流畅的外文，这值得我们赞赏，但由于语言认知、文化身份等原因，他们对道教典籍所蕴含的文化思想的把握必定存在不够准确或不够完善之处，仍需要国内学者本着求真务实的学习态度，对这些道教典籍翻译文本展开科学理性的翻译批评，对其中存在的"问题翻译"正本清源，切实有效地推进道教典籍的海外传播。

基于上述研究思路，本书围绕海外学者"融翻译与研究为一体"这一显著特点，分经验总结和实践操作两大主体进行海外道教典籍英文翻译的方法论研究，既有对海外已有道教典籍英文翻译文本的批评解析，也有对从事道教典籍英文翻译实践新问题的探索性研究。除绪论和结语之外，本书共计七章内容。

第一章从宏观层面对海外道教典籍英文翻译方法论展开研究。该部分探讨了道教典籍中的类比思维与翻译问题，分析了海外道教典籍英文翻译中的两种突出现象：中国英语模式和民族中心主义倾向，还在整理当代美国汉学家马绛（John S. Major）和柏夷（Stephen R. Bokenkamp）在译作序跋中所谈到的翻译原则与思考的基础上归纳总结了道教典籍独特的英译机制。

第二至第七章从微观层面探讨海外学者译介道教典籍的具体方法。该部分节选了一些代表性英译文本展开翻译批评，分哲学、善书、戒律、仙传、炼养、综合类六个专题，从语言学、文化传播学角度进行翻译个案研究。分析所选译本的成败得失，对其中的"问题翻译"进行正本清源，旨在归纳海外道教文化研究范式，以总结国内学者从中可获取的从事道教典籍英译的启示和可资借鉴之处。鉴于道教典籍皆为古文创作，且有较多的道教术语，每章均包含原作导读内容，包括背景介绍、解析对象基本信息、文字注译、术语解读或典故阐释等，旨在帮助读者较好地理解原文文意。各章对道教典籍分类文本在海外的译介概述以及对作为解析对象的译本特色简介可有效帮助读者了解海外学者研究道教文化时对选题的取舍和价值的诉求，深入理解他们解读异质文化的路径方法以及译本存在的误读与误解背后的原因。对具体译本内容进行解析时，或是以句为单位解析英文用词和句子的特点以及翻译依据，或是以段落为单位对文本进行鉴赏，兼评其译笔特点和译文得失，顺便指出或纠正个别漏译误译之处。如有必要，还对一些词句提供现代汉语翻译，以对照英译内容，说明它们之间的差异。针对同一部道教经典有不同译本的情况，本书在选取一种译本进行重点解析的同时，还会涉及与其他译本的对比研究。此外，作为副文本的译注和译评皆为道教译本的有机组成内容，因此译作解析部分也涉及该部分内容的鉴赏。

中共中央办公厅、国务院办公厅2017年1月印发了《关于实施中华优秀传统文化传承发展工程的意见》，明确了实施中华优秀传统文化传承发展工程的总体目标、基本原则、主要内容、重点任务、组织实施和保障措施。推动中外文化交流互鉴为该工程七项重点任务之一，其基本原则是：以我为主、为我所用，取长补短、择善而从，既不简单拿来，也不盲目排外，吸收借鉴国外优秀文明成果，积极参与世界文化的对话交流，不断丰富和发展中华文化。本书第七章为道教综合类文本《抱朴子内篇》的翻译研究，选取的解析对象为美国学者魏鲁男英译文本中的《畅玄》《微旨》两篇。魏鲁男译本是这部作品在海外的首部全译本，为海外道教学者的研究提供了极大的便利，但因译者缺乏典籍英译者应有的文化自觉意识，导致译本缺失必要的注释内容，使得该译本成为西方学界诟病的焦点。因此，为响应中共中央办公厅、国务院办公厅《关于实施中华优秀传统文化传承发展工程的意见》的号召，笔者在解析魏译本的合理翻译和问题翻译的同时，有时会附上自己的新译，并在综合考察其他译者的相关译文基础之上尝试了这两篇内容的完整新译，借以探讨道教典籍的翻译机制，助推中华优秀传统文化的国际传播。完整的新译内容置于书后附录部分，抛砖引玉，供感兴趣的读者对照阅读。

（二）研究特色与价值

本书首次对海外道教典籍英文翻译文本进行语言学层面的系统研究，分析西方研究者对选题的取舍、价值的诉求以及中西道教学研究的互动与借鉴，借此分析海外学者翻译道教典籍的成败得失，在此基础上尝试道教典籍《抱朴子内篇》部分章节的英语翻译。这种"文化搭台、翻译唱戏"的模式，始终将道教典籍的翻译问题纳入中西文化和两种语言的对比和兼容的范式之中，可为同类研究提供有益参考，具有前瞻性意义。其突出特色体现在两个方面。

（1）专题归类，系统展示海外道教学研究成果。本书分哲学、善书、戒律、炼养、仙传、综合类六个专题对海外道教典籍英文翻译成果进行归类解析，较全面地反映海外学者对中国道教学的研究成果。

（2）经验借鉴，有理有据地探索道教文化译介的方法策略。本书提炼了海外汉学家在序言、导论、跋语中呈现出的翻译思考或在具体的翻译文本批评解析中解读译者遵循的翻译原则，这种理据性探讨是对以古汉语为载体的道教典籍英译方法策略的探讨，对构建科学合理的道教典籍翻译机制提供良好的素材。

由于历史原因和学科限制，翻译道教典籍的几乎都是海外学者。相对而言，国内学者这方面的工作非常欠缺，无论是将道教典籍翻译为他国文字，向国外介绍中国这一传统文化，还是将海外道教学研究成果翻译为中文，以深化国内道教学研究，或是对比研究海外道教典籍翻译的不同译本，这些领域都有很大的努力空间。基于这样的背景，本书的学术价值和应用价值体现在三个方面。

（1）深化国内道教学研究。对海外学者道教典籍翻译成果的研究，有助于国人了解他们的研究立场，从而反省自己的缺失，可帮助中国学者打开更开阔的视角。

（2）丰富典籍翻译研究体系。本书提炼了海外汉学家在序言、导论、跋语中呈现出的翻译思考或在译文行文中遵循的翻译原则，这种理据性探讨为构建道教典籍英文翻译机制提供丰富的实证理据，能深化典籍翻译理论体系建设。

（3）译评结合，以评促译。对海外道教典籍英译文本进行翻译批评，了解中国道教文化因海外学者误读误译在异域所遭受的损失，从而为真实有效"讲好中国故事"提供实证支撑。借鉴他国学者译介道教典籍的成功经验基础之上的道教典籍的对外翻译实践开启了中国人自己翻译道教典籍的新模式，其中应用的翻译技巧可供国内同行借鉴学习。

在全球化加速的当今世界，不同文化之间的相互影响和渗透日益加剧，研究道教的全球化传播轨迹和规矩，对于中国大国地位的体现和中国文化的传播具有现实意义。为此，本书的社会影响和效益主要体现在三个方面。

（1）道教是中国文化的重要组成部分，道教典籍中包含许多中华文化的精髓，如，隐含在教义文本中的中国古人关注现实、积极的参与意识，把遵循基本道德规范当作修道成仙的首要步骤的修行思想等，这些皆为人类社会关注的共同话题，深入探究中国文化基因的传播轨迹和方式，对弘扬中华文明与文化，对青年一代的教育，以及民族自豪感的提升具有现实意义。

（2）研究道教在国外的传播和影响，从道教文化语言层面充实中国文化"走出去"的研究内容，是揭示中国文化全球传播的案例与缩影，对中国走向世界有探索价值。

（3）基于经验总结的道教典籍英文翻译实践，开展中国传统文化（道教范畴）的跨文明传播，能更好地服务于道教文化的国际交流，能较好地促进中国文化国际影响力的提升，顺应时代要求，为中国文化走向世界助一臂之力。

主动参与世界文化的对话交流，吸收借鉴海外道教研究优秀成果和积极推动中国道教文化的对外译介需齐头并进。为推动海外道教学研究，海内外一批道教学者组成《道教学译丛》编委会，希望能逐步地将百年来海外道教学的所有优秀成果都翻译成中文出版，近几年已陆续出版了一些译作，在一定程度上帮助了国内道教学者拓宽研究视角。虽然专门针对海外道教典籍翻译成果的系统性研究相对欠缺，主动将道教典籍翻译成外语也只是初步尝试，但这一研究无疑是对"推进中华优秀传统文化传承发展，实施中国文化'走出去'战略"的积极响应。

第 一 章

海外道教典籍英文翻译方法论

贴切的翻译不仅仅是方法和技巧的灵活运用，更重要的是对两种文化表里虚实的透彻领悟和深入把握。翻译道教典籍的西方汉学家们通常会在其序言或导论中分析介绍原作及原作者的相关知识背景，进而说明自己翻译原作的目的、采取的翻译策略等问题。无论是采用直译、添加各种注释评论对道教典籍进行学术翻译，还是借用他者文化进行道教文化典籍的归化解读，都是译者的主观选择，关涉的是译者对待原作文化的态度问题。本章除了从道教典籍中的类比思维入手对这类典籍海外译介中的两种突出现象（中国英语模式和民族中心主义倾向）展开分析之外，还整理出当代美国汉学家马绛和柏夷在译作序跋中所谈到的翻译原则与思考，从宏观层面探讨道教典籍海外译介方法论的独特之处。这些源于道教典籍英文翻译的译者体验，是对道教典籍翻译规律性和规范性的认识，既可作为海外学者从事道教典籍英文翻译的理据探讨，亦可作为建构道教典籍翻译理论的基础性素材，指导当今中国学者从事道教典籍的翻译实践。

第一节 道教典籍中的类比思维与翻译[①]

道教文化的根本在于对"道"的信仰，"道"有天道、地道、人道，道门中人对其进行思维时，有着大量的相互类比推理，有时天道、地道推人道，有时人道推天道、地道（陈全新，2006：176）。作为人类理解和

---

① 本节主要内容发表在《外语学刊》2017 年第 4 期，第 99—103 页。

认识抽象事物的一种思维方式，类比思维在语言概念的形成和人类认知的过程中发挥了极其重要的功用。道教在神仙信仰、金丹学说、医药养生、占卜堪舆等方面都存在着显著的类比思维模式，道门中人通过比喻、象征、联想、类推等办法，把形象相似、情景相关、意义相通的事物进行类比，以此指称那些抽象深奥的意义，使之成为可以理喻的东西。道教典籍中那些记载追求长生成仙各种实践的内容皆非直抒其义，让人难以清楚其中的具体事物以及实际的操作步骤，隐语成为道教典籍最显著的语言特色，也构成了道教典籍翻译中的一大难题。充分了解道教语言的这些特征对道教典籍翻译至关重要，可以帮助我们更加有的放矢地克服理解上的偏差，降低翻译中的误读误解。

一 道教典籍语言特征解析

从最初的服食成仙到后来的内丹修炼，道教有关修道成仙的术语概念及其思想体系经历了从外丹到内丹的演化过程。道教前期通常通过化学手段以五金、八石为药物炼制长生不死仙丹，但是炼制的这些仙丹多含有剧毒，唐朝以后道教徒逐渐弃之不用，转为内丹修炼，即以人身体为炉鼎，精、气、神为药物，经过一定时间的修养锻炼，以神运炼精、气，达到三位一体，凝结成丹。内丹修炼主要是修炼者个人的身体变化以及随之而来的独特心理体验，这些基于修炼者身心体验的语言文字自然富含隐喻特征。这当然与道教内丹本身的神秘性有密切联系，为隐藏真诀，丹经用语故设迷障，让人如入云里雾里，不得其解。清傅金铨在《悟真四注》中说："丹经有微言，有显言，有正言，有疑似之言，有比喻之言，有影射之言，有旁敲侧击之言，有丹理，有口诀，似神龙隐现，出没不测，东露一鳞，西露一爪，所以读者必须细心寻求也"（王沐，2011：44）。单从语言认知角度来看，认知主体（内丹修炼者）的心理现象与实践行为都活跃在隐喻的使用过程中，他们以取象比类的思维方式记录修炼体验。这种运用带有感性、形象、直观的概念符号表达对象世界的抽象意义，通过类比、象征方式把握对象世界联系的思维方法，是丹经用语多为隐语的直接原因。

一方面，内丹修炼者通过相似联想把本来似乎无联系的事物相提并论，表达对丹道世界的认知，这种喻化思维造就大量隐喻现象。而另一方面，早期道家老庄哲学中以寓言、重言、卮言为叙事方式的中国化隐喻模式对后期形成的道教典籍隐喻表述也起到潜移默化的作用（何立芳、李丝贝，2017b：100）。庄子在《齐物论》中讲道："以指喻指之非指，不若以非指喻指之非指；以马喻马之非马，不若以非马喻马之非马也。天地一指也，万物一马也。"庄子在消解名实之争的同时，又把问题引向更为深入的言意之辨，"语之所贵者意也，意有所随。意有所随者，不可以言传也"（《庄子·天道》），明确提出言不尽意的观点，"可以言论者，物之粗也；可以致意者，物之精也。言之所不能论，意之所不能察致者，不期精粗焉"（《庄子·秋水》）。言以表意，意有言不能到者，这似乎也就框定语言的主要作用是作为意义的索隐工具而存在的。因此，庄子认为，"筌者所以在鱼，得鱼而忘筌；蹄者所以在兔，得兔而忘蹄；言者所以在意，得意而忘言"（《庄子·外物》）。如此推理，语言便是意义的"筌"或"蹄"了。庄子又提出"非言非默"的观点，"道物之极，言默不足以载；非言非默，议有所极"（《庄子·则阳》）。正是因为这种"非言非默"，对"道"的宣扬就只有通过"寓言十九，重言十七，卮言日出，和以天倪"（《庄子·寓言》）的寓言的隐喻言说方式来完成（王晓俊，2013：104—116）。

语言是人类认知对世界经验进行组织的产物，是人们在对现实世界进行"互动体验"和"认知加工"的基础上形成的（王寅，2013：52）。道教有关内丹修炼的撰述及其内丹术语概念的命名中大量隐喻的存在体现出语言的这一认知特质，《大丹直指》序言即是从人生命之形成来论述内炼成丹的原理。

> 盖人与天地秉受一同，始因父母二气相感，混合成珠，内藏一点元阳真气，外包精血，与母命蒂相连。母受胎之后，自觉有物，一呼一吸皆到彼处，与所受胎元之气相通。先生两肾，其余脏腑次第相生，至十月胎圆气足。未生之前，在母腹中双手掩其面，九窍未通，受母气滋养，混混沌沌，纯一不杂，是为先天之气。……一出母腹，双手自开，其气散于九窍，呼吸从口鼻出入，是为后天也（卿希泰，1996：73）。

人类具有相同的身体构造和感知器官，对相同的物质世界具备相同的感知、认知能力，这是能获得相似概念结构的基础，属于认知的共性。道教内丹以人身体为炉鼎，精、气、神为药物，以神运炼精、气，如此修养锻炼，达到三者复归为一，凝结成丹，称为"圣胎"，亦称"婴儿"。这是内丹家以母体结胎比喻神气凝结。内丹修炼以"凝神聚气"为要，以精神、心意之静定为基本原则，其中一条修炼要诀为"洗心涤虑，谓之沐浴"，即是将内丹修炼的静心调心比拟人体之沐浴，是修炼者在周天运转之中或之后休息时，让真气自然熏蒸全身，涤除身心污垢。炼内丹从筑基开始，真气循着任督二脉运转的整个过程都要以意念控制，内丹术语"黄婆"是媒婆、中介的隐语，这是因为黄为土色，中央为土，婆即媒婆，所以"黄婆"成为意念的别名。上述种种内丹隐喻便是内丹修炼者用以表述那些"只可意会不可言传"的修炼方法以及美妙体验的主要形式，体现出道教典籍语言显著的隐喻认知特质（何立芳、李丝贝，2017b：101）。

二 道教典籍海外译介中的隐喻认知与中国英语模式

认知语言学认为，语义是概念化的，是人们关于世界的经验和认知事物的反映，与人认识事物的方式和规律相吻合（赵艳芳，2001：12）。按照认知语言学的观点，隐喻表达的意义具有认知基础。作为我们认知世界过程中把感知转化成概念的重要手段，隐喻帮助我们通过具体的、客观的、真实的事物或物体去认知或解释虚幻的、主观的、抽象的事物或物体。认知语言学对隐喻的描写凸显出隐喻的认知性质。隐喻的基本功能是通过某一经历来理解另一经历，而"翻译过程是由有意识的综合性认知思维过程与无意识的经验性（习惯）翻译过程组合而成的"（仲伟合、朱琳，2015：72）。由此看来，翻译是一种隐喻化活动，具备隐喻的基本功能，翻译道教典籍语言中的大量隐喻表征自然要经历两次隐喻过程。

不同的文化有许多相同或类似的隐喻概念是因为人类拥有相同的生理机制和思维共性，人与人之间、人与自然之间交往有着类似经验。但由于不同民族之间的政治、历史、文化、习俗、经济和科技的发展存在不平行现象，因此也必然存在思维的差异性，自然也存在文化专有或蕴含特殊文化信息的词语。这类词语反映两种语言符号和两种文化的不对等，表现为源语词目与译语词目之间义值错位、部分对等或无等值物的对应关系，不仅是翻译界长期关注的"不可译"问题，也是双语词典释义中无法回避的一大难题（李开荣，2002：150）。道教内丹术语中出现的大量隐喻表述属于文化专有词目类型，这一类型的翻译很难做到既可以保留源语喻义又不舍弃其喻体。为使源语和目的语取得文化认知上的最大限度的对等，常用的办法是在音译或直译的基础上加注释，翻译界常把这样的译文归为中国英语（China English 或 Sino-English）。当代古籍英译大师级人物汪榕培教授认为，中国英语是英语国家使用的英语跟中国特有的文化相结合的产物，是一种客观存在（汪榕培，1991：4），常被用于翻译承载中华民族深厚文化底蕴的典籍作品。

海外学者翻译道教典籍遇到这类文化专属词目的时候，通常都是采用中国英语。如，道教修炼名词"坐忘"出自《庄子·大宗师》，庄子假借颜回与孔子的问答，提出"坐忘"的修道思想，颜回用类比手法解读了该道术的含义，具体为："堕肢体，黜聪明，离形去知，同于大通，此谓坐忘"。现摘录几位海外学者对该句的翻译。

（1）My connexion with the body and its parts is dissolved; my perceptive organs are discarded. Thus leaving my material form, and bidding farewell to my knowledge, I become one with the Great Pervader. This I call sitting and forgetting all things. （Legge，1891：257）

（2）I smash up my limbs and body, drive out perception and intellect, cast off form, do away with understanding, and make myself identical with the Great Thoroughfare. This is what I mean by sitting down and forgetting everything. （Watson，1968：90）

（3）I slough off my limbs and trunk, dim my intelligence, depart from my form, leave knowledge behind, and become identical with the Transformational Thoroughfare. This is what I mean by "sit and forget". （Mair，1994：64）

仔细分析以上译文，不难看出，海外学者在解读这段文字时都选择直译的翻译策略，都以隐喻译隐喻，在"坐忘"一词的翻译上保持高度的一致性，采用字面解读的方式。尽管隐喻的本性决定仅作字面性解读徒劳无功，但对隐喻的解读总是始于字面性解读（季光茂，2002：45）。从认知取向来讲，词语的翻译在形式上虽然表现为语码之间的转换，但本质上则应该是一个认知范畴的移植过程（肖坤学，2005a：46）。"坐忘"这一道术后来为道教所承载与发挥，在道书中屡有论述，指的是一种心法相应、物我两忘的境界。参照上述译者的翻译，该词条在《道教术语汉英双解词典》中表述如下：

> Sitting in Oblivion, also translated as Sitting and Forgetting, a Daoist term relating to cultivation and asceticism. It refers to the state of a complete neglect of oneself and his environment when he is fully absorbed in cultivation and refinement. （何立芳、陈霞，2014：230）

这是一种隐喻概念域映射的移植手段，虽然不能实现对等映射，使译文读者获得与原文读者完全相同的反应，但原文的隐喻表达方式在目的语中得到再现，体现出隐喻的认知基础（肖坤学，2005b：104）。这种再现"原生态"道教文化的中国英语，可传递汉语的文化特色，还能满足英语读者对异域文化的好奇心，帮助理解原词含义或相关文化背景。直译作为一种异化策略，是一种比较理想的保留源语思想、风格和文体形式的译出策略，按汉语原词直译而生成的"中国英语"，尤其适用于译者对文本提出哲学的认识论解读，或就关键的哲学术语或命题词项提出一系列的元文本解读。采取这种方式介绍道教文化，用异域风情吸引海外读者，有助于他们感受具有浓厚东方色彩的语言和文化特质，能让他们感受到原本生动直观的原汁原味的道教文化个性（何立芳、李丝贝，2017b：102）。

翻译作为一种文化现象，其主要意旨是满足目的文化的某种需要，弥补目的文化中的某种"缺省"。因此，翻译研究的最终目的之一应是考查翻译活动在文化意义上的效果，即翻译行为对目的语文化的各种影响，这甚至可以认为是一种最为重要的目标（范祥涛，2006：38）。感受人类文化的多元性本身是海外读者阅读译本的初衷之一。将道教文化表达形式直接纳入译文,这是一种文化植入的异化翻译,基于这种思考产生的异质性构成不同文化间取长补短、发展进步的动力,一定程度上有助于受众通过多元文化因素充实自己的文化建构,从中掌握新鲜和异质的特色,并内化为自身的文化积累。国外很多专家和学者在道教典籍翻译——尤其是其中的核心术语名称的英译上都采用音译或字面直译的办法,对于专门研究或是感兴趣于中国道教文化的西方人来说,这些中国英语对保留我国古代灿烂的文明成果未尝不是一件有意义的事情。通过这种跨文化传播的积极手段和有效途径,道教文化也可能获得形式多样而又恰当的继承与发展(何立芳、李丝贝,2017b:102)。海外学者在翻译道教典籍时倾向于采用保留原文中的语言文化元素的中国英语模式,在一定程度上说明海外受众有接受的意愿和能力,或许也能说明他们对中国文化的接受心态比我们的预期要开放得多,在道教典籍翻译中适当运用音译或直译法,随之进行说明和阐释,不仅有助于最大限度地传播道教文化,也能满足英语读者对道教文化的好奇和期盼。

第二节 道教典籍海外译介中的民族中心主义[①]

尽管多数海外道教学者在译介道教典籍时基本秉承学术研究的初衷,尽可能地依据原文本自身所蕴含的意义介绍道教文化,但由于一些译者,尤其是有着天主教传教士身份的译者主观地把道教的某些教义看作西方基督宗教的变异形态,这种"中学西源说"的认知模式在一定程度上影响了他们对道教典籍的解读,借用西方基督神学知识体系解读道教典籍内容的现象时有发生,译者自身的宗教经验、宗教关怀的痕迹在译本中时有体现,也就导致了一些颇具民族中心主义(ethnocentrism)色彩的译本。最典型的案例要数美国汉学家魏鲁男(James R. Ware,1901—1977年)1966年完成的道教典籍《抱朴子内篇》英译文本。该译本将道教本体概念"玄""道""一"完全等同于基督教之"上帝",参照基督教信仰在译本中创设了各种不同属性的"上帝"形象,属于典型

---

① 本节主要内容发表在《宗教学研究》2017年第3期,第78—82页。

的异质文化挪用做法。

一 道之本体"玄""道""一"的内涵与变异

《抱朴子内篇》主要围绕道教理论（包含道之本体论和儒道之异同）、仙道可学论和成仙途径及辅助手段展开，其言说道之本体的三大概念"玄""道""一"借自《道德经》原文。

在先秦道家思想中，"玄""道""一"为名异实同的哲学术语，因此道经中有时候也会用"玄一"或"玄道"来描述道之本体。葛洪为建构道教理论体系，将"玄"拟定为宇宙的本原实体（顾久，1995：6）。《抱朴子内篇·畅玄》中写道："玄者，自然之始祖，而万殊之大宗也。眇昧乎其深也，故称'微'焉。绵邈乎其远也，故称'妙'焉。……因兆类而为'有'，托潜寂而为'无'。……胞胎元一，范铸两仪。吐纳大始，鼓冶亿类"。"玄"被视为万物的根本，与"道"之意义等同，既可通过天地万物显现为有，又可还原于虚寂而归于无，虽难以言说，却可从天地万物运行过程中得到领悟，是先天地而生的宇宙本原。《道德经》第二十五章写道："有物混成，先天地生。寂兮寥兮，独立而不改，周行而不殆，可以为天地母。吾不知其名，字之曰道，强为之名曰大。""道"被描述为衍生万物的本体。道教尊老子为教祖，将老子神仙化，其著述的《道德经》也被圣典化，自然"道"被赋予了"无所不存，无所不能"之神秘属性，若能做到与"道"合一，便可达成长生久视。虽然葛洪在《抱朴子内篇》中沿用了"道"这一概念，但其内涵已与先秦道家之"道"有了区别，被完全神秘化了。如，《抱朴子内篇·道意》中对"道"的阐释为："道者，涵乾括坤，其本无名。论其无，则影响犹为有焉；论其有，则万物尚为无焉。"这里葛洪将"道"解读为，"大道，囊括了天地，它本来是没有名字的。如果从'无'的角度来看，那么即使是影子、回声和它相比也都算是实有的；如果从'有'的角度来看，那么即使是万事万物和它相比也都算是虚无的"（张松辉，2011：287—288）。另一个意义与"道"等同的先秦道家概念"一"原先也是指天地万物产生、形成、正常运作的普遍本质，据《道德经》第三十九章记载："天得一以清，地得一以宁，神得一以灵，谷得一以盈，万物得一以生，侯王得一以为天下正。"这一思想在《抱朴子内篇·地真》篇体现为：

"道起于一,其贵无偶,各居一处,以象天地人,故曰'三一'也。天得一以清,地得一以宁,人得一以生,神得一以灵"。显然也是发生了变异的神秘之"一"了。

表面看来葛洪是在简单重复先秦道家的理论,但仔细分析这三大概念在《抱朴子内篇》中的应用语境,其内涵已有明显不同(何立芳、李丝贝,2017a:79)。如,"一"在《抱朴子内篇》中可分为"真一"和"玄一","真一"可解读为元神,是守之勿失的具体存在,即玄与道。"真一"有姓名服饰,有高矮尺寸和具体的位置。据《地真》篇详载:"一有姓字服色,男长九分,女长六分;或在脐下二寸四分下丹田处;或在心下绛宫金阙中丹田也;或在人两眉间,却行一寸为明堂,二寸为洞房,三寸为上丹田也。此乃是道家所重,世世歃血口传其姓名耳"(《抱朴子·地真》)。"玄一"则是一种分身法术,"守玄一,并思其身,分为三人。三人已见,又转益之,可至数十人,皆如己身。隐之显之,皆自有口诀,此所谓分形之道"(《抱朴子·地真》)。显然道家和道教对这些概念的理解有明显差异。

二 道教"玄""道""一"与基督教"上帝"的文化等同

魏鲁男《抱朴子内篇》英译本自问世以来,最受诟病之处应是该译本没有提供必要的注解,以至于许多道教概念术语的译文让目的语读者难以理喻。此外,学者们对魏译本大量使用 God 这一基督信仰体系中的核心概念解读道教的本体概念"玄""道""一"也颇有微词,究其原因应是魏鲁男机械地理解了这三个异名同义概念的关系,不仅忽略了这三个概念在《抱朴子内篇》中的含义已发生了本质的变化,而且极其武断地将这三个概念等同于基督信仰中的"上帝"。在确定"道"的英语对等词为 God(上帝)之后,第一章的标题《畅玄》被英译为 God(the Mystery)Defined(Ware,1966:28),第九章标题《道意》被译为 What We Mean by "God"(Ware,1966:151),《地真》篇首句"人能知一,万事毕"的英文翻译为 If men Unity [God] could know, then they'll know all here below(Ware,1966:301)。"玄""道""一"都统一映射为基督信仰之 God,于是《抱朴子内篇》译本中有独立出现的 God,也有添加括号限定其属性的 God,大致有 150 处之多,除了《金丹》《仙药》《黄白》

《遐览》《祛惑》这些篇章外，几乎遍布该典籍译本的所有篇章，仿佛1600多年前基督教之"上帝"已远涉重洋而悄然存在于中国人的生活中，这大概也是康儒博先生提出该译本急需推出新译的主要原因之一（何立芳、李丝贝，2017a：79）。

译者将这三个概念与"上帝"绝对等同，并在译文中按目的语文化习俗借"上帝"概念的多种赋义对应解读（何立芳、李丝贝，2017a：79）。于是葛洪笔下的"玄""道""一"到了魏鲁男笔下就成了具备各种属性的上帝形象，有 God (the Mysterious and Marvelous) (Ware, 1966：229), God (the Mystery and the Undifferentiated) (Ware, 1966：241), God (the Unprejudiced and Uncommitted) (Ware, 1966：129), God (the Vague and Confused) (Ware, 1966：30), God (the Infinitesimal) (Ware, 1966：30)，等等。"玄妙难识""混元未分""神秘莫测""不偏不倚""寂静虚空""模糊含混""无穷渺小"都是译者根据自己的主观臆想所添加的限定词。魏鲁男认为，每位学者都应该懂得老子所说的"道"即为"上帝"，因为只有上帝才能体现种种对立面的统一性（Ware, 1966：1）。因此，在《抱朴子内篇》的翻译中，魏鲁男始终使用被赋予各种内涵限定的 God 一词翻译这三个核心概念。

在该译本相对简略的序言中魏鲁男谈到他频繁使用 God 对译"道"这一核心概念的理由。在他看来，这样翻译能让他时时牢记"上帝即生命即存在"（God = Life or Being）。这是他根据《出埃及记》中"我是自有永有的"（My name is I AM, I LIVE, I EXIST），以及《马可福音》中"上帝不是死人的上帝，而是活人的上帝"（God is not of the dead but of the living）得出的等式。《抱朴子内篇·道意》中有这样一段陈述：强名为"道"，已失其真，况复乃千割百判，亿分万析，使其姓号至于无垠，去道辽辽，不亦远哉？意思是：勉强给它起了个名字叫作"道"，已经无法描述它的本来面目，何况还要千百次地撕裂它，亿万回地分割它，使它的名号内容无限地改变分裂下去，这样一来离大道的本旨就越来越遥远，这岂不是太远离大道了吗？（张松辉，2011：288）据此，魏鲁男在译本序言中解释如下。

It is clear that the word *tao* appears frequently in this text not as a designation of God but of the process by which God is to be approximated or attained. In such cases I shall translate it as "the divine process". In instances where either this or "God" would be appropriate, a translator is obliged to be arbitrary. The term *tao shih* is rendered "processor"; *hsien* is translated "genie" rather than "immortal". Since Taoism recognizes God as ineffable, wide use is made of epithets as designations. In such cases the translation will normally be "God", and the literal epithet will be noted in parentheses. *Chen* (true) being a common epithet for God, the term *chen jen* has been rendered "God's Man". (Ware, 1966: 3—4)

在魏鲁男看来，《抱朴子内篇》中"道"在很多语境里不是指代"道"（上帝）之本身，而是指靠近"道"（上帝）或达到"道"（上帝）的过程，这种情况即翻译为 the divine process，而专门从事该活动的"道士"也对应译成 processor。道教认为"道"（上帝）是不可言喻的，其名号很宽泛。因此，通常情况下"道"可直接译为 God，其字面含义用括号加注说明，以表明不同的属性。魏鲁男把"真"看作"道"的名号之一，因此把"真人"译为 God's Man。

"上帝"的存在与属性问题是属于人们的"情感"问题，它不需要理性的证明和论证，人只能通过自己的"情感"去理解和赋义（孙清海，2012: 79）。传统基督教中的上帝是超越人的经验、理性和思想的真实存在。西方宗教学的创始人英国语言学家麦克斯·缪勒（Friedrich Max Müller, 1823—1900 年）曾写道，"古代一个殉难的基督徒说，'上帝没有名字'。从某种意义上看，这样说是正确的；但是，如果我们说上帝'有许许多多的名字'，这样说从历史观点来看，我想也是正确的"（麦克斯·缪勒，1989: 189）。在魏鲁男《抱朴子内篇》译本中读者几乎看不到"玄""道""一"的原型，却到处可见他参照基督教信仰所创设的带有各种不同属性的"上帝"，显然这是一种为维护基督教形象而有意为之的护教行为。美国汉学家柏夷曾撰文评论这种行为，"许多宗教都将其创教事件和人物认定为他们宗派中最为纯正的范例。宗教改革中亦常有着这样的说法，即通过对外来玷污的鉴别和剔除，进而重返那假定的纯洁起源。但当学者们不经批判地接受这种进化的模式时，他们所从事的是护教行为（apologetics），而非学术研究"（柏夷，2014：3）。尽管王宗昱先生认为"柏夷教授最后这个断语过于严格"（王宗昱，2016：273），但综观魏鲁男英译《抱朴子内篇》中有关"玄""道""一"的翻译处理，该论断用于评价该译本倒是非常中肯，表面上看魏鲁男是采用归化翻译法将原作"化为我有"（王秉钦，2004：234），但这一归化翻译明显隐含着"民族中心主义暴力"取向，不仅"剥夺了中国文化在西方的话语权，也揭示了中西文化交流中的不对等关系"（张景华，2015：69）。单从他对"玄""道""一"的文化挪用来看，魏鲁男堪称西方译者中"文化无意识"的典型（何立芳、李丝贝，2017a：81）。

一些秉持民族中心主义文化观的西方译者在解读道教典籍时容易"将翻译心理化（psychologize the translation），掩盖了翻译的文化和社会因素"（Venuti，1995：113），缺失典籍翻译所必需的文化自觉意识，是一种典型的"文化无意识"。他们通常会广泛利用西方的文化资源，如基督教文化、西方神话传说等诠释中国文化，这种典型的民族中心主义译者的翻译手法在文化多元并存的当今时代已变得不合时宜。罗选民教授主张从事典籍外译的译者需要持有文化自觉意识，认为：在全球化的语境中，认真理解和把握中西文化价值理念，努力发现彼此不同的思维方式及其存在的分歧，在不损害中国文化精神的前提下，以最合适的方式来解读和翻译最合适的典籍材料，从而达到消解分歧，促进中外文化的交流，极大地满足西方受众阅读中国典籍的需要（罗选民、杨文地，2012：64）。在文化的民族性不断走向国际化的今天，文化间的差异并非会完全消除，文化的多样性将会长期存在。为促进不同民族的文化交流，实现不同民族间的文化交流平等及相互尊重，译者应持有"同中求异"及"和而不同"的文化翻译态度（曾文雄，2010：226），始终保持文化自觉性。

第三节　道教典籍海外译介中的译学思考

作为外国学者研究中国道教的一门学科，经典阅读一直是海外道教研究的基础。学者们往往会依据自己或他人的翻译成果开展某个道教专题的研究，抑或是把他们研究道教的方法与见解带入道教典籍的翻译工作中，许多道教研究成果皆体现了翻译与研究交融一体的文本特征。一些海外道教学者倾向于使用比较宗教学的研究方法开展他们的道教研究，是因为将中国的道教与他们自幼所熟悉的基督教进行比较可取得事半功倍的研究效果。尽管这一方法容易导致他们在翻译道教典籍时忽略或弱化译本的道教文化要素，甚至会出现前文所谈到的异质文化挪用的做法，但在西方传统汉学界译介的中国道教典籍作品中，我们依然能看到很长的导言、详尽的注释和完备的索引，反映出研究者对读者接受度的普遍重视。这些翻译作品的学术性一般都很强，不仅仅是翻译成果，更是研究成果，具有严格而细致的学科规范。单从翻译视角来看，许多学者会采用直译方法，以准确为主，以传达原文的意思为先，强调译作须忠实于原文，这种治学方法影响了一代又一代汉学家，成为海外道教典籍翻译的一个重要特色。

虽然很少有人在其研究翻译道教典籍的著作中花大力气谈论他们的翻译思想，但一些学者会在序言部分论及他们选择翻译道教典籍的缘由及其目的，描述翻译中遇到的突出问题和各自处理这些问题的路径。虽然只是零星散论，尚且停留在叙说翻译体验的初级阶段，不足以形成系统的道教典籍翻译思想，姑且可以称之为"译学思考"，但这些散论均来自译者的亲身体验，对于我们研究翻译道教典籍的操作程序、操作方法很有帮助。译者在序跋中会描述他们的翻译动机、翻译策略，也会介绍一些关于原作者和原文的背景知识，这些要素都与译文最后呈现的面貌有密切关联，可以作为研究和评价译者以及译作的重要依据。这里略举两名汉学家在译作序跋中所谈到的译学思考，以窥全貌。

一 马绛团队的翻译五原则

1993 年，美国汉学家马绛基于《淮南子》第三、四、五篇的翻译完成他的专著《汉代早期思想中的天地观：〈淮南子〉三、四、五卷》（*Heaven and Earth in Han Thought: Chapters Three, Four, and Five of the Huainanzi*），系统阐释了《淮南子》中的自然观和宇宙观。之后，马绛与桂思卓（Sarah Queen）、麦安迪（Andrew Meyer）等几位汉学家一起，历经多年努力，于 2010 年共同推出国外第一个《淮南子》英语全译本，书名为《淮南子：西汉统治的理论与实践指南》（*The Huainanzi: A Guide to the Theory and Practice of Government in Early Han China*），译本前言记述了该团队的翻译五原则。

1. The translation would be complete and as accurate as it was possible to make it, with all Chinese words accounted for and nothing added or paraphrased.

2. The translation would use standard, highly readable English, with no jargon or esoteric vocabulary and no resort to contrived syntax.

3. The translation would preserve vital features of the Chinese original, such as parallel prose, verse, and aphoristic sayings.

4. We would identify and pay special attention to the formal characteristics (precepts, sayings, persuasions, and so on) that distinguished some chapters and use them for guidance in assessing both the text's rhetorical strategies and its philosophical meaning.

5. We would try to understand the text as much as possible on its own terms, as laid out in the chapter summaries and other features of the book's postface. （Major, 2010：33）

将这五原则翻译成汉语，其主要观点如下。

1. 译文应完整并尽可能准确，务求所有汉语文字得到正确释解，不增不改。

2. 译文应使用标准、可读性强的英语，忌用隐语、生僻词语，忌矫揉造作句法。

3. 译文应保留中文原文的骈文、韵文和格言警句这些重要的语言特征。

4. 译者需识别并特别注意一些特殊章节的形式特征，如戒律、格言、劝导等主题章节的行文特征，并依据这些特征判断文本的修辞策略及其哲学意义。

5. 理解文本意义应尽可能依据各章总结概述、原文后记所呈现的措辞特征。

马绛团队在翻译《淮南子》时所遵循的这五条原则较好地体现了他们对传统汉学治学模式的沿袭，既追求译文的可读性，也强调译文的忠实性。基于这样的翻译主张所推出的《淮南子》全译本在海外得到较高的赞誉。译本包含丰富的注释和详尽的附录内容（包括中国文化负载词、天文学术语、《淮南子》历史文献源流和研究文献索引等附录），自2010年出版以来，海外学者纷纷撰写书评对这一译作给予了高度评价，充分肯定了该项成果对西方读者深入了解中国传统文化的重要价值，认为该译本"既忠实又清晰"（accuracy and clarity）（Roberts，2011：308）、"由专业语言分析大师完美译出"（impeccably translated here by the most expert analysts working in our language today）（Kirkland，2011：150），"透彻诠释了刘安所作《淮南子》的历史意义"（the historical importance of Liu An's book can now be fully examined and explained）（Wallacker，2011：194），是西方读者"过去40年来汉代研究发展的有力证明，将会成为未来一个时期的权威译本"（This translation is a testament to the development of Han Studies over the past 40 years, and it will be the authoritative translation for some time to come）（Sellmann，2013：267）。这些积极评价在一定程度上也肯定了该团队所遵循的翻译五原则的有效性。他们在翻译过程中尽量做到译文和原文相符，不删不减不意译，使道家道教文化特色在英译本中得以保留，在世界文化大融合的今天，这种异化翻译主导策略对中国文化的对外传播大有裨益。

二 柏夷的翻译思考

作为欧美学术界中对中国南北朝时期的道教有着深厚研究造诣的权威学者，美国汉学家柏夷有关道教典籍翻译的思考点滴也颇有代表性。尽管柏夷教授最感兴趣的领域是中国文学，他也把文学翻译作为学术生涯最有价值的工作，然而他的社会形象却是道教研究方面的权威学者，或者说道教研究是他对学术界最杰出的贡献。这不仅是由于道教研究占据了他的论著的大部分，而且由于他在过去30年间一直是道教研究领域的重要学者（王宗昱，2016：272）。柏夷教授翻译了多部道教典籍，其中有7部被收录在美国哈佛大学罗柏松教授（James Robson）2015年编辑出版的《诺顿世界宗教选集》（*The Norton Anthology of World Religions*），这是目前最新的一套世界宗教资料导读丛书。1997年加利福尼亚大学出版社发行《早期道教典籍》（*Early Daoist Scriptures*）一书，为一部道教典籍翻译汇编，包括的译本有：《老子想尔注》（*The Xiang'er Commentary to* the Laozi)、《大道家令戒》(Commands and Admonitions for the Families of the Great Dao)、《三天内解经》(Scripture of Inner Explanations of the Three Heaven)、《灵书紫文上经》(The Upper Scripture of Purple Texts inscribed by the Spirits)、《灵宝无量度人上品妙经》(The Wonderous Scripture of the Upper Chapters on limitless Salvation)、《大塚讼章》(The Great Petition for Sepulchral Plaints)。这些译本除了《大塚讼章》由倪辅乾(Peter Nikerson)翻译完成以外，其余皆是柏夷所译。柏夷在这本译著的序言部分谈到自己翻译这些道教典籍的思考，译者从原文本的研究价值谈起，涉及选择翻译这些典籍的目的，翻译的困难和问题（读者群的差异、术语的翻译、文本意义的自足特性等），以及处理这些问题的策略。后来在为另一汉学家康儒博译注与研究葛洪《神仙传》的成果《与天地同寿：葛洪〈神仙传〉翻译与研究》一书作序时，柏夷再次谈到自己翻译道教典籍系列的初衷，并借用西方新文学批评术语"文本细读法"总结一名海外道教学者翻译道教典籍的体验和思考，认为"翻译即文本细读"(Translation is close reading)，从中我们可以了解译者的译学思路。

不同于马绛翻译团队在《淮南子》译本序言中具体提出了五条原则，柏夷谈及道教典籍翻译的观点为漫谈式散论。在他看来，道教典籍从不同角度书面记载了不同时期的道教思想和实践特色，研究翻译这些书面记载内容有助于读者了解道教的形成与发展。但由于道教典籍产生的年代久远，原作所针对的读者群与当今翻译作品针对的读者群有着天壤之别，读者的文化期待存在巨大的差异，理解翻译这些道教典籍存在诸多障碍。在《早期道教典籍》的序言中柏夷集中记述了他对道教典籍翻译的思考。

Translation, stigmatized in some scholarly circles as willfully obscuring the barriers of time and culture that separate us from other worlds, is in fact one way of attempting to bridge those gaps. Translation becomes problematic only when it lulls readers with false assurances, with the glitter of glib implausibilities. One such implausibility is the notion that Chinese religious texts of the third century might be rendered into English without substantial distortion or that, once translated, even a flicker of the meaning they held for their intended audience might survive absent the kindling provided by patient explication and scholarly care. Translation, like any other work of scholarship, is really a work of interpretation. One should beware of those translators who claim to "get out of the way" so as to allow their authors to "speak for themselves", for their interpretations are hidden. The interpretations presented here will be insofar as is humanly possible, open to view. By bearing constantly in mind that this work pretends to be no more than a work of interpretive scholarship, aiming to make available aspects of early Daoism as it was understood by those who participated in its formation, the reader will not go astray.

As with the problems of translation, the other problems mentioned earlier need to be confronted directly. We must be content to learn what these texts content themselves in revealing. With that principle in mind, I have chosen wherever possible to translate texts in their entirety rather than in judiciously selected fragments. This choice has further necessitated the long introductions that precede each text, which are meant to summarize and contextualize the information that we might today glean from them.

To many readers, the sober scholarly apparatus found here will seem at deadly odds with the fantastic and, yes, exotic face of the Daoist religion that might occasionally flash out of these pages and across the centuries to captivate us, as it assuredly did those living in early medieval China. We need to remember, though, that to the modern world, all belonging to that bygone age appears strange and exotic. If we are to understand the phenomenon of early Daoism, we must employ every means to understand it as it was understood in its time. If we are to avoid using Daoism's enticing images as mere stage props for our own fantasies, our understandable impulse to grasp intuitively the concerns of those so distant from us must be suppressed. The apparatus patiently assembled here, should it serve to remind us of this, will fulfill more than its explanatory purpose. We might then begin to understand the exotic appeal proper to Daoist scripture, where humans spoke so self-confidently as gods. (Boken Kamp, 1997: XIV – XVIII)

在康儒博完成的葛洪《神仙传》译著成果的序言中，柏夷写道：

Scripture can be translated, so long as we remember that this is not the original or the enduring scripture.

It was in this spirit and in the hope of uncovering more fully what Daoists made of their religion down through Chinese history that I initiated this series. As I began my own translation work, the first thing I noticed was that although the texts I had chosen to translate were those I had read perhaps dozens of times already, when I had finished the rough drafts, to my amazement, my view of them had changed entirely. This phenomenon bears consideration. It is, I think, the result of three related requirements of academic translation: First, and we in Daoist studies have been particularly guilty of this, when we write on any subject, we tend to cannibalize texts for bits useful to our current topic rather than read them through properly in search of the author's concerns. My "knowledge" of the texts I wanted to treat, formed in this way, was thus partial to begin with. I had to begin research all over again. Second, the need to translate every word of a text necessitates that one contextualize it, doing all sorts of dictionary work and extra reading to see how terms are used in cognate texts and to track down allusions. Few are very careful about this except when they translate passages for publication. The translator is, in effect, forced to write on the whole text for publication and so takes greater care at the initial stages of understanding. Third, even though literal translation is impossible, the effort of trying to translate—or even of closely paraphrasing—the argument of a text forces one to make hard choices. These push the translator back to the text again and again to see what can be brought over and what must be left behind.

All of this can be summed up in one sentence: Translation is close reading. (Campany, 2002: xxiii)

综合他在两部译作序言中涉及翻译的相关论述,可将他对道教典籍翻译的认识概括为五个要点。

1. 道教典籍是可以翻译的,但翻译描述出来的对象一定是变化的,绝非恒定不变的。

2. 译者不能想当然地理解原文思想,不能随意将道教术语替换为常用词语而忽略对它的解释。所谓"不需要细心注释,不给予学术性关注就可以大体翻译出道教典籍的微旨大意"的说法是不可信的。

3. 完全的直译是不可行的。翻译是一种学术性阐释活动。应警惕那些声称"让位于原作者，让原作者自己为自己说话"而不去附加解释的翻译行为。译者应力所能及地提供解释，帮助读者全面了解道教，以免误导读者。

4. 译者须充分依据原文本自身揭示的内容，尽量选择全文而不是片段进行翻译，以避免片面性。有必要在每个翻译文本前添加长篇导读，以方便今天的读者总结要点并了解当时发生的语境。

5. 译者须尽一切可能理解道教文本原初的意义，尽量像那个时代的人那样去理解道教的思想。如果要避免把道教文本中的诱人意象仅仅当作自己幻想的舞台道具，就不能仅凭直觉去理解那些离我们久远的人的所思所想。道经的翻译不是在真空中产生的，对它们的接受和理解是有语境的。

在柏夷看来，因时间、文化缘故导致我们与他者世界之间产生隔阂，译者的职责是力图弥补这些隔阂，而并非如某些学术圈所说的有意模糊这些隔阂。若译者误导读者，用难以置信的言论哄骗读者，这样的翻译是大有问题的。若认为公元 3 世纪的中国宗教文本可以基本无曲解地翻译成今天的英语文本，或者说，即便不提供细心阐释和学术性关注原作意图也可以在译文中丝毫不损得以留存，这便是一种让人难以置信的说法。

"文本细读法"以文为本，从文本出发获取文本意义，强调译者需细致把握原文本的语言、形式、意象与主题，对理解翻译道教典籍文本具有显著的实践价值。忠实传达原文文意是任何翻译行为最基本的要求，马绛团队提出的翻译五原则与柏夷的"文本细读法"翻译观都认同这一根本要求，将"忠实"作为道教典籍翻译的首要标准，但鉴于道教典籍翻译不同于一般概念的翻译行为，原作所针对的读者群与译作针对的读者群均有着特殊的文化期待，注定了道教典籍翻译必须是一种阐释之再阐释之学术行为，译者应尽力避免的不再仅仅是语义亏损的问题，还应考虑文化亏损的问题。

刘宓庆教授曾在其专著《中西翻译思想比较研究》中指出：翻译思想通常表现为对译事的某种原则主张或基本理念，通常经历三个深化（或提升）阶段：体验—体认—体悟（刘宓庆，2005：2）。无论是马绛团队提出的翻译五原则还是柏夷这种"文本细读法"翻译观，皆源于译者对道教典籍翻译的体验，是译者对道教典籍翻译规律性和规范性的认识，具有一定的代表性，能较好地反映海外道教典籍研究翻译工作者的心路历程，这些对翻译行为的经验观察最终可以凝练为翻译思想，是汉学家们对道教典籍翻译之"道"的经验的高层次认知，可用于指导当今中国学者从事道教典籍的翻译实践，亦可作为建构道教典籍系统翻译理论的基础性素材，以拓宽中华传统文化典籍翻译理论体系。笔者在尝试英译《抱朴子内篇》中的《畅玄》《微旨》时也深受这些汉学家翻译主张的启发，将"晓畅传译原文文意"作为该部分翻译实践的指导性纲领，力求译文在忠实性与可读性之间达成合理平衡的前提之下，尽可能降低文化亏损。

第 二 章

道教哲学文本翻译研究

引 语

詹石窗先生曾给"道教哲学"下过这样一个定义：道教哲学是以先秦道家理论为基础、以"道"为宇宙万物本原、自东汉末开始成型并且在以后的历史进程中不断创新、发展、完善的一种为修道成仙提供思想根据的宗教哲学（詹石窗，2003：139）。在欧美的汉学研究中，通常使用 Taoism 概括道家与道教，但前者习惯用"早期道家"（Early Taoism）或"哲学的道教"（Philosophical Taoism）以表示先秦的老、庄；后者则称为"新道家"（New-Taoism）或"宗教的道教"（Religious Taoism）（李刚，1995：16）。

欧美学者将以老子、庄子思想为中心的道家与作为宗教的道教视为一体，完全是因为受到中国传统观念的影响。在中国，自魏晋以来，对道家和道教这两个概念的使用便一直混乱不清，或不加区分，或有所区分也模糊，葛洪《抱朴子·自叙》中说："其内篇言神仙、方药……，属道家。"这里所谓"道家"准确地说应是"道教"，可见他把二者认作一码事。刘勰《灭惑论》有时说："道家立法，厥有三品：上标老子；次述神仙；下袭张陵。"有时又说："佛法炼神，道教炼形。"也把二者混谈。《魏书·释老志》《文献通考》《四库提要》等都把二者混同使用，这就造成某种混乱，使一般人误认为道教与道家是一回事（李刚，1995：17）。

学界通常把《道德经》《庄子》《列子》《文子》《淮南子》《田子》《黄帝四经》等书归属于道家哲学书籍。这些哲学书籍同为"道教哲学精义之所在"（蒙文通，1987：317），魏晋以后，老、庄诸书逐渐进入道教哲学体系，被道教徒奉为经典。毋庸置疑，道教哲学源于道家哲学。从语言符号上看，道教哲学的许多范畴和命题的符号形式都取之于道家，虽然道教从宗教神学的角度改造发展了道家哲学思想，将其神秘化和宗教化了，道教哲学中对老、庄的解释也多有牵强附会之处，但老、庄对于道教哲学思想体系的形成与发展有不可估量的影响（李刚，1995：19）。自然我们就不难理解中西学界常将老、庄并称，既把《道德经》和《庄子》视作道家典籍，又视为道教的"真经""真言"。这种传统也深深影响了欧美汉学家对道教典籍的解读和翻译活动，无论他们是将两者视为一体，还是区分为道家与道教，都会把解读老子、庄子思想作为他们了解道教的基础，这也是导致欧美汉学家对老子、庄子思想，尤其是对《道德经》《庄子》的翻译研究孜孜不倦从而不断推出不同译本的直接原因。在所有道家哲学书籍的海外译介中，《道德经》《庄子》这两部经典的译介最多，次之为《淮南子》《列子》等的译介。这些道家书籍既彰显了丰富的哲学内涵，又显现了鲜明的文学特征，对这类文本的译介理应兼顾其文学与哲学价值的再现。如果仅从文学视角进行译介，虽然可较好传译原文本的文学色彩，但难以如实传达文本的深层含义，透析文本的哲学思考；但如果只是哲学视角的译介，这类翻译往往能为读者提供一种"知其然"并"知其所以然"的阅读选择（朱舒然，2019：34），可为西方爱好道家哲学思想的研究者开拓阐释视野，但需繁杂的注释评价内容，影响普及推广效果。西方学者习惯于从哲学的眼光看待中国古代思想，这一学术取向深刻影响了近年来西方译者道教哲学文本译介的路径选择，导致西方译者最近出版的译本多呈现哲学翻译的特色。只有极少数学者在关注其哲学内涵的同时又强调其文学价值。

  本章选取欧美学界有关《道德经》《庄子》的英译文本片段作为道教哲学文本翻译研究的对象，具体内容为汉学家安乐哲（Roger T. Ames）、郝大伟（David I. Hall）合作完成的《让今生有意义：〈道德经〉的哲学阐释》（*Daodejing "Making This Life Significant": A Philosophical Translation*）中《道德经》第一章和汉学家梅维恒（Victor H. Mair）完成的《逍遥于道：庄子的早期道家寓言故事》（*Wandering on the Way: Early Taoist Tales and Parables of Chuang Tzu*）中《庄子·知北游》第一则寓言的译本。虽同为道教哲学文本，安乐哲、郝大伟合译的《道德经》译本侧重哲学内涵的挖掘，梅维恒完成的《庄子》译本则看重原文本文学性的体现，探讨他们基于不同视角的翻译策略和方法具有较好的参考价值。

第一节 《道德经》的英文翻译研究

老子《道德经》一书，又名《老子》《老子五千文》。该书的传本有很多，1993年郭店楚墓竹简本《道德经》甲、乙、丙是20世纪90年代所见年代最早的《道德经》传抄本。在此之前，学界通常将1973年长沙马王堆汉墓出土的帛书《道德经》认定为最早抄本。今本《道德经》八十一章，前三十七章为《道经》，后四十四章为《德经》。郭店简本《道德经》的绝大部分文句与今本《道德经》相近或相同，但不分《德经》和《道经》，而且章次与今本也不相对应。同时出土的还有另一重要的道家著作《太一生水》佚文（"太一"即先秦时期所说的"道"，该文主要论述"太一"与天、地、四时、阴阳等的关系）。马王堆帛书《道德经》有《德经》和《道经》之分，《德经》在前，《道经》在后。除此之外，通行本还有明正统《道藏》本，清《二十二子》本，注本有西汉河上公《老子章句》、三国王弼《老子注》、明焦竑《老子翼》、清魏源《老子本义》、近人高亨《老子正诂》及朱谦之《老子校释》等。本节将在简要介绍《道德经》在海外译介的基本情况基础之上，选取汉学家安乐哲与郝大伟2003年合作完成的《让今生有意义：〈道德经〉的哲学阐释》中《道德经》第一章的翻译作为解析对象，探讨海外学者翻译道教哲学文本的方法和策略。

一 《道德经》在海外的译介简况

作为中国哲学史上第一部具有完整哲学体系和辩证思想的著作，《道德经》以与先秦诸子学说迥然不同的姿态，对中华民族的性格、心态、思维产生了巨大、深远的影响。《道德经》言说方式的开放性与思想意涵的时代兼容性，彰显了道家核心思想概念的世界性意义，成为中国经典文化"走出去"、参与世界文化对话的典型范例（辛红娟，2016：134）。在《道德经》问世以来的2500年间，人们对这部享有"万经之王"美誉的哲学经典的阐释从未停止过，其世界意义的凸显也体现在西方学者不遗余力地用不同语种翻译《道德经》的各式版本中。大约 1750 年《道德经》的最早欧译本就已出现，其后，法国汉学家儒莲（Stanislas Julien，1797—1873 年）1842 年出版全译本。英译本问世相对晚于法译本，但大有后来居上之势（黄鸣奋，1995：96）。最早的英译应为 1868 年英国伦敦出版的湛约翰（John Chalmers）翻译文本，标题为《对古代哲学家老子关于形而上学、政体及道德的思考》(*The Speculation on Metaphysics, Polity and Morality of "The Old Philosopher", Lao-Tzu*)。美国汉学家梅维恒（Victor H. Mair）在其《道德经》译本的前言中指出："《道德经》是世界上仅次于《圣经》和《薄伽梵歌》被译介的经典。不包括无数的德文译本、法文译本、意大利语译本、荷兰语译本、拉丁语译本，以及用其他欧洲语言翻译的文本，仅英译本就已有一百多个"（Mair，1990：XI）。美国哈佛大学东亚语言与文明系教授罗柏松（James Robson）2015 年 11 月 6 日在北京参加"文明的和谐与共同繁荣——不同的道路和共同的责任"会议时谈到《道德经》在西方的译介，在其参会论文"Distorted Reflections: Cultural Exchange and Mutual-Misunderstanding in the Western Appropriation and Translation of the *Daodejing*"（《回光偏向：西方对〈道德经〉的挪用与翻译过程中所表现出来的文化交流与多重误解》）中，罗柏松教授将该部中国哲学经典的英语翻译数据更新为多达 300 种以上[①]。而在 2019 年美国学者邰谧侠（Misha Tadd）的最新统计数据中，这部道教哲学经典在海外的流传已涉及 73 种语言、1576 种译本，其中以英语为媒介的译本已达 452 种。邰谧侠还将这些译本分为风格不同的五大门类：（1）历史考据；（2）哲学分析；（3）宗教信仰；（4）文学欣赏；（5）个人发挥。各种复译本既有不同时代不同译者推出的译本，也有同一时代不同译者的译本，还有同一译者不同时代翻新订正的新译本。

针对《道德经》在欧美国家的翻译传播话题，国内许多学者做出了不同视角的探讨，其中硕士学位论文和博士学位论文居多。专著类研究

[①] 原文为：Regardless of the veracity of that claim, there is no denying that there are now more than 300 English translations of this classic of Chinese literature and philosophy and it has also been rendered into Dutch, French, German, Italian, Finnish, Icelandic, Yiddish, Spanish, and Esperanto, among many other languages. (Robson, 2015: 1)

成果主要包括:《从接受理论视角看〈道德经〉在英美的翻译》(易鸣,2006),《〈道德经〉在英语世界——文本旅行与世界想象》(辛红娟,2008),《英语世界的〈道德经〉英译研究》(杨玉英,2013)。这些成果系统地梳理了《道德经》在欧美国家的翻译传播情况。其中,杨玉英的《英语世界的〈道德经〉英译研究》从最早的《道德经》英译文本(1868年湛约翰的《对古代哲学家老子关于形而上学、政体及道德的思考》)一直梳理至2011年在瑞典出版的斯蒂芬·斯滕鲁德(Stefan Stenudd)完成的《〈道德经〉:老子对道的解读》(*Tao Te Ching: The Taoism of Lao Tzu Explained*),向读者展示了横跨近3个世纪中较具影响力的《道德经》英译本,较为完整地整理了《道德经》在欧美国家的译介情况。

斯蒂芬·斯滕鲁德依据王弼《老子注》完成的《道德经》英译本相对较新,译者在译文后列出了在此之前的29部《道德经》译本的书名,且就每部译本给予长短不一的简评。尽管他再三申明这些评价仅为个人观点,难免带有主观色彩,但从一个西方读者对《道德经》已有译本的批判性阅读视角出发,这些评论对于我们从众多的《道德经》英译文本中选择相对合适的版本作为学习材料也有一定的参考价值。从斯蒂芬·斯滕鲁德的简评中我们可以看出多数译本都有详尽的解释,从英国汉学家韦利(Arthur Waley,1889—1966年)1934年完成的《道德经》英译版本《道与德:〈道德经〉及其在中国哲学思想中的地位之研究》(*The Way and its Power: a Study of the Tao Te Ching and its Place in Chinese Thought*),美国汉学家布莱克尼(Raymond B. Blakney)1955年的译本《生活之道:老子》(*The Way of Life: Lao Tzu*),梅维恒1990年的译本《道德经:道与德之经典》(*Tao Te Ching: The Classic Book of Integrity and the Way*),到2003年汉学家安乐哲与郝大伟合作完成的《让今生有意义:〈道德经〉的哲学阐释》以及德国海德堡大学教授鲁道夫·瓦格纳(Rudolf G. Wagner)基于王弼《老子注》的译本《〈道德经〉的中国读本》(*A Chinese Reading of the Daodejing*),等等,无一不具有这一共同的特点,即注释详尽(elaborate comments),背景知识丰富(knowledgable)。斯蒂芬·斯滕鲁德2011年《道德经》译本的译介路径与上述译本也有较大程度的一致性,除了提供关键术语的注释之外,译本附加了评说内容,阐释每一节译文的主旨大意。提供注释、添加评论是这些《道德经》译作最大的共性，充分说明传统汉学研究模式在道教典籍翻译中得到了较好的沿袭。

二 安乐哲、郝大伟《道德经》译本特色

在斯蒂芬·斯滕鲁德列出的《道德经》翻译文本中，汉学家安乐哲与郝大伟 2003 年合作完成的《让今生有意义：〈道德经〉的哲学阐释》列首位，斯蒂芬·斯滕鲁德的评价，"该译本知识量丰富（knowledgeable），译者勇于创新（rather daring），很好地呈现了郭店楚墓竹简本的最新发现内容"（Stenudd，2011：310）。安乐哲与郝大伟的这部《道德经》译作是一部比较哲学视域的翻译文本，译者以 1973 年马王堆汉墓出土的《道德经》帛书本为底本，同时参阅了 1993 年郭店楚墓出土的《道德经》竹简本的最新发现，以及被视为对《道德经》思想最具哲学意味阐发的王弼（226—249 年）的《老子注》的内容，完成这部道家哲学典籍《道德经》的新译。该译本被视为 "富含知识量"，主要应指译本有详细的背景知识体系。参照新近出土的郭店楚墓《道德经》竹简本内容，译者在译文后附上《太一生水》（*The Great one gives birth to the Waters*）的原文和译文，这是该译本不同于其他《道德经》译本的特征之一。此外，译者还对标题的翻译做了大胆尝试，不同于绝大多数译者只是音译标题的做法，安乐哲与郝大伟将标题译为《让今生有意义：〈道德经〉的哲学阐释》，在哲学导论部分，译者给出了这样解读的理由：

> Were we to give priority to the cosmological insights provided by the text, we might render *Daodejing* as "The Classic of This Focus (*de* 德) and Its Field (*dao* 道)". If instead we wanted to emphasize the outcome of living according to this cosmology, we might translate it as "Feeling at Home in the World". But with deliberation we choose to underscore the human project that has prompted the articulation of Daoist cosmology and is inspired by it. Thus we translate *Daodejing* as "Making This Life Significant". (Ames, Hall, 2003：13)

译者认为，如果关注的重点是《道德经》的宇宙观，标题可以译为

"现实关注与视域之经典"〔*The Classic of This Focus*（*de* 德）*and Its Field*（*dao* 道）〕。如果想强调遵循这种宇宙观生活所带来的效应，可以把标题翻译成"舒适自在于大千世界"（*Feeling at Home in the World*），但译者刻意选择强调《道德经》对"人类工程"的价值，将标题翻译成"让今生有意义"（*Making This Life Significant*）。在译文与评注之前，译者提供了详细的背景知识，包括历史导论、历史语境、《道德经》的本质与应用、哲学导论、核心哲学术语词表以及翻译简介。其中哲学导论部分又分为9个话题，为目标语读者理解《道德经》原旨提供一系列互为关联的上下文语境。译本副标题明确了这是一部哲学视角的《道德经》新译（A philosophical translation），表明翻译的重心是老子的哲学思想。在译本序言和致谢部分，译者将这部《道德经》英译本描述为一种"有自觉意识的阐释性翻译"（a self-consciously interpretive translation），并申明"这种自觉意识不是对《道德经》的曲解，而是对该典籍所有缘起内容的核准"（Ames，Hall，2003：xi - xii）。译者在译文之前提供术语阐释，在译文后添加评注，既是为了帮助读者较好地理解老子的哲学内涵，也是向读者说明不同于其他译者的独特译法之理由。在译者看来，如果英语译本不提供导入内容和术语词表，中文文本的哲学意义会受到严重损害。如果自认为译文使用的是"客观陈述"（事实上却是带有严重文化偏见的），翻译时往往会缺乏一种自觉意识，进而不去好好思考伽达默尔所谓的"先入之见"（prejudice）所带来的影响，其后果将是对读者的背叛。整部译作皆体现了译者力图回归中国古汉语话语体系进行《道德经》的哲学释义的种种努力。

  该译本引入"语言群"（linguistic clustering）这一概念作为直译（literal translation）的替代策略。在译者看来，假定每个术语都有不同的侧重点，"语言群"策略有助于读者根据上下文解析一个术语的语义范围，从而将该术语的语义值放在首位。术语的语义值及其意义的细微差别是特定语言语境的产物。语境不同，术语的意思往往也不同，因此译本中提供了关键术语的罗马拼音，书的末尾还附上主题索引内容，便于读者对这些术语进行交叉参照（Ames，Hall，2003：56）。在翻译中"让文本自言其说，就是在这些不同的术语中找到它们的联系，这种联系使这些术语有共生的丰富意义"（常青、安乐哲，2016：92）。

《道德经》以"道"为最高哲学本体论范畴，构成了与"器"（现象界）相对应的形而上体系，用以解释宇宙万物的本体和本源，又用有无相生的辩证思想建立起中国哲学的存在论（王宏印，2009：67）。因此，从哲学视角对《道德经》进行解读更符合原文旨意。然而，正如"一千个读者眼中就会有一千个哈姆雷特"一样，欧美学者因各自所站的立场不同，对《道德经》的解读也出现了意境迥然不同的版本。即便是同一译者也会因自己阅历的增加和意识形态的改变而做出差异很大的解读。

安乐哲眼中的翻译即是阐释，在他看来，翻译并不是改变原文本，翻译是把原文本的意思呈现出来，比如翻译出来的《道德经》就是老子所言说的《道德经》；评论和解释是原文本生命的一部分（常青、安乐哲，2016：91）。安乐哲与郝大伟合译的《道德经》译本有详细的背景知识介绍，译文按中文原文－英语翻译－译者评论的顺序呈现，附有译文注释。译者在英译文之后添加了评论，类似于中国学者注译古代典籍时惯用的添加按语（案语）做法，除了对篇章主题和要义进行阐释之外，还对译者解读原文的具体手法做了说明。该部分与解释字句的翻译注释一起构成译文的副文本内容，是目的语读者深刻理解译文传译内涵的必要补充材料。安乐哲借用当代意大利学者瓦蒂莫（Gianni Vattimo）的观点"解释与评论都不是第二位的，评论是全书生命的一部分"说明在翻译《道德经》中添加这些副文本的必要性，认为，阐释域境并不意味着文本的意义就此限制在历史的背景中，文本会随着时代有所生长，这是文本的本性（常青、安乐哲，2016：89）。笔者认为，无论是通过注释疏解某些字词的含义，或是指出前期其他译本的不同解读之处，还是以评论的方式阐释主旨，为某些翻译策略做出说明，皆是为了帮助目的语读者深入理解译文试图传译的内容，应被视为翻译的有机组成部分。

三 安乐哲、郝大伟《道德经·第一章》译文解析
[原文]

道，可道也，非恒道也。[1]名，可名也，非恒名也。[2]无名，万物之始也；有名，万物之母也。[3]故恒无欲也，以观其妙；恒有欲也，以观其所徼。[4]两者同出异名，同谓之玄。[5]玄之又玄，众妙之门。[6]

[注释]

1. 道：可作名词，也可作动词。作名词时指宇宙的本原和实质，引申为原理、原则、真理、规律等；作动词时实指言说或表述。恒：永恒的、不变的。

2. 名：可兼作名词和动词，既可指名字、言词，也可指命名。

3. 无名：无可名状，指原始虚无状。有名：（物）获得其名称，指以言词表存在。母：母体，根源。

4. 徼：边际、边界，指万物的终极。

5. 二者：指无名与有名。同出而异名：来源相同，名称不同。谓：称谓，此为"指称"。玄：深黑色，这里指"玄妙深远"。

6. 众妙之门：通向神秘的总门径，比喻宇宙万物的唯一原"道"的门径。

[译文]

Way-making (*dao*) that can be put into words is not really way-making,

And naming (*ming*) that can assign fixed reference to things is not really naming.[1]

The nameless (*wuming*) is the fetal beginnings of everything that is happening (*wanwu*),

While that which is named is their mother.[2]

Thus, to be really objectless in one's desires (*wuyu*) is how one observes the mysteries of all things,

While really having desires is how one observes their boundaries.[3]

These two—the nameless and what is named—emerge from the same source yet are referred to differently.

Together they are called obscure.[4]

The obscurest of the obscure,

They are the swinging gateway of the manifold mysteries. (Ames, Hall, 2003：77)

[解析]

1. 该句的译法很多，其关键在于如何理解核心术语"道"的含义。关于"道"的解释，需回溯到产生"道"这个范畴的最初语言环境。古汉语中的"道"字,如果按照现代语法理论来看,则既是一个名词,同时也是一个动词。作为一个名词,或中国古代所谓"名","道"有其所指称的对象。"道"字最初所指称的对象,就是人们行走的道路。由道路的意思引申为指称通达某个目标、实现某种目的的途径、方法,由此再抽象为道理、规则之义。同时"道"又是个动词。作为动词,"道"的意义即在于意指某种动作、行为,或动作、行为的意念,这主要有两个方面:一是"行",二是"言",也即行动与言说(徐克谦,2000:67)。基于这样的认识,现有的译本中有译为"道路"(Way),也有译为"道理"(Reason),还有译为"自然"(Nature)或"自然法则"(Principle of Nature)的,或译为"过程"(Course),当然也有选择音译为"Tao"或是"Dao"的,几乎每位译者都给自己的翻译匹配了一个正当的理由。安乐哲和郝大伟追寻"道"字本来的语源学意义,将"道"译为"引领之道"(Way-making),其理由是:从字形结构来看,"道"由两部分构成,即"辶"(同"辵")和"首"。"辵"即"足",是人脚的象形,可引申为行走,因此有"行走、经过、疏导"(to pass over、to go over、to lead through on foot)之意。"首"本义为"头",指代头发和眼睛,进而表示"最前面的"(foremost)。"首"的字形构造有"引领""带头"的暗示意义(carries the suggestion of "to lead" in the sense of "to give a heading"),"道"与"導"("导"的繁体字)同源,意思为"带领"(to lead forth)。因此该词具备动名词特征,表示过程,是动态的。基于这样的字形结构分析,安乐哲、郝大伟选择将"道"翻译为"Way-making",这一译法与以往的各种译法大相异趣,也为"道"的其他派生意义提供了合理的解释,即从"引入"(to lead through)可引申出"道路、途径、方法、言说、阐释、教义、原则、术"(road, path, way, method, to put into words, to explain, teachings, doctrines, art)等。但其最基本的意思有:"领先"(moving ahead in the world)、"开辟"(forging a way forward)、"筑路"(road building),皆有积极主动的意蕴(Ames, Hall, 2003:57)。这种直接面对老子哲学文本中的"道"字本身,对其作一番语源学意义上的考察,不失为研究"道"之真意的必要途径。

2. 该句的断句有两种,若在"无"和"有"之后断句,该句的译文则为:The indeterminate (*wu*) is the beginning of everything that is happen-

ing; While the determinate (*you*) is the mother of everything that is happening。但根据《道德经》第三十二章"道常无名，朴。……始制有名，名亦既有，夫亦将知止，知止可以不殆"，译者认为这里应在"名"后面断句，因此译为：The nameless (*wuming*) is the fetal beginnings of everything that is happening (*wanwu*), While that which is named is their mother.

"万物"通常被译为"the ten thousand things"或"the myriad things"，但根据安乐哲、郝大伟的理解，在《道德经》的宇宙学中，"过程优先于物质实体，连续性优先于离散性"（In the *Daodejing* cosmology, process is privileged over substance, and continuity over discreteness）。因此，"物"不应理解为静态之"物"，更适合理解为"过程和那些促成过程最终完成的形成性事件"（Thus, *wu* is more appropriately understood not as static "things", but as processes, and the always transitory punctuation of these processes as consummatory events）。"物"既指"事情的发生过程"（processes），也指"取得相对完善结果的事件（events）"（happenings that have achieved some relative consummation），因此"万物"应翻译为"正在发生的一切事物"（everything that is happening）。

3. 原文"故恒无欲也，以观其妙；恒有欲也，以观其所徼"被翻译为：Thus, to be really objectless in one's desires (*wuyu*) is how one observes the mysteries of all things, while really having desires is how one observes their boundaries，译者认为"无欲"的哲学意义应为"有欲望，但无具体对象"（be objectless in one's desire），而不是普通意义上的"没有欲望"（have no desire）。这种解读肯定了欲望的存在，只不过限定了欲望的非客体性，与直接译为"不带任何欲望"（be free from desire 或 be without desire）有着实质性的区别。

《道德经》原文中有许多类似的与"无"字搭配的概念，如"无名""无为""无知""无欲""无心""无争"等，安乐哲将这些表述统称为"无"字结构（*Wu*-forms），并结合自己的哲学理解，从文本意义出发，对这些"无"字结构做出了与其他译本完全不同的阐释。

比如：

无名（wuming），"Naming without fixed reference"（没有固定指

代的命名)。

无事(wushi),"To be non-interfering in going about your business"(做事不干预)。

无为(wuwei),"Noncoercive action that is in accordance with the *de* of things"(符合事物之"德"的非强制性行为)。

无心(wuxin),"Unmediated thinking and feeling"(没有他方干预的思考和感觉)。

无争(wuzheng),"Striving without contentiousness"(无争的努力)。

无知(wuzhi),"Unprincipled knowing"(非本体论决定的知识)。[①](Ames,Hall,2003:67-68)

这些都是译者在哲学的框架下所做出的不同于其他译本的阐释。尽管以上这些译法皆"远离了现有的语汇,远离了现有的词典解释和现有的翻译范式",但安乐哲并不赞成那些因此就认为他的翻译是创造性的说法,在他看来,把一个传统连根拔起并移植到另一个传统的阐释框架中才是创造性的和激进的,而他的翻译是力图保守的(常青、安乐哲,2016:88)。从哲学典籍英译的特定语境而言,中西哲学词语不能简单地画等号。西方已经存在一套哲学传统,每个哲学术语都有其特定的历史、文化背景,一旦用来翻译中国哲学典籍中的相关观念,容易给西方读者造成一种错觉,认为中西方哲学探讨的是相同的问题(郭晨,2019:9)。安乐哲认为中西哲学词语不具备对等性,为避免与西方哲学中相关观念混淆,他对道家哲学概念的解读截然不同于其他译者的理解,引起了国内外广泛的关注和讨论。

4. 该句用破折号引出"二者"的具体所指,作同位语之用,指明"二者"即"无名"与"有名"。此外,安乐哲将"玄"译为 obscure,这一译法与其他译者的翻译也有较大的区别。通常"玄"被英译为:secret, mystery(mysterious), profound, abstruse, dark-enigma(darkness),等等。"玄"为道教教义的重要概念之一,《道德经》中多次使用"玄",

---

① 括号内的汉语为笔者翻译。

如这里的"玄之又玄,众妙之门"以及第五十一章的"玄德深矣,远矣",其意义都为"渺冥幽远",是对"道"或"德"的一种形容。东晋时葛洪建构道教教义理论体系,将"玄"提升为宇宙的本原实体,"玄"成为先天地而存在、产生万物的根本,基本上等同于"道"。隋唐之际,重玄思潮兴起,义理之学盛行,一些道教学者将"玄"发展成为认识体悟"至真大道"的一种精神境界。他们用重玄思想去看待世间的一切事物和现象,主张从心智认识上取消刚与柔、动与静、有与无、善与恶、是与非的一切对立,以达到"境智双泯""能所都忘"的虚无境界(钟肇鹏,2010:74)。安乐哲将"玄"译为 obscure 应是与这种心智认识观一致。不过,基于"玄"字有着丰富的内涵和外延,对"玄"的正确解读应根据上下文语境。因此,安乐哲将第六章的"玄牝"译为 the dark female,第十五章的"玄通"译为 dark and penetrating,第五十一章和第六十五章的"玄德"译为 profound efficacy,第五十六章的"玄同"译为 the profoundest consonance,这种语境化翻译方法贯穿整个译本,体现了安乐哲的翻译即诠释的理念。

第二节 《庄子》的英文翻译研究

庄子祖述老子,记录其思想的《庄子》一书内容庞杂,分内篇、外篇和杂篇,据《史记·老子韩非列传》载:"其学无所不窥,然其要本归于老子之言。"《庄子》原有 52 篇,计十万余言,现存《庄子》仍有 33 篇,7 万多字,其中内篇 7 章,外篇 15 章,杂篇 11 章。在道家典籍中,《庄子》的地位仅次于《道德经》。郭象在其《庄子序》中评论庄子思想为"通天地之统,序万物之性,达死生之变,而明内圣外王之道,上知造物无物,下知有物之自造也。其言宏绰,其旨玄妙。至至之道,融微旨雅;泰然遗放,放而不敖。故曰不知义之所适,猖狂妄行而蹈其大方;含哺而熙乎澹泊,鼓腹而游乎混芒"(唐雄山,2005:11),足见庄子思想之博大精深。

先秦诸子的思想在东学西渐的过程中,最让西方学者感到不可思议却深深着迷的非《庄子》莫属,《庄子》妙语如珠、譬喻精彩,其解读似尚待开采的宝藏,具有开放性特征,为读者提供了各种可能(姜莉,

2018：114）。人们普遍认为，若以寻常文字读《庄子》，很难得其要旨，缘由除了可归结于其思想博大精深之外，另一重要原因应归结于庄子所采取的"大辩不言"（《齐物论》）的言说方式。这种独特言说方式在创作实践中的运用便是"寓言""重言""卮言"，这种言说方式为人们提供了多层交错的理解和阐释空间（王晓俊，2014：121）。

《庄子·外篇》最后一章《知北游》主旨谈道，由十一则寓言组成。本节节选的解析内容为其中第一则寓言的英译文本。该则寓言围绕两个主题展开，一为"知者不言，言者不知，故圣人行不言之教"，认为知道的人不说话，说话的人不知道，所以圣人施行不说话的教导；二为"通天下一气耳"，认为气是自然界的基本物质粒子，人的生死，就是气的聚散。许多富有哲理的典故、成语出自该寓言。

一 《庄子》在海外的译介简况

《庄子》在海外的传播有近130年的历史，已被翻译为英语、法语、日语、德语、俄语、西班牙语等多个语种。在东亚文化圈内，《庄子》传播起步最早、影响最大，其中日本、韩国不仅保存了许多《庄子》汉语古本，而且各种形式的译本和注本也最多。在西方国家，由于传教士等文化交流群体的译介，《庄子》的注本和译本也不断增加，甚至一些小国都有自己的《庄子》译本，如瑞典、波兰、匈牙利等（高深，2016：86）。仅从英语世界的传播来看，尽管《庄子》英译本没有《道德经》多，但鉴于其篇幅更长，兼有深邃的哲理思想内涵和崇高的文学艺术，"英语著译者们对《庄子》的文学性给予了比对《道德经》更多的关注，而且所作的评价似乎日益增高"（黄鸣奋，1995：97）。最早的英译文本当属19世纪英国汉学家巴尔福完成的《南华真经：道教哲学家庄子之作》（*The Divine Classic of Nan-Hua*，*Being the Work of Chuang Tze*，*Taoist Philosopher*）一书，1881年由别发洋行（Kelly and Walsh, Ltd.）在上海和伦敦出版发行，但由于该书早已绝版，学界通常把英国汉学家翟理斯1889年出版的《庄子：玄学家、道德家和社会改革家》（*Chuang Tzu*：*Mystic*，*Moralist*，*and Social Reformer*）看作英语世界第一个《庄子》的全译本。在此之后，汉学家理雅各1891年英译《庄子》（*The Writings of Chuang Tzu*），与《道德经》《太上感应篇》的英译一起合称《道家文本》

(Texts of Taoism)，收录在英国语言学家、宗教学家穆勒主编的系列丛书《东方圣书》中。理雅各重视对原文的考据研究，该译本可谓是学究式的忠实译本，为西方译界公认的权威译本，乃是西方人研究道家和道教思想的重要参考资料。其后的《庄子》英译与研究都少不了参考这一重要文献（黄中习，2009：182）。

自 20 世纪起，《庄子》在海外的译介逐渐增多，其译介形式也多样化，包括全译、简译、编译、摘译、述译等。黄中习、朱舒然对《庄子》的英译本进行了较好的梳理（黄中习，2009：180—190；朱舒然，2019：25—26），从中我们可以了解到 20 世纪英语世界陆续产生了 5 部《庄子》全译本。

（1）美国汉学家魏鲁男 1963 年在纽约出版的《庄子故事集》(The Sayings of Chuang Chou)。

（2）美国汉学家华兹生 1968 年出版的全译本《庄子》(The Complete Works of Chuang Tzu)，为华兹生四年前选译本《庄子》(Chuang Tzu: Basic Writings) 的补全本。

（3）美国汉学家梅维恒 1994 年的《逍遥于道：庄子的早期道家寓言故事》(Wandering on the Way: Early Taoist Tales and Parables of Chuang Tzu)，1998 年再版。

（4）英国学者帕尔玛（Martin Palmer）1996 年出版的《庄子》英语全译本（The Book of Chuang Tzu），2006 年再版。

（5）美国学者科里亚（Nina Correa）2006 年在其互联网网站"开放论道"（http://www.daoisopen.com）上登出《庄子：无限境界》(Zhuangzi: "Being Boundless")，是《庄子》全译本的第一部电子图书。

鉴于原文篇幅较长，选译本比全译本略多，罗列十余部其中较有影响力的选译本。

（1）英国汉学家翟林奈（Lionel Giles，1875—1958 年）1906 年出版的《中国神秘主义者沉思录：庄子哲学选读》(Musings of a Chinese Mystic: selections from the philosophy of Chuang Tzu)。

（2）英国汉学家韦利 1939 年在伦敦出版哲学专著《中国古代的三种思维方式》(Three Ways of Thought in Ancient China)，其中有为普通读者而作的《庄子》部分故事和论辩情节译介内容。

（3）华裔美国学者陈荣捷（Wing-tsit Chan，1901—1993 年）1969 年出版《中国哲学资源》（*A Source Book in Chinese Philosophy*），其中完整翻译了《庄子》中的《齐物论》和《大宗师》，此外还节译了包括《应帝王》《天地》《秋水》《至乐》《知北游》等篇章中富有哲理的寓言典故片段。

（4）华裔美国学者冯家福（Gia-fu Feng，1919—1985 年）与简·英格利希（Jane English）1974 年合作翻译出版《庄子·内篇》（*Chuang Tsu：Inner Chapters*）。

（5）英国汉学家葛瑞汉（Angus Charles Granham，1919—1991 年）1981 年出版《庄子：内七篇及其它》（*Chuang-tzu：The Seven Inner Chapters and Other Writings from the Book Chuang-tzu*），这是已出版的《庄子》选译本中选译内容最多的一种。

（6）英国学者布赖斯（Derek Bryce）1992 年从维格（Leon Wieger）1913 年版的法译本《道家思想之父》（*Les Peres du Systeme Taoiste*）转译了《庄子》中的 27 篇内容，题为《庄子南华真经》（*Chuang-Tzu Nan-Hua-Ch'en Ching, or The Treatise of the Transcendent master from Nan-Hua*）。

（7）美国当代诗人希顿（David Hinton）1997 年英译出版了《庄子》内七篇（*Chuang Tzu：The Inner Chapters*），该译本多作意译。

（8）美国当代诗人哈米尔（Sam Hamill）和席顿（Jerome P. Seaton）1998 年合译出版《庄子精华》（*The Essential：Chuang Tzu*），翻译《庄子》的 22 篇内容，还附有简短的术语索引，是一部通俗易懂的《庄子》选译本。

（9）美国当代翻译家克利里（Thomas Cleary）1999 年在其四卷本《道家典籍》（*The Taoist Classics*）中译出了《庄子》内七篇。

（10）美国学者施耐沃夫（Gerald Schoenewolf）2000 年翻译出版了《老子之道、庄子之道和僧璨之道》（*The Way：According to Lao Tzu, Chuang Tzu, and Seng Tsan*），其中精选了《庄子》中的 37 个故事或寓言。

（11）美国学者伊凡豪（P. J. Ivanhoe）和诺藤（B. W. Van Norden）2001 年编译了《庄子》中的 19 篇内容，收录于《中国古典哲学读本》（*Readings in Classical Chinese Philosophy*）中。

（12）美国学者任博克（Brook Ziporyn）2009年翻译出版了《庄子：重要著作及注疏选译》（*Zhuangzi*: *The Essential Writings with Selections from Traditional Commentaries*）。该选译本广泛采用历代学者《庄子》注疏内容，通过脚注、尾注等形式帮助读者理解《庄子》内涵意义，在海外的接受度较高。

总体来看，西方译者通常是借鉴传统的中文注解来翻译、评注《庄子》，也有译者试图从中国古代思想史和宗教史入手，对传统评注加以更新或是精致化的研究，或是偏重于文本的考据学研究，关注文本的传承、来源以及真伪等问题，当然还有一些研究者试图将《庄子》当中某些提法与西方某哲学家，特别是当代哲学家的某些观点加以类比，由此构织新的论述。绝大多数译本将《庄子》首先作为哲学著作来翻译，也有译者努力兼顾《庄子》的哲学内涵与文学美感，但是当两者发生冲突的时候，往往采取首先将其哲学思想阐释清楚的策略（徐来，2008：15）。关于翻译标准和原则的探讨很多都出现在译本序跋中。在《庄子》各译本的序言中，很多译者，特别是力图展现《庄子》文学性的译者，都提及各自翻译《庄子》时的原则和方法。其中涉及最多的就是原文的形式如何再现，意义如何传达。《庄子》独特的语言魅力使得译者很想把这种奇妙的言说方式传达给读者，直译是他们最多用到的翻译方法，译者们在译序中多次提到直译（刘妍，2015：97）。但译者们所说的直译一定是基于不违背原文旨意的前提条件，要想兼顾《庄子》的文学性和哲学性，翻译过程中译者需要不断调整翻译方法，努力寻求原文形式再现和意义准确之间的平衡。

二 梅维恒《庄子》英译原则及译本主要特色

《庄子》一书呈现出鲜明的文学特征与强大的哲学张力，西方译者最近出版的《庄子》译本多呈现哲学翻译的特色，只有极少数译者在关注其哲学内涵呈现的同时又强调其文学价值的挖掘。美国汉学家梅维恒《庄子》译本可归属于这一类别，由他完成的《逍遥于道：庄子的早期道家寓言故事》自1994年出版发行后一直受到读者的广泛关注和认可，1998年由夏威夷大学出版社再版发行。梅维恒强调《庄子》的文学价值高于它的哲学价值，在译本的序言部分，译者写道：To ignore the poetics of the *Chuang Tzu* by treating it simply as a piece of philosophical prose would do it a grave injustice（Mair，1994：xli），认为忽略《庄子》的诗学特征，把它简单地当作一篇哲学散文，是对《庄子》严重的不公。翻译《庄子》的首要任务是忠实再现原文旨意，除此之外，他希望能呈现庄子作为一位杰出的文学家形象，而不是一个高谈玄学的哲学家或是有着道家信仰的悲情牧师形象。因此在翻译中译者尽最大努力再现原文的诗性语言和各种修辞表达手法，在他看来，《道德经》在美国"已经完全成为了一部归化版的美国经典著作"（a thoroughly domesticated American classic），相比之下，《庄子》在西方却没有得到应有的关注。除了学术圈之外，美国人很少听说过《庄子》，更不用说有深入了解其旨趣的美妙体验了。基于这样的背景，梅维恒决定推出《庄子》的另一复译本。作为一名以研究中国语言和文学为专长的学者，梅维恒眼中的《庄子》首先是一部伟大的文学作品，译者在陈述翻译《庄子》的初衷时讲道：My aim throughout has been to duplicate as closely as possible in English the experience that a trained student of Classical Chinese would have when he or she reads the *Chuang Tzu*（Mair，1994：xlvii），努力"使译文读者的阅读体验与一个研习中国古典文学的学生阅读《庄子》原文时所获得的感受一致"是译者一贯的翻译理念。然而，基于《庄子》中体现的绝妙想象力及其独特的语言表现方式，要把这样一部作品翻译成英语，需要做较多的转换，而不仅仅是机械的翻译。有责任心的译家需对庄子的乖张语言作出创造性的回应，尽可能兼顾一致性和准确性。

在译序中，梅维恒还谈到了自己的翻译原则：

> My policy is always to stay as close as possible to the Chinese text without becoming unintelligible or overly awkward in English. Occasionally, I have had to add a few words for grammatical or syntactical clarity in English. As a rule, however, I have endeavored to keep such additions to a minimum, not going beyond what is in the Chinese text itself. This accounts for the spareness of the English rendition, which is a deliberate attempt to convey a sense of the terseness of the Chinese original. In a few cases, I have provided brief parenthetical explanations to help the reader who has no background in Chinese history or culture. The notes in the

Glossary should suffice to solve most of the remaining difficulties initiates will encounter. (Mair, 1994: li)

在梅维恒看来，在保障英语译本具可读性，不显得那么笨拙的前提下，译者应尽量忠实于中文原文。然而，很少有英文译本能保留中文原创的简洁性，因此，有时译者不得已要添加一些词语以保证语法或句法的清晰性，但他通常会努力将这种增译控制到最小程度。有时也会用括号的方式插入一些简要的解释，以帮助那些对中国历史文化一无所知的读者。书后附上的词语表也有注释，也可以帮助这类读者解除阅读障碍。为了不影响英语读者阅读的流畅性，梅维恒尽量避免添加过多的注释和评论。只在书后词语表中列出他认为比较陌生，会给读者带来理解障碍的人名、地名、术语和典故的注释。

梅维恒力求体现《庄子》一书的文学色彩，对《庄子》文学性的看重使得他在翻译中尽最大努力来再现原文的诗性语言和各种修辞表达手法。他的翻译使庄子及其思想走出汉学家的小圈子，扩大了在美国的知名度，也给后来译者提供了有益的借鉴（刘妍，2011：47）。这是一部力求兼顾"忠实性"和"可读性"的《庄子》英译文本，本节选取其中的《庄子·知北游》的第一则寓言英译文作为解析对象。鉴于译者主要参考国内学者陈鼓应的《庄子》注译本和日本古汉语专家赤塚忠（Akatsuka Kiysoshi）的《庄子》译注本，并尽可能自始至终以英语复制作为一个对古代汉语训练有素的学者阅读《庄子》的经验体会，准确传译庄子的文学特点和哲学思想（黄中习，2009：188），故本节的原文注译内容参考了陈鼓应先生注释的《庄子今注今译》。

三 梅维恒《庄子·知北游》译文解析
[原文]

知北游于玄水之上，登隐弅之丘而适遭无为谓焉。[1]知谓无为谓曰："予欲有问乎若：何思何虑则知道？何处何服则安道？何从何道则得道？"[2]三问而无为谓不答也，非不答，不知答也。

知不得问，反于白水之南，登狐阕之上，而睹狂屈焉。[3]知以之言也问乎狂屈。狂屈曰："唉！予知之，将语若，中欲言而忘其所欲言。"

知不得问，反于帝宫，见黄帝而问焉。黄帝曰："无思无虑始知道，无处无服始安道，无从无道始得道。"

知问黄帝曰："我与若知之，彼与彼不知也，其孰是邪？"

黄帝曰："彼无为谓真是也，狂屈似之；我与汝终不近也。夫知者不言，言者不知，故圣人行不言之教。[4]道不可致，德不可至。仁可为也，义可亏也，礼相伪也。故曰，'失道而后德，失德而后仁，失仁而后义，失义而后礼。礼者，道之华而乱之首也。'[5]故曰，'为道者日损，损之又损之以至于无为，无为而无不为也。'[6]今已为物也，欲复归根[7]，不亦难乎！其易也，其唯大人乎！

"生也死之徒，死也生之始，孰知其纪！[8]人之生，气之聚也；聚则为生，散则为死。若死生为徒，吾又何患！故万物一也[9]，是其所美者为神奇，其所恶者为臭腐；臭腐复化为神奇，神奇复化为臭腐。故曰，'通天下一气耳。'[10]圣人故贵一。"

知谓黄帝曰："吾问无为谓，无为谓不应我，非不我应，不知应我也。吾问狂屈，狂屈中欲告我而不我告，非不我告，中欲告而忘之也。今予问乎若，若知之，奚故不近？"

黄帝曰："彼其真是也，以其不知也；此其似之也，以其忘之也；予与若终不近也，以其知之也。"

狂屈闻之，以黄帝为知言。

[注释]①

1. 知、无为谓：假托的人名。知，意指分别智。无为谓，意指道之本质，即无为无谓。

玄水、隐弅：假托的地名。玄，黑色，深奥的意思，和《道德经》第一章中的"玄之又玄"同义。隐，意指深远难知，弅则指郁然可见。

2. 予：我。若：同"汝"，你。服：行。从：途径。

3. 白水：寓托的水名。狐阕：寓托的地名，有疑心已空之意。狂屈：寓托的人名，意指猖狂而屈然。

4. 知者不言，言者不知，故圣人行不言之教：分别出自《道德经》

---

① 该部分注释综合参考了陈鼓应注译《庄子今注今译》（商务印书馆 2016 年版）第 646—650 页内容。

第五十六章、第四十三章。意思为：知道的人不说话，说话的人不知道，所以圣人施行不说话的教导。

5. 失道而后德，失德而后仁，失仁而后义，失义而后礼。礼者，道之华而乱之首也：出自《道德经》第三十八章。意思是：失去了道而后才有德，失去了德而后才有仁，失去了仁而后才有义，失去了义而后才出现礼。礼是道的虚华而祸乱的开端。

6. 为道者日损，损之又损之以至于无为，无为而无不为也：语出《道德经》第四十八章，意指：求道的人贪欲一天比一天减少，日渐减少一直达到无为的境地，无为就没有什么事情做不成的了。

7. 复归根：《道德经》第十六章作"复归其根"，指返回到本根。

8. 死之徒：出自《道德经》第五十章与第七十六章，意指死的延续。纪：规律。

9. 万物一也：意指万物有共通性、一体性。

10. 通天下一气耳：意指天下通于一气。

[译文]

Knowledge wandered north to the banks of the Dark Water, where he climbed the hill of Obscure Prominence and happened to meet Dumb Nonaction.[1] Knowledge said to Dumb Nonaction, "I have some questions I wish to ask you. By what thought and what reflection may we know the Way? Where shall we dwell and how shall we serve so that we may be secure in the Way? From what point of departure and by what way may we attain the Way?" He asked three questions and still Dumb Nonaction did not answer. Not only did he not answer, he did not know how to answer.

Being unsuccessful with his questions, Knowledge went back south to White Water, where he climbed up Solitary Confine and caught sight of Mad Stammerer. Knowledge asked the same questions of Mad Stammerer. "Ah!" said Mad Stammerer, "I know the answers and will tell you." But right when he started to speak, he forgot what he wanted to say.

Being unsuccessful with his questions, Knowledge went back to the imperial palace where he saw the Yellow Emperor and asked him the questions.

The Yellow Emperor said, "Don't think and don't reflect—only then may you begin to know the Way. Don't dwell and don't serve —only then may you begin to be secure in the Way. Have no departure and no way—only then may you begin to attain the Way. [2]

Knowledge asked the Yellow Emperor, saying, "You and I know the answers, but those two do not. Who's right?"

The Yellow Emperor said, "It's Dumb Nonaction who's truly right. Mad Stammerer seems like he is, but you and I come last and are not even close. Now,

One who knows does not speak;
One who speaks does not know. [3]

Therefore, the sage practices a doctrine without words. The Way cannot be compelled and integrity cannot be forced. Humaneness may be practiced; righteousness may be slighted; but ceremony is for being false to one another. Therefore, it is said,

When the Way is lost,
　afterward comes integrity.
When integrity is lost,
　afterward comes humaneness.
When humaneness is lost,
　afterward comes righteousness.
When righteousness is lost,
　afterward comes ceremony.
Ceremony is but the blossomy ornament of the Way,
　and the source of disorder'. [4]

Therefore, it is said,
　The practice of the Way results in daily decrease.
　Decrease and again decrease,
　　Until you reach nonaction.

Through nonaction,
　　No action is left undone.

　　Now, is it not difficult for what has already become a thing to return to its roots? Could anyone but the great man find it easy?

　　For life is the disciple of death and death is the beginning of life. Who knows their regulator? Human life is the coalescence of vital breath. When it coalesces there is life; when it dissipates there is death. Since life and death are disciples of each other, how should I be troubled by them? Thus the myriad things are a unity. What makes the one beautiful is its spirit and wonder; what makes the other loathsome is its stench and putrefaction. But stench and putrefaction evolve into spirit and wonder, and spirit and wonder evolve once again into stench and putrefaction. Therefore it is said, 'A unitary vital breath pervades all under heaven.' Hence the sage values unity."[5]

　　Knowledge said to the Yellow Emperor, "When I asked Dumb Nonaction and he didn't respond, not only didn't he respond, he didn't know how to respond. When I asked Mad Stammerer and he didn't tell me just when he was starting to do so, not only didn't he tell me, he forgot the questions just when he was starting to do so. Now, when I asked you, you knew the answers. Why did you say you weren't even close?"[6]

　　"The reason Dumb Nonaction was truly right," said the Yellow Emperor, "is because he didn't know. The reason Mad Stammerer seemed to be right is because he forgot. The reason you and I came last and were not even close is because we knew."

　　Mad Stammerer heard of this and considered the Yellow Emperor someone who knew how to speak. （Mair, 1994: 210 - 212）

［解析］

1. 中国文学作品中的人名和地名常常带有隐喻、双关的修辞效果。这些被赋予了特殊含义的名字往往寓示了作者的创作意图，或能揭示人物性格及其命运，或能交代作品的背景和结局，熟悉中国文化的读者很容易联想其隐指的寓意。《庄子》中人名、地名很多，其中不少人名、地名是庄子虚构出来的，一般都被赋予了象征意义。翻译人名、地名的基本原则是"名从主人"和"约定俗成"，通常的翻译方法包括：音译，音译+注释，意译（也叫"释义译法"），意译+注释。单纯的音译体现不出汉语人名、地名的寓意和联想，会使译文读者失去了解这些名字蕴意的机会，所以译者们更倾向采用音译+注释，意译，意译+注释。梅维恒的译文中对虚构的人名、地名一般都采用意译，译本后面所附的人名、地名和术语典故的词语表有简明扼要的解说，可减轻对中国文化不甚了解的读者的阅读障碍。在他看来，"这些名字都有双关意义，对寓言故事的展开密切相关，如果不翻译出来，就等于切除了原文文辞的重要特征"（Mair，1994：lii）。但遗憾的是，译者为了简洁起见，该词语表只包含部分词语。在译者看来，若读者可根据上下文或通过阅读引言内容便可理解的词语不必列出，如该句的"知""无为谓"皆为寓托的人名，译者意译为"Knowledge"，"Dumb Nonaction"即属这一类型。译者对该句中寓托的地名"玄水""隐弅"也如法炮制，翻译为"the Dark Water""Obscure Prominence"。下文出现的地名"白水""狐阕"，人名"狂屈"也是如此，译者意译为"White Water"，"Solitary Confine"，"Mad Stammerer"。

2.《庄子》书中有许多关于如何才能"有道""得道"的玄妙之说，如："道不可知""道不可闻""道不可得而学"等。故也有人引用庄子的这些说法，把"道"解释为类似于康德所谓"物自体"那样的东西，是完全外在于人的，与人的知识经验相隔绝的。但是《庄子》书中又的确经常讨论如何"知道""闻道"，并记录了一些"知道""闻道"的人（徐克谦，2000：70）。这一段"三问而不答"的寓言便是讨论该话题，三问的内容为：何思何虑则知道？何处何服则安道？何从何道则得道？而答案是：无思无虑始知道，无处无服始安道，无从无道始得道。问答之间，结构平衡，字词对应，给读者以简洁明快之感。翻译时应尽量谋求对应关系，选择核心词语时也应考虑这些词语是否适应句法变化的要求，是否适合语篇构成和交际环境，以此来努力保持原文简洁的语言结构特征。除了采用部分重复的手段之外，梅维恒还通过选用think（思）、reflect（虑）及其派生词thought、reflection等实现了前后对应，其他译者也都有这样的考量，在此摘录华兹生译本中相应部分的译文，读者可对照阅读，并体会不同译者是如何体现原文的语言特征的。

  What sort of pondering, what sort of cogitation does it take to know the Way? What sort of surroundings, what sort of practices does it take to find rest in the Way? What sort of path, what sort of procedure will get me to the Way?

  Only when there is no pondering and no cogitation will you get to know the Way. Only when you have no surroundings and follow no practices will you find rest in the Way. Only when there is no path and no procedure can you get to the Way. (Watson, 1968: 234—235)

  3. 原文"夫知者不言，言者不知，故圣人行不言之教"中的"知者不言，言者不知"语出《道德经》第五十六章，"不言之教"在《道德经》第二章、第四十三章皆有提及。作为老子思想的继承者，《庄子》中有不少思想直接沿用《道德经》的说法，但并无明确标示。《庄子》英译者通常是依据原文的行文，忠实再现原文结构，而不会刻意凸显哪些语句出自《道德经》，哪些才是庄子的原话。但也有少数细致的译者在忠实再现《庄子》原文结构的基础上，通过注解的形式说明这些沿用老子思想的特征，如华兹生的译文为 Those who know do not speak; those who speak do not know. Therefore the sage practices the teaching that has no words (Watson, 1968: 235)，在"不言之教"的译文后译者添加了注解内容："该句与上句分别出自《道德经》第二章和五十六章"(This and the sentence that precedes it appear in *Tao-te-ching* Ⅱ and LⅥ respectively)，向读者阐明"知者不言，言者不知"和"不言之教"的出处。梅维恒则是通过排版格式的改变来凸显这些文字的不同源头，与意译带有寓意的人名地名并大写首字母一样，其目的在于提醒读者需加以辨别。安乐哲《道德经》译本中将"不言之教"等同于"无为"的表征，译为"teachings that go beyond what can be said"，这种理解与梅维恒"圣人行不言之教"之译"the sage practices a doctrine without words"大同小异。

  4. 原文"失道而后德，失德而后仁，失仁而后义，失义而后礼。礼者，道之华而乱之首也"语出《道德经》第三十八章，庄子借用这般充满诗意的语言强调"德"是建立在人性本真之上的，否定儒家提倡的道德之美，反对以仁义礼教来约束人性。无论是选词还是语句的诗体排列方式，梅维恒译本皆力图传达出原文的文学特色。其中的哲学概念"道""德""仁""义""礼"分别对应为"the Way""integrity""humaneness""righteousness""ceremony"，这样的意译保障了读者阅读的流畅性，译者只在书后的词语表列出他认为可能让初学者产生歧义的词条"道"和"德"的注释，从词源学和道教语境角度进行补充释义。译本对"道"的解释为：The most etymologically precise equivalent in English is "track". Since the Tao is essentially ineffable, the authors of the *Chuang Tzu* often avoid mentioning it directly（Mair，1994：386）。涉及"德"的解释时，译者对比了儒家和道教的不同释义，即：In Confucian or conventional contexts, te is translated as "virtue." In Taoist or unconventional contexts, it is translated as "integrity". The most etymologically precise equivalent in English is the archaic word "dough [tiness]"（Mair，1994：383）。

《庄子》总体上属于散文，但有韵文夹杂其中，它们或在文章之首，或在文章之末，既存在于对话中，也夹杂在段落之中，非对韵文极有研究之人很难注意到或是辨别出。这些韵文对整个《庄子》文本所呈现的文风起着画龙点睛的作用。《庄子》的英译者当中也有少数译者注意到了韵文在全文中的地位。梅维恒无疑是所有译者中最为重视《庄子》韵文翻译的（刘妍，2011：44）。通过均衡的句子构造译者完美呈现了原文的韵律文体，基本做到以诗译诗，逢诗必译。其他重视《庄子》语言修辞特色传达的译者还有华兹生、帕尔玛等，华兹生《庄子》译本中该段的译文是：So it is said, when the Way was lost, then there was virtue; when virtue was lost, then there was benevolence; when benevolence was lost, then there was righteousness; when righteousness was lost, then there was rites. Rites are the frills of the Way and the forerunners of disorder（Watson，1968：235），这种处理手法与梅维恒译本异曲同工。

5. 若将原文"生也死之徒，死也生之始，孰知其纪！人之生，气之聚也；聚则为生，散则为死。若死生为徒，吾又何患！故万物一也，是其所美者为神奇，其所恶者为臭腐；臭腐复化为神奇，神奇复化为臭腐。故曰，'通天下一气耳'。圣人故贵一"翻译为白话文，即是："生是死的连续，死是生的开始，谁知道其中的规律！人的出生，乃是气的聚积，聚积便成生命，消散便是死亡。如果死生是相属的，我又有什么忧患呢！

所以万物是一体的,这是把所称美的视为神奇,把所厌恶的视为臭腐;臭腐又化为神奇,神奇又化为臭腐。所以说:整个天下就是通于一气罢了。所以圣人珍视〔无分别的〕同一"(陈鼓应,2016:650)。陈鼓应先生将"纪"译为"规律"。但参照《古代汉语字典》对"纪"的解释,除了表达"事物发展的规律"之外,"纪"还有"事物的端绪""纲要、关键""准则、法度""治理、经营"等含义,为此,《庄子》的英译者们根据各自理解的侧重点而做出了不同的翻译选择。梅维恒译本译为"regulator",既有"标准制定者、管理者"之意,又可指代"标准、原则",有一语双关的效果。而华兹生译本对应为"workings"(运行方式),侧重的是"治理、经营"过程的一面。

需要注意的是,现代汉语中也有"臭腐化神奇"之说,意思是"将腐败臭恶之物转化为神奇美好之物",比喻坏事变为好事,无用变有用。显然,现代语境中的"神奇"与"臭腐"的含义已发生了些许变异,已然不是《庄子·知北游》中"神奇""臭腐"之原义,演变后的词义所反映的客观事物的范围明显有了扩大。汉学家们比较重视字词语义的词源学考证,古今词义的演变在他们的翻译中得到了较好的反映,比如梅维恒就把"神奇"与"臭腐"译为"spirit and wonder"(神灵与奇迹)、"stench and putrefaction"(恶臭和腐烂),而我国著名典籍翻译家汪榕培译本选择泛化处理,分别对应为"something miraculous"(不可思议之物)和"something obnoxious"(令人厌恶之物),显然是受了现代汉语解释的影响。汪译本该段的译文为:Thus, beauty can be considered as something miraculous while ugliness can be considered obnoxious. Something obnoxious can be transformed into something miraculous and something miraculous can be transformed into something obnoxious(汪榕培,1999:363)。

6. 原文"吾问狂屈,狂屈中欲告我而不我告,非不我告,中欲告而忘之也"意思为:我问狂屈,狂屈心里要告诉我却不告诉我,并不是不告诉我,心中想说却忘记了。梅维恒译本基本是亦步亦趋地将该句翻译为:When I asked Mad Stammerer and he didn't tell me just when he was starting to do so, not only didn't he tell me, he forgot the questions just when he was starting to do so. 汪榕培译文中该句为:I asked Wild the Witless some questions, but he did not tell me what he was going to say. It was not because he

did not want to say but because he forgot what he was going to say to me（汪榕培，1999：365）。同样的亦步亦趋翻译，但各自的理解也不尽然一致。

小　结

　　冯友兰先生在《中国哲学简史》中谈到阅读中国哲学著作的语言障碍，他说："一个人若不能读哲学著作原文，要想对它们完全理解、充分欣赏，是很困难的，对于一切哲学著作来说都是如此。这是由于语言的障碍。加以中国哲学著作富于暗示的特点，使语言障碍更加令人望而生畏了。中国哲学家的言论、著作富于暗示之处，简直是无法翻译的。只读译文的人，就丢掉了它的暗示，这就意味着丢掉了许多"（冯友兰，1985：19）。冯友兰眼中的翻译不过是一种解释。他以《道德经》《论语》的翻译为例对此观点进行说明，认为有人翻译一句《老子》，就是对此句的意义作出自己的解释，这句译文只能传达一个意思。而在实际上，除了译者传达的这个意思，原文还可能含有许多别的意思。原文是富于暗示的，而译文则不是，也不可能是。所以译文把原文固有的丰富内容丢掉了许多。《老子》《论语》现在已经有多种译本。每个译者都觉得别人的翻译不能令人满意。但是无论译得多好，译本也一定比原本贫乏。需要把一切译本，包括已经译出的和其他尚未译出的，都结合起来，才能把《老子》《论语》原本的丰富内容显示出来（冯友兰，1985：19—20）。这段话不光道出了道教哲学文本翻译中的语言表达障碍与困境，也为包括本章选取的安乐哲、郝大伟《道德经》译本和梅维恒的《庄子》译本在内的诸多道教哲学文本新译本中的不同译注选择作出了合理的解释。

　　当《道德经》被放在哲学视域去解读的时候，受关注的不仅是译文本身，还包括文本的哲学属性和哲学意义是如何被阐释的（常青，2015：39）。安乐哲和郝大伟合作完成的《道德经》译本分历史的导论和哲学的导论，为译入语读者提供详细的背景知识，在《道德经》每一章译文后又添加哲学范式的注评，凡此种种，皆说明了译者深刻体会到解读道教哲学文本的障碍以及力图克服这些障碍所作的努力，对其中的核心概念进行词源学考察，依据语境的变化对这些含义丰富的概念进行合理变通，这种处理方法贯穿整个译本，体现了安乐哲的翻译即诠释的理念。为了能呈现庄子作为一位杰出的文学家形象，而不只是一个高谈玄学的哲学家或是有着道家信仰的悲情牧师形象，英译《庄子》的梅维恒努力维持原文形式与寓意传达之间的平衡。虽然梅维恒多采用直译法，也尽量避免添加过多的注释和评论，却因《庄子》各篇大都充满比喻例证，有时不得已也添加了一些词语以保证语法或句法的清晰性，有时也会用括号的方式插入一些简要的解释，以帮助那些对中国历史文化一无所知的读者。但《庄子》一书的重点并不完全在文学想象力。文学翻译也许的确可以体现文本的语言特色、句型结构等文学色彩，只是难以透析文本的哲学深度，仅从文学、文化的视角来翻译《庄子》恐难完整体现其思想价值（朱舒然，2019：2）。显然，翻译道教哲学文本仅从语言层面还远远不够，为减少非母语读者的阅读障碍，深挖道教哲学文本的思想价值，除翻译和文字注解本身之外，需要发挥各种有效手段，尽量弥补完善仅靠译文本身不足以表达的内涵。

第三章

道教善书文本翻译研究

引 语

　　道教劝善书又称道教善书，是以因果报应的说教宣传伦理道德、劝人从善去恶的通俗教化书籍，简称"善书"，民间也将该类书籍称为"劝世文"或"因果书"（陈霞，1999：2）。劝善书其名取自《太上感应篇》"诸恶莫作，众善奉行"之意，正式形成于宋代，以《太上感应篇》的出现为标志。除《太上感应篇》外，其他道教善书还有：《福寿论》《文昌帝君阴骘文》《文帝孝经》《太微仙君功过格》《关圣帝君觉世真经》《阴德延寿论》《除欲究本》等。

　　修道成仙是道教的最高追求，道教相信积善可以成仙，因此大多数劝善书都围绕"积善成仙"这一宗旨展开说教，宣扬积累善行可以获得福报，积累功德可以成仙了道。因为道教赋予神仙赏善罚恶的能力，劝善书通常会假托神仙的名义，认为天上、地下、家中及人体内都驻有各级神灵，这样的神灵可以监督和记录人的善恶行为，可以约束人的行为。借神灵能赏善罚恶的论断来陈述道教的伦理要求是道教劝善书的一大特色，既能防范恶念恶行的产生，还能引导人们积极向善行善。因儒家和佛教都对道教劝善书产生过极大的影响，因此该类书籍同时具有"明显的三教合一和民间化特征"（陈霞，1999：21）。道教善书融儒家伦理、仙道学说、民间信仰于一体，主体围绕修道成仙的终极目标演绎三纲五常的传统伦理。善书中所列善恶的具体表现和相应的奖惩内容，尤其是其中关涉全社会公德的内容在今天仍然具有参考价值。这些道德观念贯穿于我国数千年历史之中，可以调节个人与社会的关系，在一定程度上和一定范围内依然可以为社会主义精神文明服务，对当今世界的伦理道德建设有很好的借鉴意义。

道教劝善书具有强大的社会教化功能，不仅影响了明清乃至民国时期的中国社会，还影响了日本、朝鲜等邻国。日本江户时代（1603—1867年）就有《太上感应篇》日语本。为发掘道教劝善书对当今中国乃至世界文明的现实关照意义，发挥其应有的劝善功能，国内学者已将这些善书类书籍阐释简化为各种版本，不少国外学者也对这类书籍展开专题研究，将它们翻译成包括英语在内的其他语种。单从海外学者专题研究这类道书的成果来看，日本筑波大学名誉教授酒井忠夫（Sakai Tadao）先生在昭和35年（1960年）出版的专著《中国善书研究》堪称善书研究的经典之作，该书对《太上感应篇》、《功过格》、《文昌帝君阴骘文》和《了凡四训》等善书做了专门研究。此外，较为典型的善书研究成果还包括：（1）德裔美国汉学家艾伯华（Wolfram Eberhard）1967年在加利福尼亚大学出版社出版了《中国传统社会中的罪恶观》（*Guilt and Sin in Traditional China*）一书，用西方心理学的方法专门研究善书中的罪恶问题；（2）美国哈佛大学东亚研究所的包筠雅（Cynthia J. Brokaw）从明清的社会分层出发，探讨由各阶层所制作的功过格的不同功能，其专著标题为《功过格：中国封建社会后期的社会变迁与道德秩序》（*The Ledgers of Merit and Demerit: Social Change and Moral Order in Late Imperial China*），于1991年在普林斯顿大学出版社（Princeton University Press）出版；（3）美国汉学家孔丽维的道教伦理著作《宇宙与教团：道教的伦理维度》（*Cosmos and Community: The Ethical Dimension of Daoism*）以道教戒律为研究对象，同样讨论了劝善这一主题，涉及戒律中各种善恶表现形式及其奖惩报应效果，该成果于2004年在美国三松出版社（Three Pines Press）出版。孔丽维在她的这部伦理专著附录部分陈列了一些道教规诫经籍的英文翻译文本，既是为其研究提供佐证，也方便读者深入理解其论述内容。上述这些成果的研究结论都基于作者对关涉劝善话题的道教典籍的理解，自然需借助这类道书的翻译内容。

凝聚中国文化价值观的道教劝善书在海外的成功译介，在一定程度上可影响目的语国家人民的价值观，从某种角度来说也是一种文化的本质性影响。本章选取道教劝善书中的《太上感应篇》和《文昌帝君阴骘文》的英译文本作为研究对象，采取原文、注释、英译和译文解析的模式，从语言层面分析原文与译文在用词造句上的契合度，解读其中的翻译技能的综合运用，以探讨该类典籍翻译汉英转换的内在逻辑，借此探讨这些译者英译道教劝善书中的得失及其对中国文化"走出去"的启示意义。

第一节 《太上感应篇》英文翻译研究[①]

《太上感应篇》又称《太上老君感应篇》，简称《感应篇》，相传为北宋李昌龄所作，大致产生于北宋末年，其主要内容是劝人遵守道德规范，时刻止恶修善自利利他，旨在劝善，被誉为"古今第一善书"。上至朝廷，下至民间，刊印传播者众多，到明清时期达到高峰。全文篇幅不大，共计 1200 多字，开篇 16 字"祸福无门，惟人自召，善恶之报，如影随形"为全篇总纲，部分内容与《抱朴子内篇》《易内戒》《赤松子中诫经》等道教经书相同或相似。从具体内容与基本框架来看，《太上感应篇》文本的编纂与《赤松子中诫经》《抱朴子内篇》等魏晋道书有密切的渊源关系，大量内容都可在晋代葛洪《抱朴子内篇》中找到。

《太上感应篇》问世后，由于得到历代统治者的大力提倡，在社会上产生了很大的影响，成为人们社会生活不可分割的部分，以至于在明清时期几乎"家有其书"，达到家喻户晓的程度。向善从善从来都是人类共有的主题，从这个意义上讲，以"诸恶莫作，众善奉行"为纲领的《太上感应篇》在海外的译介研究不容小觑。

一 《太上感应篇》的海外传播

《太上感应篇》被公认为是道教善书之集大成者，其影响甚至波及朝鲜、日本及其他一些东南亚国家（唐大潮等，2004：1）。与以往许多道书所讲述的道教成仙术不同，《太上感应篇》不再是所谓的"外炼丹药、内练真气、服食神果仙花"，而是把"行善"作为成仙唯一的、现实的手

[①] 笔者曾撰文《试析理雅各〈太上感应篇〉英译》，载《内蒙古农业大学学报》（社会科学版）2010 年第 5 期，第 209—211 页，本节部分观点源自该文。

段，指出人要长生多福，必须行善积德，并列举了 20 余条善行和近 170 条恶行，作趋善避恶的标准。这些规诫与基督教劝人行善从善的思想不谋而合，部分内容和《摩西十诫》大体一致（何立芳，2010：209）。加之该文本浅显易懂，广为流传，儒、释、道三教戒律被巧妙地杂糅其中，自然引发了诸多西方汉学家的关注。

早在 1816 年，法国汉学家雷慕沙就将《太上感应篇》翻译为法语，标题译为 Le Livre des Recompenses et des Peines。该译本收录于英国语言学家、宗教学家穆勒主编的系列丛书《东方圣书》（The Sacred Books of the East）第 3 卷。在此之后，雷慕沙的德国学生尤利乌斯·海因里希·克拉普洛特（Julius Heinrich Klaproth，1783—1835 年）于 1828 年复译了《太上感应篇》，其标题为 Chrestomathie Mandchou ou Reveil de Textes Mandchou。作为雷慕沙在法兰西学院的继任者，汉学家儒莲于 1872 年再次翻译了《太上感应篇》，题目译为 Le Livre des Recompenses et Desines，译本包含中文文本、正文翻译、中文评注者的注释翻译，之后的其他西方汉学家在复译《太上感应篇》时多会提及该译本的一些解读方法。此外，《太上感应篇》还被多名汉学家翻译为英语，主要有：（1）1879—1881 年，英国汉学家巴尔福在《中国评论》（China Review）第八、九、十期上发表的《太上感应篇》英译本。（2）英国驻华外交官、汉学家罗伯特·道格拉斯（Robert Douglas，1838—1931 年）基于儒莲的法文译本完成的《太上感应篇》节译本，标题为：The Book of Rewards and Punishments，载于他撰写的著作《儒家与道家》（Confucianism and Taouism）第 256—271 页。（3）英国汉学家理雅各完成的《太上感应篇》全译本，标题为 T'ai Shang, Tractate of Actions and their Retributions，载于《东方圣书》第 40 卷第 233—246 页。（4）日本禅学大师铃木大拙（Teitaro Suzuki，1870—1966 年）和美国学者保罗·凯拉斯（Paul Carus，1852—1919 年）合作完成的《太上感应篇》全译本，标题译为 Treatise of the Exalted One on Response and Retribution。

本节选择理雅各的《太上感应篇》英译本（以下简称理译本）作为解析对象，将其与日本禅学大师铃木大拙与美国学者保罗·凯拉斯合作完成的译本（以下简称铃译本）做一对照研究，探讨不同译者的翻译共识与差异。铃木大拙也是一位对中国古代宗教文本颇有钻研的学者，在和凯拉斯合作翻译《太上感应篇》进程中，除了给目标语读者提供一个既忠实准确又通俗易懂的逐字翻译文本（the verbatim translation）之外，译者还从词源学、语法学、训诂学角度在译文后附加补充了诸多注解，整个译本的编排模式也借鉴了理雅各译本的做法，依据自己的理解按主题划分段落，并添加相应的标题。译者在每句英文翻译后标识对应的汉字的数序，说明该句译自原文的第几到第几字，使得该译本一定程度上更适合作为英语读者研习中文的教材，这样的翻译模式和编排体例在典籍翻译中有其独特性，也有一定的参考价值。

二 理雅各《太上感应篇》译本特色

作为 19 世纪中国儒学经典翻译大师，理雅各先后翻译了五卷本《中国经典》等。其翻译的中国经典在数量上前无古人，在学术质量和影响力上至今仍有重要地位，开创了英国汉学新时期（张西平，2017：38—39）。美国学者吉拉尔多（Norman J. Girardot）将理雅各称为"在西方创建道教传统的先驱"（inventor of Daoist tradition in the west）（Girardot，2002：420），盖应归结于他在晚年时期英译了一系列道教典籍，较为详细地向西方介绍了中国古代道教文化的重要典籍。由他翻译的《道教文本》（*The Texts of Taoism*），收录了《道德经》《庄子》《太上感应篇》《清静经》《玉枢经》《日用经》《阴符经》在内的道教典籍英译文本，载于《东方圣书》第 39、第 40 卷。

理雅各是一个介于传教士汉学家和专业汉学家之间的人物，这样一种身份使他对中国经典带有自己的独特理解，这种理解直接反映在他对中国经典的翻译之中（张西平，2017：44）。在他看来，《道德经》各章节内容反映的是老子的哲学思辨和实践意义，《庄子》宏篇叙事中的肆意挥洒虽有其独特魅力，但多数为荒诞不经的内容，而《感应篇》与《道德经》《庄子》的风格迥异，具有鲜明的文体特征，类似于西方基督教的布道文书或是民间小册子（a sermon or popular tract）（Legge，1891：39 - 40）。基于这样的认识，理雅各《太上感应篇》的翻译自然别具特色。

除译文之外，理雅各还以"论《太上感应篇》"（"On the Tractate of Actions and Their Retributions"）为题，专文介绍了《感应篇》与《道德经》《庄子》的不同旨趣，置于整个英译《道教文本》的绪论部分。译文配有大量的注释内容,从词源学、训诂学,以及其他译本的不同解读等视角为译本提供补充材料。理雅各中国经典翻译活动的视角重点是对中国宗教的研究,为的是"揭开中国的儒教、道教与佛教之面纱","揭示其教义并探究教义与原则的关系,把其中的真理与谬误区分开来"(Legge,1905:40-41)。他的这篇《太上感应篇》英译本融"学术性"和"通俗性"为一体,堪称语义翻译的典范。就翻译策略而言,他更倾向于异化翻译,"直译加注"是他英译该经籍的主流翻译方法,较好地保留中华民族的文化要素(何立芳,2010:211)。

三 理雅各《太上感应篇》译文解析

[原文]

太上曰:祸福无门,惟人自召。[1]善恶之报,如影随形。是以天地有司过之神,依人所犯轻重,以夺人算,算减则贫耗,多逢忧患,人皆恶之,刑祸随之,吉庆避之,恶星灾之,算尽则死。[2]又有三台北斗神君,在人头上,录人罪恶,夺其纪算。[3]又有三尸神,在人身中,每到庚申日,辄上诣天曹,言人罪过。[4]月晦之日,灶神亦然。[5]凡人有过,大则夺纪,小则夺算,其过大小,有数百事,欲求长生者,先须避之。是道则进,非道则退。[6]不履邪径,不欺暗室。[7]积德累功,慈心于物。[8]忠孝友悌,正己化人,矜孤恤寡,敬老怀幼,昆虫草木,犹不可伤。[9]宜悯人之凶,乐人之善,济人之急,救人之危,见人之得,如己之得,见人之失,如己之失。不彰人短,不衒己长。遏恶扬善,推多取少,受辱不怨,受宠若惊,施恩不求报,与人不追悔。所谓善人,人皆敬之,天道佑之,福禄随之,众邪远之,神灵卫之,所作必成,神仙可冀。[10]欲求天仙者,当立一千三百善;欲求地仙者,当立三百善。[11]苟或[12]非义而动,非理而行,以恶为能,忍作残害,阴贼良善,暗侮君亲,慢其先生,叛其所事,诳诸无识,谤诸同学,虚诬作伪,攻讦宗亲,刚强不仁,狠戾自用,是非不当,向背乖宜,虐下取功,谄上希旨,受恩不感,念怨不休,轻蔑天民,扰乱国政,赏及非义,刑及无辜,杀人取财,倾人取位,诛降戮服,贬正排贤,凌孤逼寡,弃法受赂,以直为曲,以曲为直,入轻为重,见杀加怒,知过不改,知善不为,自罪引他,壅塞[13]方术,讪谤圣贤,侵凌道德,射飞逐走,发蛰惊栖,填穴覆巢,伤胎破卵,愿人有失,毁人成功,危人自安,减人自益，以恶易好，以私废公，窃人之能，蔽人之善，形人之丑，讦[14]人之私，耗人货财，离人骨肉，侵人所爱，助人为非，逞志作威，辱人求胜，败人苗稼，破人婚姻，苟富而骄，苟免[15]无耻，认恩推过，嫁祸卖恶，沽买虚誉，包贮险心，挫人所长，护己所短，乘威迫胁，纵暴杀伤，无故剪裁，非礼烹宰，散弃五谷，劳扰众生。破人之家，取其财宝；决水放火，以害民居；紊乱规模，以败人功；损人器物，以穷人用；见他荣贵，愿他流贬；见他富有，愿他破散；见他色美，起心私之；负他货财，愿他身死；干求不遂，便生咒恨；见他失便[16]，便说他过；见他体相不具而笑之，见他才能可称而抑之。埋蛊厌人[17]，用药杀树，恚怒[18]师傅，抵触父兄，强取强求，好侵好夺，掳掠致富，巧诈求迁，赏罚不平，逸乐过节，苛虐其下，恐吓于他，怨天尤人，呵风骂雨，斗合争讼，妄逐朋党，用妻妾语，违父母训，得新忘故，口是心非，贪冒于财，欺罔其上，造作恶语，谗毁[19]平人，毁人称直，骂神称正，弃顺效逆，背亲向疏，指天地以证鄙怀[20]，引神明而鉴猥事[21]，施与后悔，假[22]借不还，分外营求，力上施设，淫欲过度，心毒貌慈，秽食馁人，左道惑众，短尺狭度，轻秤小升，以伪杂真，采取奸利，压良为贱，谩蓦[23]愚人，贪婪无厌，咒诅[24]求直，嗜酒悖乱，骨肉忿争，男不忠良，女不柔顺，不和其室，不敬其夫，每好矜夸，常行妒忌，无行于妻子，失礼于舅姑，轻慢先灵，违逆上命，作为无益，怀挟外心，自咒咒他，偏憎偏爱，越井越灶[25]，跳食跳人[26]，损子堕胎，行多隐僻[27]，晦腊歌舞，朔旦号怒[28]，对北涕唾及溺[29]，对灶吟咏及哭，又以灶火烧香，秽柴作食，夜起裸露，八节行刑，唾流星，指虹霓，辄指三光，[30]久视日月，春月燎猎，[31]对北恶骂，无故杀龟打蛇。如是等罪，司命[32]随其轻重，夺其纪算。算尽则死，死有余责[33]，乃殃及子孙。又诸横取人财者，乃计其妻子家口以当之，渐至死丧，若不死丧，则有水火盗贼，遗亡器物，疾病口舌诸事，以当妄取之直。[34]又枉杀人者，是易刀兵而相杀也。[35]取非义之财者，譬如漏脯救饥，鸩酒止渴，非不暂饱，死亦及之。[36]夫心起于善，善虽未为，而吉神已随之。或心起于恶，恶虽未为，而凶神已随之。其有曾行恶事，后自改悔，诸恶莫作，众善奉行，久久必获吉庆，所谓转祸为福也。故吉人语善、视善、行善，一日有三善，三年天必降之福。[37]凶人语恶、视恶、行恶，一日有三恶，三年天必降之祸。胡不勉而行之。[38]

[注释]①

1. 太上：本意最上。这里指太上老君，即老子。门：门路，有进口、出口之意。祸福无门比喻灾祸和福祉没有必定的来源和去处。

2. 司过之神：道教神灵。专门考察人的行为过失，根据过失大小而予以不同的惩罚。算：人的寿命计算单位，据葛洪《抱朴子内篇·微旨》，三日为一算。也有学者将一算解读为100日。

3. 三台北斗神君：道教神灵，执掌人的夭寿、生死、祸福。纪：人的寿命计算单位，据葛洪《抱朴子内篇·微旨》，三百日为一纪。也有学者将一纪解读为12年。

4. 三尸神：道教神灵。道教认为，人的身体中有三种作祟的神，称为上尸、中尸、下尸，又称"三彭"或"三虫"，分别居于上、中、下三丹田内，属魂魄鬼神。据说三尸神每到庚申日便上天庭诉人罪过，欲使人早死。故求仙之人必须除去三尸，广积众善，才能得道成仙。去除三尸的方法为，在庚申日这天，修道者须昼夜静坐不眠，持经诵咒，防止三尸神待人熟睡后离开人体上天告状。这样持之以恒，可使三尸自灭。道教称此为"守庚申"。庚申日：庚为天干第七位，申为地支的第九位。古人以天干（甲乙丙丁戊己庚辛壬癸）和地支（子丑寅卯辰巳午未申酉戌亥）相互搭配，组合成六十个干支数，用来纪年、纪日，周而复始，循环使用。在这六十干支数中庚申日排列第五十七位。道教认为，每个庚申日是天神判断人的善恶的日子。天曹：天上的衙门。曹，官府、衙门。

5. 月晦：指一个月的月末，即农历每月的最后一天。

6. 道：道理。这里具体指该篇所提出的善恶标准。

7. 履：践踏、踩，引申为实行、做之意。邪：不正当、邪恶。径：小路。欺：欺骗。暗：昏暗、不公开。室：房室。

8. 慈心：慈悲之心。物：天地间存在的一切，即人与万物的总称。

9. 忠孝友悌：一种伦理道德观念，即尽忠君主，孝顺父母，友爱朋友，顺从兄长。正：端正、纠正。化：教化、感化。矜：怜悯、同情。

---

① 本节注释参考了唐大潮《太上感应篇注译》中的内容，载《劝善书注译》（中国社会科学出版社2004年版）第45—50页。

孤：幼年失去父亲的儿童，老来无子的人。恤：体恤、怜悯。

10. 福禄：福，全寿富贵。禄：福气、官位、赏赐。冀：望，即期望、盼望。

11. 天仙：飞升天上的神仙，即道教认为的功德最为圆满而得道白日升天者，神仙等级中的最高级。地仙：长生在世、游行于人间的神仙，神仙等级中第二级，次于天仙。

12. 苟或：假设、如果。

13. 壅塞：堵塞、阻塞。

14. 讦：攻击或揭发别人的短处。

15. 苟免：侥幸逃脱。

16. 失便：有不得意、不顺遂的事。

17. 蛊：古人所说的害人的毒虫，后来引申为一种妖术，即用木头刻人像，写上所憎恨对象的名字，并书写符咒在上，埋于地下，使其遭受病痛或死亡。厌：厌胜，为一种妖术或诅咒。

18. 恚怒：怀恨在心。恚，恨，抵触、冲撞。

19. 谗毁：说别人的坏话，造谣生事。毁，诽谤，讲别人的坏话。

20. 鄙怀：心中所蕴藏的庸俗、浅薄的感情。鄙，庸俗、浅陋。怀，心里包藏着的某种思想感情、情绪。

21. 鉴猥事：察照鄙陋、污秽的事情。鉴，察、照。猥，鄙陋、污秽。

22. 假：借。

23. 谩蓦：欺骗。谩，欺。蓦，骗。

24. 咒诅：向神灵告状，罚咒以明心迹。咒，祝告。诅，诅咒。

25. 越井越灶：从井灶上跨过，被道教认为是一种对神极端无礼的亵渎行为。越，跨。

26. 跳食跳人：浪费、糟蹋粮食，戏侮人。跳，跨过。

27. 行多隐僻：做事不光明正大。行，做、行为。隐，不光明。僻：不正大。

28. 晦：农历每月的最末一天。腊：农历年的最后一月，即农历十二月。朔：每月的初一。旦：清晨。号：怨恨之声。怒：发脾气、恼怒。

29. 涕：挤鼻涕、流泪。唾：吐唾沫。溺：小便。

30. 八节：指农历的立春、立夏、立秋、立冬、春分、秋分、夏至、冬至八个时节。虹霓：彩虹。古人认为是斗星的余气，红白色的叫虹，青白色的叫霓。三光：日、月、星。流星、虹霓、日、月、星都是天的精气灵光，如对它们吐唾沫、用手指，是一种不敬的行为，对它们的不敬，就是对天神的不敬，是要受到神的惩罚的。

31. 春月：春天。燎：放火，此指放火烧山。猎：打猎。古人认为春季是万物生发、鸟兽虫鱼孕育的时节，此时放火烧山、打猎是违背天道的。道教认为这是莫大的罪愆。

32. 司命：道教所指的掌管人的寿夭之神灵。

33. 余责：剩余的罪责。道教有"承负"之说，认为今人受到的福祸源自祖先的善恶行为。如犯下种种罪恶，天神不仅要对此人进行责罚，这种责罚还要延及其子孙后代。

34. 当：判罪。直：通"值"，价值。

35. 易：换。

36. 漏脯：指被从房屋顶上漏下的雨水而弄脏、有毒的干肉。脯，干肉。鸩酒：把毒鸟的羽毛放入酒中而制成的毒酒。鸩，有毒的鸟。及：至，到来。

37. 吉人：善人，得善报的人。

38. 凶人：恶人，不得善报的人。胡：为什么。勉：尽力、努力。

[译文]

The Thesis[1]

1. The Thâi-Shang[2] (Tractate) says, "There are no special doors for calamity and happiness (in men's lot); they come as men themselves call them. Their recompenses follow good and evil as the shadow follows the substance.[3]

Machinery to secure retribution

2. "Accordingly, in heaven and earth there are spirits that take account of men's transgressions, and, according to the lightness or gravity of their offences, take away from their term of life. When that term is curtailed, men become poor and reduced, and meet with many sorrows and afflictions. All (other) men hate them; punishments and calamities attend them; good luck and occasions for felicitation shun them; evil stars send down misfortunes on them.

When their term of life is exhausted they die.[4]

"There also are the Spirit-rulers in the three pairs of the Thâi stars of the Northern Bushel over men's heads, which record their acts of guilt and wickedness, and take away (from their term of life) periods of twelve years or of a hundred days.

"There also are the three Spirits of the recumbent body which reside within a man's person. As each kang-shän day comes round, they forthwith ascend to the court of Heaven, and report men's deeds of guilt and transgression. On the last day of the moon, the spirit of the Hearth does the same.[5]

"In the case of every man's transgressions, when they are great, twelve years are taken from his term of life; when they are small, a hundred days.

"Transgressions, great and small, are seen in several hundred things. He who wishes to seek for long life must first avoid these.

3. "Is his way right, he should go forward in it; is it wrong, he should withdraw from it.[6]

The way of a good man

"He will not tread in devious by-ways; he will not impose on himself in any secret apartment. He will amass virtue and accumulate deeds of merit. He will feel kindly towards (all) creatures. He will be loyal, filial, loving to his younger brothers, and submissive to his elder. He will make himself correct and (so) transform others. He will pity orphans, and compassionate widows; he will respect the old and cherish the young. Even the insect tribes, grass, and trees he should not hurt.[7]

"He ought to pity the malignant tendencies of others; to rejoice over their excellences; to help them in their straits; to rescue them from their perils; to regard their gains as if they were his own, and their losses in the same way; not to publish their shortcomings; not to vaunt his own superiorities; to put a stop to what is evil, and exalt and display what is good; to yield much, and take little for himself; to receive insult without resenting it, and honour with an appearance of apprehension; to bestow favours without seeking for a return, and give to others without any subsequent regret: —this is what is called a good man.[8]

All other men respect him; Heaven in its course protects him; happiness and emolument follow him; all evil things keep far from him; the spiritual Intelligences defend him; what he does is sure to succeed.

Happy issues of his course

"He may hope to become Immaterial and Immortal. He who would seek to become an Immortal of Heaven ought to give the proof of 1300 good deeds; and he who would seek to become an Immortal of Earth should give the proof of three hundred. [9]

The way of a bad man

4. "But if the movements (of a man's heart) are contrary to righteousness, and the (actions of his) conduct are in opposition to reason; if he regard his wickedness as a proof of his ability, and can bear to do what is cruel and injurious; if he secretly harms the honest and good; if he treats with clandestine slight his ruler or parents; if he is disrespectful to his elders and teachers; if he disregards the authority of those whom he should serve;[10] if he deceives the simple; if he calumniates his fellow-learners; if he vent baseless slanders, practise deception and hypocrisy, and attack and expose his kindred by consanguinity and affinity; if he is hard, violent, and without humanity; if he is ruthlessly cruel in taking his own way;[11] if his judgments of right and wrong are incorrect; and his likings and aversions are in despite of what is proper; if he oppresses inferiors, and claims merit (for doing so); courts superiors by gratifying their (evil) desires; receives favours without feeling grateful for them; broods over resentments without ceasing; if he slights and makes no account of Heaven's people; if he trouble and throw into disorder the government of the state; bestows rewards on the unrighteous and inflicts punishments on the guiltless; kills men in order to get their wealth, and overthrows men to get their offices; slays those who have surrendered, and massacres those who have made their submission; throws censure on the upright, and overthrows the worthy; maltreats the orphan and oppresses the widow; if he casts the laws aside and receives bribes; holds the right to be wrong and the wrong to be right; enters light offences as heavy; and the sight of an execution makes him more enraged (with the criminal); if

he knows his faults and does not change them, or knows what is good and does not do it; throws the guilt of his crimes on others; if he tries to hinder the exercise of an art (for a living)[12]; reviles and slanders the sage and worthy; and assails and oppresses (the principles of) reason and virtue; if he shoots birds and hunts beasts, unearths the burrowing insects and frightens roosting birds, blocks up the dens of animals and overturns nests, hurts the pregnant womb and breaks eggs; if he wishes others to have misfortunes and losses; and defames the merit achieved by others if he imperils others to secure his own safety; diminishes the property of others to increase his own; exchanges bad things for good; and sacrifices the public weal to his private advantage; if he takes credit to himself for the ability of others; conceals the excellences of others; publishes the things discreditable to others; and searches out the private affairs of others; leads others to waste their property and wealth; and causes the separation of near relatives[13]; encroaches on what others love; and assists others in doing wrong; gives the reins to his will and puts on airs of majesty; puts others to shame in seeking victory for himself; injures or destroys the growing crops of others; and breaks up projected marriages; if becoming rich by improper means makes him proud; and by a peradventure escaping the consequences of his misconduct, he yet feels no shame; if he owns to favours (which he did not confer), and puts off his errors (on others); marries away (his own) calamity to another, and sells (for gain) his own wickedness; purchases for himself empty praise; and keeps hidden dangerous purposes in his heart; detracts from the excellences of others, and screens his own shortcomings if he takes advantage of his dignity to practise intimidation, and indulges his cruelty to kill and wound; if without cause he (wastes cloth) in clipping and shaping it; cooks animals for food, when no rites require it; scatters and throws away the five grains; and burdens and vexes all living creatures; if he ruins the families of others, and gets possession of their money and valuables; admits the water or raises fire in order to injure their dwellings; if he throws into confusion the established rules in order to defeat the services of others; and injures the implements of others to deprive them of the things they require to use; if, seeing others in glory and honour, he wishes them to be banished or degraded; or seeing them wealthy and prosperous, he wishes them to be broken and scattered; if he sees a beautiful woman and forms the thought of illicit intercourse with her; is indebted to men for goods or money, and wishes them to die; if, when his requests and applications are not complied with, his anger vents itself in imprecations; if he sees others meeting with misfortune, and begins to speak of their misdeeds;[14] or seeing them with bodily imperfections he laughs at them; or when their abilities are worthy of praise, he endeavours to keep them back; if he buries the image of another to obtain an injurious power over him[15]; or employs poison to kill trees; if he is indignant and angry with his instructors; or opposes and thwarts his father and elder brother; if he takes things by violence or vehemently demands them; if he loves secretly to pilfer, and openly to snatch; makes himself rich by plunder and rapine; or by artifice and deceit seeks for promotion; if he rewards and punishes unfairly; if he indulges in idleness and pleasure to excess; is exacting and oppressive to his inferiors; and tries to frighten other men; if he murmurs against Heaven and finds fault with men; reproaches the wind and reviles the rain; if he fights and joins in quarrels; strives and raises litigations; recklessly hurries to join associate fraternities; is led by the words of his wife or concubine to disobey the instructions of his parents; if, on getting what is new, he forgets the old; and agrees with his mouth, while he dissents in his heart; if he is covetous and greedy after wealth, and deceives and befools his superiors (to get it); if he invents wicked speeches to calumniate and overthrow the innocent; defames others and calls it being straightforward; reviles the Spirits and styles himself correct; if he casts aside what is according to right, and imitates what is against it; turns his back on his near relatives, and his face to those who are distant;[16] if he appeals to Heaven and Earth to witness the mean thoughts of his mind; or calls in the spiritual Intelligences to mark the filthy affairs of his life; if he gives and afterwards repents that he has done so; or borrows and does not return; if he plans and seeks for what is beyond his lot; or lays tasks (on people) beyond their strength; if he indulges his lustful desires without measure; if there be poison in his heart and mildness in his face; if he gives others filthy food to eat; or by corrupt doctrines deludes the multitude; if he uses a short cubit, a narrow measure, light weights, and a small pint; mixes spurious articles with the genuine; and (thus) amasses illicit gain;[17] if he degrades (children or others of) decent condition to mean positions; or deceives and ensnares simple people; if he is insatiably covetous and greedy; tries by oaths and imprecations to prove himself correct; and in his liking for drink is rude and disorderly; if he quarrels angrily with his nearest relatives; and as a man he is not loyal and honourable; if a woman is not gentle and obedient; if (the husband) is not harmonious with his wife; if the wife does not reverence her husband; if he is always fond of boasting and bragging; if she is constantly jealous and envious; if he is guilty of improper conduct to his wife or sons; if she fails to behave properly to her parents-in-law; if he treats with slight and disrespect the spirits of his ancestors; if he opposes and rebels against the charge of his sovereign; if he occupies himself in doing what is of no use; and cherishes and keeps concealed a purpose other than what appears; if he utter imprecations against himself and against others (in the assertion of his innocence); or is partial in his likes and dislikes; if he strides over the well or the hearth; leaps over the food, or over a man; kills newly-born children or brings about abortions; if he does many actions of secret depravity; if he sings and dances on the last day of the moon or of the year, bawls out or gets angry on the first day of the moon or in the early dawn; weeps, spits, or urinates when fronting the north; sighs, sings, or wails when fronting the fire place and moreover, if he takes fire from the hearth to burn incense, or uses dirty firewood to cook with; if he rises at night and shows his person naked; if at the eight terms of the year he inflicts punishments;[18] if he spits at a shooting star; points at a rainbow; suddenly points to the three luminaries; looks long at the sun and moon; in the months of spring burns the thickets in hunting; with his face to the north angrily reviles others; and without reason kills tortoises and smites snakes:

"In the case of crimes such as these, (the Spirits) presiding over the Life, according to their lightness or gravity, take away the culprit's periods of twelve years or of one hundred days. When his term of life is exhausted, death ensues. If at death there remains guilt unpunished, judgment extends to his posterity. [19]

Conclusion of the whole matter

5. "Moreover, when parties by wrong and violence take the money of others, an account is taken, and set against its amount, of their wives and children, and all the members of their families, when these gradually die. If they do not die, there are the disasters from water, fire, thieves, and robbers, from losses of property, illnesses, and (evil) tongues to balance the value of their wicked appropriations. Further, those who wrongfully kill men are (only) putting their weapons into the hands of others who will in their turn kill them. To take to one's self unrighteous wealth is like satisfying one's hunger with putrid food, or one's thirst with poisoned wine. It gives a temporary relief, indeed, but death also follows it. [20]

"Now when the thought of doing good has arisen in a man's mind, though the good be not yet done, the good Spirits are in attendance on him. Or, if the thought of doing evil has arisen, though the evil be not yet done, the bad Spirits are in attendance on him.

"If one have, indeed, done deeds of wickedness, but afterwards alters his way and repents, resolved not to do anything wicked, but to practise reverently all that is good, he is sure in the long-run to obtain good fortune:—this is called changing calamity into blessing. [21] Therefore the good man speaks what is good, contemplates what is good, and does what is good; every day he has these three virtues:—at the end of three years Heaven is sure to send down blessing on him. The bad man speaks what is wicked, contemplates what is wicked, and does what is wicked; every day he has these three vices:—at the end of three years, Heaven is sure to send down misery on him.—How is it that men will not exert themselves to do what is good?" [22] (Legge, 1891: 235 - 246)

[解析]

1. 理译本将原文的1200多字按主题划分成五个部分完成，并在相应内容旁边添加小标题，作点题之用，让读者一目了然，凸显了道教劝善书作为官方推行的社会教育基本教材的功能。为排版方便，本书将这些小标题文字加粗,置于相应内容之前,以别于译文正文。分别为:(1) 论点(The Thesis);(2) 善恶报应机制(Machinery to secure retribution);(3) 善人善行(The way of a good man);(4) 善行福报(Happy issues of his course);(4) 恶人恶行(The way of a bad man);(5) 结论(Conclusion of the whole matter)。

铃译本也有同样的考虑,只是分得更细,在相应内容的前面用括号添加了说明要旨或特征的小标题,分别是:(1) 引言(Introduction);(2) 道德规诫(Moral Injunctions);(3) 行善福报(Blessings of the Good);(4) 恶人恶行(A Description of Evil-Doers);(5) 明喻一则(A Simile);(6) 善神恶神(Good and Evil Spirits);(7) 引文(Quotations)(8) 结束语(Conclusion)。

2. 该文的"太上"指称太上老君,即老子。作为先秦道家学派创始人、道教教主,老子被尊为至高无上的神灵,享有"道德天尊"之誉。理译本采用音译法翻译"太上",其缺陷是体现不出该名称的寓意和联想。而铃译本选择直译法,将"太上"译为 the Exalted One,凸显该名词尊老子为"至高无上的神灵"的指称内涵,也符合费尔巴哈关于上帝(神灵)是人类美德的绝对化和人格化的认识,宗教崇拜的神,实际上是作为人类各种美德的总和。

3. 原书以"太上曰……"开篇,表明所示内容为太上老君之训诫。据此,译者将全篇内容处理为一直接引语,只是按主题将这一直接引语分为多个段落逐一列出。首句"祸福无门,唯人自召,善恶之报,如影随形"为全篇总纲,翻译为:There are no special doors for calamity and happiness (in men's lot); they come as men themselves call them. Their recompenses follow good and evil as the shadow follows the substance,这样的译文采用的是语义翻译法。根据英国翻译理论家彼得·纽马克(Peter Newmark)的描述,语义翻译法"力图准确再现原文风格和语气。文字是神圣的,不是因为它们比内容更重要,而是因为形式和内容是一体的"(Newmark, 2001:47)。在他看来,语义翻译法适合用于表达功能文本类的翻译,通常指"由公认的权威或具有神圣地位的作者创作的哲理性和学术性作品"(Newmark, 1988:39)。尽管理雅各翻译中国古代经典是在纽马克提出的语义翻译观之前一个世纪,但他尊重源语文化,确实将

《太上感应篇》这类作品视为有神圣地位的作者创作的哲理性文本，不作归化处理，最大限度地传达了源语的文化要素，最大限度地保存了该经文的语言特色。译者努力在形式和语义上与原文保持一致，在兼顾语法正确和意义可解的基础上多是采用较小的翻译单位，甚至逐字翻译，在需要补足语义语法方面的缺损之处还做了必要的增译，通常以括号形式标识，以提醒目标语读者。译者在译文中尽可能保留了原文的词序和句序，较好地反映出原文的语言特色（何立芳，2010：210）。这一翻译思想贯穿理雅各的整篇译文，也影响了之后的译者。铃木大拙在他的《太上感应篇》英译本中沿用了这一翻译思想，相较而言，铃译本用词更简洁，尤其是在逐字翻译法的应用方面有过之而无不及，比如上句的翻译，铃译本译文：Curses and blessings do not come through gates, but man himself invites their arrival. The reward of good and evil is like the shadow accompanying a body（Suzuki, Carus, 1906a：52）。

4. 原文"是以天地有司过之神，依人所犯轻重，以夺人算。算减则贫耗，多逢忧患，人皆恶之，刑祸随之，吉庆避之，恶星灾之，算尽则死"。这里的"是以"从逻辑上引入结论，相当于"因此"，说明前面的陈述是对以下断言的真实性的证明。理译本选择副词"Accordingly"，铃译本选择短语结构"and so it is apparent"，皆为正解。鉴于中英文都有很多同义反复的词语，原文中出现的同义反复的词语，如"忧患""刑祸""吉庆"，一般情况下译者都是用同义反复的表达与之对应，所以理译本分别译为 sorrows and afflictions, punishments and calamities, good luck and occasions for felicitation；铃译本除了"吉庆"一词有简化之外，其余皆是用同义反复的表达，分别为 calamity and misery, punishments and curses, good luck。

5. 这里涉及多个道教术语的翻译。通常情况下，道教术语的翻译多是以直译为主，辅以注释或增词来明确该术语的意义，以较好地传播中华民族的文化要素。如：道教术语"三台北斗神君"被译为，"the Spirit-rulers in the three pairs of the Thai Stars of the Northern Bushel"，采用的是直译法，不过理雅各还依据《马礼逊词典》(*Morrison's Dictionary*) 中关于星星和星座的命名附加了这样的注释：The Northern Peck or Bushel is the Chinese name of our constellation of the Great Bear, the Chariot of the Supreme

Ruler. The three pairs of stars, ι, κ λ, μ ν, ξ, are called the upper, middle, and lower Thâi, or "their three Eminences" see Reeves's Names of Stars and Constellations, appended to Morrison's Dictionary, part ii, vol. i (Legge, 1891: 236)。作为道教神名的"北斗神君",又称"北斗星君"或"北斗真君",源于古代星辰崇拜,实乃北斗七星的神化,掌管人间生死祸福、消灾招福之职能。理雅各不仅补充解释了"北斗神君"在中国文化中的含义,还将它和西方的星象进行了比拟,让西方读者不至于感觉太陌生(何立芳,2010:209)。后来的西方学者对"三台北斗"也有不同的译法,如孔丽维的《赤松子中诫经》译文就翻译为 constellations of the Three Terraces and the North Culmen,在直译的基础上添加了类属词 constellations。

作为古人寿命计算单位的"纪"和"算"存在不同的解读,译者可以根据语境做出适合的选择。理译本译为(terms of life)periods of twelve years or of a hundred days,这样浅白的释意说明了"算"在某些情况下泛指"寿命",也可具体指代12年或100天的周期。

再看道教用语"三尸神"(也称"三彭""三虫")的翻译。据《抱朴子内篇·微旨》云:"身中有三尸,三尸之为物,虽无形而实魂灵鬼神之属也。""三尸神",能记人之过,至庚申日,乘人睡去,而谗之上帝。故学道者至庚申日,辄不睡,谓之"守庚申"。理雅各把"三尸神"译为 the three Spirits of the recumbent body,又担心这样翻译会让读者不得要领,所以在脚注里补充了康熙字典对"三尸"的解读,内容为 The Khang-hsî Dictionary simply explains *san shih* as 'the name of a spirit'; but the phrase is evidently plural. The names and places of the three spirits are given differently. Why should we look for anything definite and satisfactory in a notion which is merely an absurd superstition? (Legge, 1891: 236) 因为关于"三尸"的说法不一,所以他认为没必要对这样一个荒唐的迷信概念作一个具体而满意的解读,也算是解释他泛化英译该术语的理由。虽然铃译本也是采用直译加注的模式翻译"三尸神""庚申日",分别译为 the three body-spirits, Kêng Shên day,但相较而言,铃译本对这两个道教术语的注释更透彻,译者详细说明了"三尸神"的命名、功能和位置,对庚申日"守庚申"的道教习俗也有相应的描述。

灶神监管室内的行为，他的清算日是每个月的最后一天，中文称之为"月晦之日"，理雅各意译为 the last day of the moon。

6. 原文"是道则进，非道则退"的"道"在这里具体指该篇所提出的善恶标准。该句在儒莲的法译本中译为 Avancez dans la bonne voie, et reculez devant la mauvaise voie（往正确的道路前进，从错误的道路退回）。理雅各译为 Is his way right, he should go forward in it; is it wrong, he should withdraw from it（若为正道，即可砥砺前行；若为邪道，则需及时退出）。尽管这些翻译从逻辑上都讲得通，铃译本还是不认可这两个翻译，所以做出了完全不同的解读，译为 The right way leads forward; the wrong way backward（正确的道路使人进步，错误的道路使人落后），确定主语为"是道"，突出主题，更符合原文主旨。

7. 涉及道教徒善行和恶行的规诫内容在原文中多数都是采用四言、五言的平行结构，语言形式简洁规整，理译本将这种对称平行结构转换为英语中的平行结构"he will（not）…"翻译原文的"不履邪径，不欺暗室……"等善行，尽显原文作为道教规诫所具有的简洁有力的语言风格。铃译本则选择祈使句翻译这些简洁规整的句式结构，同样能达到简洁之效力。铃译本该段的译文如下。

> Do not proceed on an evil path.
> Do not sin in secret.
> Accumulate virtue, increase merit.
> With a compassionate heart turn toward all creatures.
> Be faithful, filial, friendly, and brotherly.
> First rectify thyself and then convert others.
> Take pity on orphans, assist widows; respect the old, be kind to children.
> Even the multifarious insects, herbs, and trees should not be injured.
> (Suzuki, Carus, 1906a: 53)

8. 这里涉及外位语结构的翻译问题。汉英两种语言都有外位语结构存在，指独立于句外，同时又和句中的某个成分指代同一事物。原文

"宜悯人之凶，乐人之善，济人之急，救人之危，……受辱不怨，受宠若惊，施恩不求报，与人不追悔。所谓善人……"列举了若干善行，其中"……施恩不求报，与人不追悔"为外位语。"所谓善人"中的"所谓"指"这就是"，可视为本位语，理译本用破折号隔开，套用同样的句式，译为 this is what is called a good man，保留了原文的外位语结构，以达到强调外位语的作用。

需要指出的是，原文"受辱不怨，受宠若惊"意思为：受到侮辱不生怨恨，受到宠爱应有诚慎恐惧之心。两个四字词语共享同一汉字"受"，从形式到内容都给读者带来一种规整自然之视觉和听觉体验，理雅各英译为 to receive insult without resenting it, and honour with an appearance of apprehension，紧紧抓住了原文的词句搭配结构，堪称形神兼顾之妙译。相较而言，铃译本译为 Show endurance in humiliation and bear no grudge. Receive favors as if surprised（Suzuki, Carus, 1906a: 54），语义上虽是忠实了，但给读者的阅读体验似乎也逊色了些。

9. 道经中对于神仙的分类各有不同。如，《天隐子》将神仙分为人仙、天仙、地仙、水仙、神仙这五类。《仙经》把神仙分为三等，即天仙、地仙、尸解仙。一般认为，那些"超脱尘世，神通变化，长生不死"的人即可称为神仙，该术语通常被译为"immortal"，理雅各并不认同"immortal"一词足以包含"神仙"这一概念的全部内涵，所以选取 immaterial and immortal（回译过来意思为"无形和永生"）分别对应"神"和"仙"两个概念，力图接近"神仙"一词的内涵，"天仙""地仙"也就相应译为 immortal of heaven 和 immortal of earth。许多西方学者都选择用 immortal 对译"神仙"这一概念。的确，immortal 一词更多反映的是"长生不老"这一面，而缺失"具有超自然能力，逍遥自在"的内涵。铃译本选择翻译为 spiritual saintliness，强调神仙"道德高尚圣洁"的一面，将"天仙""地仙"对应译为 heavenly saintliness 和 earthly saintliness。近年来又有学者将"神仙"翻译为 divine transcendent，或是翻译为 supernatural being 或 heavenly being，凡此种种，皆为译者力图最大限度地接近道教"神仙"概念本意的尝试。

10. 原文"阴贼良善，暗侮君亲，慢其先生，叛其所事"意思是：偷偷地陷害正直善良的人，暗地里欺侮君主、父母，做不忠不孝之事，不敬重长者，背叛侍奉之官长。其中"先生"字面意思为"出生在先之人"，指长辈或长者，外延意义指有学问的人，理雅各在脚注中解释道：Literally, "those born before himself", but generally used as a designation of teachers（Legge, 1891：238）。因此将"先生"英译为 elders and teachers, 以求完备再现其内涵。铃译本将这句话翻译为 Insidiously they injure the good and the law-abiding. Stealthily they despise their superiors and parents. They disregard their seniors and rebel against those whom they serve（Suzuki, Carus, 1906a：55）。对照这两版译文不难看出，除了句型选择不同之外，相较而言铃译本表达更简练，其词语的锤炼也更好地体现了在不影响读者理解的前提下，字对字翻译模式在兼顾原文的形式和语义方面的优势，不过这种情况在典籍英译中实属少见。

11. 原文"虚诬作伪，攻讦宗亲，刚强不仁，狠戾自用，……"的意思：无中生有，造谣生事，以假作真，奸诈欺人，攻击、宣扬别人宗族亲戚的隐私，气质刚暴，残忍刻薄，凶狠乖戾而又自以为是。尽管许多汉学家在进行中华典籍翻译时对直译法情有独钟，但单纯的字对字的直译模式在很多情况下会显得生硬，容易导致语义表达不畅。理雅各的这一《太上感应篇》译本具有典型的语义翻译特征，采用的是与直译法非常近似但比它灵活的语义翻译策略。相较而言，铃译本则为典型的直译结果，译者把直译的概念应用到极致，不光完全依原文的字面意义翻译，而且文字的次第几乎无更动，这样直译的后果就是有些句子的翻译语义不够透彻。该句在铃译本中的译文为 Liars they are, bearing false witness, deceivers, and hypocrites; malevolent exposers of kith and kin; mischievous and malignant; not humane; cruel and irrational; self-willed（Suzuki, Carus, 1906a：55）。

12. 这里涉及"方术"（指古代方士所行之术，包括天文、历算、占验、星象、医药等）的翻译问题，理译本译为 the exercise of an art（for a living），铃译本译为 the professions and crafts（Suzuki, Carus, 1906a：57）。两位译者都没有按字面翻译为 divinations and crafts, 而是根据语境泛化了该术语的意义，因为这里应是指普通意义上的谋生之道，而非狭义的那些医卜星相等方术。

13. 出于表达的需要或便于读者的理解和接受，翻译时可套用译入语中现有的表达，前提是必须尽量避免使用具有民族特色很强的说法，尤其要避免那种望文生义的套用，否则会误导读者，影响他们的理解。原文的四字词语"以恶易好"意思很明白，就是用坏的换取别人好的，无论是译为 exchange bad things for good（理译本），还是译为 For worthless things they exchange what is valuable（Suzuki, Carus, 1906a：56），都是正确的理解，切忌译为 return evil for good，这样会带来错误的联想，容易让人想到《圣经·箴言》第 17 章中有关"以恶报善，祸患必不离他家"（Whoso rewardeth evil for good, evil shall not depart from his house）之说教。同样，四字词语"离人骨肉"的意思为：挑拨离间，搬弄是非，使得他人父子、夫妇、兄弟至亲之间不和。尽管英文中有 bone of bones and flesh of flesh（《圣经·创世记》）这样的短语表达"至亲骨肉"的意思，但这里如果套用过来，直译为 separate men's bones and flesh 会导致歧义，因此理译本和铃译本都是采用意译法，铃译本译为 cause divisions in his family（Suzuki, Carus, 1906a：57）。同样，在该文的另一处作者还列举了"骨肉忿争"这一罪过，理雅各将"骨肉"翻译为 nearest relatives，而铃译本则对译为 the members of their own family，译文为 With the members of their own family they are angry and quarrelsome（Suzuki, Carus, 1906a：62）。

14. 原文"见他荣贵，愿他流贬；见他富有，愿他破散；见他色美，起心私之；负他货财，愿他身死；干求不遂，便生咒恨；见他失便，便说他过；……"采用排比句式"见他……，愿他……"，干净利落，掷地有声。理译本保留了这一句式，用 if 条件从句对应翻译"见他……"，与铃译本中使用 when 引导的时间状语从句有异曲同工之妙。铃译本中该段译文如下。

  When seeing the success and prosperity of others they wish them to run down and fail. Seeing the wealth of others, they wish them bankrupt and ruined. They cannot see beauty without cherishing in their hearts thoughts of seduction. Being indebted to others for goods or property, they wish their creditors to die. When their requests are not granted they begin to curse and wax hateful. Seeing their neighbor lose his vantage they gossip of his failure. (Suzuki, Carus, 1906a: 59)

该段文字在《赤松子中诫经》也有类似表达。

见他人家荣贵，说他往日风尘，起心愿他流贬；见人富贵，笑他往日贫穷，愿他破散；见他财帛丰盈，起心教人劫夺；见他妻妾美丽，起心欲作奸非；见他屋宅宏壮，起心欲拟焚烧；欠他债负，起心愿债主身亡；借贷他人财物不得，起心懊恼恨多；见他偶有危难，说他往日之非。

虽个别内容有所差异，但多数概念相同。现摘取孔丽维《赤松子中诫经》英译本中的对应内容，供读者对照阅读，以体会不同译者翻译同一概念时选词和句法结构的异同。

— when they see another person prosperous and noble, they say that he ultimately came from wind and dust in the past and in their minds pray that he will become homeless and deprived.

— when they see another wealthy and noble, they laugh saying that he was poor and destitute in the past and pray that he will be destroyed.

— when they see another have money and rich silks in great abundance, they develop the intention to encourage others to steal from him.

— when they see another have beautiful wives and concubines, they develop the intention to commit adultery.

— when they see another live in a big home and large estate, they develop the intention to set fire to it and burn it down.

— when they are burdened by debt to someone, in their hearts they wish that the moneylender may die and the debt expire.

— when they cannot obtain the wealth and property of others, they develop a mind that is full of affliction and hatred.

— when they see another accidentally fall into danger, they say this is because of his wrongdoing in the past. (Kohn, 2004: 165 – 166)

15. 原文"埋蛊厌人"的意思是埋蛊咒人早夭。蛊，古人所说的害人的毒虫，后来引申为一种妖术，即用木头刻人像，写上所憎恨对象的名字，并书写符咒在上，埋于地下，使其遭受病痛或死亡。厌：厌胜，为一种妖术或诅咒。翻译这种带有浓厚的汉语民族文化色彩的表述时不得不舍弃形象，采取意译加注释的模式，因为意译可使英译文言简意赅、地道而又符合英语习惯表达，而注释能补充必要的文化背景知识，加深译语读者的理解。所以，出于同样的理由，理雅各将"埋蛊厌人"翻译为 buries the image of another to obtain an injurious power over him，添加脚注：The crimes indicated here are said to have become rife under the Han dynasty, when the arts of sorcery and witchcraft were largely employed to the injury of men（Legge，1891：241），交代该罪过的背景、性质和应用范畴。铃译本则译为 use charms for the sake of controlling others（Suzuki，Carus，1906a：60），后面添加注释：Among the Chinese superstitions which are common also in other countries, is the habit of burying figures or worms, which are intended to represent some person, for the purpose of inflicting injury upon them, being a kind of black magic. This is called in Chinese "to bury vermin"（Suzuki，Carus，1906a：77），解读更详细，与理译本有殊途同归之妙。

16. 汉语中常见一些正反概念并置的情况，意思鲜明，表达有力，能凸显事物的特点，给读者留下深刻的印象。原文"弃顺效逆，背亲向疏"即为这样的典型结构，意思为不顺天理，却反而专做不合天理的事情；背弃父母兄弟至亲骨肉，专一结交有怨有仇的人。英译时，需要在正确理解的基础上尽量保存原文的结构。理译本准确把握了"弃"与"效"、"顺"与"逆"、"背"与"向"、"亲"与"疏"这些对立概念的意思，在形式上也努力保持原文的对偶，译文为 if he casts aside what is according to right, and imitates what is against it; turns his back on his near relatives, and his face to those who are distant。尽管铃译本在行文上更为简洁，译文为 They reject a good cause and espouse a wrong cause, spurning what is near, longing for the distant（Suzuki，Carus，1906a：61），但这种典型的字对字翻译在传达原文真实内涵方面还是有其缺陷，译文概念模糊，容易导致歧义。

17. 原文"短尺狭度，轻秤小升，以伪杂真，采取奸利"意思为用短尺、少称、小升、掺杂使假、以劣充好等害人的手段获取暴利。其中"尺""度""秤""升"既可指度量衡器具，又可指度量衡单位，理译本译为 if he uses a short cubit, a narrow measure, light weights, and a small pint; mixes spurious articles with the genuine; and (thus) amasses illicit gain。铃译本为：They shorten the foot, they narrow the measure, they lighten the scales, they reduce the peck. They adulterate the genuine, and they seek profit in illegitimate business（Suzuki, Carus, 1906a：62）。皆为正解。

18. 原文"晦腊歌舞，朔旦号怒，对北涕唾及溺，对灶吟咏及哭，又以灶火烧香，秽柴作食，夜起裸露，八节行刑"中包含中国历法中的几个特殊节气的忌讳问题。在道教看来，晦、腊是天神考察人善恶的时候，人们应当端洁正行，不能歌舞以亵渎神灵。朔、旦是总结自己功过的时候，应当倍加虚心静气，细检自己的行为得失。在这个时候气恼怒骂，是对神灵大不敬。八节是诸神记录人罪过的日子，各种刑罚都应禁绝，否则会招致祸患。此外，天的北方是众神所居之地，因此，朝向北方流眼泪、挤鼻涕、吐唾沫、小便等，都是对神的亵渎。单纯的直译而不交代道教的这些文化背景可能导致译文读者无法领悟文字背后的真实内涵，需做必要的注解。理译本和铃译本都是采用直译或意译附加注解的办法，以帮助译文读者了解文字背后的道教禁忌文化，如理译本中"八节"直译为 the eight terms of the year，在脚注中明确其具体内容，即 The commencements of the four seasons, the equinoxes and solstices（Legge, 1891：244）。"八节"在铃译本中译为 the eight festivals of the seasons，译者同样补充了一些注释内容，虽没有说明这八节的具体指代，但译者通过比较犹太律法让读者了解其内涵，其注释内容如下。

It is considered as irreligious to have executions take place on festivals, a custom which is paralleled in the Jewish law, according to which it is unlawful to have a man stoned or crucified on the feast day.（Suzuki, Carus, 1906a：79）

尽管翻译中的解释或加注在翻译中国文化特色词时能起一些作用，如这里的注释内容在一定程度上帮助了读者了解道教禁忌文化，但其作用远远低于期望值，直译加注翻译法不过是译者不得已的选择。

19. 原文"如是等罪，司命随其轻重，夺其纪算。算尽则死，死有余责，乃殃及子孙"所表达的思想源自《易经·坤卦·文言》："积善之家，必有余庆；积不善之家，必有余殃"。理译本在完整再现该句语义的同时，还通过注解的模式补充包括《易经》《论语》在内的有相同或类似思想的其他典籍，以帮助译语读者能尽可能多地了解中国传统思想文化。该句附加的脚注内容如下：

The principle enunciated here is very ancient in the history of the ethical teaching of China. It appears in one of the Appendixes to the Yî King, "The family that accumulates goodness is sure to have superabundant happiness; the family that accumulates evil is sure to have superabundant misery." We know also that the same view prevailed in the time of Confucius, though the sage himself does not expressly sanction it. This Tractate does not go for the issues of Retribution beyond the present life. （Legge, 1891：244）

试比较铃译本中该句的翻译：

For all these crimes the councilors of destiny deprive the guilty, according to the lightness or gravity of the offence, of terms from twelve years to a hundred days, and when the lease of life is exhausted they perish. If at death an unexpiated offence be left, the evil luck will be transferred to children and grandchildren. （Suzuki, Carus, 1906a：65）

20. 原文"又枉杀人者，是易刀兵而相杀也。取非义之财者，譬如漏脯救饥，鸩酒止渴，非不暂饱，死亦及之"内含一个明喻，一个暗喻。原文作者把平白无故枉杀人比喻为换刀相杀，是由自己的恶行导致的冤冤相报，把用不正当手段获取不义之财比喻为吃污染有毒的肉充饥，喝毒酒止渴，不但不能充饥止渴，反而会促使死亡到来。理译本该句中的两个比喻都保留了原文修辞形式，只是对喻体做了泛化处理，"刀兵"译为 weapons，"漏脯"译为 putrid food（若按字面意思"漏脯"可翻译为

soaked food that has been spoiled by dripping water)。铃译本同样也是采用明喻翻译明喻的手法,译文如下:

> Further, those who unlawfully kill men will in turn have their weapons and arms turned on them; yea, they will kill each other. Those who seize property, are, to use an illustration, like those who relieve their hunger by eating tainted meat, or quench their thirst by drinking poisoned liquor. Though they are not without temporary gratification, death will anon overcome them. (Suzuki, Carus, 1906a: 66)

对"又枉杀人者,是易刀兵而相杀也"这句的理解,两位译者都对原文的句法做了分析。理雅各认为中文表述有点复杂,对照儒莲的法译文"那些杀害无辜人民的人就像敌人交换武器自相残杀"(Ceux qui font périr des hommes innocens ressemblent à des ennemis qui échangent leurs armes et se tuent les uns les autres) (Legge, 1891: 245),理雅各做出了相似的解读。铃译本则分两层解读该句,一为"枉杀人者,是易刀兵",二为"而相杀",译文为 Further, those who unlawfully kill men will in turn have their weapons and arms turned on them; yea, they will kill each other (Suzuki, Carus, 1906a: 65)。文后的译注如下:

> I understand the sentence, "those who slay, exchange weapons," to mean that "he that killeth with the sword must be killed with the sword"; and further, adds the Chinese moralist in the following sentence, "such evil-doers will turn their swords against one another and mutually kill themselves", which is a gradation, for it is stated that not only will they be killed, but they will slay one another. (Suzuki, Carus, 1906a: 79 – 80)

这样的解读导致他的译文和理雅各译文有较大的区别。

21. 原文"其有曾行恶事,后自改悔,诸恶莫作,众善奉行,久久必获吉庆,所谓转祸为福也"中的"所谓"意思是"这就叫作",为典型的外位语结构标识语,通常这种结构在英语中用破折号引出,理译本在这里即采用了这种句型。铃译本将"所谓"译为"so to speak",应是出于对应原文行文的考虑,译文为 Those who have hitherto done evil deeds should henceforth mend and repent. If evil be no longer practiced and good deeds done, and if in this way a man continues and continues, he will surely obtain happiness and felicity. He will, indeed, so to speak, transform curses into blessings(Suzuki, Carus, 1906a: 66 - 67)。作为禅学大师的译者在该段译文前用括号添加"引文"(Quotations)字样,除了想说明该段文字为他引内容,更重要的是想通过注释指明该句引自佛典《法句经》,《法句经·爱身品》讲到:行恶得恶,如种苦种;习善得善,亦如种甜。译者添加的注释为 These passages are quotations from the Dhammapada which has become a household book of religious devotion all over China(Suzuki, Carus, 1906a: 83)。

22. 原文"故吉人语善、视善、行善,一日有三善,三年天必降之福。凶人语恶、视恶、行恶,一日有三恶,三年天必降之祸,胡不勉而行之"意思为:能够获得善报的人,言语、思想、行为无不体现出其善良的本性,每天能够做到这三善,积累满三年至善行圆满,天神必定会将幸福降临与他。不得善报的人,言语、思想、行为都显现出其凶恶的本性,每天都犯有这三恶,积满三年至恶贯满盈,天必定会将灾祸下降与他。如此看来,人们为什么不尽力向善呢?关于"语善、视善、行善"三善的翻译,理译本和铃译本都准确理解了原文的意义,只在选词造句上略有不同。铃译本译为(the man)who speaketh what is good, who thinketh what is good, who practiceth what is good(Suzuki, Carus, 1906a: 69)。不过铃译本还补充译者自己的理解,认为这三善为伊朗先知拜火教创始人琐罗亚斯德(Zarathushtra)首先提出的,注释内容为 The threefold way of good thoughts, good words, and good deeds, is a proposition which, so far as we know, was first taught in the West by Zarathushtra, the great prophet of Iran(Suzuki & Carus, 1906a: 83)。

《赤松子中诫经》也有类似表述,具体内容为:修身制命,治性之法,清朝常行,吉气专心,记念善语善行善视。一日之内,三业不生,三年之内,天降福星,皆为福报也。孔丽维《赤松子中诫经》英译本中这段文字的译文如下:

The various methods of self-cultivation, life-preservation, and the control of one's inner nature, when undertaken regularly from the clear morning onward, will bring auspicious qi to concentrate in one's heart and be recorded in one's thoughts. Speaking good, doing good, and seeing good all day long will prevent the three karmic causes from arising. In three years Heaven will send down a special star of good fortune and in all cases will bring fortunate rewards. (Kohn, 2004: 158)

"眼睛是心灵的窗户"是人类共有的认知,孔译本将"视善"直译为"seeing good",这一译法与理译本和铃译本的变通译文"contemplates what is good"和"thinketh what is good"相比,更能形神兼顾传达原文之意。

第二节 《文昌帝君阴骘文》英文翻译研究[①]

《文昌帝君阴骘文》是一部说理性与纪事性结合的道教善书,又称《文昌帝君丹桂籍》,简称《阴骘文》或《丹桂籍》。把这本书称为《丹桂籍》,其由来是因为旧时以登科为折桂,因以"丹桂"比喻考试及第的人(陈霞,1999:60)。该书不过700余字,托名文昌帝君而作,说教的对象以官僚士大夫为主。与其他善书一样,该书借用神的名义和神能奖善惩恶的威慑力,主要从正面诱导人们行善积德,书中谈到禁恶之事有14条,正面诱导行善之事有30条,这一点与《太上感应篇》略有不同(《太上感应篇》惩罚条例约有170条,劝善之事例只有20余条)。此外,相比于《太上感应篇》,该书的世俗化程度更深,回避了积善成仙之说,重点是借文昌帝君之口讲述善恶报应观点,针对的是凡间事务和道德问题。

---

① 何立芳:《铃木大拙〈文昌帝君阴骘文〉英译本解析》,《当代外语研究》2011年第10期,本节部分观点源自该文。

一 《文昌帝君阴骘文》的海外传播

"文昌帝君"是东晋大善人张亚子和天上文曲星的综合体,以文昌"降笔"名义编撰的《文昌帝君阴骘文》《文昌大洞仙经》等诸多善书广为流传,不仅在中国大陆和台、港、澳都有着广泛的影响,并且进而漂洋过海,远播国外(王兴平,1996:105)。单从在海外的传播情况来看,或许是因为地理位置占优势的缘故,国外最早接受文昌文化的国家要算朝鲜,《文昌帝君阴骘文》流传到邻国日本的时间也相对较早。根据王兴平教授的研究,大约在江户时代(1603—1867 年)初期,文昌经籍已引起日本学界的注意。被视为日本阳明学鼻祖和教育大家的中江藤树(Nakae Toju,1608—1648 年)曾为文昌帝君劝善书《阴骘文》作注,并在专著《鉴草》中加以引用。另一著名哲学家贝原益轩(Ekiken Kaibara,1630—1714 年)也研读过《阴骘文》,并在其著述中有所反映。江户时代末期,日本出现不少文昌经籍的翻刻本和日译本。如文政三年(1820 年)翻译出版的《日语阴骘文绘钞》,文政十二年(1829 年)刊印后又由须原屋源助(Suharaya Gensuke)译印的《丹桂籍》(明·颜正注,清·颜文瑞补案)等(王兴平,2000:53)。《阴骘文》还被作为世界文化遗产收入日文本《世界圣典全集》。

最早的西文译本应是法国学者罗斯奈(Leon de Rosny)1854 年的法译本《阴骘文》(*Le Livre de La recompense des Biengaits secrets*),刊登在当年的《东方与殖民地阿尔及利亚评论》(*Revue l'Orient et de l'Algerie et des colonies*)杂志第 16 期。1879 年,英国汉学家道格拉斯(Robert Kennaway Douglas,1838—1913 年)在其专著《儒教和道教》(*Confucianism and Tauism*)中对《阴骘文》进行了简介和选译,日本禅学大师铃木大拙与美国学者保罗·凯拉斯 1906 年合作完成的《文昌帝君阴骘文》英译本应是该善书在西方国家的首部完整英译作品。本节所选解析内容即为铃木大拙与凯拉斯共同完成的《文昌帝君阴骘文》英译本(以下简称铃译本)。

二 铃木大拙、凯拉斯《文昌帝君阴骘文》译本特色

该译本由封面、目录、引言、译文、中国学者注释翻译、译者注解

这几部分组成，最后还附有关键词索引，在中国典籍英译方面可谓独树一帜。在引言部分，译者不仅对《文昌帝君阴骘文》有简要的介绍，还针对标题的翻译做了说明，考证了"阴骘"一词的解释与翻译。此外，译者还考证了文昌帝君其人其号，将文昌帝君比拟为目的语读者所熟知的圣经人物加百利（Gabriel），这是一位给人类传送好消息的上帝的信使，方便了西方读者对中国文化人物的认知和了解（何立芳，2011：39）。在该译本的出版说明中译者明确谈到翻译该文的目的：

> We hope that the publication of this book will help Western readers to understand better the Chinese character and especially its undeniable fervor for moral ideals. Though the Chinese mind, especially among the uneducated classes, is filled with superstitious notions, we cannot help granting that the character of their moral maxims ranges very high; and we must confess that among all the nations of the world there is perhaps none other so seriously determined to live up to the highest standard of ethical culture.
>
> An appreciation of the virtues of the Chinese will help Western people to treat them with more consideration, and so we contribute our interpretation of this treatise as a mite towards a better understanding between the East and the West, between the white races of Europe and America and the natives of Asia. We hope that the day will come when the mutual distrust will disappear, and when both in reciprocal appreciation of their natural good qualities, will be anxious to treat each other with fairness and brotherly kindness. （Suzuki, Carus, 1906b：14）

对"善"的追求是人类共有的永恒主题，推出该译本的目的即是让西方读者了解中国传统美德、促进中西文化沟通，达成中西方对人类共有的"善"的共识。虽然译本中也存在一些误解和错译，但总体来讲，该译本堪称是一"熔资料、考据、研究、翻译为一炉"的成功译本，既兼顾了文本语义的翻译，也照顾了文化信息的交流。就文本翻译而言，译者在正确理解原文的基础上，主要采用直译或与直译有关的既传达原文语义又保存原文文化特色的方法。而针对其中的文化元素，为避免由于中西文化之间的巨大差异可能造成的损失,译者采取了不同的补偿手段,借助注释、考据和研究等重要手段,较为成功地完成了该典籍英译中的文化译介工作,基本达到了"失之东隅,收之桑榆"的效果,最大限度地实现了文化信息的转换,为从事典籍英译的学者提供了一些有益且有效的启示(何立芳,2011:42)。

三 铃木大拙、凯拉斯《文昌帝君阴骘文》译文解析
[原文]

帝君曰:吾一十七世为士大夫身,未尝虐民酷吏。[1]救人之难,济人之急,悯人之孤,容人之过,广行阴骘,上格苍穹。[2]人能如我存心,天必锡汝以福。[3]于是训于人曰:昔于公治狱,大兴驷马之门;[4]窦氏济人高折五枝之桂;[5]救蚁中状元之选;[6]埋蛇享宰相之荣。[7]欲广福田,须凭心地,行时时之方便,作种种之阴功,利物利人,修善修福。[8]正直代天行化,慈祥为国救民,忠主、孝亲、敬兄、信友。[9]和睦夫妇,教训子孙,毋慢师长,毋侮圣言;或奉真朝斗,或拜佛念经,报答四恩,广行三教。[10]谈道义而化奸顽,讲经史而晓愚昧。济急如济涸辙之鱼,救危如救密罗之雀,矜孤恤寡,敬老怜贫,举善荐贤,饶人责己。[11]措衣食周道路之饥寒,施棺椁免尸骸之暴露。[12]造漏泽之仁园,兴启蒙之义塾。家富提携亲戚,岁饥赈济邻朋。[13]斗称须要公平,不可轻出重入。奴仆待之宽恕,岂宜备责苛求。印造经文,创修寺院,舍药材以拯疾苦,施茶水以解渴烦。或买物而放生,或持斋而戒杀;[14]举步常看虫蚁,禁火莫烧山林。点夜灯以照人行,造河船以济人渡。勿登山而网禽鸟,勿临水而毒鱼虾,勿宰耕牛,勿弃字纸,勿谋人之财产,勿妒人之技能,勿淫人之妻女,勿唆人之争讼,勿坏人之名利,勿破人之婚姻,勿因私仇使人兄弟不和,勿因小利使人父子不睦,勿倚权势而辱善良,勿恃富豪而欺穷困。依本分而致谦恭,守规矩而遵法度,谐和宗族,解释冤怨,善人则亲近之,助德行于身心;恶人则远避之,杜灾殃于眉睫。[15]常须隐恶扬善,不可口是心非,恒记有益之语,罔谈非礼之言。翦碍道之荆榛,除当途之瓦石,[16]修数百年崎岖之路,造千万人来往之桥。垂训以格人非[17],捐资以成人美,做事须循天理,出言要顺人心;见先哲于羹墙,慎独知于衾影。[18]诸恶莫作,众善奉行,永无恶曜加临[19],常有吉神拥护,近报则在自己,远报则在儿孙。百

福骈臻，千祥云集[20]，岂不从阴骘中得来者哉？

[注释]①

1. 世：父子相继为一世。士大夫：指读书做官的人。未尝：从来没有。虐：虐待。酷：暴虐。吏：指低级的官员。

2. 济：帮助，接济。急：危急，困难。悯：怜悯，同情。孤：失去父母的儿童。广：大，扩大。行：做，执行。格：到。苍穹：天。

3. 存：保有。锡：赐给。

4. 昔于公治狱，大兴驷马之门：据传，于公（汉代东海郯人于定国之父）曾经做管理县狱的官员，在职期间，善于判断冤狱，不草菅人命，鉴于他的善举，其子孙后代均得以兴旺发达。驷马：套着四匹马的车，此为做高官者的象征。

5. 窦氏济人高折五枝之桂：相传窦氏（全名窦禹钧）年三十无子，其祖父曾托梦告之，"汝无子，又不寿，宜早修德"。于是窦禹钧广行善事，不可胜计，后获子嗣，并高寿，其五个儿子皆登科入仕，为朝廷高官。

6. 救蚁中状元之选：相传宋郊、宋祁两兄弟同在太学读书，有一个和尚预言说，宋郊能登科甲，宋祁却能中状元。但后来却是宋郊中了状元，原因就在于宋郊曾在一次大雨中救了遭水淹的蚂蚁，积下了阴德，故上天给予嘉奖。

7. 埋蛇享宰相之荣：楚人孙叔敖，幼时出外玩耍，曾见一两头蛇死于路旁，遂将其掩埋。由此积下阴德，长大之后做了楚国的宰相。

8. 福田：指种植福报的田地。行：做。阴功：以至诚之心，做各种好事而不求人知晓，但天却是知道的。利：有利于。

9. 正直：公正无私。慈：慈爱。祥：吉利，吉祥。

10. 真：道教名词，泛指一切神祇。斗：指北斗神。四恩：指天地恩、国王恩、生身父母恩、师长恩。三教：汉代儒者认为夏朝崇尚忠，商代崇尚敬，周朝崇尚文，故以忠、敬、文为三教。自东汉佛教传入我国后，称儒、佛、道为三教。

---

① 本节注释参考唐大潮注译的《文昌帝君阴骘文注译》，《劝善书注译》（中国社会科学出版社2004年版）第55—59页。

11. 涸辙：水干了的车辙。罗：捕鸟的网。矜：怜悯，同情。恤：体恤，怜悯，救济，周济。

12. 措：安置，安排，筹划办理；周：周济，救济。

13. 提携：带领，携带。赈：救济。

14. 持斋：坚持斋戒，吃素、不杀生、诵经等都被称为持斋。

15. 睦：和好，亲近。眉睫：形容事情的急迫、紧急。

16. 荆榛：泛指丛生的荆棘。当途：占着道路。

17. 垂：流传。训：教导，教诲。格：正，纠正。

18. 羹：用肉或菜等做成的带汁的食物，即我们现在所说的"汤"。《后汉书·李固传》谓："舜食则见尧于羹，坐则见尧于墙。"尧、舜都是古代有德行的圣人。此句意为：时时处处都要以圣人为自己行为的楷模。衾：被子。影：身体的影子。

19. 曜：指日、月、星。恶曜：指专司灾祸的神灵。

20. 骈：两马并驾一车，成双，成对的。臻：到，到达。云集：比喻许多人或事物聚集在一起。

[译文]

The Lord says:

For seventeen generations I have been incarnated as a high mandarin[1], and I have never oppressed my people nor maltreated my subordinates. I have helped them in misfortune; I have rescued them from poverty; I have taken compassion on their orphans; I have forgiven their transgressions; I have extensively practised secret virtue (*yin chih*) which is attuned to heaven above.[2] If you are able to keep your hearts as I have kept mine, Heaven will surely bestow upon you blessings. Therefore, these are the instructions I declare unto mankind:[3]

He who wants to expand the field of happiness,[4] let him lay the foundation of it on the bottom of his heart.

Practise benevolence wherever you find an opportunity, and let your deeds of merit be unheeded (*yin*)[5].

Benefit all creatures; benefit the people.

Practise goodness: acquire merit.[6]

Be honest like Heaven in conducting your affairs.

Compassionate and auspicious, the state government must be devoted to the salvation of the people. [7]

Let your heart be impartial and wide of range.

Fulfil the four obligations; impartially observe the three doctrines.

Be faithful and reverential to the ruler. Be filial and obedient to parents. Be congenial and friendly to brothers. Be sincere in your intercourse with friends.

Let some worship the Truthful One, and revere the Northern Constellation, while others bow before the Buddha and recite sutras. [8]

By discoursing on morality and righteousness, convert both the cunning and the dull. By preaching on the canonical books and histories, enlighten the ignorant and the benighted.

Relieve people in distress as speedily as you must release a fish from a dry rill [lest he die]. Deliver people from danger as quickly as you must free a sparrow from a tight noose.

Be compassionate to orphans and relieve widows. Respect the old and help the poor.

Promote the good and recommend the wise. Be lenient with others and exacting with yourself.

Save your clothing and provisions that ye may befriend the hungry and cold on the road.

Give away coffins and cases lest the dead of the poor be exposed.

Build charitable graveyards for unclaimed corpses.

Establish philanthropic institutions for the education of children.

If your own family is well provided, extend a helping hand to your relatives. If the harvest fails, provide for and relieve your neighbors and friends.

Let measures and scales be accurate; and be neither chary in selling nor exacting in buying.

Treat your servants with generosity and consideration. Do not expect perfection nor be too strict in your demands.

Publish and make known sutras and tracts. [9] Build and repair temples and shrines.

Distribute medicine to alleviate the suffering of the sick. With tea or water relieve the distress of the thirsty.

Light lanterns in the night to illuminate where people walk. Keep boats on rivers to ferry people across.

Buy captive animals and give them freedom.

How commendable is abstinence that dispenses with the butcher! [10]

While walking be mindful of worms and ants.

Be cautious with fire and do not set mountain woods or forests ablaze.

Do not go into the mountain to catch birds in nets, nor to the water to poison fishes and minnows.

Do not butcher the ox that plows thy field.

Do not throw away paper that is written on. [11]

Do not scheme for others' property.

Do not envy others' accomplishments.

Do not approach thy neighbor's wife or maids.

Do not stir thy neighbors to litigation.

Do not injure thy neighbor's reputation or interest.

Do not meddle with thy neighbor's conjugal affairs.

Set not, for personal malice, brothers at variance with one another.

Set not father and son at variance for trifles.

Never take advantage of your power, nor disgrace the good and law-abiding.

Presume not, ye that are rich; nor deceive the needy and suffering. [12]

While attending to your duty, be humble and modest. [13]

Live in concord with your relatives and clansmen.

Let go hatred and forgive malice. [14]

Those that are good, seek ye for friends; that will help you to practise virtue with body and soul. Those that are wicked, keep at a distance; it will prevent evil from approaching you.

Pass in silence over things wicked, but promulgate all that is good.

Do not assert with your mouth what your heart denies.

Always have in mind helpful sayings.

Do not use improper language.

Cut the brambles and thorns that obstruct the highway. Remove bricks and stones that lie in the path.

Repair the defiles though for many hundred years they have remained unimproved.

Build bridges to be traversed by thousands and ten thousands of people. [15]

Expound moral maxims to correct the people's faults.

Supply the means to give instruction to people of talent.

Let your work conform to Heaven's reason, and let your speech express humaneness. [16]

Keep the ancient sages before your eyes even when at supper or while looking over the fence.

Be mindful when you are alone in the shadow of your coverlet. [17]

Anything evil refrain ye from doing; all good deeds do! So will you be released forever from the influence of evil stars, and always be encompassed by good guardian angels. [18]

Rewards may be immediate, and you will receive them in person, or rewards may be remote, and will devolve upon your posterity.

Blessings come a hundredfold in loads as if drawn by horses; good fortune is piled up a thousandfold like a mass of clouds. [19]

Do not all these things accrue to the heart of the quiet way? （Suzuki, Carus, 1906b: 17 – 22）

[解析]

1.《梓潼帝君化书》记载帝君有十七世化为士大夫，所以《阴骘文》开篇即说"吾一十七世为士大夫身"，译为"For seventeen generations I have been incarnated as a high mandarin"。译者用"incarnate"一词翻译"为……身"，该词具有强烈的宗教意味，在基督教领域作"道成肉身"之解，指耶稣是道，通过童贞女玛利亚取肉身成人，而在佛教中又通常解读为佛的三身之一"化身"（其余二身为"法身"和"报身"）。译者在注释部分也对此说了说明，认为这一说法受传入中国的印度佛教的影响。此外，古代将官吏和士人统称为"士大夫"，该句用"high mandarin"翻译"士大夫"也是因循古意，因为 mandarin 除了指称"普通话"之外，还指代中国官僚，源自葡萄牙语中的 mandarim（早期拼写 mandarin）。该词最早出现在 16 世纪葡萄牙人报道中国的一些信札中。

2. 原文"广行阴骘，上格苍穹"意为：做大量的善事，就能飞升上天。在道教看来，飞升上天即为修道成仙，意味着能与天相配，获得福报。该句体现了道教的积善成仙思想，英译文"I have extensively practised secret virtue (*yin chih*) which is attuned to heaven above"抓住了原文内涵，尤其是用"be attuned to"（与……合拍）而不是用"reach"或其他表示"到达"含义的动词翻译"格"字，更是体现了译者对原文的深刻考究。该句还涉及关键术语"阴骘"一词的翻译。这里"阴"是"默"的意思，"骘"是"定"的意思，指的是天虽不言，但于冥冥中监督人的善恶行为而降赏罚。后来人们称"阴骘"为"阴德"。《汉英双语现代汉语词典》对该术语的英文解释是：secretly seek stability through doing good deeds for merit in the netherworld。这只能算是一种释义，谈不上是"阴骘"一词的对应英文表述。铃译本深知不可能在英文中找到一个像中文这般既简洁又意义深刻的对应词语，所以在引言部分提出"阴骘"英译的三种选择：(1) secret virtue，(2) heaven's quiet dispensation，(3) mysterious workings，并对这三种译法都做了相应的评说，认为，虽说这三种翻译都可作为正译，但都不能算是足额翻译。综合看来，第三种译法似乎是实现第一、第二译文意图的途径，所以译本最终标题译为 The Tract of the Quiet Way。并指出，这一选择也只是一个过渡性翻译，虽然简洁但很宽泛，仍需进一步提供解释才能让读者懂得该文的含义（Suzuki, Carus, 1906b：4）。为了帮助目的语读者较好地理解该文，铃译本还在注释中拆解了"阴骘"二字，将"阴"解释为"不引人注意"（in secret or unheaded）或"不夸耀"（unostentatious），并引用基督教颂歌中的"God moves in a mysterious way, His wonders to perform"这句话来佐证选择译为"the quiet way"的依据。指出，如果要将这两行诗文译为中文，其中"in a mysterious way"可以等同于中文的"阴骘"。因为基督教严厉禁止基督徒做事招摇，教义中有"不让我们的右手知道左手在做什么"（not let our right hand know what the left hand is doing）这类戒条，所以在解读"阴骘"一词的来源时译者引用《尚书·洪范》"惟天阴骘下民，相协厥居"这句，其英文翻译为 Heaven alone, in a quiet or mysteriously unnoticeable way, directs the affairs of mankind living below on earth。

3. 这里省译了原文的"昔于公治狱，大兴驷马之门；窦氏济人高折五枝之桂；救蚁中状元之选；埋蛇享宰相之荣"四句讲述于公、窦禹钧、宋郊、孙叔敖这几个历史上有名的灵验故事，是为不影响目的语读者阅读的流畅性。不过，身为"世界禅者"的铃木大拙深知典籍翻译的核心应是其中所蕴含的文化元素的译介，因此译本选择在后面的注解部分用几倍于原文的篇幅向读者解释了这些文化典故，并给每一典故附加了小标题以点明主旨。如在阐释汉朝时的地方官于公"多积阴德，从不冤枉好人"的故事时添加了"A Good Judge"这一标题，对于公的身份与行为做一评判。而在叙述五代时的窦禹钧"力行善事，救济别人，广积阴功，获得厚报"的事迹后用"Humaneness Rewarded"点明了积善的好处，用"Saving Many Lives"为题向译文读者叙说了宋郊"救蚂蚁中状元"的故事，最后则以"The Double-Headed Snake"为题讲述了仁义之士孙叔敖埋蛇的事迹。即便如此，译者并没忘记对原文应有的忠实之责，所以选择在讲述每一典故时，其首句或首段采用直译法翻译了原文本中的四句话。

原文：昔于公治狱，大兴驷马之门。

译文：In olden times, Yu King, judge of the criminal court, was held in such high esteem (on account of his virtue) that a gateway for four-horse carriages was erected in his honor.

原文：窦氏济人高折五枝之桂。

译文：The Tou family saved people and thus nobly obtained the five-branched olea.

原文：救蚁中状元之选。

译文：He who took pity on ants attained the highest literary honor.

原文：埋蛇享宰相之荣。

译文：He who buried (out of sight) the snake (of bad omen) was

deemed worthy of the honor of premiership.

通过这些辅助性手段把需要注释的地方都做了解释，对文化缺省部分进行了填补性解释。这些翻译策略表面上看好像很烦琐，却阐明了掩盖在原文字面后的文化内涵，方便了读者的理解，也给译语读者提供了一个了解异域文化的机会（何立芳，2011：41）。

4. "福田"为佛教术语，梵文为 punyakshetra，谓可生福德之田；凡敬侍佛、僧、父母、悲苦者，即可得福德、功德，犹如农人耕田能有收获，故以田为喻，则佛、僧、父母、悲苦者，即称为福田，直译为"field of happiness"，既保留原文的喻体，也译出了内涵。

5. "行时时之方便，作种种之阴功"译为：Practise benevolence wherever you find an opportunity, and let your deeds of merit be unheeded (*yin*)。原文中的"方便"为佛教用语，意为"方法，达到某一结果的成功途径"，主要用于大乘佛教，可以直译为 deeds of benevolence。而为了忠实于原文的形式结构，译者运用了两个祈使句，把"作阴功"处理为 let your deeds of merit be unheeded (*yin*)，从形式上到内容都与原文保持了一致（何立芳，2011：40）。

6. 原文"利物利人，修善修福"中的"物"泛指"万物"，译为"creatures"可指"all objects about us"。此外，译者根据具体语境，将"修善修福"理解为因果关系，译为 Practise goodness: acquire merit，传达了原文作者的真实意图，实谓正解。

7. "正直代天行化，慈祥为国救民"这句的译文：Be honest like heaven in conducting your affairs. Compassionate and auspicious, the state government must be devoted to the salvation of the people. Let your heart be impartial and wide of range。回译过来意思是：政府的行为处事要像上天一样诚实，拯救百姓需持有同情心，要公正要广博。实际上这句话的意思是"做君主的，应当公正无私，替天教化百姓；应当怀着慈爱之心治理国家，造福于百姓"。该句可改译为 On behalf of heaven monarchs should be impartial and compassionate in conducting their teachings and governings for the benefit of the people.

8. 依据英文先总后分的表达习惯，原文"忠主孝亲，敬兄信友。或奉真朝斗，或拜佛念经。报答四恩，广行三教"在译文中调整为：报答四恩，广行三教，忠主孝亲，敬兄信友，或奉真朝斗，或拜佛念经。译文为Fulfil the four obligations; impartially observe the three doctrines. Be faithful and reverential to the ruler. Be filial and obedient to parents. Be congenial and friendly to brothers. Be sincere in your intercourse with friends. Let some worship the Truthful One, and revere the Northern Constellation, while others bow before the Buddha and recite sutras。佛教、道教均有"四恩"之说，但内容不尽相同。《大乘本生心地观经·报恩品》记载："世出世恩有其四种：一父母恩，二众生恩，三国王恩，四三宝恩。如是四恩，一切众生平等荷负。"明全真道士周玄贞编撰的《高上玉皇本行经》写道："天地盖载，日月照临，皇王水土，父母生身，为四重恩。""三教"则指"儒、释、道"。这里译者并未译出具体内容，但在注解中详细说明了"四恩"和"三教"的具体所指，同时指明"心善"为三教共有，即儒教之"仁"，佛教之"慈"，道教之"感应"。道教概念中"真"意为"自然之本性"，尽管译者将之译为"the Truthful One"，似乎可以对等"真"的原意，但译者仍加注说明"真"可指道教，也有可能指代道教始祖老子，抑或是道教圣贤，或道教圣书《太上感应篇》。由此可以看出译者对道教概念术语翻译的审慎。

9. "印造经文，创修寺院"中的"经文"译为"sutras and tracts"，sutras通常指代"佛经"，译者用该词想指代儒释道的所有经典，其实可以改用"scriptures"，泛指宗教圣典。

10. "或买物而放生，或持斋而戒杀"译为"Buy captive animals and give them freedom. How commendable is abstinence that dispenses with the butcher"，回译为中文即指购买被关押监禁的动物，给它们自由。不杀生的禁欲（行为）值得赞美。"放生"和"戒杀"都是佛教情怀，俗语有云"救人一命胜造七级浮屠"，佛经里常把放生视为发慈悲之心的善举，为永劫长乐、长寿之善因；而把杀生看作怀残忍之心的恶行，为永劫冤冤相报之本。原文的"物"指"有生命之物"，这里指"被人捕捉而出售的有生命之物"，译为"captive animals"堪称妙译。不过"持斋"的意思是"坚持斋戒"，不茹荤食、不杀生都是道教认为的持斋行为，译者用"abstinence"（禁欲）翻译"持斋"是可行的，但忽略了"持斋"与

"戒杀"之间的相互包含关系。若要考虑与译者采用的祈使句式保持一致，可将"或持斋而戒杀"译为 Do not kill and be abstinent。

11. "勿弃字纸"是中华传统美德之一。劝人敬惜字纸的劝善书大多以《惜字律》命名，主要是劝诫人们不可随意丢弃、践踏写有字的纸，需专门收集后焚烧成灰，并妥善保存字灰。单纯把"勿弃字纸"译为"Do not throw away paper that is written on"虽浅显易懂，但如果不提供相应的文化背景知识，该句的译文也就失去了意义，因此译者在注释部分补充了这一点，现摘录其注释内容如下：The Chinese show great respect for writing and writing materials, because, they say, by them we become acquainted with the virtues, wisdom and sayings of ancient sages. Any writing, to the Chinese, partakes of the nature of spirit, and there is a special order of monks who make it their duty to collect written scraps of paper and burn them, to save them the disgrace of any disrespectful treatment（Suzuki, Carus, 1906b：41）。因为文昌帝君是读书人信奉尊崇的神，因此《阴骘文》有"无弃字纸"这样的与读书人相关的内容，翻译时需补充背景文化知识。

12. 原文"勿倚权势而辱善良，勿恃富豪而欺穷困"中的"而"为连词，可表并列关系、相承关系、递进关系、转折关系或修饰关系。依据上句"勿因私仇，使人兄弟不和；勿因小利，使人父子不睦"，这里应表相承关系，译者理解为并列关系不符合上下文逻辑，可改译为 Never abuse your power to disgrace the good and law-abiding. Nor deceive the needy and suffering on the strength of your wealth。

13. "依本分而致谦恭，守规矩而遵法度"译为 While attending to your duty, be humble and modest，用"attending to one's duty"翻译"依本分"可谓准确达意，这里省译了"守规矩而遵法度"，丝毫不影响该句意义的完整。

14. "解释冤怨"应理解为"解怨释冤"，因此译为 Let go hatred and forgive malice。汉语有"结怨"（to owe a grudge）之说，可直译为 tie (the knot of) hatred or enmity。"解"为"结"的反义词，可对应为"loosen"或"untie"，译者译为"let go"，也算是一种灵活变通。

15. "修百年崎岖之路，造千万人来往之桥"翻译为 Repair the defiles though for many hundred years they have remained unimproved. Build bridges

to be traversed by thousands and ten thousands of people，其中"崎岖之路"被对应为 defiles（该词通常用来指山中弯曲而窄小之路），这样精准的选词充分体现了译者深厚的中英文语言功底。

16. "做事须循天理，出言要顺人心"的译文 Let your work conform to Heaven's reason, and let your speech express humaneness 与原文形式和内容保持高度一致。虽然译者把"天理"和"天道"都翻译为 Heaven's Reason，但译者专门加注说明，这里指通常意义上的"天之道义"，可译为 reason 或 rationality。

17. "见先哲于羹墙，慎独知于衾影"意思是"吃穿住行，时刻想念圣贤教诲；独行独卧，始终慎如众目睽睽"。该句借用《后汉书·李固传》中所记载的古代圣人尧舜的逸事："舜食则见尧于羹，坐则见尧于墙"，强调在日常生活中要事事以圣人为榜样，谨慎自己的行为，不可欺人欺己。译者选择直译法，保留了原文意象"羹墙"（when at supper or while looking over the fence）、"衾影"（in the shadow of your coverlet），依然通过注释补充解读该句的内涵，译者虽没有直接翻译典故内容，但在阐释原文旨意的基础上引用《论语·里仁》"君子无终食之间违仁，造次必于是，颠沛必于是"和《中庸》第一章"道也者，不可须臾离也；可离，非道也。是故君子戒慎乎其所不睹，恐惧乎其所不闻"，以说明原文的内涵。该句译文的注释内容如下：

> This means not to forget for a moment the deeds or instructions of wise men of old, "to be always on guard lest the heart might go astray." Says Confucius (*Lun Yü*, IV, 5): "The superior man does not, even for a space of a single meal, act contrary to virtue. In moments of haste his mind dwells on it. In time of danger his mind dwells on it." In the *Chung Yung*, (*Doctrine of the Mean*), it is said that the *tao* ("path" or "doctrine") is not for a moment to, be ignored, for that which can be ignored is not the *tao*. (Suzuki, Carus, 1906b: 42)

18. "永无恶曜加临，常有吉神拥护"译为 So will you be released forever from the influence of evil stars, and always be encompassed by good guard-

ian angels。"神"通常译为"god"或"spiritual being",译者依据上下文在这里译为"angel",并通过动词"encompass"和"guardian"的巧妙结合翻译"拥护",可见译者的匠心独运。

19. 原文"百福骈臻,千祥云集"采用明喻的修辞手法描述"阴骘"给人带来的诸多福气和吉祥,选择的喻体为"骈臻"(两马并驾所带来的)和"云集"(像成片的云般聚集),译者保留了原文喻体,以明喻翻译原文的明喻,译文为 Blessings come a hundredfold in loads as if drawn by horses; good fortune is piled up a thousandfold like a mass of clouds。

小　结

道教劝善书是道教逐渐世俗化、逐渐与民众生活结合的产物(陈霞,1999:3),已在中国社会存在近千年之久。"通俗易懂、简单易行"是这类典籍的共同属性,因其蕴含丰富的宗教伦理道德内容常被用作道德教材,在民间广泛流传,即能规范约束教内人士的思想行为,又能教化普通大众趋善从善。在明清时代乃至民国时期,道教劝善书均发挥过显著的社会教化作用。选择这类文本进行翻译研究的海外学者,尤其是有着传教士翻译家双重身份的学者,重点关注的也是这类典籍的社会教化功能,因此翻译时通常会把文中简略提及的道德教化故事附录其后,依据原文蕴含的主旨大意添加相应的小标题,作点题之用,以凸显道教劝善书作为官方推行的社会教育基本教材的功能,最大限度保持译文和原文之间的功能对等。至于具体的翻译方法,以本章解析的《太上感应篇》译本和《文昌帝君阴骘文》译本为例,原文浅显易懂,文字简约,言简意赅,英译者尽量保留了这一平易直白的文体特征,主体采用的是以达意为前提的直译法,既向读者传播了中华民族的文化要素,也在一定程度上丰富了译文语言的表达力。需要指出的是,这种直译是有条件的,必须以传旨达意为前提,允许因中英语言差异而表现在译文上的不同,如果完全依原文的字面意义翻译,甚至不改变文字的次第,定会出现有些句子的语义不够透彻,这样的直译法是行不通的。

第 四 章

道教戒律文本翻译研究

引 语

作为一个成熟的组织化的宗教，道教拥有一套以道教戒律为载体的宗教道德体系。这些戒律既可以约束教徒的思想行为，又可维系教团稳固，还有助于国家的稳定和团结。通常我们把约束规范道教徒思想行为准则的条文内容统称为道教戒律，但从"戒"和"律"的内涵与功能来看，又可分而论之。据《中华道教大辞典》所给出的定义，"戒"为规戒，主要以防范为目的；律为律文，主要以惩罚为手段。"戒""律"合用构成对道教徒言行的防范和制裁（胡孚琛，1995：564）。可见，道教戒律是道教内部为构建和谐的教团环境所设立的一系列规定和训诫，其重要性仅次于教义。

道教戒律类文本可分为戒经、律文、科文、清规、功过格、善书六种（丁培仁，2006：5）。这种将功过格和善书都归为道教戒律类文本的论断自有其道理，其中最充足的理由是这类劝善止恶的文本与早期道教戒经的基本精神完全吻合。而一些道教戒经作品，如《赤松子中诫经》，也会被列为善书之一，原因应归结于该文以劝善为专题行文的特点，可见戒经与善书在主题和功能上具有难以区分的一致性。人们通常称道教戒律书为"戒经"，其中出自正一道的戒经常以"律"冠名，如《女青鬼律》，有禁制劾鬼的功用，这是道教招神劾鬼的特色所在。道教的科文通常被称为"明科"（或称"盟科"），意思是与神盟誓，永不犯戒，是奉道者尤其是道士的行为规范。清规是金元间全真道受到佛教禅宗丛林制度影响后才有的说法，指日常修行规范，通常有惩处条例，由住持、道众对犯过道士予以惩罚。宋代以后流行功过格和劝善书。功过格是道教戒律更为具体化的一种文本形式，始于南宋金代《太微仙君功过格》，要求信徒（不限于道士）自己填写每日所行善事和恶事，月终以过除功，以功折过，然后总计，检查功过多少。因这种书提供了定量计算每一功过的轻重及折除的固定格式，故名"格"。可见，道教戒律品类繁多，单从名称上来看就有约二十种，如戒、律、科、愿、念、劝、格、行、品、忌、禁、规、清规、清约、式、诰、德、诀、病、药等（刘绍云，2006：25）。被丁培仁教授归入道教戒律范畴的功过格和劝善书是道教后期世俗化进程中的产物，融摄儒释道三教思想，虽本于早期戒律，和戒经、律文、科文、清规同为道教教徒的规诫内容，但其适用范围更广，已广泛流传于民间，为普通百姓所熟知，因此本书将劝善文本单列出来，已在第二章进行了讨论，本章所讨论的戒律文本主要为戒经文类。

道教认为，戒律就是道，想学道就必须严守戒律，遵从规诫。道教戒律中的这些规诫有警告、劝告、告诫、劝诫等功能，在过去起到过调节个人与社会关系的作用，到今天对现实社会也有一定的关照意义，仍然有可能在一定程度上和一定范围内服务于现代社会的精神文明建设。因此，不少学者开始关注道教戒律的研究，除了从宏观层面对道教戒律进行知识性介绍之外，还从微观层面对其历史发展、传授、与律法道德的关系，以及其中涉及的生态思想、女性观等展开研究。不过，相对于体系庞大的道教戒律文本而言，中西学界针对道教戒律的研究还不够全面，不成体系，多数为零散话题的探讨。这种状况是与道教诸多戒律书很不相称的（丁培仁，2006：4）。

单从西方学者对道教戒律书的关注度来讲，作为欧美道教学研究的先驱之一，法国汉学家马伯乐（Henri Maspero，1883—1945 年）开启了西方学者从道教内部系统研究道教的时代，在他撰写的《道教》一书的附录《文献一览》中，戒律类仅列两部（杜光庭《金箓斋启坛仪》一卷应归入科仪类）。在吕鹏志先生编译的《法国道教研究文献目录（1831—2002）》亦难见欧洲道教学界的这方面信息。当然，贺碧来（Isabelle Robinet）在《道教史上的上清降经》二卷、司马虚（Michel Strickmann）在《茅山的道教——降经编年史》中考定了包括戒律类道经在内的上清派经书的年代，这对于我们研究上清派戒律有着十分重要的意义。另外，贺碧来先生在《神圣经书的流传》、索安（Anna Seidel，1938—1991 年）在《皇家宝藏和道教圣物》、施舟人先生在《敦煌抄本中的道教职位》中还探讨了道教的传经禁戒以及道士等级阶位与所受戒律的关系（唐怡，2006：13）。相较而言，海外学者完成的第一部系统研究道教清规戒律的著作是当今知名汉学家、道教研究学者孔丽维 2004 年出版的《宇宙与教团：道教的伦理维度》（Cosmos and Community：The Ethical Dimension of Daoism）一书，该书分主题从 6 个维度解读了道教戒律条文所折射的道教伦理思想，具体包括：（1）人类行为与宇宙之善（Human Behavior and Cosmic Goodness）；（2）道德法则与感官转换（Moral Rules and Sensory Transformation）；（3）欲望克制：食物、酒和性（Impulse Control：Food，Wine，and Sex）；（4）向善之戒条（Admonitions toward Goodness）；（5）教团模式（Forms of Community）；（6）修身束行之道门规诫（Monastic Discipline：Changing Body and Behavior）；（7）从教团到宇宙（From Community to Cosmos）。孔丽维是活跃在西方中国道教经籍研究领域的女学者，集教师、翻译家、汉学家、道教徒等多个身份于一体，成果颇丰（姜莉，2018：34）。她不仅编撰了一些综合介绍道教概要的书籍，还撰写了一批关涉道教神秘主义、道德准则和身体修炼的成果，其研究成果《宇宙与教团：道教的伦理维度》则是一部针对道教社团组织管理模式的专题研究，书后附有 11 篇道教清规戒律文本的翻译，分别包括：（1）《太上老君说一百八十戒》（The 180 Precepts of Lord Lao）；（2）《太上老君戒经》（Precepts of the Highest Lord Lao）；（3）《赤松子中诫经》（The Essential Precepts of Master Redpine）；（4）《上品大戒》（Great Precepts of the Highest Ranks）；（5）《十戒经》（Scripture of the Ten Precepts）；（6）《三元品戒》（Precepts of the Three Primes）；（7）《太清五十八愿文》（The Fifty-Eight Prayers of Great Clarity）；（8）《观身大戒》（The Great Precepts of Self-Observation）；（9）《禁戒经》（Scripture of Prohibitions and Precepts）；（10）《十事威仪》（Ten Items of Dignified Observances）；（11）《初真戒律》（Precepts of Initial Perfection）。此外，孔丽维还在她的电子出版物《〈宇宙与教团〉补充读物》（Supplement to Cosmos and Community）一书中摘录了部分包含在道教经籍中的戒律内容的译文，涉及的道教经籍主要有：《老子想尔注》（*Xiang'er Commentary to the Laozi*），《女青鬼律》（*Demon Statutes of Nüqing*），《天师教戒科经》（*Precepts and Rules Taught by the Celestial Master*），《正一五戒》（*Five Precepts of Orthodox Unity*），《玄都律文》（*Statutes of Mystery Metropolis*），等等。澳大利亚学者芭芭拉（Barbara Hendrischke）和裴凝（Benjamin Penny）发表在《道教资源》（*Taoist Resources*）1996 年第 2 期上的《〈太上老君说一百八十戒〉译文及文本研究》（*The 180 Precepts Spoken by Lord Lao— A Translation and Textual Study*）一文，也有《太上老君说一百八十戒》的完整翻译。这些都是西方学者了解道教戒律的极好研究素材。

本章选取孔丽维完成的《赤松子中诫经》和《洞玄灵宝天尊说十戒经》英译本作为解析对象。

第一节 《赤松子中诫经》英文翻译研究

《赤松子中诫经》（简称《中诫经》）托名道教神仙赤松子，以他与黄帝之间的对话形式讨论祸福报应这一劝善书的共同主题。《易经·坤卦·文言》中说："积善之家，必有余庆；积不善之家，必有余殃"，《中诫经》反复宣扬天人感应和因果报应，劝诫人们要多行善事、积累功德，通常被归于道教戒律类，收入《道藏》洞真部戒律类。原文不足 4000 字，共计 12 段，文风平易直白，采用问答形式探讨了九个问题：（1）万民受生何不均匀？（Why are people different in their fortunes?）（2）人生寿命合得几许？（How long is a typical human life?）（3）或有胎中便夭，或得数岁而亡，犯何禁忌？（Why are there miscarriages and the deaths of infants?）（4）神仙善恶之兆，见蒙福佑（How can one improve one's lot?）（5）司命夺人算寿，世人作何罪所招？（Which sins are punished by subtractions from the life expectancy?）（6）人犯天地禁忌夺算，有数人之罪，如何？（Do sins and punishments match one another?）（7）世人违犯，卧不安席，罪可解乎？（How can one dissolve the sins already accumulated?）（8）更有人间至妙之道，可得闻乎？（Can one find the Dao even in ordinary human life?）（9）智人何等次之（What types and ranks of wise ones are there?）①。通过枚举各种善恶的表现行为及其奖惩报应效果，为道教徒厘定了一份详尽的"善恶奖惩条例"，是现存道经中最早以劝善为专题行文的道教戒经。

一 孔丽维对道教戒律的认知和解读

收录在《道藏》和《藏外道书》中内容涉及道内人士行为规范准则的道经达70多种，孔丽维在《宇宙与教团：道教的伦理维度》一书的附录中选取了部分代表性文献进行译介，并通过引言简要介绍了这些戒律文本的内容、大致撰写年代以及学界已有的一些相关研究等。这些戒律文本译文是她研究道教伦理的基础素材，译者将其作为附录文本，供感兴趣的读者阅读了解，方便读者结合这些道教戒律文本内容深入领会她论著的思想，这种思路沿袭了西方汉学家融研究与翻译为一体的惯常做法。

孔丽维既是一名翻译家，也是一名道教徒，她对所翻译对象的行文特点及其文字背后所蕴涵的意义有较为充分的理解。该书的引言部分有如下内容：

> Daoism shares with other religions the emphasis on ethical guidelines requisite to serious attainment and its support of three fundamentally different types of community: lay organizations, monastic institutions, and the closed communities of millenarian or utopian groups. It is unique in that its rules, which make use of both traditional Chinese values and Buddhist precepts, are highly varied and specific not only to these communities as they change over time but also to different levels of ordination and types of rituals. Furthermore, the rules are manifold, there are numerous different terms for them, and they appear in different grammatical formats. On the basis of their terminology and grammar, four types can be distinguished:

---

① 括号内英译文是孔丽维在该篇译文的引言部分介绍《中诫经》主旨大意时依据中文内容翻译的，详见文献（Kohn, 2004: 155）。

prohibitions formulated as "do not" (*bude* 不得); admonitions including the term "should" (*dang* 当) or "should always" (*changdang* 常当); injunctions that deal with concrete daily behavior; and resolutions that focus on a specific mindset, are phrased in the first person, and usually contain expressions like "pray" (*yuan* 愿), "be mindful" (*nian* 念), or "bring forth [the good] intention" (*faxin* 发心). (Kohn, 2004: 1-2)

在她看来，同其他宗教一样，道教将遵从道德准则作为修道的必要条件，这些准则适合用于世俗社会、寺院庙宇和封闭的千年王国或乌托邦团体的管理。其独特之处在于融合了中国传统价值观和佛教戒律，内容丰富，且形式多样，会因时代变迁或使用场合不同而发生变化。孔丽维谈到了道教戒律的表述特征，认为道教戒律涉及范围广，术语众多且说法不一，语法句式也多种多样。依据戒律各不相同的术语表述和语法句式，孔丽维将特征显著的道教戒律归为四类，即：(1) 禁 (prohibitions)，常以否定词"不得"(do not) 开头；(2) 劝 (admonitions)，常包含情态词"当"(should) 或"常当"(should always)；(3) 科 (injunctions)，指向具体的日常行为规范；(4) 愿 (resolutions)，专注明确的思维模式，常用第一人称，常使用动词"愿"(pray)、"念"(be mindful)、"发心"(bring forth [the good] intention)。

至于这些道教戒律的内涵差异，孔丽维写道：

The most general word for rule in China is *jie* 戒, commonly translated "precept..." More psychologically, the word means to be prepared for unforeseen dangers, to guard against unwholesome influences, and to abstain from harmful actions. ...

Beyond this, *jie* in China also include prohibitions (*jin* 禁) of certain socially disruptive behaviors and detailed taboos (*ji* 忌) of time and space. Unlike the universal rules, prohibitions focus on specific social actions and attitudes that are considered detrimental to the group and may lead to the disruption of social bonds and the destruction of integration and harmony. Represented by the ancient Confucian tradition, they are geared toward the upholding of propriety and social order, controlling sex, aggression, greed, and so on. Violations are punished by preventing people from attaining the established social goals of long life, prosperity, respect, and well-being. ...

Beyond *jie*, a second form of Daoist rules is found in positively formulated guidelines, encouraging followers to develop virtues of kindness and compassion and to become considerate toward others. Often called admonitions (*quan* 劝), they are the Daoist equivalent of what moral philosophers call supererogatory rules. ...

A third type of Daoist rules appears as practical injunctions or rules (*ke* 科; *gui* 规 after the Song), dignified observances (*weiyi* 威仪), and statutes (*lü* 律). They prescribe in detail how and when to perform a certain action. Injunctions regulate every aspect of life and physical activity, causing the submission of the individual to the communal pattern and enabling the complete transformation of personal reality toward a celestial level. (Kohn, 2004: 2 – 5)

孔丽维认为最常用的戒律称"戒"（对应英文为 precept），"戒"包含"禁"（prohibitions）、"忌"（taboos），"禁"一切对社会有危害之行为，"忌"特定时间、特定场合之忌讳。第二类别常被称为"劝"（admonitions），是一种正面的引导，鼓励信众培养美德，要善良，要有同情心，会体谅人。第三类道教戒律为一系列约束人的日常行为举止的具体操作规范，包括"科"（injunctions）、"威仪"（dignified observances）、"律"（statutes）等，"科"在宋以后称作"规"（rules）。第四类戒律被称作"愿"（resolutions），为道教戒律中最高层次的道德约束，通常是一些以第一人称发出的善愿善念（prayers or good wishes）。这些对道教戒律语言的认知皆反映在她翻译的戒律文本中，同时我们也了解到了"戒""禁""忌""劝""科""威仪""律""愿"这些道教戒律不同概念的对应英文。

二　孔丽维《赤松子中诫经》译本的篇章结构特点

汉英篇章组织结构有着本质的差异，通常看来，英语的一个段落只允许容纳一个话题，一个段落基本只表达一个中心思想，而汉语的一个段落可以容纳一个或一个以上的话题，因此一个段落出现多个主题在道教典籍文献中尤其突出，翻译时就需要考虑典籍段落的划分重组问题。钟书能指出"以意合为主的汉语在建构篇章时可以将多个具有关联的话题链镶嵌在同一段落中，而以形合为主的英语却倾向于让每个话题链独立建构于一个段落中"（钟书能，2016：90）。英语中的段落是约定俗成的单位，其自然段与篇章的组织原则是一致的。因此，在汉英篇章翻译过程中，译者须对镶嵌了多个话题链的汉语段落解构，再在英语语篇中按独立段落重构每个话题链（钟书能、徐晶晶，2018：39）。道教典籍翻译是一个极其复杂的过程，译者既要注意英汉结构差异以保证译文段落与话题的一一对应和主题的突出，又要对原文复杂话题链进行解构，并在译文中重新建构并调整，以适应译入语读者的阅读习惯。

从篇章层次来看，孔丽维翻译《赤松子中诫经》时按英语的表达习惯依主题细分段落，全文不过 12 个段落，英译本则演变为 63 个自然段。此外，译者采用不同的编排模式，突出她认为需要特别强调的内容，如，在翻译赤松子解答黄帝提问"司命夺人算寿，世人作何罪招致"时，译文按先总后分的思路，把赤松子列举的世人触犯的罪行条例（原文从"不敬天地鬼神"一直到"欺诳谩人"）逐条翻译出来，并独立成行与译文的其他部分区别开来，同样，在翻译赤松子言说"古人"的善良品质（原文从"无不亲"一直到"无自可"），"世人多行五背，心常九念"中"九念"，"心行五德之人，常怀九思"中的"九思"的具体所指时，译者都如法炮制，这种篇章处理模式不仅逻辑清楚，更重要的是突出醒目，值得中国译者效仿。

以《中诫经》开篇两段为例，作者借赤松子之口解答了"万民受生不均"的终极根源，并列数了一些人"胎中便夭"或"得数岁而亡"所犯的禁忌条例，其核心旨意为："自古英贤设教，留在《仙经》，皆劝人为善，知其诸恶，始乃万古传芳，子孙有福"，提出了道教趋善去恶的教育思想。作者用量化的方式列出了行恶所应受到的"夺算"后果，强调弃恶为善的重要性，以便让天下百姓能够一目了然，清楚其中的利害关系，自觉做到趋善远恶。该部分最显著的特点是从人们普遍存在的畏天、敬天、顺天的心理因素出发，塑造了一个能赏善惩恶的天地之神，作者运用因果报应的逻辑公式，借助"天"的威严和力量，通俗易懂地向人们进行了一番劝善的教育。虽然有着浓厚的宗教色彩，但它所能达到的教育效果是显而易见的（马丽涛，2001：26）。译者将这两个段落解构为15个自然段，除了英语读者习惯于将问答分列这个缘故之外，依主题分立成段才是译者作出这一选择的根本原因。本节解析内容即为孔丽维翻译这两段的英译文本。

三　孔丽维《赤松子中诫经》译文（节选）解析
[原文]

轩辕黄帝稽首，问赤松子曰："朕见万民，受生何不均匀，有富贵，有贫贱，有长命者，有短命者，或横罹枷禁，或久病缠身，或无病卒亡，或长寿有禄，如此不等，愿先生为朕辩之。"[1]赤松子曰："生民茕茕，各载一星，有大有小，各主人形，延促衰盛，贫富死生。[2]为善者，善气覆之，福德随之，众邪去之，神灵卫之，人皆敬之，远其祸矣。[3]为恶之人，凶气覆之，灾祸随之，吉祥避之，恶星照之，人皆恶之，衰患之事，病集其身矣。[4]人之朝夕，行心用行，善恶所为，暗犯天地禁忌，谪谴罪累事非，一也。[5]人之朝夕为恶，人神司命，奏上星辰，夺其算寿，天气去之，地气著之，故曰衰也。[6]"

黄帝又问曰："人生寿命合得几许？"[7]对曰："人生堕地，天赐其寿，四万三千八百日，都为一百二十岁，一年主一岁，故人受命皆合一百二十岁，为犯天地禁忌，夺算命终。"[8]又问："或有胎中便夭，或得数岁而亡，此既未有施为，犯何禁忌？"赤松子对曰："此乃祖宗之罪，遗殃及后。自古英贤设教，留在《仙经》，皆劝人为善，知其诸恶，始乃万古传芳，子孙有福。[9]夫人生在天地之中，禀阴阳二气，皇天虽高，其应在下，后土虽卑，其应在上，天不言而四时行，地不言而万物生，人处其中，恣心情欲，凡人动息，天地皆知，故云天有四知也。[10]人不言报天地之恩，发言多怨天地，天生烝民，以乾坤表父母，日月表眼目，星辰表九窍，风动火力为煖气，寿命终时，总还归土。[11]天上三台、北辰、司命、司录差太一直符,常在人头上,察其有罪,夺其算寿:若夺一年,头上星无光,其人坎坷多事;夺算十年,星渐破缺,其人灾衰疾病;夺其算寿二十年,星光殒灭,其人困笃,或遭刑狱;夺其算寿三十年,其星流散,其人则死;时去算尽,不周天年,更殃后代子孙,子孙流殃不尽,以至灭门。[12]人不自知过犯,只言短寿。故天不欺物,示之以影,昼夜阴阳,雷电雨雪,虹霓交晕,日月薄蚀,彗孛飞流,天之信也;[13]地不欺物,示之响应及生万物,江河流注及至枯涸,山崩地动,恶风拔木,飞沙走石,水涝虫蝗,饥荒天旱,瘴疠灾疫,地之信也。[14]鬼神不欺物,示之以祸福、怪异、灾祥,是鬼神之信也。国主不欺物,示之天地和,星辰顺,灾殃灭,四方归,万姓安,人君之信也。人之所行,发言用意,莫言天地如此,故圣人云:'皇天无亲,惟德是辅。'[15]畏天命,畏大人,畏圣人之言。凡人逐日私行,善恶之事,天地皆知其情。暗杀物命,神见其形;心口意语,鬼闻人声;犯禁满百,鬼收其精;犯禁满千,地录人形;日行诸恶,枷锁立成,此阴阳之报也。[16]皇天以诚议,故作违犯,则鬼神天地祸之也。[17]"

[注释]①

1. 稽首:古时的一种跪拜礼,即叩头到地,是九拜中最恭敬者。罹:遭遇不幸的事。枷:旧时一种套在脖子上的刑具。禄:福气。辩:通"辨",辨明,辨别。

2. 生民:人。茕茕:即惸惸,孤孤单单的样子。载:通"戴",头顶着。

3. 德:恩惠。神灵:神明。

4. 吉祥:亦作"吉羊"。成玄英疏:"吉者,祥善之事;祥者,善庆之征。"恶:厌恶。

5. 暗:不显露。谪谴:责罚谴责。

6. 人神司命:人的司命神,为星宿神灵,属虚宿。

7. 合:应当。几许:多少。

8. 堕地:即落地出生。都:总共。

---

① 注释参考曾传辉《赤松子中诫经注译》,载《劝善书注译》(中国社会科学出版社2004年版)第17—19页。

9. 遗殃：流传下来的祸害。设教：设施教化。《仙经》：道教经书名，今已失传。芳：美好的名声。

10. 皇天：天，旧时常与"后土"并用，合称天地。卑：低下。四时：春、夏、秋、冬四季。恣：放纵，听任。四知：具体内容各书所说不完全一致，一般指天知、神知、你知、我知。四知之说沿袭下来，意指恶行不可掩藏。

11. 烝民：众民。乾坤：天地。九窍：中医学名词，亦作"九孔"，即"阳窍七（眼、耳、鼻、口）和阴窍二（大小便处）"。煖：通"暖"。总：全。

12. 三台：星名，也作"三阶"或"泰阶"，即上台、中台、下台，共六星，两两相对，起文昌，列抵太微。北辰：北极星。司录：星名，即司禄，文昌宫第六星。差：差使。太一：方仙道与黄老道的最高天神。直符：亦书作"值符"，又名"符""值星"，指当值的星符。坎坷：不得志，不顺利。殒：通"陨"，堕落。困笃：病重垂危。流散：游移散开。不周：这里是"没到"的意思。天年：人的自然年寿。更：再。流：衍播、牵连。

13. 欺物：欺骗万物。影：隐晦现出。晕：光泽四围模糊的部分。这里作动词用。日月薄蚀：日月相掩食。彗孛飞流：彗星在宇宙间飞散流动。彗星，俗称扫帚星。

14. 响应：回声相应。涸：干枯。水涝：水淹。瘴疠：山林温热地区流行的恶性疟疾等传染病。

15. 恠：同"怪"。国主：即国君。归：归附。万姓：百姓。

16. 畏：敬服。天命：古代把天当作神，称天神的意志为天命。大人：道德高尚的人。逐日：按日，天天。私：不公开。录：逮捕。

17. 诫议：警诫，评论是非。

[译文]

Xuanyuan, the Yellow Emperor[1], knocked his head to the ground and asked Master Redpine: I have seen the myriad people receive life, but why is it not equal? There are those rich and noble, there are those poor and humble. There are those with a long life, there are those with a short life. Some are met by obstruction and troubles and undergo punishment in the cangue [punishment board]². others again suffer from extended illness and have their bodies all tied up. Some die suddenly without apparent disease, others live a long life with good emoluments³. Like this, people are not equal. I pray you, sir, to explain the situation to me.

Master Redpine said: People coming to life are all in isolation, each depending on one particular star. There are big stars and small, each governing a specific person's longevity and shortness [of life], decline and prosperity, poverty and wealth, death and life. As for those who do good, good qi^4 will cover them, good fortune and virtue will follow them, all nasty evils will leave them, the spirits and numinous forces[5] will guard them, other people will have respect for them, and all misfortunes will stay far away from them. As for those who do evil, bad qi will cover them, disasters and misfortunes will follow them, all lucky and auspicious signs will avoid them, baleful stars will shine on them, other people will detest them, and all sorts of unpleasant and disastrous affairs will crowd around them.

Day or night, whatever people do in their actions and minds, all the good and evil they commit, whether they secretly violate the prohibitions and taboos of Heaven and Earth, or give rise to personal blame and the accumulation of sins, is not the same at all. Day or night, whenever people do evil, the body gods and the Director of Fates [Siming] will submit a report to the stars and constellations above.[6] They in turn will effect a subtraction from the sinners' lives, so that the [light] qi of Heaven will leave them and the [heavy] qi of Earth will cluster around them. This is why they go into decline.

The Yellow Emperor asked: Altogether, how long should a human life expectancy be?

The Master replied: When people first come to earth, Heaven endows them with a life expectancy of 43,800 days, that is 120 years of life, each of which corresponds to one calendar year. So people originally receive a total life expectancy of 120 years. But if they violate the prohibitions and taboos of Heaven and Earth, certain amounts of time are subtracted from it and it will come to an end.[7]

The next question was: On occasion there are those dying while still in the womb or those who only live to see a few years. They have not yet done anything in the world, so what prohibition or taboo could they have violated?

Master Redpine explained: Things like these happen because the sins of the ancestors and forebears bequeath calamities upon their descendants. Ever since antiquity, heroes and wise men have established a corresponding teaching, which has remained in the books of the immortals. They all admonish people to do good and to know the very incipience of evil, so that even in ten thousand ages they give nothing but good fortune to their numerous generations of descendants. [8]

Now, human beings live between Heaven and Earth and are endowed with the two *qi* of yin and yang. Sovereign Heaven, although high, yet has its correspondence down below. Mother Earth, although low, yet has its correspondence far above. [9] Heaven does not speak, yet the four seasons move in order. Earth does not speak, yet the myriad beings come to life. People reside right between the two. All their licentious intentions and passionate desires, whatever they do or do not do, Heaven and Earth know all about it. For this reason we say that Heaven has four-sided [all-round] knowledge. [10]

Normally, people never say anything to recompense the grace Heaven and Earth have shown to them; on the contrary, they utter frequent complaints against them. Still, Heaven brings forth people and endows them with the trigrams Qian and Kun manifest in their father and mother, with the sun and the moon manifest in their two eyes, with the stars and constellations manifest in their nine orifices, and with the movement of wind and the power of fire manifest in their warm [body] *qi*. Then, when life ends, all these return to the soil.

In addition, Heaven houses the [constellations of the] Three Terraces and the North Culmen as well as the offices of the Director of Fates and the Director of Emoluments. They commonly take the perfected talisman of the Great One and place it on people's heads to examine if they are full of sins. [11] In accordance with their finding, they make a subtraction from the life expectancy.

If the celestials subtract one year, the star [essence] above the person's head loses its luster and he or she runs into lots of difficulties. If they take off ten years, the star gradually fades and the person encounters disasters, decline, and various diseases. If they subtract twenty years, the star's radiance is reduced significantly and the person runs into legal trouble and is imprisoned. [12] If they take off thirty years, the star dissolves and the person dies. If at this time, the subtractions are not complete and Heaven needs to ruin further years, they will be taken from the person's descendants, sons and grandsons. Should that not be sufficient either, they extend destruction to his married relations and retainers. [13] The latter, of course, have no idea where they went wrong or what they violated; they can only say that they have a reduced life expectancy.

In this way Heaven never cheats on living beings but shows them its inclinations, like a shadow following its object, through day and night, light and darkness, thunder and lightning, rain and snow, intertwining rainbows, eclipses of the sun and the moon, and floating characters of wisdom. All these are signs given by Heaven. [14]

Similarly Earth never cheats on living beings but shows them its inclinations, like an echo follows the sound, by making rivers and streams dry up and bringing forth landslides and earthquakes, hurricanes and tornadoes, sandstorms and moving stones, floods and locust plagues, famines and droughts, epidemics and other disasters. All these are signs given by Earth. The demons and spirits never cheat on living beings either. They show them their inclinations through good and bad fortune, strange omens and auspicious signs. These are the signs given by demons and spirits. Nor does the ruler cheat on living beings. Rather, shows them his good inclinations by making sure that Heaven and Earth are in harmony, the stars and constellations follow their course, disasters and calamities end, all in the four directions take refuge, and the myriad people are at peace. These are the signs of a good ruler among men. [15]

Typically people's actions, speech, and intentions do not make any reference to these activities of Heaven and Earth. For this reason the sages often say: Sovereign Heaven has no personal feelings, only virtue. This is just it. Thus people should be in awe of the mandate of Heaven, in awe of the great man, and in awe of the words of the sages.[16]

Whatever good and evil people egotistically commit in their daily lives, Heaven and Earth know all about their inner feelings.[17] Even if they secretly harm the life of another being, the spirits can clearly see it in their bodies. Also, whatever they say in body, speech, and mind, the demons always listen to their voices.[18] Then, if they violate the prohibitions a hundred times, the demons take away their essence. If they violate them a thousand times, the Earth registers their form. It they commit nothing but evil every day, they will be imprisoned and put into the cangue. Such is the retribution enacted through yin and yang.[19] Sovereign Heaven thus has its set of precepts and agreements, any violation of which will be punished by misfortune through either spirits and demons or Heaven and Earth.[20] (Kohn, 2004: 156 – 158)

[解析]

1. 轩辕黄帝是中华民族的缔造者和人文始祖，有着十分复杂的内涵和起源，仅仅采用音译加直译的方法翻译为"Xuanyuan, the Yellow Emperor"，不足以反映该文化概念的全部意思。类似于这样的基本术语和关键词语在道教典籍中有很多，因富含多层意义往往很难在一个上下文中给出完整而确切的印象，这是典籍翻译的一个突出问题。针对这一问题，王宏印教授建议采用"文外注释"的方法，认为添加一个比较全面的词条，可以弥补这一缺陷。以"轩辕黄帝"为例，比较全面的词条注释可以包含下列内容。

Huangdi（黄帝）, literally the Yellow Emperor in translation, was one of the legendary yet a real historical figure in the Chinese civilization. Actually Huangdi was the son of Shaodian（少典）and his family name was Gongsun（公孙）. He used to live by the Ji River（姬水）, and so he got another family name Ji（姬）. But since he was born in a hill named Xuanyuan（轩辕）, he was also named thereafter, and was even more often called Xuanyuan Huangdi（轩辕黄帝）. Huangdi had his kingdom founded in a place named Youxiong（有熊）, and he got one more name Youxiong（有熊）. And most importantly, Huangdi, for his greatest merits and virtues, was embraced and supported by all the surrounding tribes as the central king. And since his kingdom in the central region of China took the yellow color of earth as the auspicious sign, the Yellow Emperor（黄帝）his most popular name. For all these reasons, we know that Huangdi was once and forever is worshiped as the first ancestor of the Chinese nation.（王宏印，2009：17-18）

不过这样的词条虽然全面但也略显冗长，只适合作为文外注释，或者像一些海外译者那样在译本后面附一个词语表加以注解了。

2. 原文"或横罹枷禁"中的"枷禁"指"戴上枷锁被监察"。"枷"为旧时一种套在脖子上的刑具，译为"punishment in the cangue"原义表达已经很充分，但译者仍用方括号的模式添加［punishment board］在后用于补缺或订误，似有画蛇添足之嫌。

3 将"久病缠身"译为"suffer from extended illness and have their bodies all tied up"太过受制于原文字面，其实只需保留前半句"suffer from extended illness"即已清楚达旨。而"长寿有禄"中的"禄"指"福气"，译为"good emoluments"（报酬，薪水）缩小了原文的范畴，可改译为"good fortune"，也和下文的"富德随之"的英译保持一致。

4. "气"被古代中国人看着生命元素之一。道教养生学认为，"气"作为生命运动的能量，有气则生，无气则死。"气"的英文翻译有"pneuma"和"breath"，也有音译为"qi"，但都需提供一个注释。这里统一采用音译法，因而"善气"译为"good qi"，"凶气"则为"bad qi"，下文的"阴阳二气"译为"the two qi of yin and yang"，吉气为"the auspicious qi"，妖气为"the qi of early death"。如果能采用文外注释的方式，提供以下这样的解释进行补充，效果会更好，具体为 qi was regarded as a vital force inhering in the breath and bodily fluids by early Daoist philosophers and alchemists who developed techniques to alter and control the movement of qi within the body in order to achieve physical longevity and spiritual power。

5. 古代传说、宗教及神话中"神灵"是指天地万物的创造者和主宰者，或指有超凡能力、无所不知、无所不能、可以永恒不死的人物，如下文提到的能主宰人的生命祸福的"司命神"即为星宿神灵，所以译者将"神灵"译为"the spirits and numinous forces"。

6. 依据上下文的逻辑，原文"暗犯天地禁忌，谪谴罪累事非，一也"的正确断句应为"暗犯天地禁忌，谪谴罪累，事非一也"，因此译文"…whether they secretly violate the prohibitions and taboos of Heaven and Earth, or give rise to personal blame and the accumulation of sins, is not the same at all"对原文做出修正，这种现象在典籍翻译中时有发生，因为古代典籍在流传过程中难免会传抄有误，英译典籍时译者需细读文本，不能盲目遵从原文本内容，如果有不合逻辑之处则需做出修正。

"人神"是居于人体内部器官的诸神，译为"the body gods"，颇得要旨。"司命"有多重意思，或为星名，或为神名，也有掌握命运、主管诏令等意，直译为"the Director of Fates"，并在括号内加以拼音注明，这种直译加音译的方法是处理该类专有名词的常见手法。

7. "为犯天地禁忌，夺算命终"中的"算"为古代计数的筹码，道教用以指称人的寿命计算单位，人活百日叫作一算，通常直译为"one reckoning"。这里模糊处理为"certain amounts of time"是因为没有具体的寿命数量。

8. 汉语原文"自古英贤设教，留在《仙经》，皆劝人为善，知其诸恶，始乃万古传芳，子孙有福"属典型的意合表述，故需厘清其中的逻辑关系，可分句翻译。译文"使人了解恶的起源"（to know the very incipience of evil）而不是"使人了解诸多恶行"（to know the variety of evils），虽与原义略有出入，倒也符合"防微杜渐"这样的逻辑思维，这样处理更容易让读者理解接受。

9. 用"Sovereign Heaven"和"Mother Earth"分别对应"皇天""后土"即明示了原概念的具体指代，也译出了天地能主持公道、主宰万物的神性，胜过单一地译为"Heaven"和"Earth"。

10. 尽管译者可以通过调整语序来明晰句与句之间的关系，但主张直译的译者会首选亦步亦趋翻译原文，前提条件是不影响译入语读者的理解，这种现象在道教典籍翻译中比较常见。"人处其中，恣心情欲，凡人动息，天地皆知，故云天地有四知也"的译文即为这样的例证，译者力求在忠实传达原文意思的基础上，不改变原文的形式结构。原文是倒装结构，译文保留了原文的语序，甚至还直译"四知"为"four-sided knowledge"，只是以括号补充"all-round"的形式加以解读。

11. "三台、北辰、司命、司录"皆为天上的星宿名。"太一"是方仙道与黄老道的最高天神，其职能是"摄御百神"，"内安精气，外攘灾殃，却除死籍，延命永长"，等等。该句意指"天上的这些星宿差使太一神君持符在头上，察到谁有罪，就夺他的算纪"。译文分两步完成，一是说明"天"与三台、北辰、司命、司录的依存关系，"house"一词作动词用，很有画面感。二是说明这些星宿的作为，对应为 They commonly take the perfected talisman of the Great One and place it on people's heads to examine if they are full of sins，意思准确到位。

12. 该句漏译了"其人困笃"。基于上文"夺算十年，星渐破缺，其人灾衰疾病"（夺算十年，星辰渐渐变得破缺，这个人将会遭灾衰败得疾病）和下文"夺其算寿三十年，其星流散，其人则死"（夺算三十年，其星游移流散，这个人就会死去），这里的"其人困笃（个人病重垂危）"的信息不宜漏掉，需补译。改译为 If they subtract twenty years, the star's radiance is reduced significantly and the person becomes seriously ill or runs into legal trouble and is imprisoned。

13. 原文"不周天年"指"没活到人的自然年寿"。道教认为，有罪之人会被夺去算纪，如果一个人的算纪终了，没活到自然的寿数，就会殃及后代子孙，子孙承传的祸害没完没了，就会遭灭门之灾。译者抓住夺算的主线，加以变通，将原文的"不周天年"译为 Heaven needs to ruin further years，将原文的"子孙流殃不尽，以至灭门"译为 Should that not be sufficient either, they extend destruction to his married relations and retainers。这样一来，有一气呵成之感，意义更加完整。

14. 原文"故天不欺物，示之以影，昼夜阴阳，雷电雨雪，虹霓交晕，日月薄蚀，彗宇飞流，天之信也"意思是，所以上天不欺骗万物，用隐晦的方式显示自己的意图。昼夜阴阳，雷电雨雪，彩虹光晕，日月薄蚀，彗星流动等，这是上天昭示世人的预兆。"示之以影"意为"用隐晦的方式显示自己的意图"，译者将"影"变通解读为"如影随形"（like a shadow following its object），切合下文的天象描述，可谓灵活却不逾矩的妙译。同样的做法也见于下一句"示之响应"的译文"like an

echo follows the sound"。至于"彗宇飞流"（指"彗星流动"）译为 "floating characters of wisdom"就有待商榷了，尽管"彗宇"有"大智慧"之解，但依据语境，这里应指天文术语"彗星"，因此改译为 the floating of comets，任何词语的语义确定离不开上下文的正确分析。

15. 将"四方归，万姓安"译为 all in the four directions take refuge, and the myriad people are at peace，可谓传神达意，译出了"四方归附，百姓安定"的祥和国态，其中"take refuge"有"寻求依附或庇护"，极好地传译了"归"的意思。

16. 原文"皇天无亲，惟德是辅"出自《尚书·蔡仲之命》，意思是上天对人不分亲近远疏，只帮助那些有德行的人。翻译为 Sovereign Heaven has no personal feelings, only virtue，只是凸显皇天的"大德"，没有正确反映原文的意思。可改译为 Sovereign Heaven has no personal feelings, only helping the virtuous people。这样理解也与全文的"奖善罚恶"的主旨一致。"This is just it"为增译，以承上启下之用。"大人"在中国文化典籍中有不同的理解，《周易》《庄子》《荀子》各有其解，常见的解说有"伟大、崇高、高明之人"，译为"the great man"不如译作"the virtuous man"更符合该段主题，考虑到前面的天命（the mandate of Heaven）和后面的圣人之言（the words of the sages），不妨添加"the deeds of"。因此改译为 Thus people should be in awe of the mandate of Heaven, in awe of the deeds of the virtuous man, and in awe of the words of the sages。

17. 原文"凡人逐日私行，善恶之事，天地皆知其情"意思是"世俗人每天私下的言行，无论善恶，天地皆知"。译者巧妙地将"凡人逐日私行，善恶之事"合译，译为"Whatever good and evil people egotistically commit in their daily lives, Heaven and Earth know all about their inner feelings"。但"私行"非"自私之行"，而是"私下行为"，"情"非"感情"，而是"情况"，所以可改译为 Whatever good and evil people privately commit in their daily lives, Heaven and Earth know all about it。

18. 尽管原文的"心口意语"只是提及"心里想的、嘴里说的"，但译者译为"whatever they say in body, speech, and mind"，补充了肢体语言这部分，带有译者自己的诠释，属创造性翻译，虽有过余解读之嫌，但在上下文语境中却有增强话语效果之功效。

19. 词句意义的解读是翻译的关键，译者需仔细掂量词句的指称意义、语内意义和语用意义。该句将"鬼收其精"直译为"the demons take away their essence"，"地录人形"直译为"the Earth registers their form"，虽只停留在指称意义的解读层面，但丝毫不影响译文读者的理解，可若把"枷锁立成"直译为"the shackles are ready immediately"，却无法体现原文的联想意义，意译为 they will be imprisoned and put into the cangue 是明智之举，能较好译出原文的语用意义。

20. "诫议"包含"警诫"和"评论是非"两层意思，译者对应为"precepts and agreements"，其中用"agreements"（协议）翻译"议"而非用"judgement"（评判），与后面的"violation"搭配，共同传译"皇天具备训诫评判之权威，任何违反行为都将受到惩罚"的交际语境。

第二节 《洞玄灵宝天尊说十戒经》英文翻译研究

《洞玄灵宝天尊说十戒经》（简称《十戒经》），篇幅不长，核心内容由"十戒"和"十四持身之品"两部分组成。《十戒经》中的十戒，特别是前五戒（不杀、不淫、不盗、不醉、不欺），可以说是儒、释、道三教共同遵守的行为规范。而十四持身之品的前十条是说明君臣、父子、兄弟、夫妇、师友等言谈时所应遵守的规范，加上十戒中的"宗亲和睦，无有非亲；见人善事，心助欢喜；见人有忧，助为作福"等内容，表现出鲜明的儒家色彩。在儒家文化一直占据主流地位的中国社会里，这些带有浓厚儒家色彩的内容的加入，可能是道教自身对儒家文化做出主动适应而出现的结果（朱大星，2007：50）。该经托名道教最高尊神"三清"之一的上清灵宝天尊（玉清元始天尊、上清灵宝天尊、太清道德天尊合称"三清"），针对的是在家的初级信仰者清信弟子，属道教戒律类。整个经文内容共计四段：天尊授戒序说（首段）、十戒条目（第二段）、十四持身之品（第三段）、天尊说持戒功德（末段）。原文浅显易懂，直接明了，借天尊之口向在俗的道教信徒传授需要践行的宗教戒条，辅之以简单直接的宗教功能、宗教目的和义理的说明，方便初入道门者理解接受。

一 《洞玄灵宝天尊说十戒经》在海外的传播

《十戒经》在敦煌道教文献中连抄在《道德经》之后，并各自附有传授盟文。有学者据此推断该经文与道家道教的根本经典《道德经》有着相辅相成之影响力，认为这一经戒传授针对的是在家的初级信仰者清信弟子，于是成为道教通往社会的一座重要桥梁，从而有利于道教的传播，并对社会基层的宗教信仰乃至道德教化产生一定的影响（刘永明，2016：178），这样的戒律文本自然会引起海外学者的关注。日本学者山田利明（Yamada Toshiaki）、大渊忍尔（Ōfuchi Ninji）、楠山春树（Kusuyama Haruki）、吉冈义丰（Yoshioka Yoshitoyo）等在研究道教灵宝派、敦煌道经、道教戒律时都介绍和考证了该道经，施舟人（Kristofer Schipper）、傅飞岚（Franciscus Verellen）编撰的《道藏通考》（*The Taoist Canon*）三卷本也收录了该文，将该标题直译为 *Lingbao Scripture on the Ten Rules, Spoken by the Heavenly Worthy*，并大致介绍了该经的行文结构以及在敦煌八卷本中的存留情况，其中"十四持身之品"译为 the Fourteen Rules for Self-Control，"清信弟子"译为 Adept of Pure Faith。同《赤松子中诫经》一样，该文被孔丽维收录在其专著《宇宙与教团：道教的伦理维度》的附录中，作为研究道教伦理思想的佐证辅助材料。

二 孔丽维《洞玄灵宝天尊说十戒经》译文解析

[原文]

天尊[1]言：善男子、善女人[2]，能发自然道意，来入法门[3]，受我十戒、十四持身之品[4]，则为大道清信弟子[5]，皆以勇猛飞天齐功[6]，于此时进心不懈退者，即超凌三界[7]，为上清真人[8]。

一者不杀，当念众生[9]；二者不得妄作邪念；三者不得取非义[10]财；四者不欺，善恶反论；五者不醉，常思净行；六者宗亲[11]和睦，无有非亲；七者见人善事，心助欢喜；八者见人有忧，助为作福；九者彼来加我，志在不报[12]；十者一切未得，我不有望[13]。

次说十四持身之品：

与人君言则惠[14]于国，与人父言则慈于子，与人师言则爱于众，与人臣言则忠于上，与人兄言则友于弟，与人子言则孝于亲，与人友言则信于交，与人夫言则和于室，与人妇言则贞于夫，与人弟言则恭于礼，与野人[15]言则勤于农，与贤人言则志于道，与异国人言则各守其域，与奴婢言则慎于事。

天尊言曰：修奉清戒，每合天心，常行大慈，愿为一切，普度厄世，谦谦尊教，不得中怠，宁守善而死，不为恶而生，于是不退，可得拔度五道[16]，不履三恶[17]，诸天所获，万神所敬，长斋奉戒，自得度世。而为偈[18]曰：

一切修学人，誓愿[19]成真道。慈悲念戒文，道声断烦恼[20]。

[注释]

1. 天尊：道教对最高天神的尊称。"三清"指居于三清天、三清境的三位最高尊神，即玉清元始天尊、上清灵宝天尊、太清道德天尊。

2. 善男子、善女人：佛典中对在家的信男、信女之美称。

3. 法门：佛教用语，指修行者入道的门径。道教用以借指众生入道的门径，如："天尊慈悲，大开法门"。

4. 身：立身，修身，指对自身言行的把握。语出《列子·说符》："子列子学于壶丘子林。壶丘子林曰：'子知持后，则可言持身矣。'"品：本意为种类、品种，这里引申为法则。

5. 清信弟子：泛指品阶较低的道教信徒。

6. 齐：达到。功：与"过"相对，指功绩、功业、功劳。

7. 超：超出，胜过，引申为离世脱俗。凌：凌驾；超过；越过。三界：佛教术语，指众生所居之欲界、色界、无色界，或指断界、离界、灭界等三种无为解脱之道。

8. 上清：与玉清、太清一起合称道教三清。真人：天尊的别名，道教称存养本性或修真得道的人为真人；亦泛称"成仙"之人。

9. 念：佛教术语。指心中泛起的念头、主意。这里作动词，指惦记，常常想。众生：泛指人和一切动物。

10. 非义：不合乎道义。

11. 宗亲：以姓氏为区分的同宗亲属。

12. 加：凌驾，侵凌。报：报复。

13. 望：盼望；希望。

14. 惠：本意是恩，好处；给人财物或好处等。

15. 野人：古时指生活在乡间的人。

16. 拔度：亦作"拔渡"，指超度、拯救。五道：佛教谓天、人、畜生、饿鬼、地狱五处轮回之所。道教承袭此轮回转世说，亦有"三尸三恶门""三尸五恶门""五苦五道门"，借指阻碍人成仙的色、爱、贪、竞、身五种负累。

17. 三恶：为佛教的"六道轮回"说中的"三恶道"，指地狱道、饿鬼道、畜生道。六道指因造作善恶各种业（行为、语言、思想皆称为业）而带来的六类果报，并随顺当时世界称轮回至某一道为"生"，离开某一道为"死"。

18. 偈：佛经中的唱词，这里指奉戒颂。

19. 誓愿：立誓发愿，以示决心。

20. 烦恼：佛教语，指迷惑不觉，包括贪、嗔、痴等根本烦恼，能扰乱身心，引生诸苦，为轮回之因。

[译文]

The Heavenly Worthy said：

Oh, you good men and good women! You were able to develop an intention for the Dao of spontaneity and have come to enter the river of the divine law[1]. Now receive my ten precepts and fourteen principles of self-control to become Disciples of Pure Faith in the great Dao, gaining courage and strength to fly to the heavens and increase your merit. [2]

From here onward you will never slide back again but most certainly attain transcendence and go beyond the Three Worlds to become perfected of Highest Clarity. [3] For this, now bow down and receive [the precepts], repeating them with truth in your hearts：

The Ten Precepts

1. Do not kill but always be mindful of the host of living beings.

2. Do not be lascivious or think depraved thoughts.

3. Do not steal or receive unrighteous wealth.

4. Do not cheat or misrepresent good and evil.

5. Do not get intoxicated but always think of pure conduct.

6. I will maintain harmony with my ancestors and family and never disregard my kin.

7. When I see someone do a good deed, I will support him with joy and delight.

8. When I see someone unfortunate, I will support him with dignity to recover good fortune.

9. When someone comes to do me harm, I will not harbor thoughts of revenge.

10. As long as all beings have not attained the Dao, I will not expect to do so myself.[4]

The Fourteen Principles of Self Control

1. When I speak with another's lord, I shall feel gracious toward his country.

2. When I speak with another's father, I shall feel kind toward his son.

3. When I speak with another's leader, I shall feel loving toward his followers.

4. When I speak with another's older brother, I shall behave as a younger brother should.

5. When I speak with another's minister, I shall feel loyal toward his lord.

6. When I speak with another's son, I shall feel filial toward his parents.

7. When I speak with another's friend, I shall feel trusting toward his companions.

8. When I speak with another's wife, I shall feel virtuous toward her husband.

9. When I speak with another's husband, I shall feel harmonious toward his family.

10. When I speak with another's disciple, I shall feel respectful toward his formalities.

11. When I speak with a farmer, I shall feel conscientious about agriculture.

12. When I speak with a senior Daoist, I shall feel orthodox about the Dao.

13. When I speak with a stranger, I shall feel protective about his country's borders.

14. When I speak with a slave or maid, I shall feel concerned about his or her affairs. [5]

The Heavenly Worthy said:

To cultivate and venerate the pure precepts [of the Dao], always keep your mind linked with Heaven and always act with great compassion.

Solemnly vow that you will strive for the liberation of all living beings of the world, humbly and modestly venerate the teaching, never allow yourself to be lazy or lax. Whatever happens, calmly stick to the good, thus you can die. Never do anything bad, thus you can live.

Following these guidelines, you will never fall behind. Instead you will attain complete liberation of the five realms of suffering and the three bad rebirths. You will be protected by all the heavens and supported by the myriad gods. Keep on performing the purgations and honoring the precepts, and naturally you will go beyond the world. [6]

Concluding Verse[7]

All you who practice cultivation and study properly

Vow to perfect the Dao of true realization.

Full of compassion, be mindful of the words of my precepts

And the very sound of the Dao will put an end to your vexation. (Kohn, 2004: 184 – 186)

[解析]

1.《十戒经》为灵宝派经典，而灵宝派是中古道教派别中受佛教影响最深的道派，诫经的许多内容实际上直接受到大乘佛教经典的影响。如，这里的"善男子、善女人"本为佛典用语，指在家的信男、信女，"善"是对信佛、闻法、行善业者之美称。译者直译了该称谓，加脚注指明来源，也是对原文融儒释道思想为一体的说明。此外，原文的"入法门"在译文中变通为"入法河"（enter the river of the divine law），盖是顺应英语读者的认知，以适合交际语境之故。

2. 这里涉及"清信弟子"的翻译。孔丽维同样采用的直译，将"清信弟子"译为"Disciples of Pure Faith"，大写首字母是为了强调该短语为专有名词，有其特指意义。译者还根据日本学者楠山春树的研究成果，在脚注中补充了以下解释内容：This title *qingxin dizi* 清信弟子 is an adaptation from Buddhism that applies to first-level ordinands who have taken the ten precepts，较好地帮助了读者理解这一道教称谓名词。另外，用"self-control"译"持身"既译出了该词涵盖的"把握自身言行"之义，又与"品"的英译"principle"形成很好的对应，堪称妙译。

3. "超凌"字面上本为同义反复词，译者依据上下文将该词对应为"attain transcendence and go beyond"，在概念上设法区分了"超"与"凌"，也从逻辑上补充了上句"飞天"即可超脱凡尘的效应。同"清信弟子"的翻译处理一样，"三界"直译为"the Three Worlds"，"上清"译为"Highest Clarity"，但遗憾的是这里没有添加一定的注解。

4. 这部分为核心内容之一的"十戒"的翻译，除了逐条分行译出这十条戒律内容的文体特征之外，译者从前五条所包含的"不得"二字读出这些戒律的禁止语气，将前五条内容统一用"Do not…"祈使句型翻译，同时又从后五条中的"无有非亲""心助欢喜""助为作福""志在不报""我不有望"析出原文含有"我"的主动性，因而统一采用第一人称的陈述句。汉语作为意合语言，常常缺乏明晰主语，汉译英时常需补充主语，译者从省略主语"you"的祈使句转到以第一人称"I"为主语的陈述句，这种逻辑转换的做法对我们有很好的启示意义。根据原文的意义结构重新构思句子之间的关系，使得原文思想借助译入语能合乎逻辑地进行下去，既能做到大意不爽，又能实现小处有别的语义迁移，这是典籍英译的关键。

古文言简意赅，英文周密而意少，如何同时照顾和体现这两种语言特点是古汉语英译时经常会遇到的实际问题。这里译者既有针对若干字句的变通处理，也有按照原文句子的信息含量重新安排译句的词量和结构。如，将简单的一个"取"字译为"steal or receive"，将"不得妄作邪念"译为"Do not be lascivious or think depraved thoughts"，将"善恶反论"中的"反论"对应为"misrepresent","众生"译为"the host of living beings","宗亲"译为"my ancestors and family",等等,皆为不可多得的妙译。

5. "十四持身之品"的内容最早见于古灵宝经旧经《太上洞玄灵宝智慧罪根上品大戒经》(简称《罪根上品大戒经》),这一点孔丽维通过脚注进行了说明。单从内容上看,该部分传达了与人为善、积善成仙的思想宗旨。译者统一采用主从复合句"When I speak with …, I shall feel … toward …"对应原文"与人君言则惠于国……"等这些包含"与……言则……"的句型,兼顾了原文的形和意。至于其中涉及君臣、父子、兄弟、夫妇、师友等言谈时所应遵守的儒家伦理规范,原文用"惠、慈、爱、忠、友、孝、信、和、贞、恭、勤、志、守、慎"这些动词,简练而意丰,译者通过共享动词"feel"和介词"toward"或"about"的短语结构,保留原文的排比句式。原文是简略紧凑的,译文也有一气呵成的紧凑感。

6. 译者按主题将原文的一段文字析出三层内容,分三段完成。"修奉清戒,每合天心,常行大慈"为第一层,是奉戒的总体要求。"愿为一切,普度厄世,谦谦尊教,不得中怠,宁守善而死,不为恶而生"为第二层,是更为具体的要求。"于是不退,可得拔度五道,不履三恶,诸天所获,万神所敬,长斋奉戒,自得度世"为第三层,谈的是可以达到的目的。其中"于是不退,可得拔度五道,不履三恶"译为 Following these guidelines, you will never fall behind. Instead you will attain complete liberation of the five realms of suffering and the three bad rebirths,增译"Following these guidelines"是为了让上下文语义的逻辑更加连贯自然。用同一个动词短语"attain complete liberation"翻译原文的两个谓语动词"拔度"和"不履",既清楚又达意,便于译入语读者理解,是切合实际且有效的作法。"五道""三恶"则分别意译为"the five realms of suffering"和"the three bad rebirths"。"获"通"护","诸天所获,万神所敬"的译文为 You will be protected by all the heavens and supported by the myriad gods,这里涉及典籍中"所+动词"结构的翻译问题。"所+动词"结构在古典时期的文本中非常常见,根据当代美国知名哲学与宗教学家、汉学家任博克(Brook A. Ziporyn)教授的分析,"所"在很多时候指代"处所",如《道德经》第六十二章的"道者万物之奥。善人之宝,不善人之所保"。马王堆甲本写得更清楚："善人之保也，不善人之所保也。"只有理解为"处所"，"之保"和"之所保"才会出现差别。《庄子》中"万物之所造"不是"万物造出的东西"，而是"万物从那里造出"（万物之"能"造）（郭晨，2019：11）。依此解析，这里的"所"与后面的动词构成名词性结构，意指"诸天、众神庇护的对象"，用被动语态可直达原义。

7. 用 Concluding Verse 译"偈曰"，与文意的转折和篇章的结语都很吻合。"真"的本义为道教修真得道的仙人，称为"真人"，《庄子·大宗师》云："何谓真人？古之真人，不逆寡，不雄成，不谟士。"《庄子·天下》称："虽未至极，关尹老聃乎！古之博大真人哉！"汉晋以后，道教将"真人"神格化。《淮南子·本经训》："莫生莫死，莫虚莫盈，是谓真人"。《云笈七签》记述上清仙境有"高真""玄真"等九种真人（钟肇鹏，2010：170）。"真人"的对应英文有两种，一为"the True Man"，二为"the Perfected"，这里用"perfect the Dao of true realization"翻译"成真道"，综合了这两种对道教真人的理解。

小　结

道教戒律规诫的对象囊括个体、社会、自然、超自然，需天、地、神、人共同遵守，既是道教的伦理规范、组织规范，同时也是一个体现教义思想的理论体系，其中蕴含着道教的基本哲学认识（刘绍云，2006：22）。戒律条款名目繁多，主题多样，涉及道教徒修炼生活，也关联传统的家庭伦理、经济伦理、法律伦理，等等。翻译道教戒律文本既要洞悉戒律不同品类的内涵异同，也要对其形式表征有清楚的认知，方能达其要旨。本章选取的解析文本的英译者孔丽维教授集汉学家、翻译家、道教信徒多种身份于一身，对道教戒律主题有着深厚的了解，在系统研究各类道教戒律文本的基础之上孔丽维完成了伦理维度的道教学研究，作为附录内容的戒律文本翻译以及以补充读物出现的其他道教戒律的译本体现了这位博学学者对道教教团管理模式的熟知程度。

作为调节人们行为规范的准则，道教戒律文本常用"不得""常当""当"等规定性语言，句法简明扼要，条理清晰。孔丽维在透彻理解原文意义的基础之上，重新构思句子之间、段落之间的关系，逻辑清楚地呈现了原文思想。最典型的做法就是按条目逐条译出戒律内容，分主题细分段落，区分层次，合理使用祈使句和英语情态动词，以凸显道教戒律文本简单凝练、逻辑分明等语言特征，既能做到大意不爽，又能实现小处有别的语义迁移，对当今法律条文的翻译也有较好的借鉴价值。

第 五 章

道教仙传文本翻译研究

引 语

  神仙思想由来已久,成书于战国时期记述古代志怪的古籍《山海经》就有不死民的记载,《庄子》中也充满仙人、仙境的种种描绘。自《汉书·艺文志》方技略著录神仙书以来,记载神仙事迹的传记文学《列仙传》《神仙传》《洞仙传》《续仙传》《疑仙传》《集仙传》等相继问世。此外,还陆续出现一些收录道教神仙事迹的文献汇编,如,《三洞群仙录》《仙苑编珠》《墉城集仙录》《历世真仙体道通鉴》等,以及记载神仙灵异事迹的志怪小说《搜神记》《三教源流搜神大全》《新搜神记》等。托名刘向所著的《列仙传》乃现存问世最早的道教神仙传记书籍,篇幅虽小,但文笔洗练,内容丰富,晋以后流传甚广,历代道教仙传多取材此书,而托名东晋著名道士葛洪所著的《神仙传》乃中国古代仙传的巅峰之作,上承《列仙传》,下启《续仙传》《洞仙传》《墉城集仙录》《女仙传》《历代真仙体道通鉴》等,标志着神仙传记已趋成熟,后世仙传无不效仿和借鉴其文本形式和思想内容。

  作为道教信仰系统中不可或缺的重要组成部分,神仙真人自始至终都起着连接天人关系的桥梁作用。整个道教史围绕神仙真人向方士(道士)传授天帝之意的信仰建构,朝着修道成仙的终极目标发展,而教徒中流传的神仙故事及其文字形式神仙传记正是这种轨迹最重要的记录。各个历史时期都有各自的神仙传记,他们的具体内容和风格都不会完全相同。这些神仙的故事,与其说是对各位神仙真人生平事迹的记录,不如说是对各个历史时期变化着的神仙观念的记录,是所在历史时期老百姓，尤其是知识阶层的精神世界的生动写照（邱鹤亭，2004：92）。《列仙传》现有《道藏》《说郛》《四库》等各种版本，记载了早期神仙道教的相关史料，囊括了上自神农时雨师赤松子，下至西汉时方士玄俗共计70位道教神仙的生平事迹。而《神仙传》是继刘向《列仙传》后进一步撰写神仙事迹的书籍，按照葛洪《神仙传》自序中的讲述，葛洪写作此书，一是为了解答弟子们对世间是否真有神仙的疑惑，二是对自己所著的《抱朴子内篇》的补充说明，三是因为署名西汉刘向所著的《列仙传》过于简略，并且多有遗弃，所以葛洪写作此书，也是对《列仙传》遗漏的神仙人物进行补充完善（谢青云，2017：1）。流传至今的《神仙传》版本仅《中国丛书综录》著录的就多达16个版本。这16个版本按其来源与内容，又可分为《四库全书》本（传84人）和《广汉魏丛书》本（传92人）两大系统（周文晟，2012：81）。这些神仙传记因其版本众多，加之流传过程中各方引用传抄时的增删改写，现存的神仙传记内容已非原著原貌。

　　道教神仙传记既有一些原始宗教的成分，也有一些社会政治、风土人情等方面的内容，其叙事结构独特，具有相当重要的文学审美价值，早已受到国内外诸多学者的关注。学者们纷纷对这些道教辅教书籍的版本内容、神仙思想、叙事结构等展开研究，挖掘它们蕴含的宗教学价值和文学价值。早在20世纪初，道教神仙传记即已引发了海外汉学家的研究兴趣。据向群在其博士学位论文《葛洪〈神仙传〉研究——以文本流变为中心的考察》的介绍，日本学者对道教神仙传记文本的研究注重文献实证、考辨源流，如福井康顺、下见隆雄、小南一郎、泽田瑞穗、土屋昌明、龟田胜见等都曾考证过以《神仙传》为主的道教仙传文学的版本问题（向群，2015：2—5）。欧美学者对神仙传记的研究通常以文化对话的方式展开，翻译与研究相辅相成，各不偏废。单从海外学者解读神仙传记内容的情况来看，最早有关神仙传记的英文译本出现在英国汉学家翟林奈（Lionel Giles，1878—1958年）1948年出版的著作《中国列仙集锦》（*A Gallery of Chinese Immortals*）中，法国汉学家康德谟（Maxime Kaltenmark，1910—2002年）在1953年完成了最早（汉代）的仙传《列仙传》的法文译注，并对其中的神话做了研究。贺碧来（Isabelle Robinet）在其论文《道教神仙——光与影、天与地的弄臣》（*The Taoist Im-*

mortal：Jesters of Light and Shadow，Heaven and Earth）中研究了神仙的各种神话意象。德国汉学家甘奇（Gertude Guntsch）1988 年的著作《〈神仙传〉与仙的形象》（Das Shen-hsien chuan and das Erscheinungsbild eines Hisen）包含了部分神仙传记的德文翻译，美国华裔学者王艺文是一位虔诚的道教修炼者，她 1997 年出版的著作《从道教神仙系统谈道教教义》（Teaching of the Tao：Reading from the Taoist Spiritual Tradition）也载有一些神仙传记内容的英译。

　　成仙了道是道教的核心教义，承载道教思想记录道教历史的诸多典籍或是为了论证神仙实有，或是为了说明仙可学致，多数会涉及道教神仙人物，因而海外道教学者在进行中国道教学专题研究时或多或少都会涉及典籍中记录神仙事迹的传记文本内容的理解和翻译。如，美国学者汉学家魏鲁男 1966 年出版的译作《公元 320 年中国的炼丹术、医学和宗教：葛洪的内篇》（Alchemy，Medicine，Religion in the China of AD 320：The Nei P'ien of Ko Hung），虽然书中翻译的内容是葛洪的《抱朴子内篇》，但因葛洪在书中列出一些道教神仙的成仙事迹作为"仙可学致"的佐证，因此魏鲁男这一译本中包含少数神仙人物传记的英译。此外，意大利汉学家玄英 2004 年的著作《太清：中国中古早期的道教和炼丹术》（Great Clarity：Daoism and Alchemy in Early Medieval China）虽然主题是炼丹，但作者在引论中为道教炼丹史清本溯源时，曾追溯左慈、葛玄、郑隐等道教神仙人物的生平事迹，因此也有这些人物介绍的英文翻译。相较而言，美国汉学家康儒博 2002 年所著《与天地同寿：葛洪〈神仙传〉翻译与研究》（To Live as Long as Heaven and Earth：A Translation and Study of Ge Hong's Traditions of Divine Transcendents）称得上是海外第一个相对完整的译介道教神仙传纪内容的翻译文本。基于这部对道教神仙传记文献的翻译研究，2009 年康儒博完成了另一部以道教修仙为主题的研究专著，书名为《修仙：古代中国的修行与社会记忆》（Making Transcendents，Ascetics and Social Memory in Early Medieval China），探讨了道教修仙的不同方式、神仙形象运作和被识别的社会环境等话题。本章在简要介绍康儒博《与天地同寿：葛洪〈神仙传〉翻译与研究》这一著作的基础之上，选取其中的两则传记内容的英译文本作为解析对象，分别为道教教祖老子和五斗米道创建人、天师道祖天师张道陵传记内容的英译文本，以此探讨道教仙传文本的翻译方法和策略。

第一节　康儒博《与天地同寿：葛洪〈神仙传〉翻译与研究》简介[①]

《神仙传》是东晋道教学者葛洪广泛取材仙经道书、百家之说以及当世所传神仙故事而编撰的一部神仙传记。美国汉学家康儒博在其专著《与天地同寿：葛洪〈神仙传〉翻译与研究》中完整推出《神仙传》的英译文本。该成果将疏解内容、前期对《神仙传》以及葛洪的另一作品《抱朴子内篇》的相关翻译研究、译文等文本内容同置于一个开放、交叉、吸收、转化的动态网络之中，这种互文关联的翻译模式有效引导读者从《神仙传》源文本语言所彰显的神仙文化研究走向翻译研究（何立芳、李丝贝，2020：77）。当代著名道教学者汉学家柏夷为该书作序，高度评价了这一研究成果中包含的《神仙传》译文内容，认为该译本已接近他心目中的理想译文，是典型的学术型翻译，每一传记的翻译后面都附有诠释与评论，为凡夫俗子提供了一份清晰翔实的译文。

全书由三部分组成。第一部分和第三部分为译本的副文本（paratext），即疏解内容，是译文读者充分了解《神仙传》内容的必要补充材料。作者除了开宗明义陈述对道教系统命名法的观点以及翻译研究《神仙传》的原因所在之外，还在第一部分不惜笔墨为读者呈上葛洪作品所折射的道教修仙的主要元素。文本翻译与评论为该书的第二部分。康儒博认为，翻译《神仙传》除需添加必要的注解之外，还需要有批判性眼光。因此，每一传记的翻译除了附有大量注释之外，整个译本都带有很强的"批判性"特色，尤其体现在源文底本选择方面（何立芳、李丝贝，2020：78—79）。

就一部典籍的翻译准备而言，译者可以选择一个底本，参校其他版本进行校勘，以便产生一个比较可靠的通行本，个别异文的处理可以在注解中加以说明（王宏印，2009：14）。《神仙传》有两大版本系统，一为文渊阁《四库全书》本，一为《广汉魏丛书》本。康儒博英译这些神

[①] 本节部分内容发表在《国际汉学》2020年第1期，第77—83页。

仙传记内容的底本并不是葛洪所著内容的原版，有些内容综合了后来学者们汇编的其他版本。这种现象在康儒博的这部翻译作品中比比皆是，有时候我们根本无法直接选定某个文本作为他翻译的底本，只能依据他的译文和注释重构一个源文。康儒博尽可能广泛地搜集《神仙传》佚文，确定它们在源文献中的位置及源文献产生的时间，然后对比这些引文，选择其中的一种或多种作为翻译底本，并根据源文献所示指出各传记中每一特定叙事要素的相对早晚。对于每一则传记，康儒博皆列出其所有来源，并分析各版本间的相似与差异。无论是兼采百家为翻译选定底本，还是不惜笔墨为读者提供注释，最终目的只是向读者推出一个较为清楚明白的完整译本（何立芳、李丝贝，2020：80）。这一翻译特色贯穿他的整部《神仙传》英译文本。

这本翻译研究著作穿插了源文版本差异研究内容和其他学者相关神仙传记的翻译研究内容，译者从各种关系中考察道教神仙传记文本的意义与价值，属于典型的"互文性"翻译模式。因此，尽管本章我们依然还是从原文、注释、英译、解析的模式展开道教神仙传记文献翻译的批评解析，与其他章节不同的是，分析其中一些具体的语言文化翻译现象时主要是探讨译者解读源文本的互文模式及其翻译策略的有效度问题。因该英译本依据的底本主要取自《太平广记》卷八的汉魏本，因此，本章选用的原文注释参考了谢青云译注的《神仙传》内容。需说明的是，如果将康儒博译文与这里提供的原文进行比照，会发现有些文字信息根本不对称，这是由于康儒博参阅的文献版本不仅仅是汉魏本的缘故，读者不能简单用忠实与背叛的标准予以评判。

第二节 《神仙传·老子》英语翻译研究

春秋末年著名的思想家老子被尊为道家学派创始人。他所撰述的道家经典哲学著作《道德经》与被奉为儒学圣典的《周易》一起共同开启了我国古代哲学思想之先河，对中国哲学、政治、经济、军事、宗教等方面产生了深远的影响，其世界意义也得到西方学界的认同，成为世界上除《圣经》以外，译本最多的一部经典（邰谧侠，2019：7）。

老子被视为道家学派的鼻祖，同时也被尊奉为道教的始祖，被赋予了神仙的属性。老子神仙形象的描述见诸《庄子》《史记》《抱朴子内篇》等典籍中，这些作品给读者塑造了一位长相奇异、年命延长、神迹灵异、不可接近的神秘人物形象。但史籍对老子的生平记载都颇为简略，多数为一些片段记载。今存《道藏》收录的《列仙传》中的"老子"传记内容不过寥寥 100 余字，原文如下。

> 老子姓李名耳。字伯阳，陈人也。生于殷，时为周柱下史。好养精气，贵接而不施。转为守藏史。积八十余年。史记云："二百余年时，称为隐君子。"谥曰聃。仲尼至周见老子，知其圣人，乃师之。后周德衰，乃乘青牛车去，入大秦。过西关。关令尹喜待而迎之，知真人也，乃强使著书，作《道德经》上下二卷。

葛洪《抱朴子内篇·杂应》中的老子形象如下。

> 老君真形者，思之，姓李名聃，字伯阳，身长九尺，黄色，鸟喙，隆鼻，秀眉长五寸，耳长七寸，额有三理上下彻，足有八卦，以神龟为床，金楼玉堂，白银为阶，五色云为衣，重叠之冠，锋铤之剑，从黄童百二十人，左有十二青龙，右有二十六白虎，前有二十四朱雀，后有七十二玄武，前道十二穷奇，后从三十六辟邪，雷电在上，晃晃昱昱，此事出于仙经中也。见老君则年命延长，心如日月，无事不知也。

因为老子身份的不确定，历史上与老子相关的各种传说层出不穷。葛洪在《神仙传》这部作品中收集了当时关于老子的各种传说，将老子的神仙形象塑造得更为完整，《神仙传》中的老子已然是一位因"得道"而成仙的人。经多年流传过程中的增删改写，到了宋代，第一部古代汉族文言小说总集《太平广记》中收录的老子传记内容已增加到 2500 多字，对老子神仙形象的描述越来越翔实，以至于读者可以几乎全面地了解到关乎神仙老子的各种奇闻。虽然《太平广记》属小说性质，更注重叙事之精彩有趣，对原材料文字的改动更具随意性，但也不能据此而否定其更可靠地保存了葛洪《神仙传》原貌的可能性。汉学家康儒博翻译葛洪《神仙传·老子》主要依据的底本就是《太平广记》中的内容。

一 康儒博《神仙传·老子》译文底本的说明

有关老子的传记内容在许多古代类书中都有涉及，翻译这则传记时，康儒博尽可能参阅了这些书籍，在译本的第三部分译者对该传记译本的源文本及不同时期文章段落的差异进行说明，具体包括：欧阳询等编撰的《艺文类聚》，郦道元编撰的《水经注》，李昉等编撰的《太平御览》和《太平广记》，释道世的《法苑珠林》，徐坚的《初学记》，李贤注解的《后汉书》，蔡梦弼评注杜甫诗歌的文集《草堂诗笺》，先由白居易编撰后经孔传续撰的《白孔六帖》，吴淑注释的《事类赋》，陈葆光的《三洞群仙录》，曾慥的《类说》，马骏良辑录的丛书《龙威秘书》。不过他主要依据《太平广记》这个版本完成《神仙传·老子》篇传记内容的译文，只是里面个别在译者看来不合逻辑或有错漏的内容，译者参照《法苑珠林》的内容作了修正，并在译文后面的文本注解中加以说明。译文中有些内容被置于"〈〉"中，有些内容被置于"{}"中，这是译者为提示那些对文本内容的历史演变感兴趣的读者所作的特别说明，注明标识"〈〉"的内容为唐代之后被证实的部分，用"{}"标识的译文为公元1300年之后的内容，单从语言文化层面欣赏译文的读者可以忽略这些标识。被置于"[]"中的译文为译者增译，采用"[]"呈现原文没有而译者认为需添加以求语义完整的内容，充分显示了译者对待原文本的严谨态度。

二 康儒博《神仙传·老子》译文解析

[原文]

老子者，名重耳，字伯阳，楚国苦县曲仁里人也。其母感大流星而有娠，虽受气天然，见于李家，犹以李为姓。[1]

或云，老子先天地生。或云，天之精魄，盖神灵之属。[2]或云，母怀之七十二年乃生，生时，剖母左腋而出，生而白首，故谓之老子。或云，其母无夫，老子是母家之姓。或云，老子之母，适至李树下而生老子，生而能言，指李树曰：以此为我姓。

或云，上三皇时为玄中法师，下三皇时为金阙帝君，伏羲时为郁华子，神农时为九灵老子，祝融时为广寿子，黄帝时为广成子，颛顼时为赤精子，帝喾时为禄图子，尧时为务成子，舜时为尹寿子，夏禹时为真行子，殷汤时为锡则子，文王时为文邑先生，一云，守藏史。[3]

或云，在越为范蠡，在齐为鸱夷子，在吴为陶朱公。[4]皆见于群书，不出神仙正经，未可据也。

葛稚川云：洪以为老子若是天之精神，当无世不出。俯尊就卑，委逸就劳，背清澄而入臭浊，弃天官而受人爵也。[5]夫有天地则有道术，道术之士，何时暂乏？是以伏羲以来，至于三代，显名道术，世世有之，何必常是一老子也。[6]皆由晚学之徒，好奇尚异，苟欲推崇老子，故有此说。

其实论之，老子盖得道之尤精者，非异类也。按《史记》云：老子之子名宗，仕魏为将军，有功，封于段。至宗之子汪、汪之子言、言之玄孙瑕，仕于汉。瑕子解，为胶西王太傅，家于齐。[7]

则老子本人灵耳，浅见道士，欲以老子为神异，使后代学者从之，而不知此更使不信长生之可学也。何者？若谓老子是得道者，则人必勉力竞慕；若谓是神灵异类，则非可学也。

或云：老子欲西度关，关令尹喜知其非常人也，从之问道。老子惊怪，故吐舌聃然，遂有老聃之号。亦不然也。今按《九变》及《元生十二化经》，老子未入关时，固已名聃矣。老子数易名字，非但一聃而已。[8]

所以尔者，按《九宫》及《三五经》及《元辰经》云：人生各有厄会，到其时，若易名字，以随元气之变，则可以延年度厄。[9]今世有道者，亦多如此。

老子在周，乃三百余年，二百年之中，必有厄会非一，是以名稍多耳。欲正定老子本末，故当以史书实录为主，并老仙经秘文，以相参审。其他若俗说，多虚妄。

洪按《西升中胎》及《复命苞》及《珠韬玉机》《金篇内经》，皆云：老子黄白色，美眉，广颡长耳，大目疏齿，方口厚唇；额有三五达理，日角月悬；鼻纯骨双柱，耳有三漏门；足蹈二五，手把十文。以周文王时为守藏史，至武王时为柱下史。[10]时俗见其久寿，故号之为老子。夫人受命，自有通神远见者，禀气与常人不同，应为道主，故能为天神所济，众仙所从。

是以所出度世之法，九丹八石，金醴金液；次存玄素守一，思神历藏，行气炼形，消灾辟恶，治鬼养性，绝谷变化，厌胜教戒，役使鬼魅之法，凡九百三十卷，符书七十卷，皆《老子·本起》中篇所记者也，自有目录。其不在此数者，皆后之道士，私所增益，非真文也。[11]

老子恬淡无欲，专以长生为务者，故在周虽久，而名位不迁者，盖欲和光同尘，内实自然，道成乃去，盖仙人也。[12]

孔子尝往问礼，先使子贡观焉。[13]子贡至，老子告之曰："子之师名丘，相从三年，而后可教焉。"

孔子既见老子，老子告曰："良贾深藏若虚，君子盛德若愚。去子之骄气与多欲淫志，是皆无益于子也。"[14]

孔子读书，老子见而问之曰："何书？"

曰："《易》也。圣人亦读之。"[15]

老子曰："圣人读之可也，汝曷为读之？其要何说？"[16]

孔子曰："要在仁义。"[17]

老子曰："蚊虻噆肤，通夕不得眠。今仁义惨然而汨人心，乱莫大焉。[18]夫鹄不日浴而白，乌不日染而黑，天之自高矣，地之自厚矣，日月自明矣，星辰固自列矣，草木固有区矣。夫子修道而趋，则以至矣，又何用仁义！若击鼓以求亡羊乎？夫子乃乱人之性也。"

老子问孔子曰："亦得道乎？"

孔子曰："求二十七年而不得也。"

老子曰："使道可献人，则人莫不献之其君矣；使道可进人，则人莫不进之其亲矣；使道可告人，则人莫不告之兄弟矣；使道可传人，则人莫不传之其子矣；然而不可者，无他也，中无主而道不可居也。"

孔子曰："丘治《诗》《书》《礼》《乐》《易》《春秋》，诵先王之道，明周、召之迹，以干七十余君而不见用，甚矣人之难说也。"[19]

老子曰："夫六艺，先王之陈迹也，岂其所陈哉？今子所修者，皆因陈迹也。迹者，履之出，而迹岂异哉？"[20]

孔子归，三日不谈。子贡怪而问之。孔子曰："吾见人之用意如飞鸟者，吾饰意以为弓弩而射之，未尝不及而加之也；人之用意如麋鹿者，吾饰意以为走狗而逐之，未尝不衔而顿之也；人之用意如渊鱼者，吾饰意以为钩缗而投之，未尝不钓而制之也。至于龙，乘云气，游太清，吾不能逐也。今见老子，其犹龙乎，使吾口张而不能翕，舌出而不能缩，神错而不知其所居也。"[21]

阳子见于老子，老子告之曰："虎豹之文，猿猱之捷，所以致射也。"[22]

阳子曰："敢问明王之治？"

老子曰："明王之治，功盖天下而似不自己；化被万物而使民不恃；其有德而不称其名；位乎不测而游乎无有者也。"[23]

老子将去，而西出关，以升昆仑。关令尹喜占风气，逆知当有神人来过，乃扫道四十里，见老子而知是也。老子在中国，都未有所授，知喜命应得道，乃停关中。[24]

老子有客徐甲，少赁于老子，约日雇百钱，计欠甲七百二十万钱。甲见老子出关游行，速索偿不可得，乃倩人作辞，诣关令，以言老子。而为作辞者，亦不知甲已随老子二百余年矣，唯计甲所应得直之多，许以女嫁甲。甲见女美，尤喜，遂通辞于尹喜。得辞大惊，乃见老子。[25]

老子问甲曰："汝久应死，吾昔赁汝，为官卑家贫，无有使役，故以'太玄清生符'与汝，所以至今日，汝何以言吾？吾语汝，到安息国，固当以黄金计直还汝，汝何以不能忍？"[26]

乃使甲张口向地，其"太玄真符"立出于地，丹书文字如新，甲成一聚枯骨矣。喜知老子神人，能复使甲生，乃为甲叩头请命，乞为老子出钱还之。老子复以太玄符投之，甲立更生。喜即以钱二百万与甲，遣之而去。并执弟子之礼，具以长生之事授喜。

喜又请教诫，老子语之五千言，喜退而书之，名曰《道德经》焉。

尹喜行其道，亦得仙。汉窦太后信老子之言，孝文帝及外戚诸窦，皆不得不读，读之皆大得其益。故文景之世，天下谧然，而窦氏三世保其荣宠。[27]

太子太傅疏广父子，深达其意，知"功成身退"之义，同日弃官而归，散金布惠，保其清贵。及诸隐士，其遵老子之术者，皆外损荣华，内养生寿，无有颠沛于险世。其洪源长流所润，洋洋如此，岂非乾坤所定，万世之师表哉！故庄周之徒，莫不以老子为宗也。[28]

[**注释**]①

1. 里：街巷。有娠：怀孕。见：同"现"，出现。

---

① 因康儒博英译《神仙传·老子》篇时主要依据的底本《太平广记》源自《广汉魏丛书》，本节选用的原文和注释参考了谢青云 2017 年译注的《神仙传》中第 22—44 页内容，该译注以《道藏精华录》中所收录的《神仙传》为底本，属《广汉魏丛书》本一系。

2. 或：某人，有人。精魄：精神魂魄。魄，指依附形体而存在的精神。

3. 上三皇：道教所演化的上古皇帝，相应的还有"中三皇""下三皇"。既可代表上古传说中拥有不同名号的天皇、地皇、人皇，也可指他们分别所在的时代。伏羲、神农、祝融、黄帝、颛顼、帝喾、尧、舜、夏禹、殷汤、文王：皆为古代传说中的中华民族人文始祖。葛洪认为，后人为推崇老子编造了许多不可考证的奇闻异说，包括老子在不同时期拥有的各种不同名号，如：玄中法师，金阙帝君，郁华子，九灵老子，广寿子，广成子，赤精子，禄图子，务成子，尹寿子，真行子，锡则子，守藏史，范蠡，鸱夷子，陶朱公等，都是一些"浅见道士"为了吸引别人来学习老子，而对老子进行的神化。守藏史：《史记》中称老子为"周守藏室之史也"，一般认为是掌管周朝图书典籍的官吏。

4. 越：即春秋时的越国。范蠡，春秋时期楚国人，被后人尊称为"商圣"。相传他出身贫贱，但博学多才，曾辅佐越王勾践消灭了吴国（周朝时诸侯国之一，约在今江苏苏州、无锡及浙江湖州一带）。传说他功成名就之后隐居到齐国（周朝时山东半岛的一个诸侯国），化名为鸱夷子，其间三次经商而成巨富，又三散家财，后老死于陶地，世称陶朱公。

5. 稚川：即葛洪，东晋著名道教学者，炼丹家。他总结和发展了东晋之前的神仙方术。爵：古代君主赐予贵族的封号，分为公、侯、伯、子、男五等，此处代指官位。

6. 三代：原指夏、商、周三个朝代，此处指离作者最近的汉、魏、晋三个朝代。

7. 魏：战国时诸侯国之一，约在今河北魏县和河南开封一带。段：地名，今山西运城夏县东部。胶西王：即刘印，汉朝刘邦之孙，汉文帝时被立为胶西国王，汉景帝时因参与叛乱，兵败被杀。其地约在今山东高密西南一带。太傅：又称太子太傅，为辅导太子的官员。封：指帝王把爵位及土地赐给臣子。

8. 聃：耳长而大，这里指吐舌时伸出舌头的状态。《九变》及《元生十二化经》：道教著作，今已不传，内容不详。

9. 尔：如此，这样。《九宫》《三五经》《元辰经》：道教著作，今已不传，内容不详。厄会：众灾会合，犹言厄运。道教有一种说法，修道之人达到某一阶段或在人世存活太久时，会遭遇到特别的灾难。元气：古人指产生和构成天地万物的原始物质，同时能推动世界的变化和运行。

10.《西升中胎》《复命苞》《珠韬玉机》《金篇内经》：道教典籍，今已不传，内容不详。颡：指额头。达理：通贯的纹路，指皱纹。日角月悬：额角两端似有日月的形状。文：同"纹"，指手上有特别的纹理，也可指文字。柱下史：一种与秦汉以后御史相当的官职，主管历法阴阳五行之书。

11. 九丹：外丹名词。用草木、矿石烧炼而成、服之可以长生成仙的九种丹药。八石：炼丹用的八种矿石药物，具体说法不一，一般指朱砂、雄黄、云母、空青、硫黄、戎盐、硝石、雌黄。金醴：在道教炼养术中指口中津液，一些道教养生家认为，通过吞咽口中津液可以滋养五脏，延年益寿。金液：道教内丹术中指肺之液，也有指元气。外丹术中指用药物所炼成的药液，也代指水银。藏，通"脏"，脏腑。行气：又称服气、炼气，分外息法和内息法两大类。外息法一般是以呼吸吐纳结合闭息所进行的炼养活动，内息法是以静坐养神、养气的方式进行的训练。炼形：指通过导引动作使身体气血运行通畅、身体柔和、健康长寿的锻炼方法。鬼：原指人死后的灵魂，此处指人身中一些不良的习性。绝谷：即辟谷，古人认为可以通过此法养生延年。一般绝谷期间不吃谷类食物，但会吃一些药物并配合导引服气等方法。鬼魅：泛指鬼怪之物。符：道教驱使鬼神或帮助人与神进行沟通交流的秘文，图形一般为文字和符号的结合体，使用时用笔墨写在纸上。《老子·本起》：一本介绍老子的书，今已不存，内容不详。

12. 恬淡：指人内心清心寡欲的一种状态。和光同尘：出自《道德经》第四章"和其光，同其尘"一句，原意为不对事物有尊和卑的偏向，以免引起贵和贱的分别心，后引申为与世浮沉，随波逐流而不立异。

13. 孔子（前551—前479）：名丘，字仲尼，春秋时期鲁国人，儒家学派的创始人。尝：曾经。礼：指周代的礼教。子贡：孔子的弟子，姓端木，名赐，字子贡，善雄辩，有政治才能，曾任鲁国、卫国相辅。他还善于经商，并因经商而成巨富，被认为是儒商的始祖。

14. 贾：做买卖的商人。

15.《易》：即《周易》，被称为群经之首，本为古代占卜的书，后被列入儒家经典，主要是用阴阳卦象来表示事物演进变化的过程，包含了一定的哲学辩证思想。《史记》中称孔子晚年喜欢读《周易》。

16. 曷：怎么，为什么。

17. 仁义：儒家的重要伦理范畴，其本意为仁爱与正义，后成为儒家道德的最高标准，有"杀身成仁，舍生取义"之说。

18. 虻：昆虫的一科，种类很多，身体灰黑色，生活在野草丛里，雄的吸植物的汁液，雌的吸人、畜的血。噆：叮咬。惨：狠毒，凶残。泪：扰乱。

19. 周、召：亦作"周邵"，周成王时共同辅政的周公旦和召公奭的并称。两人分陕而治，皆有美政。

20. 六艺：含义有二，一指礼、乐、射、御、书、数六种技能，是周朝的贵族教育体系中教授的主要内容。二指六经，即《诗》《书》《礼》《乐》《易》《春秋》，是春秋时期孔子开私学所教授的六部经典。此处指后者。

21. 麋鹿：俗称"四不像"，是一种中国特产的珍稀动物。缗：钓鱼绳。太清：这里指天空。翕：合，聚。

22. 阳子：即孙阳，字伯乐，相传为秦穆公时人，善相马。猱：古书上说的一种猿猴。

23. "功盖天下而似不自己"几句：这几句化用《道德经》第二章中的一段话："是以圣人处无为之事，行不言之教。万物作焉而不辞，生而不有，为而不恃，功成而弗居。夫唯弗居，是以不去。"这是道家理想中的"无为而治"的政治状态。即一个国家的领导者顺其自然，不做过多干预，整个国家也能依道而行，井井有条而不混乱。

24. 昆仑：原为道教神山，被称为"百神之乡"，相传为西王母所居之处。今昆仑山在新疆和西藏之间，西接帕米尔高原，东延入青海境内。占风气：即风角占候术，是古代占卜术中很重要的一支，主要通过对风的分析而占卜所要发生的事。中国：上古时，华夏族建国于黄河流域一带，以为居天下之中，故称中国，而把周围其他地区称为四方。后泛指中原地区。

25. 客：这里指佣人。赁：租借，此处意为被雇佣。倩：请别人代自己做某事。诣：到，特指到尊长那里去。

26. 太玄清生符：一种能起死回生的符。安息国：西方作"帕提亚"（英语为 Parthia），伊朗高原古代国家，作为国家存在的时间约为公元前 248—224 年，中国史籍称"安息""安息国"，盖取自其开国者 Arsacids 汉语音译"安息"；与汉朝关系密切，为丝绸之路的必经之地。直：通"值"。酬劳。

27. 窦太后：即汉文帝刘恒的皇后，汉景帝刘启的母亲。史载窦太后好黄老之说，要求景帝和窦氏国戚都要读老子的书，并用老子休养生息的理念治国，形成了汉代文帝和景帝时期国家繁荣昌盛的稳定局面，史称"文景之治"。谧：安宁，平静。

28. 疏广：字仲翁，号黄老，东海兰陵（今属山东临沂）人，西汉名臣。疏广从小好学，精于《论语》《春秋》，汉宣帝地节三年（前 67）封为太子太傅。疏广信奉黄老之学，任太傅五年后，因感老子"知足不辱，知止不殆"，"功遂身退，天之道"之说，称病辞官与侄子俱还乡。还乡后将皇帝所赐黄金遍赠乡里，教化一方。乡人感其散金之惠，在二疏宅旧址筑一座方圆三里的土城，取名为"二疏城"；在其散金处立一碑，名"散金台"，在二疏城内又建二疏祠，祠中雕塑二疏像，世代祭祀不绝。庄周：即庄子，姓庄名周，字子休（亦说子沐），春秋时宋国蒙（今河南商丘，一说安徽蒙城）人。他在哲学思想上继承和发展了老子"道法自然"的观点，使道家真正成为一个学派，他也成为道家的重要代表人物。著有《庄子》一书，道教中也称《南华经》。

［译文］

Laozi（Master Lao, or the Old Master）had Chong'er 重耳 as his name, Boyang 伯阳 as his style. [1] He was a native of Quren hamlet, Ku district, in the kingdom of Chu. His mother felt a great meteor enter her, and thus she conceived. But, although he received his pneuma from Heaven, since he was born into the Li 李 family he took Li as his surname. [2] Some say Laozi was born before Heaven and Earth were. Some say he was produced from celestial cloud-souls or essences and that he must have been some sort of deity or numen. [3] Some say his mother carried him seventy-two years before finally giving birth and that when he was born he emerged by piercing through her left armpit; and that he was born with white hair, hence was called Laozi. Some say that his mother

< had no husband and that > Laozi was the surname of her family. Some say that his mother gave birth to him under a plum tree and that, being able to speak at birth, he pointed at the tree and said, "I'll take this as my surname."

Some say that in the Upper [portion of the] Era of the Three Sovereigns he was Ritual Master of the Mystic Center; that during the Lower [portion of] that era he was Thearch-Lord of the Golden Porte; that during the era of Fu Xi (伏羲) he was Master Denseflower (Yuhua zi 郁华子); that during the era of the Divine Husbandman he was Old Master Nine-Numina (Jiuling 九灵 Laozi); that during the era of Zhu Rong (祝融) he was Master Far-reaching Longevity (Guangshou zi 广寿子); that during the era of the Yellow Thearch he was Master Far-reaching Attainment (Guangcheng zi 广成子); that during the era of Zhuan Xu he was Master Red Essence (Chijing zi 赤精子); that during the era of Thearch Ku he was Master Lutu; that during the era of Yao he was the Master Who Has Completed His Striving (Wucheng zi 务成子); that during the era of Shun he was Master Yin Shou (Yin Shou zi 尹寿子); that during the era of Yu of the Xia [dynasty] he was the Master Who Has Perfected His Practice (Zhenxing zi 真行子); that during the era of Tang of the Yin [dynasty] he was Master Xi Ze (锡则子); and that during the era of King Wen [of the Zhou dynasty] he was Master Wen Yi (文邑先生)—and one version adds that [under the Zhou] he served as Archivist. < Some say that in [the kingdom of] Yue he was Fan Li (范蠡); that in [the kingdom of] Qi he was Master Chi Yi (鸱夷子), and that in [the kingdom of] Wu he was Tao Zhugong (陶朱公). Such opinions appear in all sorts of books, but they do not appear in the correct scriptures of divine transcendence, and > they are unreliable.[4]

< My own view is that, if Laozi were indeed a celestial essence or deity, then there would have been no era in which he did not appear.[5] And he would indeed have stepped down from positions of honor to occupy lowly stations; he would have lowered himself from lofty reclusion to assume laborious tasks; he would have abandoned [celestial] purity and entered into [earthly] impurity, he would have relinquished his celestial post and accepted human rank. Now as long as there have been a Heaven and an Earth, so long have there been arts of

the Dao. How could there ever have been a period when practitioners of arts of the Dao were lacking? Therefore it is hardly surprising that, > in every era from Fu Xi down to the three ancient dynasties, various persons have become noted for their arts of the Dao. < But why must we regard them all as the same, single person, Laozi? These sorts of speculations are the product of recent generations of practitioners, lovers of what is marvelous and strange, who have created them out of a desire to glorify and venerate Laozi. To discuss it from a basis in fact, I would say that > Laozi was someone who was indeed particularly advanced in his attainment of the Dao < but that he was not of another kind of being than we.

According to the *Records of the Historian*, Laozi's son was named Zong; he served as a general in the Wei kingdom, and thanks to his merit was enfeoffed at Duan.[6] Zong's son was Wang; his son was Yan; Yan's great-grandson was Xia, an official under the Han. Xia's son Jie was the Grand Mentor of the Prince of Jiaoxi, and his family lived in Qi.[7] From this it can be seen that the view that Laozi was originally a deity or numen must stem from practitioners of the Dao of shallow views who wished to make Laozi into a divine being of a kind different from us, so as to cause students in later generations to follow him; what they failed to realize was that this would cause people to disbelieve that long life is something attainable by practice. Why is this? If you maintain that Laozi was someone who attained the Dao, then people will exert themselves to imitate him. If you maintain that he was a deity or numen, of a kind different from us, then his example is not one that can be emulated by practice. >

Some say that as Laozi was about to head out west through the pass, the keeper of the pass, Yin Xi （尹喜）, realizing that he was no ordinary man, followed after him and asked for his Dao, and that Laozi, shocked and amazed by this, stuck out his tongue a very long way (*danran*), and that this is how he came to be called Lao Dan.[8] This is also false. According to today's *Scripture of the Nine Transformations* (*jiubian jing* 九变经) and *the Scripture of the Twelve Transformations of the Primordially Engendered One* (*Yuansheng shierhua jing* 元生十二化经), Laozi definitely already had the name Dan before he entered the pass. [And] Laozi changed his name and style several times; he was not only called Dan. Bearing this in mind, it may also be noted that according to *the Scripture on the Nine Palaces* 九宫[经], *the Scripture on the Three and Five* 三五经, and *the Scripture of the Primordial Epochs* 元辰经, each person in his or her life has certain perilous conjunctions; when he reaches these times, he (should) change his name and style according to the sound corresponding to < the changes in > his birth pneuma. [9] In this way he can extend his years and escape the peril. Nowadays there are still practitioners of the Dao who do this. Laozi was alive in the Zhou for over two hundred years. In over two hundred years' time there must surely have been more than one perilous conjunction. This explains why his names and styles are relatively many.

If one wishes correctly to determine the facts about Laozi, one should take historical writings and records of actual events, along with the scriptures on transcendence and esoteric writings, as primary, and compare these with one another. Any other sources may be vulgar speculations, containing much that is false. < I note that in the [*Scripture of*] *Western Ascension*, the [*Scripture on*] *Laozi in the Embryonic State*, the [*Scripture on*] *Returning to the Shoots of One's Life-Allotment*, > *The Pearly Scabbard and the Jade Tablet*, and the *Esoteric Scripture on Golden Slips*, it is stated—by all of them alike—that Laozi was of a yellow < and white > hue, had elegant eyebrows, a broad forehead, long ears, large eyes, and widely spaced teeth, as well a square mouth and thick < lips >. On his forehead there were patterns [symbolizing] the three [powers] and the five [phases], the sun and the moon. His nose was high and straight. His ears had three apertures each. On the soles of his feet were [patterns symbolizing] yin and yang and the five [phases], and in the palms of his hands there was the character "ten". [10]

During the reign of King Wen of Zhou, Laozi served as Palace Librarian; under King Wu, he served as Archivist. [11] Common people of that time, noting his longevity, called him Laozi (the Old Master).

< Now when people receive their allotted life spans, some are naturally endowed with the capacity to communicate with spirits and perceive distant phe-

nomena; the pneumas with which they are blessed are not the same as those of ordinary people. Such people are fit to become lords in the Dao (道主), such that they come to be aided by celestial spirits and followed by numerous transcendents. As such a person, Laozi made available many methods for transcending the world, including, [first of all,] [formulas for] nine elixirs and eight minerals, Liquor of Jade and Gold Liquor, next, methods for mentally fixing on the mystic and unsullied, meditating on spirits and on the Monad, successively storing and circulating pneumas, refining one's body and dispelling disasters, averting evil and controlling ghosts, nourishing one's nature and avoiding grains, transforming oneself [so as to] overcome trouble, keeping to the teachings and precepts, and dispatching demons. [12] In all, [the writings on these methods) came to nine hundred thirty fascicles, plus seventy fascicles of talismanic texts. All of these texts are listed in the *Central Slips on Laozi's Origins* (*Laozi benqi zhongpian* 老子本起中篇)[13]. Since this text gives a bibliographic catalog, any texts that are not found among these titles [can be identified as] > something that later Practitioners of the Dao have added on their own initiative; they are not authentic writings.

< Laozi was tranquil and yielding, and harbored no desires. He devoted himself wholly to the pursuit of long life. This is why, although he [served] under the Zhou for a long time, he never rose in rank. He seems to have wished [outwardly] to blend in with others while > inwardly realizing naturalness. [14] < Then, when his way was completed, he departed, surely as a transcendent.

Confucius once went to ask Laozi something about the rites. At first he sent [his disciple] Zigong ahead to him. When he arrived, Laozi said to him, "Your master is the one named Qiu. If he follows me for three years, then at that point he should be teachable."

When Confucius himself met Laozi, Laozi told him, "A good merchant hides his goods so that [his shop] appears empty. A true gentleman hides his integrity so that he appears dull. [15] Quit your haughty bearing! You are spoiling your aim with too many desires. None of these is of any benefit to you!" >

[On another occasion] Laozi came upon Confucius while he was reading.

"What book is that?" he asked. "The [*Book of*] *Changes*," answered Confucius; "the [ancient] sages also studied it. " "It's all right for the sages to have studied it," Laozi said, "but for what purpose are you studying it? < What is the gist of it?" "The gist is in goodwill and duty," Confucius replied. Laozi responded, "When mosquitoes and gadflies sting the flesh, we lie awake all night long. If we let goodwill and duty torment our hearts and keep them restless, there is no disorder worse. [16] The snow goose wants no daily bath to make it white, the rook no daily inking to make it black. It is inherent in Heaven to be high, in Earth to be thick, in the sun and moon to shed light, in the stars to form constellations, in trees and plants to have their distinctions. [17] If you too go forward cultivating the Dao, you will already have attained the utmost. Why be so busy proclaiming good will and duty, like the man banging the drum as he goes looking for lost sheep? You are disrupting human nature, sir. "

[On another occasion,] Laozi asked Confucius, "Have you after all attained the Dao?" "I've searched for it for twenty-seven years and have not found it," answered Confucius. Laozi said, "Supposing the Dao could be offered up, there is no one who would not offer it to his lord. Supposing the Dao could be presented as a gift there is no one who would not present it to his relatives. Supposing the Dao could be told to others, there is no one who would not tell it to his brothers. Supposing the Dao could be bequeathed, there is no one who would not bequeath it to his children. That we cannot do so is for this reason alone: unless you have an appropriator within to make it your own, the Dao cannot take up residence in you. "

[On yet another occasion,] Confucius said, "I have studied the [classics of] *Songs*, *Documents*, *Rites*, *Music*, *Changes*, and *Spring and Autumn Annals*. I have chanted the way of the former kings and made plain the imprints of the Dukes of Zhou and Shao in order to introduce myself to over seventy rulers, but still I have not been employed. How hard people are to persuade!" Laozi replied, "The Six Classics are the worn footprints of the former kings, not what they used to imprint. What you are cultivating yourself in now is all worn footprints, and footprints are where the shoes have passed, they are not the shoes!"[18]

When Confucius returned [from seeing Laozi], he did not speak for three days. Zigong thought it strange and asked him why. Confucius said, "When I see that someone is thinking like a bird in flight, I refurbish my thinking into a bow and shoot at him, and never have I failed to hit and retrieve him. When I see that someone is thinking like a deer, I refurbish my thinking into a running dog and pursue him, and never have I failed to catch him. When I see that someone is thinking like a fish in the deep, I refurbish my thinking into a hook and line and cast for him and never have I failed to hook him and reel him in. But when it comes to a dragon, riding clouds and vapor, roaming about in the Grand Purity empyrean, I am unable to pursue him. Today I saw Laozi, and how like a dragon he is! My mouth gaped so wide I could not get it shut; my tongue protruded so far I could not get it back in. My spirits were thrown into confusion and did not know where to lodge."[19]

When Yangzi 阳子 went to see Laozi, Laozi told him, "It's the elegant mark of the tiger and leopard and the spryness of monkeys which draw the hunter's shot." "May I inquire how an enlightened king rules?" Yangzi asked.

"When the enlightened king rules

His deeds spread over the whole world but seem not from himself.

His riches are loaned to the myriad things but the people do not depend on him.

He has integrity, but no one mentions his name or station.

Immeasurable, he roams where nothing is." >[20]

When Laozi was about to leave [China][21] and head west through the pass to ascend [Mount] Kunlun, the keeper of the pass, Yin Xi, having divined from the wind and pneumas, knew that a godlike person was due to pass through. So he swept the road < for forty *li* >. Upon seeing Laozi, < he realized he was the one whom he expected. In China, Laozi had never bestowed his teachings on anyone. But, > recognizing that Yin Xi was fated to obtain the

Dao, Laozi stopped [for a while] beneath the pass.

< Now Laozi had a retainer named Xu Jia 徐甲 who, from his youth, had been hired out to Laozi for the price of a hundred pieces of cash per day. By this time Laozi owed him 7,200,000 pieces. When Xu realized that Laozi meant to exit through the pass very soon and travel on, and that he would not obtain what he was owed, he solicited someone to name Laozi in a complaint to the keeper of the pass. But the person making the complaint did not realize that Xu had been following Laozi for over two hundred years; he only reckoned on the large sum Xu was due to receive, and on this basis he betrothed his daughter to Xu. Xu, for his part, was delighted upon seeing that the girl was comely.

When the complaint was communicated to Yin Xi, he was shocked and saw Laozi about it, Laozi said to Xu Jia, "You were due to die long ago. When I hired you, you were an official's slave from a poor family, and I lacked an attendant, so I gave you a Grand Mystery talisman for living purely[22], and that is how you have lived down to this day. How can you speak against me now? And I told you before that when we reach Parthia I would settle with you in gold. Why couldn't you wait?"

With that, Laozi had Xu Jia open his mouth toward the ground. The Grand Mystery perfected talisman at once emerged onto the ground, the cinnabar writings on it as good as new, and Xu became a pile of dried-up bones. Yin Xi, knowing that Laozi was a divine person and that he was capable of bringing Xu back to life, knocked his head on the ground on Xu's behalf, pleading for his life and also requesting to make the payment to Xu on Laozi's behalf. Laozi then tossed the Grand Mystery talisman onto the bones once more, and Xu immediately returned to life. Yin Xi then gave Xu Jia two million in cash and sent him off.

Yin Xi then performed the rites due from a disciple to a master. > Laozi bestowed on him all of the matters pertaining to long life. < Yin Xi further asked for teachings and precepts, whereupon Laozi spoke five thousand words to him. Yin Xi then withdrew and > wrote these down, titling them the *Classic of the Way and Its Power* (*Daodejing*). < He practiced Laozi's way and so came to obtain transcendence himself. >

Han Empress Dou believed in Laozi's words, so Emperor Wen and all the members of the Dou clan could not but read them. < Upon reading them, they all benefited greatly, and that is why the empire was at peace during the reigns of [Emperors] Wen and Jing and why the Dou clan preserved its glory for three generations more.

The Grand Mentor of the Crown Prince, Shu Guang 疏光, and his son deeply understood the meaning [of Laozi's words] and so perceived the relative value of withdrawing oneself [from service] versus completing one's merit [in office]. They quit their posts on the same day and returned home, distributing their money and dispensing kindness, and thus protected their purity and honor.

And so it goes for all practitioners who seclude themselves. All who venerate the arts of Laozi scorn glory and ornamentation without while nourishing life and longevity within; they avoid falling into the dangerous world. Seeing that his abundant spring has flowed down for so long and has formed such a vast ocean, how could Laozi be anything other than an exemplary teacher and standard established by Heaven and Earth for a myriad successive generations? > That is why all followers of Zhuang Zhou [Zhuangzi] take Laozi as their ultimate progenitor.[23] (Campany, 2002: 194 – 204)

［解析］

1. 在中国古代，人名比现在复杂，分为名、字、号。"字"是根据人名中的字义另取的别名。古代人的名字中的字是由名演化而来，字与名有着密切的关系。如，诸葛亮，字孔明，明与亮意义相同。在通常情况下，字是下对上、少对长的面称和对他人的尊称。号是士大夫和文人墨客的自称，以委婉曲折、幽默含蓄的方式，表达自号者的超凡脱俗、潜然物外的情趣和志向，是正名之外的美称和自称（卢红梅，2006：95 – 96）。中国译者翻译古代人名时，通常有两种方式对应中文人名的名、字、号。

（1）用 name 或 real name 翻译"名"，literary name 翻译"字"，fancy name 对应"号"，如林语堂《浮生六记》译本中"乙丑七月，琢堂始自都门回籍。琢堂名韫玉，字执如，琢堂其号也"的对应英文为 In the Seventh moon of the year 1805, Chot'ang returned home from the capital. This was his "fancy name", while his real name was Yünyü and his literary name Chihju.

（2）用 name/courtesy name/pen name ——对应汉语的名、字、号。如杨宪益《红楼梦》译本中的"姓贾名化，表字时飞，别号雨村者"的对应英文为：His name was Jia Hua, his courtesy name Shih-fei, and his penname Yu-tsun。

多数西方译者通常笼而统之地采用"name"一词翻译古代人名中的名、字、号，如霍克斯（David Hawkes）将《红楼梦》中的句子"庙旁住着一家乡宦，姓甄，名费，字士隐"英译为 Next door to Bottle-gourd Temple lived a gentleman of private means called Zhen Shi-yin。译者将"老子者，名重耳，字伯阳"英译为 Laozi（Master Lao, or the Old Master）had Chong'er 重耳 as his name, Boyang 伯阳 as his style, 除了提供了英文中三种常见的"老子"译文之外，译者用"name"对应"名"，"style"对应"字"，凸显了"字"作为基于本名含义另取别名的语用功能，也传译出中国古代人名的命名特征。这种处理手法也是为了照顾原文多处提到"老子数易名字"这一记载，使译文前后统一说法。

2. 道教认为气为生命之本、性命之源。早期道教经典《太平经》讲到："夫气者，所以通天地万物之命也；天地者，乃以气风化万物之命也"（王明，1960：317）。"气"在英文中常被译为"breath"或"energy"，也有采用音译"qi"，康儒博选择古希腊哲学术语"pneuma"翻译这一概念，以等同作为"生命的根本动力"之元气，"pneuma"兼具"元气、精神、灵魂"之意。原文"虽受气天然，见于李家，犹以李为姓"译为 But, although he received his pneumas from Heaven, since he was born into the Li 李 family he took Li as his surname。

3. 原文"天之精魄，盖神灵之属"意思是：如果老子是天地的精灵神魄，那么他自然就是神灵了。古人认为能离开人体而存在的精神，阳神为魂，阴神为魄。道教有"三魂七魄"之说。道教百科词典（The Encyclopedia of Taoism）收录"魂魄"词条的翻译为 Yang soul(s) and Yin soul(s); celestial soul(s) and earthly soul(s)。维基百科上对"魂魄"的词源学意义和语义学意义做了详细的解读，并用表格形式列出了多达十部词典关于魂魄的翻译。其中带有共性的翻译为 soul 和 spirit，为多数译者所采用的译法，如林语堂1972年编撰的《林语堂当代汉英词典》(*Lin Yutang's Chinese-English Dictionary of Modern Usage*) 中对"魂"的解读为：Soul; the finer spirits of man，对应的"魄"的解读则为：the baser spirits or animal forces。梁实秋先生1992年编撰的《远东汉英大辞典》(*Far East Chinese-English Dictionary*) 的解读略有不同，"魂"的对应解释为 a soul; a spirit，"魄"则有三层解读：(1)(Taoism) vigor; animation; life。(2) form; shape; body。(3) the dark part of the moon。而美国学者德范克（John De Francis）2003年编撰的《ABC 汉英大词典》(*ABC Chinese-English Comprehensive Dictionary*) 上的对"魂魄"解读越发简单，两者的区分度不大，"魂"的英文为 soul, spirit, mood。"魄"的英文则为 soul, vigor, spirit。当代一些西方汉学家喜欢从词源学的角度考证中国汉字的意义，结合象形文字的考证，"魂"可拆分为"云鬼"，"魄"为"白鬼"，因而"魂""魄"可分别英译为"the cloud soul"和"the white soul"。只不过康儒博这里将原文的"精魄"译成"精魂"(cloud-souls or essences)，但并非误读误译，而是因为该段文字是译者综合《法苑珠林》和《太平广记》的内容翻译而成，《法苑珠林》中的内容为"魂"，这一点译者在注释中有说明。

  4. 该段涉及一些专有名词的翻译，包括传说中上古时代的不同名称、老子被后世道教徒牵强附会的各种别称名号等。这些文化特色表达难以在英文中找到对等语，只有退而求其次，采用添加范畴词、音译、直译、意译等手段求其近似。在此基础上，添加拼音、汉字、注释的做法成了翻译这些文化特色词语的常态。如，"玄中法师"直译为 Ritual Master of the Mystic Center，"金阙帝君"直译为 Thearch-Lord of the Golden Porte，郁华子为 Master Denseflower（Yuhua zi 郁华子），"九灵老子"为 Old Master Nine-Numina（Jiuling 九灵 Laozi），"广寿子"为 Master Far-reaching Longevity（Guangshou zi 广寿子）。因"上三皇""下三皇"分别代表两个不同的时期，所以"上三皇"译为 the Upper [portion of the) Era of the Three Sovereigns，其中"portion of the Era of"为添加的范畴词。但这些翻译仅仅只是语言层面的近似，译入语读者若想了解这些称谓背后折射的文化意蕴必须借助译者提供的注释。如，在"金阙帝君"的注释中，译者依据柏夷、柯慕白（Paul W. Kroll）、魏鲁男（James Ware）等学者的道教典籍翻译研究成果补充了以下知识点。

（1）The divine Laozi continued to be invested with this title, *jinque dijun* 金阙帝君, in the Shangqing scriptures, where he reigned as the highest of four lords.

（2）The "porte" (*que*; an alternative, etymologically elegant rendition by Paul Kroll, ruined for me by its evocation of highway construction projects, is "pylons") was a gate hung between twin timber or stone towers, often protecting access to sacred grounds such as the inner sanctuaries of palaces or temples; during the Han and in Ge Hong's time, *que* were often erected at the entrances to aristocrats' tombs.

（3）The Golden Porte in Shangqing and Lingbao macro-cosmology was "a palace in the upper reaches of the Shangqing Heavens, where they join the even higher heavens of Yuqing (Jade Clarity), peopled by the gods of the prior heavens, who have no intercourse with humanity whatsoever".

（4）Ge does once mention the Golden Porte as a microcosmic somatic site located beneath the heart at the "central cinnabar field", a site that is the occasional residence of the divine Monad. （Company, 2002: 194 – 195）

读者可以了解到:（1）老子在上清经记载的诸多尊神中享有最高地位；（2）"阙"的词源学意义，常指通往皇宫神庙的楼台，在汉代和葛洪所在的东晋时期，常被用来指代达官贵人陵墓前的石牌坊；（3）"金阙"在上清经和灵宝经中指上清境中的最高界，与玉清境毗邻，里面居住着与人类毫无交际的上天之神；（4）"金阙"在《抱朴子内篇》中指人体小宇宙中"中丹田"（心脏）之下的部位，"太一"神的居住地。这些背景知识虽然简略，但配合这些专有名字的直译，足以让译入语读者了解大意。

5. 原文"洪以为老子若是天之精神，当无世不出"为直接引语。古人常以自己的名字，或者其他的谦称，如仆、臣、愚等实指"我"，因此，译者将"洪以为"译为"my own view is that"，宾语从句用虚拟语气，以表达所有这些皆为一些学道者的主观臆断（speculations）。译者把该句中的"天之精神"译为"a celestial essence or deity"，把前文"盖神灵之属"中的"神灵"译为"a deity or numen",是因为古汉语中的"精神"和"神灵"本就是两个不同概念"精"和"神"、"神"和"灵"的组合。这里葛洪收集了当时关于老子的传说,并对其中的一些荒诞不经的说法进行了批判,认为是一些"浅见道士"为了吸引别人来学习老子,而对老子进行的神化。他认为老子是一个因"得道"而成仙的人,据此,也可考虑译为"a celestial being"。

6. 分封制是东西方都出现过的一种政治制度,指的是帝王把爵位及土地赐给臣子以加强对国家的统治,英语单词为"enfeoff",其英语阐释为 put in possession of land in exchange for a pledge of service, in feudal society,该词与原文的"封"意义几乎完全对等。

7. 古代官衔称谓词十分庞杂,体现的是被称谓者的身份和权势,通常难以在英文中找到级别相当内涵对等的称谓词,如该句中的"太傅"为中国古代职官,始于西周,为辅佐太子的官员,因此译者用释义法翻译为 the Grand Mentor of the Prince。

8. 原文"老子惊怪,故吐舌聃然"意思为:老子听了十分惊诧,竟吐出舌头来半天没收回去。耳大而长谓"聃","聃然"则指吐舌之状。译者准确把握了原意,译为 stuck out his tongue a very long way (*danran*),增加括号中的拼音只是为了让读者能更好地理解下句中的老子的别名老聃的音译 Lao Dan。

9. 原文"人生各有厄会,到其时,若易名字,以随元气之变,则可以延年度厄"意思是人一生会经历几次命运中的坎坷,遇到劫难时,如果能改一下名字,便是顺应自然的安排,就可以平安消灾、延年益寿。其中"厄会"指各种灾难汇合,译为"perilous conjunctions"恰如其分。"以"为连词,表目的关系,意思为"来""用来"等。"元气"亦称"原气",为中国道家哲学术语,指构成万物的原始物质,亦指人体组织器官生理功能的基本物质与活动能力,可英译为"primordial pneuma",也可如该文译者那样翻译为"birth pneuma"。因该句中"以随元气之变"在《法苑珠林》中的表述是"随生气之音",所以康儒博翻译为 he (should) change his name and style according to the sound corresponding to < the changes in > his birth pneuma,并在翻译文本注释中做了说明。从这一例证我们可以得到这样的启示,对译文的评判不可单从文字表面的呈现就判定译文是忠实还是背叛原文，最好能还原译者的翻译过程，基于这样的前提才能较为客观地进行评价。该句还可译为 Each person in his life has certain perilous conjunctions. If he (should) change his name and style to fit in with the changes in his birth pneuma at these times, he could extend his years and escape the perils。

10. 原文"老子黄白色，美眉，广颡长耳，大目疏齿，方口厚唇；额有三五达理，日角月悬；鼻纯骨双柱，耳有三漏门；足蹈二五，手把十文"为古籍中有关老子的肖像描写，原文突出细节，以彰显老子与凡人迥然不同，谢青云译注《神仙传》一书中该段的白话文为：老子黄白皮肤，眉毛很美，额头宽阔耳朵很长，眼睛很大，牙齿稀疏，四方大口嘴唇很厚；他的额头有十五道横贯的皱纹，额角两端似有凸出的日月的形状；他鼻子很端正，鼻骨似两根柱子挺立；耳朵上有三个耳孔，他一步可以跨出一丈远，双手上有十道纹路（谢青云，2017：34）。

译者对其中几个数字做出了自己独到的变通处理。"三五达理"译为：patterns〔symbolizing〕the three〔powers〕and the five〔phases〕，将"三五达理"阐释为额头上有象征"三才""五行"的皱纹图案，而非具体有十五道皱纹，"足蹈二五"译为 On the soles of his feet were〔patterns symbolizing〕yin and yang and the five〔phases〕，"二五"理解为象征"阴阳""五行"的脚底图案，而非具体的长度。另外，古汉语中"文"作名词时既可以指线条交错的图形，也可指文章、文字，译者将"十文"翻译为"十"这个汉字，并提供注释补充他这样理解依据的是法国学者索安的研究成果《汉代道教中老子的神话》（*La divinisation de Lao Tseu dans le Taoisme des Han*），认为"十"指代"干支"中的"十天干"（Campany，2002：199）。单从文字表面来看，康儒博的解读似乎有点牵强，但若从原文所发生的语境来看，葛洪这里引用古籍对老子的肖像描述，实是为了批判这些荒诞不经的说法，为传达原文的这一语用意义，康儒博的译文完全符合古籍对老子的神化。

11. 守藏史：周代管理藏书室的官员，对应译为"Palace Librarian"；柱下史译为"Archivist"（档案管理员）。柱下史是一种与秦汉以后御史相当的官职，掌管中央的奏章、档案、图书以及地方上报的材料，两种官职的英译皆颇为妥当。

12. 原文"夫人受命，自有通神远见者，禀气与常人不同，应为道主，故能为天神所济，众仙所从。是以所出度世之法，九丹八石，金醴金液；次存玄素守一，思神历藏，行气炼形，消灾辟恶，治鬼养性，绝谷变化，厌胜教戒，役使鬼魅之法"中的"九丹八石、金醴金液"为道教徒用矿石炼就的所谓长生药物，"存玄素守一，思神历藏，行气炼形"则是道教徒修身养性的一些法术。道教认为人身体是小宇宙，体内诸神与大宇宙中的神相统一，存想法术即可招出体内诸神，派往大宇宙中执事。道教所谓守一存真，乃能通神，这是对道士的修行要求，说明修行存想是通神的重要方法（张泽洪，1999：21）。玄素，即玄女和素女，传说她们以房中术授黄帝。守一，指在身心安静的情况下，把意念集中在身体的某个部位，思神即存想身中诸神，历藏则是存想法术具体实施的方法。译者翻译"存玄素"时对原文的表述颇有疑问，认为玄素通常引申房中术，不应该作为存想的对象，所以并未具体翻译为 mentally fixing on the mystic maiden and the unsullied maiden，而是虚化翻译为 mentally fixing on the mystic and unsullied，体现了译者对原文的理解上的修正。将"守一""思神"合译为"meditating on spirits and on the Monad"，其中"the Monad"为希腊词语，指先于万物产生的至高神，维基百科的解释是"the Supreme Being in cosmogony"，该词对译"一"这一等同道教之"道"的概念，可较好地传译道教存想通神的重要法术。"守一"还可以翻译为"hold/embrace the One"或"safeguard the Unity"。"厌胜"原为古代方士的一种巫术，谓能以诅咒制服人或物。"厌"字此处念 yā（阴平韵），通"压"，有"抑制、堵塞、掩藏、压制"的意思。译者将"变化"与"压胜"组合，译为 transforming oneself [so as to] overcome trouble，相较于原文的搭配似乎更趋合理。由于这些道教方术都无法在英语中找到合适的词汇，译者通过添加范畴词 formulas 和 methods 的方式帮助目标语读者了解其属性。这种做法，着实可资借鉴。

13.《老子·本起》是一本介绍老子的书，"中篇"并非书名中的一部分，而是指该书共有上、中、下三部，所以可修订为 the second book of Laozi's Origins (Laozi benqi 老子本起)。

14. 原文"盖欲和光同尘"指不露锋芒，与世无争的平和处世态度，出自《道德经》第四章"挫其锐，解其纷，和其光，同其尘"。多数译者翻译《道德经》中这句话倾向于保留原文形式，如汉学家安乐哲的译文为 It blunts the sharp edges and untangles the knots; It softens the glare and brings things together on the same track（Ames, Hall, 2003: 83）。康儒博选择意译法将"盖欲和光同尘"译为 He seems to have wished [outwardly] to blend in with others，也未偏离原文的思想。

15. 古人崇尚用词简略、行文对仗，原文"良贾深藏若虚，君子盛德若愚"意思是：善于经商的人虽然拥有许多财物但却藏而不露，君子虽多有道德却往往看起来比较愚笨。英译文补充了略去的内容，将原文隐含的内容明晰化，译为 A good merchant hides his goods so that [his shop] appears empty. A true gentleman hides his integrity so that he appears dull。

16. 原文"蚊虻噆肤，通夕不得眠。今仁义憯然而汨人心，乱莫大焉"出自《庄子外篇·天运》，康儒博将该句英译为 When mosquitoes and gadflies sting the flesh, we lie awake all night long. If we let goodwill and duty torment our hearts and keep them restless, there is no disorder worse。这里涉及儒家"五常"中的两个重要概念"仁"和"义"的理解。"仁""义"通常被解释为"仁爱"和"正义"，为儒家道德的最高标准。英译者们常常会根据语境做出自己不同的翻译，以至于这些概念在英文中有不同的表述，如"仁"的英译就包括：benevolence, virtue, kindness, humaneness, 等等；"义"的英文则包括：righteousness, morality, appropriateness, 等等。作为儒家学说中的核心概念，"仁"与"义"皆有广义狭义之分，因应用语境不同指称就有差异，无法统一为一个英文单词。这里译者根据语境用"goodwill"和"duty"翻译"仁"和"义"，将这两个道德范畴落实到具体的为他人着想的"仁爱"和合乎正义的"职责"上，取的是这两个概念的狭义。

读者可对照阅读其他中外译者《庄子》英译本中这句引文的译文。如，在被誉为"《庄子》英译本中的佼佼者"（汪榕培，1999: 37）的美国汉学家华兹生 1968 年英译的《庄子》全译本中，该句的译文为 A mosquito or a horsefly stinging your skin can keep you awake a whole night. And when benevolence and righteousness in all their fearfulness come to muddle the mind, the confusion is unimaginable（Watson, 1968: 163）。华兹生《庄子》译本通俗易懂，已被收入"联合国教科文组织各国代表作品丛书"。即便

如此，由于中西方文化和思维的差异，再有名的汉学家也难免会受到中国文字认识不足的局限，该句的修饰语"惨然"的词典意义有"狠毒，凶残"之意，不难理解华兹生会译为"in all their fearfulness"，但实际上"惨然"应是突出"仁义给人的毒害惨痛，以至于使我们的内心混乱不堪"。国内典籍翻译之翘楚汪榕培教授将该句译为 When you are bitten by a mosquito or a fly, you won't be able to fall asleep all night. When you are muddled by humaneness and righteousness, you will be thrown into the most serious disorder（汪榕培，1999：237），这样的译文和康儒博译文"If we let goodwill and duty torment our hearts and keep them restless, there is no disorder worse"所体现的交际意图是一致的，突出了仁义给人内心带来的影响。

17. 原文"夫鹄不日浴而白，乌不日染而黑，天之自高矣，地之自厚矣，日月自明矣，星辰固自列矣，草木固有区矣"的英译文为 The snow goose wants no daily bath to make it white, the rook no daily inking to make it black. It is inherent in Heaven to be high, in Earth to be thick, in the sun and moon to shed light, in the stars to form constellations, in trees and plants to have their distinctions。译者采用"It is inherent in ... to do sth."这一句型翻译"天之自高矣，地之自厚矣，日月自明矣，星辰固自列矣，草木固有区矣"中"自"所包含的"固有的；内在的；与生俱来的"意蕴，可谓传神之笔。

18. 原文"丘治《诗》《书》《礼》《乐》《易》《春秋》，诵先王之道，明周、召之迹，以干七十余君而不见用，甚矣人之难说也"意思为：我研究《诗经》《书经》《周礼》《周乐》《易经》《春秋》，给七十多个国家的国君讲述前代君王的治国之道，让他们明白周公、召公的辅政事迹，但却没人采用我的主张。看来说服他人实在太难了。翻译其中的历史文献与人物时需还原其真实面貌，因此，"周、召之迹"译为 the imprints of the Dukes of Zhou and Shao，其中"imprint"除了有"印痕、痕迹"之意外，还可隐射"深远影响"之意，该句译文为 I have studied the [classics of] *Songs*, *Documents*, *Rites*, *Music*, *Changes*, and *Spring and Autumn Annals*. I have chanted the way of the former kings and made plain the imprints of the Dukes of Zhou and Shao in order to introduce myself to over seventy rulers, but still I have not been employed。

原文"夫六艺，先王之陈迹也，岂其所陈哉。今子所修者，皆因陈迹也。迹者履之出，而迹岂异哉？"中"陈"和"迹"都是多义词，带有歧义性，译者较好地领悟了原文作者这般词汇的妙用，选用 worn footprints，imprint，shoes 这些词语搭配，英译文为 The Six Classics are the worn footprints of the former kings, not what they used to imprint. What you are cultivating yourself in now is all worn footprints, and footprints are where the shoes have passed, they are not the shoes。译文效果和原文分毫不爽。

这段记载孔子和老子逸事的文字也出现在《庄子外篇·天运》中，文字略有区别：

孔子谓老聃曰："丘治《诗》《书》《礼》《乐》《易》《春秋》六经，自以为久矣，孰知其故矣，以奸者七十二君，论先王之道而明周、召之迹，一君无所钩用。甚矣！夫人之难说也？道之难明邪？"

老子曰："幸矣，子之不遇治世之君也！夫六经，先王之陈迹也，岂其所以迹哉！今子之所言，犹迹也。夫迹，履之所出，而迹岂履哉？

在此附上汪榕培《庄子外篇·天运》译本该部分内容的译文，供读者对照阅读。

Confucius said to Laozi, "I've been compiling the six classics—*The Book of Poetry*, *The Book of Documents*, *The Book of Etiquettes*, *The Book of Music*, *The Book of Changes* and *Spring and Autumn Annals*—for what I'd call a long period of time. I believe that I am well acquainted with them. However, when I tried to persuade the seventy two princes by discussing the ways of government by former kings and expounding the accomplishments by Duke of Zhou and Duke of Shao, none of them adopted my suggestions. How difficult it is! Is it difficult to convince men, or is it difficult to expound Tao?"

Laozi said, "How fortunate you are! You have not met with a ruler who rules over the world in good order! The six classics are the traces left over by the former kings. How can you say that they provide the sources of their traces? What you've just said is like the traces. Traces are prints left over by the shoes. How can you say that the traces are the shoes?"（汪榕培，1999：243）

19. 原文"吾见人之用意如飞鸟者，吾饰意以为弓弩而射之，未尝不及而加之也；人之用意如麋鹿者，吾饰意以为走狗而逐之，未尝不衔而顿之也；人之用意如渊鱼者，吾饰意以为钩缁而投之，未尝不钓而制之也。至于龙，乘云气，游太清，吾不能逐也。今见老子，其犹龙乎，使吾口张而不能翕，舌出而不能缩，神错而不知其所居也"运用多个比喻修辞形容思路敏捷之人以及可行的应对措施，以凸显老子思想深邃、神秘莫测的神仙形象。原文意思：我遇见人家的心思像飞鸟一样飘逸时，我就构造一个弓箭去射他，没有不成功射落的；如果别人的心思像麋鹿一样敏捷跳跃时，我就构造一只奔跑的猎狗去追逐他，也没有不咬到嘴里并拿住他的；别人的心思要是像潜在深渊里的鱼一样深藏不露时，我就是构造一个带钓钩的绳子投下去，也没有不钓出来并制服住他的。至于龙，乘着云气往来，遨游在天空之中，我就追不上了。现在见到老子，他就像龙一样，惊得我张着嘴合不上，吐着舌头缩不回，精神恍惚，都不知道他人在哪里（谢青云，2017：39）。译者完全采用直译法，用明喻翻译明喻，其中选用的动词也十分传神，和原文一样形象生动。如下例：

原文：吾饰意以为弓弩而射之，未尝不及而加之也。
译文：I refurbish my thinking into a bow and shoot at him, and never have I failed to hit and retrieve him.
原文：吾口张而不能翕，舌出而不能缩。
译文：My mouth gaped so wide I could not get it shut; my tongue protruded so far I could not get it back in.

只是译者对最后一句"神错而不知其所居也"的理解不够准确，可改译为 My spirits were thrown into confusion and I did not know where he actually resided。

20. 阳子（或称阳子居）询问老子何为明王之治的记载在《庄子·应帝王》中也有类似内容，原文如下：

阳子居蹵然曰："敢问明王之治。"
老聃曰："明王之治：功盖天下而似不自己，化贷万物而民弗恃。有莫举名，使物自喜。立乎不测，而游于无有者也。"
汪榕培《庄子》英译本中上述文字的译文为：
Yang Ziju was embarrassed and asked, "May I ask how an enlightened king governs his state?"
Laozi said, "When an enlightened king governs his state, his meritorious deeds are felt all over the world but they do not seem to be out of his efforts; his influence reaches everyone but the people do not feel that they depend on him; his achievements are not attributed to him but all the people enjoyed themselves; he is shrouded in mystery and wanders in the land of nonexistence."（汪榕培，1999：117—119）

虽然《庄子》中的该段文字表述略有差异，但主旨思想完全一致，对照汪榕培《庄子》英译本该段的翻译，我们依然可以看到海外汉学家囿于字面理解而导致的误译，如"化被万物而民弗恃"的康儒博译文"His riches are loaned to the myriad things but the people do not depend on him"和"不测"的译文"immeasurable"。大致是因为"化"后面的动词"被"在《庄子》中写作"贷"，译者译为"His riches are loaned to"，实际上"化"应为"教化"之义。"位乎不测"虽可解读为"处于深不可测之处"，应指"明王"的行踪无人知晓，而非康儒博所理解的"无可估量"（immeasurable），这些理解不到位的地方在汪榕培译本中皆得到修正。

21. 古文"中国"非当今意义的"中国"，而是指河南及其周围地区的中原地带，所以译为"China"是不准确的，可改译为"the central parts of China"。

22. 葛洪《抱朴子内篇·遐览》写道："其次有诸符，则有《自来符》《金光符》《太玄符》三卷,……符出于老君,皆天文也,老君能通于神明,符皆神明所授。"译者据此判断《太玄清生符》可能为《太玄符》三卷之一,并依据字面意思直译为 the Grand Mystery talisman for living purely, 虽与后文出现的"太玄真符""太玄符"表述不同,但依据上下文,应为同一道符,译者为忠实于原文的表达分别翻译为"the Grand Mystery perfected talisman"和"the Grand Mystery talisman",反而容易导致歧义,可以统一译名为"the Grand Mystery talisman"。

23. 原文"其洪源长流所润,洋洋如此,岂非乾坤所定,万世之师表哉!故庄周之徒,莫不以老子为宗也。"意思是老子的学说和道术渊博深邃,流传很广,这难道不是乾坤所定,值得后代万世向他师法学习的吗?所以庄周一派的门徒,也都把老子奉为他们的宗师了。原文采用隐喻手法描述老子思想和道术的影响力,译者采用直译的方法保留了喻体,形神兼备传达了原文的含义,其中"乾坤所定,万世之师表"翻译为 an exemplary teacher and standard established by Heaven and Earth for a myriad successive generations, 颇为准确到位。

第三节 《神仙传·张道陵》英文翻译研究

张道陵,原名张陵,是东汉时期正一盟威道(简称正一道,又称天师道)的创始人,俗称张天师。正一盟威道的创立一般被视为道教教团组织建立的标志,至今有1800多年历史。张天师一生足迹广布,他不但是制度道教的首创者,且为后世留下丰富的思想、文化资源和历史遐想(詹石窗、李怀宗,2018:105-111)。立教之始,张道陵即奉老子为道祖,以《道德经》作为教化信众的基本经典,继承与弘扬了道家思想。张道陵在传统的鬼神信仰中注入了道的内涵,从而提升了信仰的层次。人们信奉神灵,不仅在于神能消灾免祸,赐福生财,更在于神与道通,由敬神进而可体悟大道。张道陵当年设置的"二十四治"大抵是以汉代行政管理机构为摹本,既是政区也是教区,体现了政教合一的管理精神,不仅为人们提供了一种新的生活方式,为社会提供了一种新的教化体系,也对中华思想文化的形成与发展产生了重要影响(张继禹,2008:33-36)。

作为天师道的教祖级人物，同时又是道教神系中的主神之一，张道陵在道教史中享有重要地位。然而，从宗教的角度看，张道陵创教鲜见于宗教正典，多为神话方式的神圣叙事。留于后世的张天师仙传中，载于历代笔记小说中的有20多篇，大多以"仙道传说""宗教人物传说""鬼狐精怪故事"等张天师传、神仙传的面目出现。晋代葛洪所撰《神仙传》中的《张道陵》，吸取了一些民间口头文学资料，如"七试赵升"，但它已被载入道教经典作为第一代天师的传记来看待（苏宁，2018：125）。"七试赵升"反映的是道教修仙思想对修道者的道德要求，即：不贪财，不好色；济人之急，救人之危；不彰人短，不炫己长；受辱不怨，受宠不惊；不嗔不怒，恕人容物；忠诚道师，有献身精神。《神仙传》中多个传记都体现了道教成仙了道的这一道德诉求。

史书《后汉书》和《三国志》虽曾提及张道陵，但十分简略，后世道教中对他的塑造多为神话叙事，迷信色彩较为浓厚。道教史与民间传说中的张天师，已成为一个富有艺术光彩的道教神仙典型。祖天师形象及创教故事，为中国道教研究、中国文学与艺术研究提供了精彩的个案（苏宁，2018：126）。鉴于张道陵在道教创建体系中的特殊地位，其神仙逸事在各典籍的记载中又表现出一定的独特性，本节对这一则传记内容的康儒博英译本展开解析。

一 康儒博《神仙传·张道陵》译文底本的说明

《神仙传·张道陵》目前见存主要有三个版本：四库本、汉魏本（取自《太平广记》卷八）、《云笈七签》本。但从三种版本的内容来看，《云笈七签》本主体仅述"七试赵升"之事，与汉魏本此部分内容基本一致。四库本与汉魏本差异较大，两种叙述对于张道陵的态度截然相反。……张道陵晚年开悟，遂学长生之道。关于修道历程，两种版本皆大致包括了入蜀前与入蜀后两个阶段，但具体所述却截然相反。相较而言，汉魏本结构清晰，而四库本此部分内容叙述繁复，并且，细察可发现前后存在矛盾，应是拼凑改编使然（向群，2015：289—295）。

汉魏本《张道陵传》相对最为齐全。《艺文类聚》中张道陵第七次试探赵升的叙述很详细，《太平御览》中记述的这一事件除了少量措辞有别之外也大体相同。据此，尽管康儒博翻译《神仙传·张道陵》时参考了

《艺文类聚》《太平御览》《初学记》《云笈七签》《类书》《龙威秘书》《四库全书》等文献，除却张道陵第七次试探赵升的叙述译者依据的是《太平御览》相关部分，其余内容的翻译底本仍为取自《太平广记》卷八的汉魏本，只是省译了结尾处的几行内容。康儒博的理由是，这几句没有出现在《云笈七签》本，由此推断应为后来评注者添加的个人感受，所以略去不译（Campany, 2002：331—332）。

二　康儒博《神仙传·张道陵》译文解析

[原文]

张道陵者，字辅汉，沛国丰人也。本太学书生，博通五经，[1]晚乃叹曰"此无益于年命"，遂学长生之道。得黄帝九鼎丹法，欲合之，用药皆糜费钱帛。[2]陵家素贫，欲治生，营田牧畜，非己所长，乃不就。[3]

闻蜀人多纯厚，易可教化，且多名山，乃与弟子入蜀。住鹄鸣山，著作道书二十四篇，乃精思炼志。[4]忽有天人下，千乘万骑，金车羽盖，骖龙驾虎，不可胜数。[5]或自称柱下史，或称东海小童，乃授陵以新出正一盟威之道。[6]

陵受之，能治病，于是百姓翕然奉事之以为师，弟子户至数万。即立祭酒，分领其户，有如官长。并立条制，使诸弟子，随事输出米、绢、器物、纸笔、樵薪什物等。领人修复道路，不修复者，皆使疾病。[7]

县有应治桥道，于是百姓斩草除溷，无所不为，皆出其意，而愚者不知是陵所造，将为此文从天上下也。[8]

陵又欲以廉耻治人，不喜施刑罚，乃立条制，使有疾病者，皆疏记生身已来所犯之罪，乃手书投水中，与神明共盟约，不得复犯法，当以身死为约，于是百姓计愈。[9]

邂逅疾病，辄当首过，一则得愈，二使羞惭，不敢重犯，且畏天地而改。从此之后，所违犯者，皆改为善矣。[10]

陵乃多得财物，以市其药合丹，丹成，服半剂，不愿即升天也。[11]

乃能分形，作数十人。其所居门前水池，陵常乘舟戏其中，而诸道士宾客，往来盈庭，盖座上常有一陵，与宾客对谈，共食饮，而真陵故在池中也。

其治病事，皆采取玄素，但改易其大较，转其首尾，而大途犹同归也。行气、服食，故用仙法，亦无以易。[12]

故陵语诸人曰："尔辈多俗态未除，不能弃世，正可得吾行气、导引、房中之事，或可得服食草木数百岁之方耳。其有九鼎大要，唯付王长，而后合有一人，从东方来，当得之，此人必以正月七日日中到。"[13] 具说长短形状。至时果有赵升者，恰从东方来，生平原，相见，其形貌亦如陵所说。

陵乃七度试，升皆过，乃受升丹经。[14]

七试者：

第一试：升到门，不为通，使人骂辱四十余日，露宿不去，乃纳之；

第二试：使升于草中守黍驱兽，暮遣美女非常，托言远行过，寄宿，与升接床，明日，又称脚痛不去，遂留数日，亦复调戏，升终不失正；[15]

第三试：升行道，忽见遗金三十饼，升乃走过，不取；

第四试：令升入山采薪，三虎交前，咬升衣服，唯不伤身。升不恐，颜色不变，谓虎曰："我道士耳，少年不为非，故不远千里，来事神师，求长生之道，汝何以尔也？岂非山鬼使汝来试我乎？"须臾，虎乃起去；

第五试：升于市买十余匹绢，付直讫，而绢主诬之，云未得。升乃脱己衣，买绢而偿之，殊无吝色；[16]

第六试：升守田谷，有一人往，叩头乞食。衣裳破弊，面目尘垢，身体疮脓，臭秽可憎。升怆然为之动容，解衣衣之，以私粮设食，又以私米遗之；[17]

第七试：陵将诸弟子，登云台绝岩之上。下有一桃树，如人臂，傍生石壁，下临不测之渊，桃大有实。陵谓诸弟子曰："有人能得此桃实，当告以道要。"于时伏而窥之者，二百余人，股战流汗，无敢久临。视之者，莫不却退而还，谢不能得。升一人曰："神之所护，何险之有，圣师在此，终不使吾死于谷中耳。师有教者，必是此桃有可得之理故耳。"乃从上自掷，投树上，足不蹉跌。取桃实满怀，而石壁险峻，无所攀缘，不能得返。于是乃以桃一一掷上，正得二百二颗。陵得而分赐诸弟子各一，陵自食一，留一以待升。[18]

陵乃以手引升，众视之，见陵臂加长三二丈，引升，升忽然来还，乃以向所留桃与之，升食桃毕。陵乃临谷上，戏笑而言曰："赵升心自正，能投树上，足不蹉跌，吾今欲自试，投下，当应得大桃也。"众人皆谏，唯升与王长嘿然。陵遂投空，不落桃上，失陵所在。四方皆仰，上则连天，下则无底，往无道路，莫不惊叹悲涕，唯升、长二人，默然无声。[19]

良久，乃相谓曰："师则父也，自投于不测之崖，吾何以自安？"乃俱投身而下。正堕陵前，见陵坐局脚床斗帐中。见升、长二人，笑曰："吾知汝来。"乃授二人道要，三日乃还。归治旧舍，诸弟子惊悲不息。[20]

后陵与升、长三人，皆白日冲天而去，众弟子仰视之，久而乃没于云霄也。[21]

初，陵入蜀山，合丹半剂，虽未冲举，已成地仙，故欲化作七试，以度赵升，乃如其志也。

[注释]①

1. 太学：中国古代的国立大学，为传授儒家经典的最高学府。汉武帝元朔五年（公元前124年）设五经博士，弟子五十人，为西汉太学建立之始。五经：指《周易》《尚书》《诗经》《礼记》《春秋》五部儒家经典。

2. 黄帝九鼎丹法：又称九鼎丹法，相传为黄帝所用的炼丹法。糜（mí）：奢侈浪费。钱帛：金钱和布帛。帛：丝织品的总称。

3. 治生：经营家业；谋生计。就：成，成就。

4. 鹄鸣山：亦作鹤鸣山，道教名山，今四川省成都市大邑县境内。精思：一种道家内修方法。

5. 骖：古代驾在车前两侧的马，这里指驾驭。

6. 柱下史：老子的别称。东海小童：上清派尊神。正一盟威：文渊阁《四库全书》为"明威"，本为与神盟誓之意，这里指具有消灾解难、降魔除妖功能的道教符箓。

7. 翕：收敛；聚会，形容一致。然：用在形容或副词后，表状态，可译为"……的样子"。祭酒：本为官名。古礼，祭祀宴飨时，由最年长者举酒以祭于地，故祭酒为尊称。战国时齐国稷下学官尊长亦称祭酒。这里指正一教在组织上的设置，初入者为"鬼卒"，管理这些"鬼卒"者

---

① 因康儒博英译本依据的底本主要取自《太平广记》卷八的汉魏本，因此，本节注释参考谢青云译注的《神仙传》（中华书局2017年版）中第168—179页的内容。

称祭酒，如果管理的人非常多，则称"治头大祭酒"。樵薪：木材和柴禾。

8. 溷：肮脏，混浊。意：意图，想法。

9. 条制：制度。疏记：分条记载。计愈：逐个治愈。

10. 辄：总是，就。首过：磕头忏悔自己的过错，即自省思过，自己承认、交代过失。

11. 市：买；购买。

12. 玄素：即玄素之道，指古代房中术。传说玄女和素女以房中术授道教始祖黄帝。行气：一种道家的内修方法。服食：按照一定的方法，进食一些药物或炼制的丹药等，道家以为可以通过长期的服食达到长生不老的功效。

13. 九鼎大要：即黄帝九鼎丹法。合：副词，意思为该，应当。日中：指正午。

14. 试：考验。

15. 草中，根据后文这里应指"草棚中"或"草屋中"。接：连接；毗连。正：正念。

16. 直：通"值"。讫：完毕，终了。吝：舍不得，过分爱惜。

17. 弊：破败。怆然：悲伤的样子。设：陈设；安排。遗：赠送。

18. 股：大腿。战：害怕，发抖。蹉跌：失足跌倒。嘿然：沉默无言的样子。

19. 投空：从空中跳下。仰：脸向上，引申为抬头看。

20. 局脚：装在器物底部的曲脚。局，同"曲"。魏晋以后，盛行在坐榻下装上曲折形的高脚，称曲脚。斗帐：小帐子。因形如倒置的斗，故名。

21. 白日冲天：即白日飞升。道教谓人修炼得道后，白昼飞升仙境成仙。

[译文]

Zhang Ling was a native of the Pei kingdom. ＜Originally he was a student in the Imperial Academy, where he became well versed in the Five Classics.[1] After this, however, he sighed and said, "None of this is of any benefit to one's years or allotted life span." So he studied the Way of long life. He obtained the Yellow Thearch's Method of the Elixirs of the Nine Tripods, and he wished to synthesize these elixirs, but the necessary medicinal ingredients cost much in cash and silk. Zhang's family was simple and poor, but, desiring to establish his hold on life, he worked the fields and raised animals incessantly. However, even after a long time he had still failed to reach his goal.[2]

Having heard that many of the people of Shu were pure and generous, easy to teach and transform, and, moreover, that country was full of noted mountains, he entered Shu with his disciples. He took up residence on Crane Cry Mountain, where he composed a work on the Dao in twenty-four sections. Then he concentrated his thoughts and refined his will.[3] Suddenly > a celestial personage descended, < with a train of one thousand carriages and ten thousand cavalry men, golden chariots with feathered canopies, dragons and tigers in the harnesses—so many they could not be counted.[4] One in the party announced himself as Archivist, another as the Young Lad of the Eastern Sea, and these two bestowed on Zhang Ling the newly promulgated Way of the Covenant of Correct Unity.[5]

Once Zhang had received this, he became able to cure illnesses. And so the common people flocked to him, hailing and serving him as their master. His disciples numbered several myriad households. He therefore established [the office of] Libationer, so as to divide and lead their households, a system of offices and supervisors and administrative sectors was established. He arranged for rice, fabric, tools, utensils, paper, brushes, lumber, firewood, and other supplies to be distributed as needed.[6] He directed some people to repair certain roads, and those among them who failed to do so he caused to become ill. [From then on,] whenever a district had a bridge or stretch of road that needed repairs, the commoners there without exception cut down the brush and removed the debris. It all happened according to Zhang's plan, but the ignorant did not realize that these things were all his doing; rather, they took them as due to the scriptural text which had descended from Heaven above.

Zhang Ling wanted to rule the people by means of honesty and shame and avoid using punishments. So, once he had set up administrative sectors, whenever people in any sector became ill, he had them compose an account of all the infractions they had committed since their birth; then, having signed this document, they were to cast it into a body of water, thereby establishing a covenant with the spirits that they would not violate the regulations again, pledging their own deaths as surety.[7] Because of this practice, the common people were extremely mindful. When they happened to become ill, they always reflected on their transgressions, [thinking that] if there was only one, they might obtain a recovery, and that if there were [as many as] two they would be mortified. Thus they did not dare to commit serious infractions but reformed themselves out of awe for Heaven and Earth; and from this time forward, anyone who did commit in fractions reformed himself to become a good person.[8]

On account of all this, Zhang Ling obtained much wealth, which he used to buy the necessary medicinal ingredients for synthesizing elixirs. > When the elixirs were completed, he ingested < only half the dosage, not wishing to ascend to Heaven immediately. > As a result, he gained the ability to divide himself < into several dozen persons. Now, there was a pond outside the gate of Zhang's residence, on which he frequently went boating to amuse himself. Meanwhile, however, many Daoist guests would be going and coming in his courtyard. There would always be one Zhang Ling in the courtyard, conversing, eating, and drinking with these guests, while the real Zhang was out on the pond.

As for his methods of curing illness, they were selected from both esoteric and ordinary sources and were modified only slightly. Of those methods that proved most effective he altered some details, but in the main his methods still conformed to the others. As for his circulation of pneumas and dietetic regimen, he relied on [standard] methods of transcendence; here, too, he made no significant changes.[9]

Zhang told most everyone, "You and your ilk have not yet been able to expunge the vulgar elements from your disposition, and so you are unable to leave the world behind. It is therefore appropriate that you obtain my procedures for circulating pneumas and arts of the bedchamber. Perhaps you will prove yourself capable of a special herbal diet, but even that is only a formula for living several hundred years."[10] But as for the most essential of his Nine Cauldrons teachings, he entrusted these only to Wang Zhang 王长, who later synthesized the elixirs.

And [Zhang predicted that] there was one other person who would receive these teachings—one who would come from the east. This man, [he predicted], would certainly arrive at noon on the seventh day of the first month. He went on to describe the man's height and physical appearance. At the time specified, a man named Zhao Sheng 赵升 did indeed show up; he arrived from the east, and once others got a look at him, they saw that his form and features were exactly as Zhang had predicted. >

Zhang then put Zhao through a series of seven trials, and after Zhao had passed them all, Zhang bestowed the scripture on elixirs on him. < The seven trials were as follows. The first trial: when Zhao arrived at his gate, he was denied entry, and Zhang had others curse and berate him. He did not leave, in daylight or at night, for over forty days. Zhang then let him in.[11]

The second trial: Zhang had Zhao watch over some livestock out in pasture lands.[12] One evening Zhang sent a woman of extraordinary beauty, who pretended to be traveling far from home and asked to spend the night there and share Zhao's bed. The following day she further feigned a foot injury and said she was unable to leave; she stayed several days, during which she repeatedly flirted with him. Through all of this, Zhao never strayed from proper decorum.

The third trial: once while Zhao Sheng was walking on a road, he suddenly noticed thirty catties of gold that someone had left behind. He walked past it and did not pick it up.

The fourth trial: Zhang sent Zhao into the mountains to collect firewood. Three tigers approached him at once and bit through his clothing without, however, injuring his body. Zhao remained fearless. Without changing the expression on his face, he told the tigers, "I am a practitioner of the Dao, and since my youth I have been nothing else. That is why I did not consider a thousand *li* far to travel to come and serve my divine teacher here, seeking the way of long life. What do you mean by this? Isn't it the spirit of this mountain who has caused you to come and test me like this?" Soon the tigers rose and departed.

The fifth trial: while in the market, Zhao Sheng bought a dozen or so bolts of fabric, paying the price that was asked. But the fabric merchant falsely stated that Zhao had not paid him. Zhao removed his own clothes and gave them to the merchant as compensation without a trace of regret.

The sixth trial: while Zhao was on duty guarding grain from [public] fields, there came a man knocking his head on the ground begging for food. His clothes were in tatters, his face was caked with dirt, his body was filthy and he stank terribly. Zhao was moved to sorrow at his condition. He removed his own clothes and clothed the man in them; he set out a meal for the man from his own private provisions; and he sent him off with grain from his personal supply. >[13]

The seventh trial: with his disciples, Zhang Ling climbed up to the top of the cliff face of Cloud Terrace Mountain. Below the top of the cliff, there was a peach tree about the [thickness of a] man's arm growing out from the rock face; the depth beneath it were unfathomable, and it was thirty or forty feet down from the top of the cliff. The tree was loaded with peaches. Zhang said to his disciples, "I will declare the essentials of the Way to whoever can obtain those peaches." The disciples all broke out in a sweat, and none dared even to look down at the tree. But Zhao Sheng said, "With the divine personage protecting me, how could there be any danger in it?" He then threw himself off the top of the cliff, landing in the tree. He picked an armful of peaches, but the cliff face was sheer and he had no way to get back up. So he threw the peaches up to the top, obtaining two hundred of them. These Zhang Ling divided, giving one to each of his disciples and reserving two; of these, he himself ate one, and one he saved for Zhao. Zhang then extended his hand as if to pull Zhao up, and at once Zhao appeared back with them. Zhang gave him the last peach. < When he had eaten it, Zhang laughed beside the clifftop and said to him, "Zhao Sheng, your heart is naturally correct, that is what enabled you to throw yourself off and not to slip. I was testing you just now by sending you down after the peaches. Now I think I'll try throwing myself off, to see if l can get a bigger peach." Everyone protested this; only Zhao Sheng and Wang Chang remained silent. Zhang then threw himself off into space. But he did not land on the peach tree, and the disciples lost sight of him. They looked everywhere—up toward Heaven, down to the ground, they searched where there were no paths. All of them were shocked and sorrowful and shed tears except for Zhao and Wang, who, after a while, said to each other, "Our master was like our father. How can we find peace when he has thrown himself off into the abyss?" So they both threw themselves off. And they landed directly in front of Zhang Ling, who was seated on a mat inside a screen. When he saw them, he smiled and said, "I knew you both would come. After I have finished transmitting the Way to you two, I will return to arrange things at my former residence; then, in three days, I shall return." The [other] disciples remained stricken with shock and grief.

Afterward, Zhang Ling, together with Zhao Sheng and Wang Chang, rose up into the heavens in broad daylight and so departed. A crowd of disciples watched them from below as they gradually vanished into the clouds. >[14] （Campany, 2002: 349 – 354）

[解析]

1. 张道陵本名张陵，早期道教文献多数采用张陵，自《太平广记》起，之后的文献多用张道陵。太学为中国古代的最高学府，译为"the Imperial Academy"，也算是言简意赅，形意皆顾。原文"晚乃叹曰"中的"晚"应指晚年时，译为"after this"虽与上下文毫无违和感，但也可以修正为"in his later years"，以贴合史籍记载事实。

2. 古文中的"乃"可作代词、动词、副词、连词，语境不同，"乃"的理解就有较大的区别。具体体现在该句的英译中，因断句不同导致语境不同，从而造成翻译的差异性。清代学者马骏良辑录丛书《龙威秘书》中该句的"非己"为"非已"，原文若断句为"用药皆糜费钱帛，陵家素贫，欲治生，营田牧畜非已，所长，乃不就"，这里的"乃"为副词，意思为竟然，却。整句解读：但炼丹的药石非常贵，张道陵家又很穷，想好好经营家业，于是勤加耕种田地、畜养牲畜，然而这般劳作过了很久也还不能达到他的预期目标。康儒博的译文即依据这一种解读，译文："Zhang's family was simple and poor, but, desiring to establish his hold on life,

he worked the fields and raised animals incessantly. However, even after a long time he had still failed to reach his goal（Campany, 2002: 350）。原文若为"用药皆縻费钱帛，陵家素贫，欲治生，营田牧畜，非己所长，乃不就"，这里的"乃"作连词用，意思：于是，就。整句解读：但炼丹的药石非常贵，张道陵家又很穷，想致富，种田畜牧他又不擅长，于是放弃了。该句可试译为 Although he wished to make riches, he was not adept in working the fields and raising animals that he had to give it up。

3. 原文"闻蜀人多纯厚，易可教化，且多名山。乃与弟子入蜀，住鹄鸣山，著作道书二十四篇，乃精思炼志"中"乃精思炼志"的"乃"有两种解读，若将"乃"理解为连词"于是"，该句译为他听说四川的老百姓性格淳朴，容易接受教育点化，而且那里名山大川很多，就带着弟子住进了鹄鸣山，在那里写了二十四篇论述道术的文章，并专心修炼求道数年。英文便如康儒博所译：Having heard that many of the people of Shu were pure and generous, easy to teach and transform, and, moreover, that country was full of noted mountains, he entered Shu with his disciples. He took up residence on Crane Cry Mountain, where he composed a work on the Dao in twenty-four sections. Then he concentrated his thoughts and refined his will（Campany, 2002: 350）。但若解读为动词，表判断，该句的意思则是他听说四川的老百姓性格淳朴，容易接受教育点化，而且那里名山大川很多，就带着弟子住进了鹄鸣山，在那里写了二十四篇论述道教内修方法这类道术的文章。这样理解的话，英译文则可改为 Having heard that many of the people of Shu were pure and generous, easy to teach and transform, and, moreover, that country was full of noted mountains, he entered Shu with his disciples. He took up residence on Crane Cry Mountain, where he composed a work on the Dao in twenty-four sections, concerning the practices of inner cultivation。

4. 原文"忽有天人下，千乘万骑，金车羽盖，骖龙驾虎，不可胜数"描述了神仙从天而降的浩荡气势。英译文"Suddenly a celestial personage descended, with a train of one thousand carriages and ten thousand cavalry men, golden chariots with feathered canopies, dragons and tigers in the harnesses—so many they could not be counted"（Campany, 2002: 350）完全沿袭

原文的语序，生动再现了原文"千乘万骑，金车羽盖，骖龙驾虎"的意象，其中采用破折号引出结尾"不可胜数"，为英语中典型的外位语句子结构，使语义晓畅明了。译者选择"celestial"和"personage"搭配翻译"天人"可谓妙译，胜过单纯译为"a celestial being"，大大凸显了天人的尊贵身份。

5. 针对原文中固有的文化专有项，如"鹄鸣山""柱下史""东海小童""正一盟威"，因在英文中无法找到对应翻译，译者按常规直译出来，在脚注中提供相应的阐释，每一条阐释都较好展示了译者对该文化专有项的研究。譬如，"正一盟威之道"直译为"Way of the Covenant of Correct Unity"，译者提供的脚注内容如下：

> This is both a text and the new, divinely dispensed religion outlined in the text. For details on its contents, see Kleeman, "Licentious Cults," 202 ff. In quoting a *Zhengyijing*, XYBZ 2/13b says that the need for this covenant arose because "at the time, in Shu, people and ghosts were not separated, so that disasters and epidemics constantly arose"; the Most High Lord Lao therefore "bestowed the *Laws of the Covenant of Correct Unity* so as to divide people from ghosts and established the twenty-four parishes. Down to today the people are still receiving the blessings [of this divine dispensation]. [This matter] appears in *Shenxian zhuan*."（Company, 2002：351）

康儒博根据祈泰履（Terry F. Kleeman）的研究成果"中国古代祭祀、互惠与暴力"（Licentious Cults and Bloody Victuals：Sacrifice, Reciprocity, and Violence in Traditional China）的解读，认为"正一盟威之道"既可指由张道陵创建的道教派别，也可指记述约定的一种文本，并引用见存于《仙苑编珠》中的正一道道经《正一经》中的记载向译入语读者介绍了道教教祖老子降授"正一盟威法文"的历史背景。这样的注释内容在康儒博的这一译本中比比皆是，属于典型的译研结合的范例。

6. "户"作为计量单位可对应为"household"。"祭酒"本义是在大飨宴时以年老宾客一人举酒祭祀地神，需长者立主位，面南酹酒祭神开席。引申为对同辈或同官中年高望重者的尊称，后用为官名，意为首席，主管。英文单词"libationer"有"以酒祭神之人"之意，但若要表达其作为官职的内涵，需添加表属性的范畴词。从结构上看，"有如官长"应是对"祭酒"这一职位的补充解释，可视为同位语。"条制"的词典意义为"条例制度"，实指张道陵创立五斗米道时为统率教民而建立的核心管理机构"二十四治"，每一"治"皆设"祭酒"以主持教务管理，译者将"条制"译为"administrative sectors"，还原了该词的本意内涵。原文"弟子户至数万。即立祭酒，分领其户，有如官长。并立条制，使诸弟子，随事轮出米、绢、器物、纸、笔、樵薪、什物等"翻译为 His disciples numbered several myriad households. He therefore established [the office of] Libationer, so as to divide and lead their household; a system of offices and supervisors and administrative sectors was established. He arranged for rice, fabric, tools, utensils, paper, brushes, lumber, firewood, and other supplies to be distributed as needed (Campany, 2002: 351)。译者将"官长"（a system of offices and supervisors）和"条制"（administrative sectors）并置，虽和原文表述有一定差异，但却是译者充分领会原文语义基础上的合理调配。补充衔接词"therefore"和"so as to"也使译文语句之间的逻辑更明晰。

7. 汉语疏于显性逻辑，呈流水句型，语义联系比较松散，尤其是古汉语中有许多似断还连的无关联语句。遇到这样的语句时，细读文本最为关键。原文"陵又欲以廉耻治人，不喜施刑罚，乃立条制：使有疾病者，皆疏记生身已来所犯之罪，乃手书投水中，与神明共盟约，不得复犯法，当以身死为约"即为这样的典型句型，需译者进行文本细读，辨清之间的逻辑关联，读者可细品下列译文中衔接词的添加以及主从结构、非谓语结构的变换处理：Zhang Ling wanted to rule the people by means of honesty and shame and avoid using punishments. So, once he had set up administrative sectors, whenever people in any sector became ill, he had them compose an account of all the infractions they had committed since their birth; then, having signed this document, they were to cast it into a body of water, thereby establishing a covenant with the spirits that they would not violate the regulations again, pledging their own deaths as surety (Campany, 2002:

351)。该句中的"条制"虽已是第二次出现,且后面为冒号,不必重复上文的还原式翻译,译出字面含义即可,但译者仍然选择增译法,以向译入语读者忠实传达该道教仪式的庄严意味。

8. 原文"于是百姓计念,邂逅疾病,辄当首过,一则得愈,二使羞惭,不敢重犯,且畏天地而改。从此之后,所违犯者,皆改为善矣"的翻译涉及数词"一"和"二"的具体所指问题。康儒博将其理解为"一桩罪""二桩罪",该部分在译文中被处理为心理活动,译者添加了肌腱式衔接内容 [thinking that],并将"羞惭"创建性解读为因犯下两桩罪行便会带来的"致命"(be mortified)后果,也导致了后面的"重犯"被理解为"重大犯错"(serious infractions)而不是"再次犯错",这样翻译虽有它的逻辑思辨道理,但体现的是译者的思路,有过度解读之嫌。其实该句的意思为:于是百姓们永远都会记得不能犯罪,犯了罪的就要生病,于是就应该交代自己的罪过,这样做一来可以使病痊愈,二来使其感到羞愧以后就不敢再重犯,而且因为慑于天地神灵而改过自新。自从张道陵实行了这个办法后,凡是犯过罪的,都改恶向善了。因此,该句译文可以略作修改,译为 Because of this practice, the common people were extremely mindful. When they happened to become ill, they always reflected on their transgressions, which might help them obtain a recovery, and moreover made them ashamed and guilty. Thus they did not dare to commit infractions again but reformed themselves out of awe for Heaven and Earth; and from this time forward, anyone who did commit infractions reformed himself to become a good person。

9. 原文:其治病事,皆采取玄素,但改易其大较,转其首尾,而大途犹同归也。行气、服食,故用仙法,亦无以易。该句的意思是:张道陵为人治病,都是用房中术,但他把房中术的主要内容更改了,保留了起始和结尾,但是大致意思还是没有变。他所教授的行气、服食等方法,还是按以前仙家的方法施行,也没有什么变化。其中"玄素"指代房中术,惯常的译法有意译为"the sexual arts",抑或直译为"the arts of the bedchamber",康儒博取"玄素"二字的指称意义将这一道教方术泛化翻译为"both esoteric and ordinary sources",若不细究原文,这样的译法也是合乎情理的。依据下文张道陵对诸弟子说的话"尔辈多俗态未除,不能弃世，正可得吾行气、导引、房中之事，或可得服食草木数百岁之方耳"，可知行气、导引、房中、服食乃张道陵修仙的主要道术，译者这样翻译"玄素"，盖是因为对神仙道教中房中术的各种别名了解不够全面的缘故，该段文字或可改译为 As for his methods of curing illness, he mainly adopted the arts of the bedchambers, which were mostly modified and yet the beginning and final parts were not altered. As for his practices of pneumas circulation and dietetic regimen, he relied on [standard] methods of transcendence; here, too, he made no significant changes。

10. 原文：故陵语诸人曰："尔辈多俗态未除，不能弃世，正可得吾行气、导引、房中之事，或可得服食草木数百岁之方耳。"译文：Zhang told most everyone, "You and your ilk have not yet been able to expunge the vulgar elements from your disposition, and so you are unable to leave the world behind. It is therefore appropriate that you obtain my procedures for circulating pneumas and arts of the bedchamber. Perhaps you will prove yourself capable of a special herbal diet, but even that is only a formula for living several hundred years"（Campany, 2002：352），该译文除了漏译"导引"（可直译为"guiding and pulling"）这一道教炼养方术之外，其余部分的翻译无论是选词还是原文逻辑的梳理都值得我们学习效仿，尤其是"尔辈""俗态""除"的对应译文，以及"正可得""或可得"的翻译堪称佳译。

11. 中文的"露宿"意指在野外住宿，译者将"四十余日，露宿不去，乃纳之"翻译为 He did not leave, in daylight or at night, for over forty days. Zhang then let him in，漏译了"露宿"这一信息，应是译者有意为之，只为凸显"四十余天"这一漫长的时间段。这种手法在文学翻译中尤其常见，在不影响读者阅读逻辑的前提下，译者可以选择性省去他认为次要的信息。

12. 黍：一年生草本植物，叶线形，子实淡黄色，去皮后称黄米，比小米稍大，煮熟后有黏性，即今北方所谓的黄米，英语单词为"millet"。原文"使升于草中守黍驱兽"本来指"张道陵让赵升在田间草屋看守庄稼、驱赶野兽"，译者却译为"张道陵指派赵升于牧场看护牲畜"（Zhang had Zhao watch over some livestock out in pasture lands），出于照顾目的语读者的阅读习惯，将农耕文化意象转换为畜牧文化意象，虽完全改变了原文的信息，但因该段主题为塑造赵升不为女色所动的形象，这样的信息调试是完全可行的。

13. 原文"升守田谷，有一人往叩头乞食。衣裳破弊，面目尘垢，身体疮脓，臭秽可憎。升怆然，为之动容，解衣衣之，以私粮设食，又以私米遗之"塑造了济人之急、救人之危的赵升形象。对照原文不难发现，译者亦步亦趋成功向译入语读者推送了一位颇有仁慈侠义心肠的道士形象，其人物形象的塑造成功体现在外貌描写和动作描写的遣词造句中，读者可从译文中细细评味那些精准的词语搭配，附译文：while Zhao was on duty guarding grain from [public] fields there came a man knocking his head on the ground begging for food. His clothes were in tatters, his face was caked with dirt, his body was filthy and he stank terribly. Zhao was moved to sorrow at his condition. He removed his own clothes and clothed the man in them; he set out a meal for the man from his own private provisions; and he sent him off with grain from his personal supply（Campany，2002：353）。

14. 相较于《太平御览》版本，《太平广记》本关于张道陵第七次考验赵升的描述更为细节化，比如为衬托赵升忠诚道师之献身精神，其他弟子胆怯退缩的样子见诸以下文字描述："于时伏而窥之者三百余人，股战流汗，无敢久临，视之者，莫不却退而还，谢不能得。"而《太平御览》该部分的叙述仅为"弟子皆流汗，无敢视者"。康儒博选用更为简略的《太平御览》卷九百六十七的内容翻译了张道陵第七试，读者可参阅下文对照阅读译本内容，附该段原文如下：

陵与诸弟子登云台山，绝岩上有一桃树，大如臂，旁生石壁，下临不测。去上三四丈，桃大有实。陵谓诸弟子曰："得此桃者，当告以道要。"弟子皆流汗，无敢视者。升曰："神人所护，何险之有？"乃从上自掷，正投桃树，取桃满怀，而石壁峻峭不得还，乃掷桃地上，得二百枚。陵分桃赐诸弟子，余二枚，陵自食一，留一以待升。陵乃伸手引升，升忽见返，以向一桃与升。升食桃毕，陵乃临谷上，戏笑而言曰："赵升心自正，能投树上，足不蹉跌，吾今欲自试投下，当应得大桃也。"众人皆谏，唯升与王长嘿然。陵遂投空，不落桃上，失陵所在。四方皆仰，上则连天，下则无底，往无道路，莫不惊叹悲涕。唯升、长二人，良久乃相谓曰："师则父也，自投于不测之崖，吾何以自安！"乃俱投身而下，正堕陵前。见陵坐局脚床斗帐中，见升长二人笑曰："吾知汝来。授汝道要，吾将归治旧舍，三日乃还。"诸弟子惊悲不息。后陵与升、长三人，皆白日冲天而去。众弟子仰视之，久而乃没于云霄也。初，陵入蜀山，合丹半剂，虽未冲举，已成地仙。故欲化作七试，以度赵升，乃知其志也。

对照《太平御览》中上述第七试的内容，除了最后一句被译者省去未译之外，英译本基本忠实传译了原文所有的细节。版本选择是任何典籍翻译中的一个重要环节，常有因版本不同导致译文差异的现象发生。因此对译文的批评解析不可单从文字表面的呈现就判定译文是忠实还是背叛原文，最好能还原译者的翻译过程，基于这样的前提才能较为客观地进行评价。

小　结

海外学者普遍重视文本研究，不少研究成果皆体现了一种更加贴近文本真相的"互文性"研究方法，这是因为基于各种资料的互文解读是保障全面正确理解原作的有效模式。道教典籍常常会有因版本不同导致个别行文出现差异的现象，无论是今译还是英译道教典籍，与文本相关的诸多注、疏内容都不容译者忽略，反复对比和参考与原作有关的各种古文注、疏内容是任何有责任心译者的首要选择。

记录道教神仙生平事迹的传记文本是神仙思想的生动教材，属于特殊类型的传记文学体裁，既有宗教典籍的私密性，又有传记文学的通俗性和艺术性，在多年流传过程中经各家传抄引用的各式变通和修订，必然会出现内容有别的不同版本。在研究翻译葛洪《神仙传》时，美国汉学家康儒博尽可能广泛地搜集了《神仙传》佚文，确定它们在源文献中的位置及源文献产生的时间，然后对比这些引文，选择其中的一种或多种作为翻译底本，并根据源文献所示，指出各传记中每一特定叙事要素的时间先后关系，重新构建一个可靠的较为完整的译文内容，这种基于互文资源的互文解读模式对神仙传记文本的翻译做了有益的尝试,具有很好的借鉴价值。

　　互文性存在于所有文本中,是一切文本的本质特征,将翻译同互文性联系起来进行研究可以拓宽视野,加深对翻译本质的理解(李明,2003:5)。康儒博在该书开场白部分谈论《神仙传》的翻译策略时说自己的翻译尽量采用直译法,努力在译文中保留源文本有时看似很奇特的叙述,目的是想让译本内容不说自明。不过,为了尽可能准确传达原文本意义,译者不惜附上长长的注释,解读其中关联到的重要道教人物、道教术语、道教方术等。此外,还给每一个人物传记添加了长短不一的评论材料,以彰显"《神仙传》文内文外的各种关联"(point out connections both outside and within the text of *Traditions*)(Company,2002:11)。就文本内的互文关联而言,作者借用和转化了《神仙传》流转过程中不同版本的内容。就文本外的互文关联来说,《列仙传》、《抱朴子内篇》以及其他学者前期翻译成果为译者重塑文本意义起到了很大的参照效应。基于这种互文解读模式的《神仙传》翻译研究成了西方汉学界翻译道教典籍的典范。如果我们从微观(译作与原作、译作与译入语等语言层面的互文)和宏观(译作文本与译入语其他各类文本之间的互文)两个角度探讨翻译经典文本与各类相关文本之间的互文性特征(于辉、宋学智,2014:135),康儒博《神仙传》译本所呈现的互文解读模式对当今中国文化外译的借鉴意义亦是显著的。

第六章

道教炼养文本翻译研究

引　语

　　长生不死是道教的中心思想，也是道教徒追求的终极目标。除"积善成仙"说之外，道教还有诸多成仙了道的修炼方术，如服食、导引、行气、辟谷、存神、诵经等，方士们坚信服食仙丹乃升仙之要，因此炼制不死仙丹常被视为最重要的方术，许多道教典籍都有道士炼制仙丹服食仙丹的记述。我们把记述这些炼制仙丹方术的文献归类为道教炼养文本。据胡孚琛和吕锡琛教授在其专著《道学通论》一书中的阐述，秦汉以来，方仙道以五金、八石为药物炼制长生不死仙丹的方术，称作炼丹术。唐代以来，道士们又将以人体的精、气、神为药物炼制仙丹的方术也称炼丹术。于是，这种人体内的炼丹术叫内丹术，原来以矿物药为原料的炼丹术则名为外丹术。在道书中，黄白是金银的隐名。方士们试图将贱金属的铜、铁、铅等点化为贵金属金银，发展出人工制造药金、药银的方术，称作黄白术，也即是炼金术。（胡孚琛、吕锡琛，2004：441）。

　　现存的道教炼养文本有许多是一些制造药金、药银的实验记录，如《正统道藏》中的《黄帝九鼎神丹经诀》《九转流珠神仙九丹经》《太清金液神丹经》《三十六水法》收录了许多丹方，积累了丰富的实验资料。而将炼丹术修炼加以理论化著述的最有影响力的作品当属托名东汉魏伯阳撰写的《周易参同契》（简称《参同契》），享有"万古丹经王"之称，与之齐名的另一内丹方术力作是托名北宋道士张伯端创作的《悟真篇》。

《参同契》借金丹术法象论男女合炁①之术，以日月运行的易学规律为内丹术和外丹术提供了一个普适的理论框架（胡孚琛、吕锡琛，2004：443）。而《悟真篇》则在总结宋代以前内丹的正统法诀的基础上，进一步提出了解读《周易参同契》的方法，抽绎出《周易参同契》的丹道理论内核，将其发挥成圆通无碍的内丹理论体系，使内丹道走向成熟（郭建洲，2005：1）。

就两部经典的文本表征而言，《参同契》和《悟真篇》在创作手法上颇有一致性，代表了该类文献的创作风格，即采用大量的隐喻修辞和使用诗词的文学体裁来记述丹道思想。整部丹经具有典型的诗性特征，既有诗的句式，又有词的韵味，作者为强化修道丹书的隐秘性和神秘性，将四言诗、骚体辞赋等传统典雅的文体与五言诗这种新兴的诗体杂糅在一起，呈现了一种全新的文本形态。此外，作者还采用大量的隐喻类创作手法，导致整个文本的文意艰深晦涩，佶屈聱牙。例如，铅和汞是炼丹者用以炼制金丹的两种常用药物，《参同契》作者冠之以各种隐名，如用金火、金木、白虎、黄芽等隐喻铅，以金水、青龙、苍液、河上姹女等隐喻汞。这种记载炼丹口诀、宣扬仙术的方法在北宋张伯端的《悟真篇》中也有较多的体现。《悟真篇》全书共有 99 首诗词，包含七律、七绝、五律、词多种诗歌文体，密集使用隐语同样是《悟真篇》的典型语言特色，这种传播炼丹之术的创作手法无疑直承《参同契》。据刘湘兰研究，借隐喻来撰写丹经，正是炼丹者们特意选择的创作手法，而诗歌又正是最擅长用意象来表达真实情感或意图的文学体裁。诗歌的审美特质，在于意象的朦胧、跳跃、留白可以让读者依凭自己的生活经历与情感体验产生联想。对于既要严守丹道精义又能传承丹道秘术的炼丹家而言，这种亦虚亦实的阅读体验正符合他们的理想。而隐喻的创作手法又完全满足了他们的实际需求。诗中隐喻的意象增强了炼丹诗文的神秘性，形成了丹书所特有的创作风格（刘湘兰，2017：70）。因此，即便那些对道教颇有研究的中国学者面对这些意象华美、意蕴幽微的炼丹文献时，也

---

① 道经中用"炁"字作先天气的代号，用"气"字作后天气的代号，在丹经中，精化之炁用炁字，吐纳导引之气用气字（王沐，1981：45）。本书遵从这一解读，并尊重原文作者的选择。

会用类似"晦涩难解"这样的字眼描述他们的阅读体验，更不用说那些虽有着浓厚的研究兴趣但只具备有限的古汉语文化知识的海外道教学者了。相较而言，海外涉足道教炼丹文献翻译研究的专家为数不多，汉学家玄英算是其中成果最为显著的一位学者。除领衔编撰《道教百科全书》(*The Encyclopedia of Taoism*)之外，2006年他还出版了第一部研究道教丹道的著作《太清：中国中古早期的道教和炼丹术》(*Great Clarity: Daoism and Alchemy in Early Medieval China*)，其中附有《九转流珠神仙九丹经》、《太清金液神丹经》和《太极真人九转还丹经要诀》三部上清派丹经的英文翻译。该著作已由山东大学历史文化学院韩吉绍教授翻译为中文，于2016年10月出版发行。玄英还翻译了《悟真篇》《参同契》《入药镜》《金丹四百字》《黄帝阴符经》《重阳立教十五论》等多部道教丹道经典，当代道教学者王沐谈及《悟真篇》渊源、丹法要旨和全文校注的学术论文集《悟真篇浅解》(*Foundations of Internal Alchemy*) 也在他的翻译之列。

总体而言，海外学者能将这般佶屈聱牙的道教炼养类文本译成英文，虽值得赞赏，但因这类文本比其他文本更难准确翻译，译本中难免会存在一些翻译质量的问题，不过，他们在处理这一独特的道教文本时所采取的翻译策略和方法值得我们学习研究。本着求真务实的态度，本章选取玄英完成的《参同契》和《悟真篇》英译文本的部分章节进行批评解析，以展现译者的翻译思路，并对其中的一些"问题翻译"正本清源，最大限度还原源文意蕴，借以探讨道教炼养文本的翻译方法和策略。

第一节 《周易参同契》英文翻译研究

《周易参同契》论述炼丹、内养之道，建立了一套完整的丹道理论与实践体系。作者魏伯阳把以前的炼丹、内养方术，与其自身体验结合起来，予以理论概括，将周易阴阳交合之道、黄老自然养性之道、炉火铅汞炼丹之道合而为一，说明人欲长生成仙，必须服食铅汞所炼还丹（外丹），或炼养自身阴阳（内养），方能成道，在肯定外丹术的同时又肯定了内养术（霍克功，2006：26）。这部道教修仙炼丹之作包含许多典故和类比，作者用诗意般的语言和丰富的意象阐释道教丹道学，不光受到教内人士的重视，也引发了包括哲学家、宇宙学家、诗人、书法家、语文学家和藏书家在内的诸多学者的研究兴趣。

注疏《周易参同契》的作品有很多，主要见于各类丛书和专辑，现存四十余种注本有十一种收于《道藏》，八种见于《四库全书》，晦涩难懂是《参同契》留给注疏家和评论家的最典型印象。也正是因为这一丹道经典"词韵皆古，奥雅难通"，学者们对《周易参同契》的解读模式也呈多元化态势，有学者从阴阳补益角度注解，有学者从外丹视角解读，也有学者选择探讨其内丹学的内涵。华裔澳大利亚学者柳存仁（Liu Ts'un Yen，1917—2009年）从这部丹道经典的外在表象和内在实质两个方面分早、中、后三个时期描述和揭示了《参同契》在历史的长河中被认知和接受的过程，即早期为外丹。"即神仙家之所谓炼丹，需要物质的原料运作，丹灶炉鼎各种设备者也。"像现代人所说在化学实验室中研究，其活动并不涉及人身。中期为阴丹。意谓应用补益之说以释《参同契》者，其对象为男女，甚者为采阴补阳，其事在个人之外，有我与彼两方合作完成。后期为内丹。只以个人本身之心、肾相交为活动，无个人外之异体，这异体既包含物质材料，如早期之外丹所用，亦包含人之异性，如中期之阴丹所为（李国来，2015：116）。柳先生对《参同契》在中国古代丹道历史上的发生发展历程的梳理可较好地帮助我们理解这部金丹之祖的丰富内涵。

当代国内学者解读这部丹经的思路基本一致。一是都会确定一个底本，同时参校其他版本，借鉴前人或同道的研究成果。二是因为原文语义晦涩难懂，多用比喻，一些经文很难直译，故只能退而求其次，以意译代之，即便采用直译，也必定提供相应的注解进行阐释。三是因历史上既有以"内丹"注解《参同契》者，又有以"外丹"注解者，故都会分别从内、外丹不同角度解释经文。海外学者译介研究该书的路径虽有差异，但主体与国内学者相似。

一 《周易参同契》在海外的传播

该书在海外的译介并不是很多，现有译本主要以英语译本为主，除此之外还有为数不多的俄语和日语译本，单从研究视角来看，科技史研究专家们的关注较多，也有少数从医学养生角度或宗教哲学层面进行译介的学者。主要有：

（1）美国化学家戴维斯（Tenney L. Davis）与中国学者吴鲁强教授（1904—1936年）合作，依据元代俞琰注本《周易参同契发挥》翻译研究了《周易参同契》，标题为《〈参同契〉——中国古代炼金术专著》（An Ancient Chinese Treatise on Alchemy Entitled Ts'an T'ung Ch'i），最初发表在国际科学史权威刊物《爱雪斯》（Isis）1932年第18期上，通过这种模式向西方介绍中国古代炼丹史，极大地发挥了联系东西方科学与文化的桥梁作用。该英译本后来被中国大中华文库系列丛书收录，于2012年在长沙岳麓书社出版发行。

（2）湘潭师范学院中国科技史研究室原主任周士一先生（1930—2008年）完成的《周易参同契》英译本（The Kinship of the Three），英国皇家学会会员、近代生物化学家和科学技术史专家李约瑟（Joseph Needham，1900—1995年）为其作序，该书用现代科学的术语、概念、符号探究古代科技史，1988年由湖南教育出版社出版。

（3）英国学者理查德·博钦格（Richard Bertschinger）从医学养生角度译介的这部道教典籍，书名为《长生之奥秘——第一部古代中国神仙文本的翻译》（The Secret of Everlasting Life: The First Translation of the Ancient Chinese Text of Immortality）。该书于1994年由英国多塞特郡元素出版社（Element Books Ltd.）出版发行。

（4）意大利汉学家玄英以元代全真道士陈致虚《周易参同契注解》为底本的同名译作《参同契》（The Seal of the Unity of the Three），于2011年由金丹出版社（Golden Elixir Press）出版。该译本由九部分组成，除第三部分为翻译文本之外，其余皆为必要补充材料，包括序言、引言、注释、附录、词汇表、参考文献等，这些阐释性文本作为译文的补充，为译文读者提供了丰厚的背景知识，有效地帮助读者理解和鉴赏道教丹道文化。

上述译本皆为全译。此外，有关《周易参同契》的翻译还散见于一些海外学者的研究成果中，如上文提到的李约瑟博士，他在《中国科学技术史》多卷本中综述了中国古代的科学技术对世界文明发展所起的巨大作用，其中第二卷（1956）、第四卷第2分册（1965）、第五卷第3分册（1976）、第五卷第4分册（1980）集中讨论了道教思想和道教炼丹术，包括外丹术和内丹术，自然少不了对《周易参同契》的引用和翻译。美国宾夕法尼亚大学科学史与科学社会学系教授席文（Nathan Sivin）1968 年研究道教内丹的著述《中国炼丹术初探》（*Chinese Alchemy：Preliminary Studies*）以及 1976 年发表在《爱雪斯》（*Isis*）上的论文《中国炼丹术对火候的把握》（"Chinese Alchemy and the Manipulation of the Time"）均包含了《周易参同契》的节译内容。华裔美国学者翻译家王艺文在其《从道教神仙系统谈道教教义》（*Teaching of the Tao：Reading from the Taoist Spiritual Tradition*）一书中论及道教炼神、修身、炼丹、长生术时也节译了《周易参同契》中的内容。因该典籍蕴含丰富的哲学思想，融老子哲学本体论、《周易》变易观以及道家的精气说为一体，哲学史家、朱子学专家、华裔美国学者陈荣捷（Chan Wing-Tsit，1901—1994 年），华裔澳大利亚学者、汉学家和道教专家柳存仁，在考证中国哲学史和道家思想的研究中也不乏许多源自《周易参同契》的理解和翻译。

二 玄英《周易参同契》译本特色

古今有许多学者都对《周易参同契》作过注解和整理，主要注本有后蜀彭晓《周易参同契分章通真义》3 卷，宋朱熹《周易参同契考异》1 卷，陈显微《周易参同契解》3 卷，以及俞琰《周易参同契发挥》9 卷等。各家注本分章结构不尽相同，譬如，后蜀彭晓《周易参同契分章通真义》3 卷本分 90 章，而元代陈致虚《周易参同契注解》分 35 章。玄英在序言部分交代了他对这些注本的使用情况，译者虽以元代全真道士陈致虚《周易参同契注解》为底本，但也参阅了其他版本内容，同时还借鉴前期其他学者有关《参同契》的翻译研究成果。需要指出的是，尽管他依据陈致虚注本，但并未遵循该注本的分章结构，而是按诗句字数、韵律、主题变化分 88 章进行翻译，并将中文分章内容附在译本后面，供读者参考。此外，为方便读者查阅，译者给每章都增添了点明主题的标题，一旦出现相同的主题，标题就保持不变，比如炼丹（Compounding the Elixir）和还丹（Inverting the Course）这样的主题就多次出现在译本中，这些标题是陈致虚注解本中没有的，其他《参同契》校订本也不包含这样的标题。译者又依据韵律变化将每章划分为若干诗节，通常以四行诗节为主（当然《参同契》并不完全都是四行诗节）。该译本没有采用松散的散文体，而是以诗词的形式逐句译成独立诗句，这样做虽然谈不上严格遵循诗歌翻译的要求，但也基本遵循了原文诗歌体裁的形式特征，一定程度上传译了原文的外在形式内容。译者提供的注释也分为以章节为单位的主题注释和以词句为单位的文本差异注释。尽管译者参考了包括《古本参同契》在内的多种注释版本，各章节的注释内容并不局限于这些资料来源，译者还参阅了一些当代学者的注解，比如，日本学者铃木由次郎（Suzuki Yoshijiro）译注的《周易参同契》（*Shūeki sandōkei*，明德出版社1977年版），方旭编著的《周易参同契讲解》（载《中国气功四大经典讲解》，浙江古籍出版社1988年版），以及乌恩浦撰写的《周易参同契》（载《气功经典译注》，吉林文史出版社1992年版）。尽管后期注疏家和学者们的阐释视角各有偏重，或为内丹，或为外丹，或为宇宙论，再或是其他话题，但玄英尽可能将不同的视角关联在一起，并按传统意义的三大主题——黄老道学（英文通常解读为Taoism）、《周易》大旨（英文通常解读为cosmology）、神仙炉火（英文通常解读为alchemy）对原文本进行细读、翻译和注释。

玄英的这部同名著作融翻译与研究于一体，作者撰写了长长的引言，对《参同契》原书的标题、作者、著述年代、文本形态、主要注疏等一一作了探讨，还围绕人、宇宙与道，无为之道，《参同契》中的炼金术，从外丹到内丹这些主题展开研究。这些背景知识能较好帮助读者深入理解《参同契》的文本内涵。此外，为了不影响读者阅读的流畅性，译者将其翻译的文本和注释部分完全切分。翻译文本按主题分上、中、下三部分，囿于原文语体特点，也为了尽量保留作者原有的意象，译文基本采用直译的策略；注解部分既有主题的阐释，也有语言层面的术语解读和句子解释。此外，译者还专门提供了与陈致虚版本不同的其他注疏内容的辨析，以"文本注释"（textual notes）方式对照了陈致虚注本与彭晓、朱熹、俞琰等学者的《参同契》注疏本在某些具体文字理解上的不同。这种注解与翻译文本一起共同构成一个相对闭合的文本意义系统。尽管译者也清楚《参同契》的解读模式多元，除了在该书引言中以"从外丹到内丹"为题粗略介绍了《参同契》的不同解读模式，囿于外丹视角和内丹视角的含义相去甚远，译者在实际的翻译中也只能择其一端进行解读，因此，无论是主题的阐释或语言层面的术语、句子解释，主要还是外丹学意义上的解读，只是极个别的地方补充了内丹学的不同释义。作为一名海外学者，能将如此艰涩难懂的丹经译为英语已实属不易，我们无权求全责备，反而应该高度赞赏海外学者的这一伟大尝试，积极探讨他们解读道教丹道作品之方法和策略，择其有效之法为我所用。

后文节选玄英《周易参同契》英译本中《太阳流珠章》和《关关雎鸠章》两章内容作为范例，分析其文本特点和相应的英译策略，其中文体风格的传译和隐喻修辞的处理将是该部分英译文解析的重点。

三　玄英《周易参同契·太阳流珠章》译文解析

《太阳流珠章》源自《参同契》中卷，全文采用四言句型，四字一顿，节奏鲜明，共计 26 句，描述丹药交结成丹的过程与原理。作者使用了大量的隐语，整个叙述语义模糊，难以理解，结尾句"可以口诀，难以书传"即指炼丹之道需名师指点，可口传心授，却很难诉诸笔端将其细节披露无遗，充分说明炼丹过程繁复难解，绝非简单的语言文字就可以将其阐明疏通的。有鉴于此，古今中外的注译者们都不得不借助包括题解、注释在内的各种手段，力求最大限度地传译出原文的主要旨意。北京师范大学的章伟文教授 2014 年以《道藏》所收彭晓《周易参同契分章通真义》经文为底本，并参校其他版本，在借鉴很多前辈、同道等所取得之注《参同契》成果的基础上译注了《周易参同契》，该译注每章内容包含题解、原文、注释、译文四个部分。汉学家玄英的英译模式与章教授的译经解经模式大有类同之处，唯一不同的是玄英的翻译主要基于外丹视角，而章教授的许多经文皆分别从内丹、外丹不同之角度作出解释。

中文古籍的整理者或译注者有根据首句内容而定名的习惯，如本章标题"太阳流珠章"即取首句"太阳流珠"来命名，方便读者查阅。英译者则倾向于依据主题内容来命名，玄英在基本遵从原文诗性特征的基础之上，依主题将该章分译为两个部分。第一部分标题为"金丹合成"（Compounding the Elixir），即"太阳流珠章"前 18 句内容，译者处理为 3 个诗节，另一部分以"三五"（The Three Fives）为题，英译的是该章后 8 句内容，由 2 个诗节完成。为方便读者对照了解中西译者阐释《参同契》的思维模式的异同，该部分依原文、原文注释、英译文和译文解析的顺序分别列出各部分内容。

[原文]

太阳流珠，常欲去人；卒得金华，转而相因；化为白液，凝而至坚。[1] 金华先唱，有顷之间；解化为水，马齿阑干。[2] 阳乃往和，情性自然；迫促时阴，拘畜禁门。[3] 慈母育养，孝子报恩；严父施令，教敕子孙。[4] 五行错王，相据以生；火性销金，金伐木荣。[5] 三五与一，天地至精；可以口诀，难以书传。[6]

[注释]①

1. 太阳流珠：外丹药物"汞"之别名，因其闪烁有光亮，游走不定，故称"太阳流珠"；内丹则借"太阳流珠"喻人之心、神。常欲去人：意思指汞在烧合之时，只有铅金才能制伏留存它；也指内丹意义上的"人之意识常为外物所牵引"这一现象。金华：或作"金花"，指铅金之液与流汞相合后化为白液，再复凝成坚冰之状；内丹意义上的"金华"喻先天元阳祖炁，由坎水之肾精升华而成。相因：相依之意。凝而至坚：他本或作"凝而正坚"。

2. 马齿：这里以白而坚的"马齿"比喻丹之坚、白，一说"马齿"乃借野菜中的马齿苋为喻，形容丹之状呈花瓣样排列。阑干，或言其为"琅玕"，《尚书·禹贡》有"球琳琅玕"，即宝珠；或谓其为"斓玕"，形容丹之温润。

3. 阳：即"太阳流珠"。和：指与铅液相合。"阳乃往和，情性自然"既可指汞与铅因其化学属性的缘故而自然相合，也可指人的神、炁出于自然而一唱一和。迫：逼迫。促：促动。时：时候。阴：火候中的"阴符"。拘：拘执，指火候中"采药"。畜：他本或作"蓄"，蓄聚，指火候中的"封藏"。禁门：古代的皇宫称禁中，"禁门"喻丹田、中宫之黄庭。"迫促时阴，拘畜禁门"可指外丹意义上的操作火候，指汞包裹铅液于其中，逼迫之、促动之，及时拘存、蓄止于封闭的鼎器之内，也可指人身体中的后天阴邪之气未化，修炼之士需祛除这些时不时冒出的阴邪之气，此为"迫促时阴"；护持正念，须臾不离于大道，故说"拘畜禁门"。

---

① 注释主要参阅章伟文《〈周易参同契〉译注》（中华书局2014年版）第268—275页内容，文字略有改动。

4. 慈母：比喻铅金。慈母育养：喻指铅金可以熔化为液体，也就是"金生水"，这是外丹视角的解释；从内丹意义上讲，慈母育养意指真炁孕于下丹田之坤腹，犹如母之胞育。孝子：喻指铅液与汞相配而化成的白液。孝子报恩则指这样化成的液体，后又凝成至坚之"金华"，水反为金，故说"孝子报恩"。在内丹家看来，一阳初动，真炁擒制真汞，以制伏神识所生的各种杂念；并行周天火候，经督脉飞上头顶昆仑，又复回于丹田坤母之舍，与真汞交结而成丹，此即"孝子报恩"。严父施令，教敕子孙：铅金出于土，即所谓的"土生金"；铅金又可以熔化为水，也即"金生水"。故土是铅金之父，水则是土之孙；炼丹鼎炉亦皆以土涂于内壁，使铅金、流汞不逃逸，炼丹之成实有赖于土之功，故说"严父施令，教敕子孙"。"严父"喻神识之主，即人的真性；神识纷呈，然皆源出于人之真性，故以子孙继踵喻之；思虑杂乱而不精专，则是子孙不孝，此时严父当敕令之归于正，也即从杂乱的思虑中回归到清净之真性。

5. 王，旺之意。据，凭借之意。销，熔之意。"五行错王，相据以生"意指木、火、土、金、水五行相错而旺，如木旺则克土，土旺则克水，以此类推。同时，五行又依次相生，比如金能生水，水能生木，等等。内丹家用"木"喻真性，用"火"喻神识，"五行错王，相据以生"可以喻指内丹炼精化炁，由纷乱之神识中复归清净之真性，要求火反生木，由火旺逆回到木旺，此乃"五行错王"；但真性化神识，真性与神识，也即木与火，又是"依次相生、实为伴侣"的关系，因而有"相据以生"之说。"火性销金，金伐木荣"可以解读为：以炎火炼铅金，火旺则能销熔金；铅金化为液水，以铅液之水方能制伏有丹砂、木精之喻的流汞。这是外丹意义上的解读。从内丹意义上讲，若要炼精以化炁，当以神火以烹之，方能成功，此为"火性销金"；神识杂乱，当以精、炁以制伏之，方能呈现出莹洁之真性，此为"金伐木荣"。

6. 三五与一：外丹以水喻铅液，其数为一，以火喻流汞，其数为二。炼丹之炉灶由土垒成，一些炼丹之鼎，其内壁亦涂有土，土之生数为五。铅、汞乃炼丹最主要、最常用的药物，合铅与汞，其数为三；鼎、炉皆与土相关，土数为五，此即"三五"。"一"指铅、汞投入鼎炉中，所熔化而成之液，此鼎中之液其数亦为一，故说"三五与一"。也有将"三五"解读为"三性""二味"。三性，指炉火、铅金、木汞；或谓铅水、汞火与鼎炉之土，称为"三性"；铅、汞入鼎炉中锻造，称"三性会合"。二味，指铅、汞，或者龙、虎。此"三性""二味"即所谓"三五"，"一"指金丹，此为天地至精。自内丹言之，坎水之精、炁，其生数为一；离火之神，其生数为二，合坎、离即水、火而成三，谓取坎填离，也就是神与炁、精相抱；戊己之脾土喻真意，其数为五，"三五与一"，指坎水之精、炁与离火之神，在脾土真意的调节下，混融化为真一之炁。或谓"三"，指心、肺、肝之炁，"五"指脾之炁，"一"指肾之炁，欲成金丹，须凭借此五炁，所谓"五炁朝元"。

[译文]

Compounding the Elixir[1]

The Flowing Pearl of Great Yang
desires ever to leave you.
When, at last, it finds the Golden Flower,
it turns about, and the two rely upon each other.
They transform into a white liquid,
coagulate and are perfectly solid.[2]

The Golden Flower is the first to sing:
in the space of an instant
it dissolves into water—
horse-tooth and *langgan*.
The Yang is next to join it:
qualities and natures are so of themselves.[3]

Approach it forthwith,
seize it and store it within the Forbidden Gates.
The loving mother will nurture and nourish it,
and the filial child will reward her with love;
the stern father will issue orders,
to teach and admonish his children and grandsons.[4]

The Three Fives[5]

The five agents rule in alternate order,
each overtaking the other in order to live.
Fire by its nature melts Metal;
when Metal cuts it, Wood blooms.

The Three Fives combine into One,
the ultimate essence of Heaven and Earth.
Oral instructions are possible;
hardly can this be transmitted in writing.[6] （Pregadio, 2011: 104 – 105）

[解析]

1. 译者冠以"金丹合成"（*Compounding the Elixir*）之题，提示该部分内容是炼养金丹的过程和原理，符合英语文化以主题为纲的行文习惯。

2. 译文基本为直译，如"太阳流珠"翻译为"the Flowing Pearl of Great Yang"，"金华"取其别名"金花"直译为"the Golden Flower"。不过，译者借鉴了中国学者译注《参同契》的通常做法，在该节译文之前提供了相应的题解内容。大致内容如下。

该部分主题与炼丹术有关，阐释炼丹中的主要特征，这一点在《参同契》第 39—40 章①已有论述，描述"真阴"（"流珠"，即"易挥发的汞"）与"真阳"（"金华"，即"坚固的铅"）的结合。汞受热易挥发说明了"真阴"本性是"常欲离人而去"。"流珠"即"真阴、真汞"，即丹砂（汞），代表五行之"火"离卦（☲）中间的阴线（离卦二阳在外，一阴在内），象征"太阳"，因此得名"太阳流珠"。"金华"即"真阳、真铅"，即黑铅，是五行之"水"坎卦（☵）中间的阳线，象征"太阴"，一旦遇热化为白色液体（五行中

---

① 这是译者的划分法，对应中国学者的划分法应为《以金为堤防章第三十七》和《捣治并合之章第三十八》两章，在译者看来，这两章都是关于道教炼丹的内容，因此标题同样为"金丹合成"（"Compounding the Elixir"）。

与真铅对应的"金"为白色)。铅金之液与流汞相合便不再逃逸,两物合其质地与性情,凝结成一种干燥的混合物(或称"汞合金")。将此物捣碎置于炉鼎烧炼,开始时只需用如"慈母"一般的温和之火,之后则需如"严父"一般的旺盛之火,至此,"流珠"与"金华"即可合成金丹。①

通过这一题解,读者可以了解"太阳流珠"和"金华"在外丹修炼中的实指,以及"金液还丹"的炼养过程,对其中的丹道原理也略有知晓。这样的题解是对原文直译内容的补充,也仅是从外丹学意义上解读了这几句诗文的意思。所谓"太阳流珠"即指汞,因汞为液体金属,且化学性质不稳定,故言其"常欲去人"。"金华"指铅,将铅、汞进行烧炼,汞即可化为白液,冷凝成稳定性很强的固体。若从内丹修炼角度来看,所谓"真汞"又非原初物质意义上的砂汞,而是特指人体内的"元神",将人体内之元神比喻成化学性质不稳定、挥发性高的汞。"真铅"特指"元精",即"天地之母气"(王沐,1990:43)。人的元神常想离开人体,如果元神突然得到了生命中的元精能量,于是,元神元精就会互依互存,神气交融,化为金液,神气愈凝愈坚,聚而不散。神气相融之后,第一个明显变化是口腔内分泌神气所化"玉液""金液",五行中金与玉都属金,金为白色(五行之色),故言"白液"。神气既凝之后,

---

① 原文:The remainder of Book 2 (sections 62 – 74) is concerned with alchemy. The present section reiterates the main features of the alchemical process already illustrated in sections 39 – 40. It describes the conjunction of True Yin and True Yang, the Flowing Pearl and the Golden Flower, volatile mercury and firm lead. The volatilization of Mercury when it is heated illustrates the principle that True Yin, by its own nature, tends to leave and become dispersed. The Flowing Pearl is True Yin and True Mercury, it is the central Yin line within Li ☲, the trigram associated with cinnabar and the agent Fire, which in turn are emblems of Great Yang (*taiyang*); hence the name Flowing Pearl of Great Yang. The Golden Flower is True Yang and True Lead; it is the central Yang line within Kan ☵, the trigram associated with black lead and the agent Water, which are emblems of Great Yin (*taiyin*). When the Golden Flower is heated, it liquefies and takes on a white color (white is the color of Metal, the agent corresponding to True Lead). Then it joins with the Flowing Pearl, which as a consequence will not escape and vanish. The two ingredients coagulate into a dry amalgam, merging their natures and their qualities. The amalgam is pounded and is placed in the tripod. Controlled and nurtured by fire, which at first should be as mild as a "loving mother" and then as vigorous as a "stern father," the Pearl and the Flower transmute themselves into the Golden Elixir. (Pregadio, 2011:199 – 200)

第二个效应便是骨节坚强（陈全林，2004：100—101）。

　　针对原文独特的外部语言特征和内涵实质，译者选择直译法。这里译者提供的题解内容和国内学者的解读基本一致，对原文主题做出了浅显的正解，对其中的专业术语进行阐释，共同构成一个既能保留原文风格又能传译原文内涵的译文体系。如遇到需要做特别说明的句子，译者会单独列出注释内容加以凸显，如，原文的第5—6句"化为白液，凝而至坚"描述了炼丹的两个步骤，一为"化"（solve），二为"凝"（coagulate），译者按字面译为 They transform into a white liquid, coagulate and are perfectly solid，并在注释中专门说明这句话与第三十九章（即《以金为堤防章第三十七》）中的"先液而后凝，号曰黄舆焉"同出一辙。这种提示为译入语读者提供了另一阅读选择，加深对原文意蕴的理解。

　　3. 译者通过注解对诗文中"马齿""琅玕"的意象做了简明而精要的解读，谓"马齿"喻金丹之坚、白，谓"琅玕"是位于世界中心昆仑山中的神秘宝石①，这样的解读简单易懂，其依据应该是源自中国学者的相关注解，如前面引用的章伟文译注中也有几乎同样的解读，章伟文注解"马齿琅玕"的内容为：无质生质，凝结成丹，犹如马齿、阑干之状，故说"马齿阑干"（章伟文，2014：271）。

　　4. "禁门"直译为"Forbidden Gates"，但注释补全了其实质含义，即："禁门"本为"皇宫"之义，从外丹视角可解读为炼丹之"炉鼎"，而其内丹学意义则为人体之下丹田②。这一内容与章伟文的译注完全对应，章伟文对"禁门"的解释为：禁门，古代的皇宫称禁中，"禁门"喻丹田、中宫之黄庭（章伟文，2014：272）。同理，译者将原文中的"慈母""孝子""严父""子孙"直译为"the loving mother"、"the filial child"、"the stern father"、"his children and grandsons"，但这些称谓名词绝非其字面意义所指代的内容，而是具有外丹或内丹的意蕴。译者在该节的主题注解中已有交代，虽说相较于章伟文提供的汉语注释（详见中

---

① 原文：Horse-tooth is a metaphor of its strength and whiteness. Langgan is a mythical gemstone, said to be found on Mount Kunlun at the center of the world. （Pregadio, 2011：200）

② 原文："Forbidden gates"（*jinmen*）is a common name for the king's or the emperor's palace. In a Waidan reading, this term refers to the tripod; in a Neidan reading, the lower Cinnabar Field. （Pregadio, 2011：200）

文注释4），译者这样的注解略显简单，但对于一个汉学家而言，能基本厘清这些喻体的真实指代内容以及他们之间的关系已实属不易。

5. "五行错王，相据以生；火性销金，金伐木荣。三五与一，天地至精；可以口诀，难以书传"这八句其实也是在讲述丹药合成之事，只不过是用五行相生相克的原理来描述炼丹过程，译者另起一章独立译出，冠之以标题"三五"（The Three Fives），并在注释部分详细解读该主题，读者需借助这一题解内容才能领会这八句诗文的含义。

为解读何为"三五"，何为"一"，译者首先叙述了最为常见的五行顺生的原理，如水生木、木生火、火生土、土生金、金生水。再解读炼丹过程沿用的两个原理，一为相克原理，即土克水、木克土、金克木、火克金、水克火；二为五行逆生原理，特别是其中的火生木和水生金两条。译者回溯上一章提到的"金华"（五行之"金"）、"流珠"（五行之"木"）遇火而合是五行相克的作用，但炼丹过程中"相克"并不仅仅消熔金华与流珠，更是将其转化成金丹。"金华"受热液化（火性销金，因其属性使然），这样才能与流珠相合。同理，一旦"流珠"为"金华"所制伏，流珠不但不消失反而会更繁荣，此所谓"金伐木荣"，此时"金华"与"流珠"才能最终合成丹药①。其主旨和章伟文译注（详见中文

---

① 原文：In addition to the alchemical emblems, the compounding of the Elixir can also be described by means of the five agents. The most common arrangement of the agents is the generation sequence (*xiangsheng*), in which Water generates Wood, Wood generates Fire, Fire generates Soil, Soil generates Metal, and Metal generates Water. Instead of this sequence, the alchemical process utilizes two others. The first is the conquest sequence (*xiangke*), in which Water is conquered by Soil, Soil is conquered by Wood, Wood is conquered by Metal, Metal is conquered by Fire, and Fire Is conquered by Water. The second consists of the reversal of the generation sequence, in which, in particular, Fire generates Wood, and Water generates Metal. The two quatrains of this section are respectively devoted to these two sequences. The frst quatrain mentions Metal, Wood, and Fire (the agents that correspond to the subjects of section 62): the Golden Flower is Metal, the Flowing Pearl is Wood, and fire makes their conjunction possible. The conquest sequence is at work here; yet in the alchemical process, the "conquest" does not merely cause the extinction of the individual ingredients, but also their transmutation into the Elixir. When the Golden Flower (Metal) is heated in the tripod, it undergoes liquefaction ("Fire by its nature melts Metal"); only because it has been subjugated by fire can it join the Flowing Pearl. Similarly, when the Flowing Pearl (Wood) is controlled by the Golden Flower, it fourishes instead of vanishing ("when Metal cuts it, Wood blooms"); only then can the Golden Flower and the Flowing Pearl merge in the Elixir. (Pregadio, 2011: 201)

注释5、6）的内容大体一致。

6. 西方学界对"金、木、水、火、土"五行的英译基本达成一致，常见的对应译法：Metal，Wood，Water，Fire，Soil，也基本认同用"generate"对应"生"，用"conquer"对应"克"来描述五行的相生相克原理。

　　这几句诗文中还涉及数词"三五"和"一"的所指问题。玄英在其注释中用五行逆生原理解释这里的数字概念，向译入语读者补充了炼丹过程中五行逆生原理，即：水生金，而非金生水；火生木，而非木生火。换句话说，阴生真阳，阳生真阴。这种排列形态体现在"三五与一"中，暗指五行各自代表的数值。木为三，火为二，火生木组成第一个五；水为一，金为四，水生金构成第二个五；而位于中心地位的土数为五，即为第三个五，代表五行的统一性和多重性之下的统一性。炼金术首先将阴阳恢复到以木和金为代表的真实状态，然后将二者结合为一体。正如最后的四行"三五与一，天地至精；可以口诀，难以书传"所指出的那样，这就是炼金术的秘密①。

　　和上文"慈母""严父"等词语的翻译一样，如果仅把"三五与一"直译为"The Three Fives combine into One"完全无法传达原文关涉丹道合成的真实内涵，翻译这样的语句时，添加注释是必不可少的。

四　玄英《周易参同契·关关雎鸠章》译文解析

　　《关关雎鸠章》取自《参同契》中卷最后一章，该章主要阐释阴阳相资相配这一重要的丹道原理。该段开篇即引用《诗经·关雎》中的首句，

---

① 原文：The other sequence active in the alchemical process is based on the inversion of the generation sequence. Water, instead of being generated by Metal, generates Metal; and Fire, instead of being generated by Wood, generates Wood. In other words, Yin generates True Yang, and Yang generates True Yin. This configuration is expressed in the sentence "The Three Fives combine into One," which alludes to the numeric values of the agents. The pair made of Wood (3) and Fire (2) forms the first 5; the pair made of Water (1) and Metal (4) forms the second 5; and the central Soil, of its own, is the third 5, representing the Oneness of the five agents and the Unity underlying multiplicity. The alchemical process first restores Yin and Yang to their authentic state, represented by Wood and Metal, then joins the Two into the One. As the last quatrain points out, this is the secret of the alchemical work. （Pregadio，2011：201 - 202）

将铅金、流汞阴阳和合于鼎器之中与雎鸠相求于水边、沙洲相比拟,同时也是阐明精、炁与神和合于丹田,即如阴阳、雌雄两情相契。该段主体为四言句式,但也杂糅了一些五言、六言文体。

[原文]

关关雎鸠,在河之洲;窈窕淑女,君子好逑。¹雄不独处,雌不孤居;玄武龟蛇,蟠虬相扶;以明牝牡,竟当相须。²假使二女共室,颜色甚姝,令苏秦通言,张仪结媒,发辩利舌,奋舒美辞,推心调谐,合为夫妻,弊发腐齿,终不相知。³若药物非种,名类不同;分刻参差,失其纪纲,虽黄帝临炉,太一执火,八公捣炼,淮南调合,⁴立字崇坛,玉为阶陛,麟脯凤腊,把藉长跪,⁵祷祝神祇,请哀诸鬼,沐浴斋戒,冀有所望,亦犹和胶补釜,以硇涂疮,去冷加冰,除热用汤,飞龟舞蛇,愈见乖张。⁶

[注释]①

1. 关关:雌鸟与雄鸟相求的和鸣之声。雎鸠:一种水鸟,在每年求偶的季节里,雄鸟与雌鸟如约聚首,双双出没于水边、沙洲嬉戏、觅食,并不时发出"关关"的和鸣之声,相传这种鸟类雌、雄情意专一。洲:水中的陆地。窈窕:美好的样子。淑女:贤淑的女孩。好逑:好的配偶。

2. 玄武:四象之一,其形为龟、蛇相合,盘虬相依。蟠虬:回旋、缠绕之意;"虬"即蛙、蟾蜍等两栖类动物的幼体,因其生活在水中,用尾巴游走,且常作旋绕运转,故"蟠虬"合而言之,喻指盘绕交错、相互交织之意。牝牡:"牝"即雌,"牡"即雄。外丹以此喻铅金、流汞阴阳相需。自内丹言之,"玄武""龟蛇""蟠虬""牝牡""雌雄",喻指身中精、炁与神阴阳之相需、相和合。

3. 苏秦、张仪:战国时期著名的纵横家,相传为鬼谷子的徒弟,以能言善辩著称。苏秦主张"合纵"以抗秦,张仪首创连横的外交策略代表秦国出使游说各诸侯国,以"横"破"纵",使各国纷纷由合纵抗秦转变为连横亲秦。

4. 黄帝:古华夏部落联盟首领,中国远古时代华夏民族的共主。据说他是少典与附宝之子,本姓公孙,后改姬姓,故称"姬轩辕";居轩辕

---

① 注释参阅了章伟文《〈周易参同契〉译注》(中华书局 2014 年版)第 319—323 页的内容,文字略有调整。

之丘，号"轩辕氏"，建都于有熊，亦称"有熊氏"。黄帝为五帝之首，被尊为中华"人文初祖"。太一：商朝开国君主成汤的祭名，也作"天乙""太乙""高祖乙"；道教中有太乙救苦天尊，乃道教尊神，居"东方长乐世界"，相传能救人度鬼，闻声救苦；或谓"太乙"即"东皇太乙"或"东皇太一"，乃先秦时楚国神话中的最高神祇。八公：淮南王刘安礼遇的八位隐士。

5. 陛：台阶。把藸：拿着祭神的礼品。长跪：古代的一种表示非常敬重的跪礼。

6. 祝：祈祷。硇（náo）：天然产的氯化铵，与炼外丹所用的硝石之类的药物性质相近，大热有毒，可入药，以其能透五金，俗称"透骨将军"。以硇涂疮，乃误用其性，不仅不能愈合创口，反而使伤口更加扩张，适助其虐。乖张："乖"即违反、背离；"乖张"，怪僻、不通情理、不顺常理的意思。

[译文]

Using ingredients of unlike kind[1]

"*Guan guan* go the ospreys,
on the islet in the river.
The modest, retiring, virtuous, young lady:
for our prince a good mate she."[2]

Cocks do not live in solitude,
nor do hens dwell on their own;
the Dark Warrior's turtle and snake
coil around and assist one another.
This shows that for female and male
each should thoroughly attend to the other.[3]

Suppose that a house is shared by two women,
of enchanting beauty and charm;
and that Su Qin, the mediator,
and Zhang Yi, the interceder,

debate with sharp tongues,
and with beautiful words propose
that they arrive at an earnest accord,
joining as husband and wife:
their hair will fall, their teeth will rot,
but not once shall they know one another.[4]

With ingredients of unlike kinds,
with names and types unmatched
and mistaken doses and measures,
your guiding thread is lost.[5]

Then even if the Yellow Emperor tends to the furnace,
 the Great One looks after the fire,
 the Eight Sirs pound and refine,
 and Master Huainan adjusts the compound;[6]

even if you set up space for a sumptuous altar,
 with steps made of jade
 and with dried meat of unicorn and phoenix fat,
 and you pay obeisance holding the records;[7]

even if you pray invoking all spirits and gods,
 beg every demon with wails,
 and you bathe, fast, and keep to the precepts,
 hoping that what you long for would finally come—

all this would be like spreading glue to repair a pot,
daubing a wound with sal ammoniac,
using cold ice to cure a chill
or hot water to heal a fever.
Even seeing a flying turtle or a dancing snake
would be easier than this![8] (Pregadio, 2011: 112–113)

[解析]

1. 本章从阴阳互配相须相依之角度论述丹道之理。从外丹炼养来看，丹药须得阴阳性情相配方能炼成金丹。而从内丹炼养来讲，阴必资阳，神与炁、精上下相交、雌雄相媾，则有生生不穷之理，孤阴、寡阳不能成丹（章伟文，2014：319）。译者给本章添加的标题为"关于异类要素的使用"（Using Ingredients of Unlike Kind），在具体论述每一诗节的翻译之前译者也提供了类似于中国学者章伟文所作的题解说明，以减轻译入语读者的阅读负担。其题解内容如下。

　　该章开篇引用《诗经·关雎》，以此隐喻阴阳互根的宇宙生成原理。玄武龟蛇把阴阳结合描绘为生命起源，玄武象征水，在五行"宇宙进化"序列中排列第一。阴与阳结合重申了"乾坤合宇宙生"这一观点。天若不赋予大地以精华，就不可能实现其天造万物的潜能，大地若不是受到天的孕育，就不可能给大地带来生机一片。这是《参同契》所阐述的阴阳和合原则模式。因此，无论是物质的、非物质的，还是象征意义的炼丹原料都能借助五行之"土"这一核心媒介确保乾坤结合。如果这些炼丹原料不能相契相合，那么任何礼仪、祈祷、抑或神仙都无济于事。①

2. 《关雎》为《诗经》的第一篇，通常被认为是一首描写自然景物和禽鸟的鸣叫求偶活动来喻指男女恋爱的情歌。《诗经》有多个英译本，

---

① 原文：Beyond its prevalent interpretation in terms of morals, the poem quoted from the *Book of Odes* (*Shijing*) at the beginning of this section is a metaphorical illustration of the male and female principles awaiting conjunction to generate the cosmos (see the notes to section 11 above). The turtle and the snake of the Dark Warrior also depict the joining of Yin and Yang as the origin of life: the Dark Warrior is the emblem of Water, the first agent in the "cosmogonic" sequence of the five agents. The conjunction of Yin and Yang in the world reiterates the joining of Qian and Kun that gives birth to the cosmos. Without bestowing its essence upon the Earth, Heaven could not achieve its potential to generate, and without being fecundated by Heaven, the Earth could not realize its gift of bringing to life. This is the model for the union of the male and female principles illustrated in the *Cantong qi*. Therefore the ingredients of the Elixir—whether they are material, immaterial, or symbolic—should guarantee the conjunction of Qian and Kun, availing themselves of the intermediation of a third principle represented by the central agent Soil. If the ingredients cannot accomplish this conjunction, no rite, prayer, deity, or immortals could be of help. (Pregadio, 2011：212)

英国汉学家理雅各和韦利，美国诗人庞德（Ezra Pound，1885—1972年）都曾翻译过《诗经》，中国学者许渊冲（1921—2021年）、杨宪益（1915—2009年）、汪榕培（1942—2017年）等著名的翻译家，也都将这部最早的诗歌总集翻译成英语，从这些译本中可以看到不同译者对《关雎》的独到见解。以下摘录两位汉学界泰斗的英译文，供读者对比阅读。

（1）理雅各译文

Hark! from the islet in the stream the voice

Of the fish hawks that o'er their nest rejoice!

From them our thoughts to that young lady go,

Modest and virtuous, loth herself to show.

Where could be found, to share our prince's state

So fair, so virtuous, and so fit a mate? （Legge，1876：1）

（2）韦利译文

"Fair, fair," cry the ospreys

On the island in the river.

Lovely is this noble lady,

Fit bride for our lord. （Waley，1996：5-6）

尽管不同译者对"雎鸠""淑女""君子"的解读各有差异，但都认同《关雎》的爱情主题，英译文也能较好地再现原诗的节奏和形式。该诗篇名同样出现在《参同契》上篇《于是仲尼章》，谓"《关雎》建始初"，意思是指：《诗经》咏《关雎》，正夫妇人伦之道。玄英把该句译为"*guan* go the ospreys" to lay the beginning，用双引号标识"关雎"充当标题之用，这里译者提供了解题注释，称：通常意义上《关雎》篇被解读为男女交往之正道，是道德观和贞操观之典范。而《参同契》引用《关雎》，是因为雎鸠这种水鸟用情专一，不到交配季节绝不媾合，因而用雎鸠这一意象代表阴阳分离等待再次会合①。

---

① 原文：The entire first quatrain of this poem is quoted section 74 below. This poem is often deemed to depict the correct relation between man and woman, and the ideals of morality and chastity. the Cantong qi, however, refers to it because ospreys are said to live on their own until the time of mating, and thus represent the state of separation of Yin and Yang while awaiting their rejoining. （Pregadio，2011：140）

无论作为篇名的翻译，还是其中具体诗句的翻译，《关雎》原文的词序和意象都在译文中得到保留，而从玄英提供的文献及其行文来看，这段诗句的翻译当综合参考了之前理雅各和亚瑟·韦利的译文。

3. 译者对该诗节中的"雌雄""玄武""龟蛇""蟠虬""牝牡"的翻译做了较为灵活的处理，其中"雄"译为cocks，"雌"对应为hens，这是把抽象概念具体化，对原概念作了浅化处理；"牝牡"指阴阳，泛指与阴阳有关的如雌雄、男女等。译者将"牝牡"译为female and male，取的是该词的指示意义。因"玄武"为道教四象之一（其余三象分别为青龙、白虎、朱雀），其形为龟、蛇相合，盘虬相依之状，故译者按字面将"玄武龟蛇"译为The Dark Warrior's turtle and snake，并用注释说明《参同契》用龟蛇两物象征"玄武"，其中"玄"指的是北方之黑暗，"武"则为龟甲鳞片，类似战士之盔甲①。译者所作的这一注释内容值得商榷。古代五行说北方属水，水色黑，因而用"玄"代指北方，但并没有北方就代表黑暗之说；"武"为会意字，从止，从戈，可释为"与军事、战争有关的事、道德或行为"，但从未有指代龟甲鳞片之说。

4. 苏秦、张仪为战国时期著名的纵横家，两人以能言善辩而著称。译者在注释中补充了这一背景知识，并简要解读了纵横家中"纵""横"概念在当时的具体所指，即"纵"（the vertical）为南北纵向的国家联盟（alliances among states），"横"（the horizontal）为东西横向的国家联盟。原文的"苏秦通言，张仪结媒"英译为"Su Qin, the mediator, and Zhang Yi, the interceder"，将"通言"和"结媒"分别作为苏秦、张仪的身份名词翻译为同位语，这种处理手法直接明确，同时也保留了古文利用简练语言引出生动形象的特点。此外，译者在该句注释中还解释了原文的"通言"和"结媒"，认为"通言"亦可译为"信使"（messenger），而"结媒"的字面意义为"媒人"（go-between），以方便读者理解苏秦、张

---

① 原文：The *Cantong qi* is one of the texts that intend the Dark Warrior as a dual emblem made of a turtle and a snake According to the traditional interpretation, "dark" refers to the obscurity of the North, and "warrior" to the scaly carapace of the turtle, which is similar to a soldier's armor（Pregadio, 2011: 213）

仪的身份。此外，译者还补充了"通言""结媒"在道教丹道文学中的内涵，即为五行之"土"，是介于阴（真汞）阳（真铅）之间的媒介物（mediator）①。用解释性译法透彻地显示简练的古文词句的丰富内涵，可谓得古文英译的要诀。

5. 性质不相同的药物不可能变化生成金丹，只有同类性质的药物，方能相互作用而成丹。《参同契》中反复重申这样的丹道原理，如《胡粉投火中章第三十三》中有"类同者相从，事乖不成宝"（Things of the same kind follow each other; if they are at odds, they cannot form the Treasure）的论断。译者在这节翻译的注释中采取互文的方式提醒读者可对照阅读《胡粉投火中章》的观点。"纪纲"本指网罟的纲绳，引申为纲领，译为"guiding thread"而非"guiding principle"，既有"绳"的意象，又有"导"的功能，可谓妙译。

6. 针对该节出现的道教先圣黄帝、太一、八公、淮南（子）等专有名词，尽管译者没有像中文注译者章伟文那样提供如此详尽的注释，但为帮助读者有效阅读，在注释中也补充说明了这些道教先圣的基本信息，但都极为简略，如黄帝的补充信息：黄帝为中国早期炼丹师的守护神。传说他曾受炼丹教义，修炼成功后即飞升为仙②。而针对淮南子的注释只说明淮南子刘安具备丹道知识，因而人们认为他是服食仙丹然后成为神仙的。针对"太一"的补充信息："太一"为至高之神，为早期丹经的神启者之一。对"八公"注释也只有一句，说他们"受雇于刘安朝廷，据称曾撰写矿物水溶之法"③。尽管这样注释比较简单，但仍然达到了简要提示以帮助理解的目的。

---

① 原文：*Tongyan* ("mediator") might also be translated as "messenger." *Hemei* ("interceder") literally means the "go-between" between future spouses. In later alchemical literature, this is one of several terms that denote the agent Soil as the central "mediator" between Yin (True Mercury) and Yang (True lead). (Pregadio, 2011: 213)

② 原文：The Yellow Emperor (*Huangdi*) was he patron deity of the early Chinese alchemists. He received alchemical teachings and, according to some versions of his legend, ascended to Heaven after compounding an elixir. (Pregadio, 2011: 177)

③ 原文：The Great One (*Taiyi*) is the supreme God and one of deities who revealed the early scriptures on the elixirs. The Eight Sirs (*Bagong*) were employed at the court of Liu An, and are known as authors of an early text on the aqueous solutions of minerals. (Pregadio, 2011: 213)

7. 原文"把藉长跪"指手持祭祀礼品跪拜礼神，以示尊敬。译者玄英将该句译为"And you pay obeisance holding the records"，选取的是"长跪"的语用意义，译文直译"把藉"为"holding the records"，错误地把"藉"等同于"籍"并提供了"籍"的解释："Records" refers to the Taoist certificates of transmission and/or ordination, or to similar document that attest the identity and attainment of a priest or an adept（Pregadio, 2011：214），因误读译者把"藉"理解为证明道士身份的"籍"（records），并将其类比记录牧师或教徒身份的名册，虽方便了读者的理解，但与原文的意义不符，可将 records 改为 sacrifice。

8. 在整个翻译过程中，译者基本上是直译原文的意思和句子，用拉丁词语 sal ammoniac 翻译天然矿物"硇"体现了译者力图追求译文古雅的风格。最后一句"飞龟舞蛇，愈见乖张"意思：想要本性爬行的龟、蛇腾升，在空中飞舞，这岂不是愈加不通情理吗？译文"Even seeing a flying turtle or a dancing snake would be easier than this"（即便是要人看见飞舞的龟蛇也比这①更容易）全然是译者字面直译的结果，这里似乎有理解深度不够的问题。试改为 It would be as irrational as you wish the crawling turtles or snakes to fly and dance in the air。

第二节　《悟真篇》英文翻译研究

作为道教内丹丹法主要经典，《悟真篇》以诗词形式总结了宋代以前内丹的正统法诀，是一部在丹道史上与《周易参同契》并列齐名的著作。最早刊本分上、中、下三卷和外集一卷：上卷含七律16首，总论金丹修炼要旨；中卷有64首七言绝句，1首五言八句，着重功夫境界、实修证验的描述；下卷为13首西江月词，5首七言绝句，虽与上卷一样也是总论金丹大要，但侧重点不同；外集收诗歌20首，词12首，均讲禅理，与前三卷无内在关联，多数《道藏》版本不收录外集，或只作为附录、拾遗看待。

---

① 指前文所说"和胶补釜，以硇涂疮，去冷加冰，除热用汤"，都是些不通情理的炼制丹药之法。

《悟真篇》沿袭了《参同契》中的内容及术语，其讲述对象为内功造诣较深的人，想达其要旨仅从表面词义研究是远远不够的。我国著名的道教学丹功专家王沐先生在追溯《悟真篇》的丹法源流时有过这样一段论述。

> 作者对自己使用《参同契》的术语，也担心会将读者引入迷途，所以在《悟真篇》"读参同契歌"中，列举书内所用"两仪、四象、八卦、乾坤、吉凶、悔吝"等卦象爻辞后，总括一句说："百姓日用不知，圣人能究本源，顾易道妙尽乾坤之理，遂托象于斯文。"这是告诉读者，术语都是托象，就是用卦象作比喻，不要拘泥在这形式上面，而是悟出它内蕴的真诀。所以在此歌中又进一步说："犹设象以指意，悟真意则象捐，达者惟简惟易，迷者愈惑愈繁，故修真之士读《参同契》者，不在乎泥象执文。"这更明确地告诉读者，"象"只是一种比喻，必须透过形式而悟其内涵真意，才能掌握内丹丹法。这也就是作者把他所著丹经命名为《悟真篇》的原因。（王沐，1981：54）

为此，王沐先生建议读者"不要在形式上打圈子，以致陷入迷阵之中，必须从正面、反面、夹缝中、边缘外、找出真正含义；更从比喻词、影射词，暗喻的隐语中，反语的机锋内，寻其含义，破其哑谜。然后六辔在手，驰骤由心，掌握主流，一以贯之，才能剥去掩饰的外衣，看到它本来的面目"（王沐，1982：32—33），这种阅读思路不仅是许多国内学者注译《悟真篇》时遵循的基本法则，也深刻影响了海外学者译介《悟真篇》的策略和方法。

一 《悟真篇》在海外的传播

《悟真篇》和《参同契》同为道教丹法之正宗，但《悟真篇》的丹法丹诀"比《参同契》更明显更完备"（王沐，1981：59），在各代丛书中均有收录，如《文献通考》《四库全书子部》《古今图书集成》《明道藏》《道藏辑要》等。虽说《道德经》《庄子》《阴符经》等早期道教经典都对《悟真篇》产生过较大影响，但从丹道史角度来看，《悟真篇》与

《参同契》的授受因缘最为密切，其内容和文体都与《参同契》有着明显的一脉相承特质。因此，研究《悟真篇》的学者通常会同时研究《参同契》，研究《参同契》的学者自然也不会遗漏对《悟真篇》的探讨，这种现象不仅存在于中国学者对道教丹道经典的注疏方面，同样也体现于海外学者的对该类典籍的译介方面。

按时间排序，海外包含《悟真篇》译介内容的作品主要如下。

（1）为揭示道教炼丹术中的科学因素，美国化学家戴维斯[①]（Tenney L. Davis）与学者赵云丛（Chao Yun-ts'ung）共同署名的系列论文在《美国艺术与科学院学术动态》（Proceedings of the American Academy of Arts and Science）上发表，分别为1939年第5期上的《天台张伯端和他的〈悟真篇〉：对中国炼丹术贡献之研究》（"Chang Po-tuan of T'ien-t'ai, His Wu Chen P'ien, Essay on the Understanding of the Truth: A Contribution to the Study of Chinese Alchemy"，该文以《悟真篇》为研究对象，包含了《悟真篇》的全文翻译；1940年第13期上的《张伯端内丹韵文三篇》（"The Three Alchemical Poems by Chang Po-tuan"）。

（2）美国学者克利里（Thomas Cleary）依据清朝学者刘一明编撰的《悟真直指》完成《悟真篇》英文译本，书名为《悟真篇：一部道教内丹经典》（Understanding Reality: A Taoist Alchemical Classic），1987年夏威夷大学出版社出版。

（3）法国汉学家贺碧来（Robinet Isabelle）1995年出版的法文专著《道教内丹：统一性和多样性》（Introduction a l'ahchilie interieure taoiste: De l'unite et de la multiplicite），里面包含了作者基于陈致虚《悟真篇》注释文本所完成的法文翻译及其评论。

（4）意大利汉学家玄英早在日本读研期间（1991—1992年）便开始研读《悟真篇》，约在1995年英译《悟真篇》上卷的16首七律诗，后经反复修改并重新做了文本注解，于2009年出版[②]，书名为《感悟真实：

[①] 戴维斯先生也曾和中国化学家吴鲁强合作译介过《参同契》。

[②] 2011年玄英完成了《参同契》的英译，同年还将王沐先生的《〈悟真篇〉丹法要旨》（原文分上、下两篇载《道协会刊》1982年第1期）翻译成英文，书名为《内炼的基础：道教内丹实践》（Foundations of Internal Alchemy: the Taoist Practice of Neidan）。

律诗〈悟真篇〉，一部道教内丹典籍》（Awakening to Reality：The Regulated Verses of Wuzhen Pian, A Taoist Classic of Internal Alchemy）。

（5）英国学者理查德·博钦格（Richard Bertschinger）2012 年完成了张伯端的《悟真篇》英译，书名叫《张伯端内丹术指南〈悟真篇〉的翻译》（Written On Awakening to Reality：A Translation of Zhang Boduan's Guide to Internal Alchemy），为了让读者逐步了解道教内丹学派的起源和发展，译者翻译该部巨著时尽可能少做阐释性翻译，并附加了一些评注内容，强调《悟真篇》在内丹理论建构方面的价值。博钦格之前也翻译过《参同契》，两译本均是从医学生理学、内丹学视角进行解读。

此外，《悟真篇》的译介还散见于海外学者的一些研究成果中，此处不赘述。

二 玄英《悟真篇》译本特色

同他后来翻译《参同契》的路径一致，玄英的《悟真篇》译本包含序言、导言、译文、刘一明注释选译、文本注释、中文术语表、参考文献。标题有两部分，大标题为《感悟真实》（Awakening to Reality），下附小标题《律诗〈悟真篇〉，一部道教内丹典籍》（The Regulated Verses of Wuzhen Pian, A Taoist Classic of Internal Alchemy），译者通过副标题开宗明义地说明了该书翻译的内容为《悟真篇》上卷的 16 首七律诗歌。该译本以收录于《道藏》中的元代学者陈致虚撰写的《紫阳真人悟真篇三注》为底本，同时还参阅了宋叶士表、袁公辅注《修真十书悟真篇》，宋翁葆光的《紫阳真人悟真篇注疏》和《悟真篇注释》，明陆西星的《悟真篇小序》，清刘一明的《悟真直指》，清仇兆鳌的《悟真篇集注》。因版本不同所导致的内容差异集中体现在文本注释部分。译者还参阅了当代一些学者的研究成果，包括：张振国的《〈悟真篇〉导读》（宗教文化出版社 2001 年版），刘国樑和连遥的《新译〈悟真篇〉》（台北：三民书局 2005 年版）以及王沐的《〈悟真篇〉浅解》（中华书局 1990 年版），译者尤其提到王沐这本校注对他翻译《悟真篇》的影响。

就翻译体例而言，译者依中文、译文、注释的顺序分别呈现每一首诗歌的翻译内容。注释包含题解和逐句注释两个部分。相对于他的《参同契》英译注释系统而言，这部《悟真篇》译本虽略为简化，但更为直观，方便读者阅读。在序言中译者讲到：该译本面向不懂汉语的读者，因此虽然不是有意化繁就简，但也省译了一些无关紧要的细节描述，在努力忠实原文的前提下尽量使译文清楚易懂。

译者选译了刘一明《悟真直指》中的部分内容，即刘一明对《悟真篇》中的内丹概念术语的阐释，与前面16首七律的翻译及注释形成互文关系，以帮助读者加深理解这些内丹口诀的内涵。《悟真直指》收于《道书十二种》中，该注"自创一系列术语，杂用理学一些名词代替铅汞龙虎名词，读起来感到生硬"（王沐，1990：6）。不过在玄英眼里这部18世纪末期的注本却是"语言清晰朴实"（distinguished by the use of a lucid and plain language）（Pregadio, 2009：1），因此译者选择性翻译了其中的术语阐释部分，作为译本注释之外的附加注释。以"金丹"为例，刘一明注本中对《悟真篇》上卷第3首诗第2句"惟有金丹最的端"和第8首诗第5—6句"潭底日红阴怪灭，山头日红药苗新"的注释能帮助读者深化这一内丹概念的理解，玄英将此内容翻译为英文，必要时补充一些自己的看法，这种双重注释的做法为目标语读者提供又一阅读选择，对于解读晦涩难懂的道教丹经不失为一种有效的尝试。

《悟真篇》原文包含大量的隐语，本着使这部深奥的内丹经典通俗化、大众化的翻译原则，中西译者只能依理意解，译文注释皆成了帮助读者阅读、理解、应用这部经典的重要必备内容。玄英《悟真篇》译本多采用直译法，甚而还有音译，尤其是其中的隐喻象征语都是采取直译法或音译法，译文注解（包括他选译的刘一明注《悟真篇》的内容）便成了译本获得意义的重要保障。

三　玄英《天仙金丹·五行情性第三》译文解析

张伯端《悟真篇》用数字分次第，原书中的诗词本无具体标题，为提纲挈领，分清层次，陈全林注译本中每首诗词前面均配有两句四言韵句作标题，既是凝练主题，也能区分次第，故借用。此处《天仙金丹·五行情性第三》即张伯端《悟真篇》上卷第三首诗。在王沐先生看来，此首叙"天仙""金丹"两词，均是上乘大法，目标必须高远。以精神二物，分先天后天，用真意导引，使精气神三者归一，以真意运之，为金丹筑基初步功夫（王沐，1990：5）。

[原文]

学仙须是学天仙[1]，惟有金丹最的端[2]。二物会时情性合[3]，五行全处虎龙蟠[4]。本因戊己为媒娉，遂使夫妻镇合欢[5]。只候功成朝北阙，九霞光里驾翔鸾[6]。

[注释]①

1. 天仙：道教所追求的最高果位。《钟吕传道集》云："仙有五等：天仙、神仙、地仙、人仙、鬼仙，皆是仙也。"

2. 金丹：道教炼丹名词，亦称"金液还丹""金液大丹"。古代方士、道士用黄金炼成"金液"，或用铅汞等八石烧炼成黄色的药金（还丹），故名。道教认为服之能长生不老。宋金以后，道教称经过人体内炼，凝结而成的大药为"金丹"，也称婴儿或内金丹。的端：正确，恰当。

3. 二物：指坎、离两卦，坎为水，乃元精之代号；离为火，为元神的代号。下文的"夫妻""龙虎"即为"二物"的象征语。道教认为，"二物"合则有金丹。会：合。

4. 五行：内丹家认为，人体内的肝、肺、脾、心、肾分别对应五行的木、金、土、火、水，主管魂、魄、意、神、志。五行全备是炼就真神的条件。蟠：盘曲。"虎龙蟠"为象征语，指元精、元神互结而言。

5. 戊己：本为天干中的戊日与己日，戊己属土，土分阴阳。内丹修炼中指"真意"，也叫"黄婆"，喻指可以促使体内体外呈阴阳道性物质的元神、元精凝合的一种下意识。媒娉：指媒妁聘娶之礼。夫妻喻二物，即坎、离，是元精、元神的代称。镇，守住。这里引申为精神内守。合，阴阳交合，丹药内凝。镇合欢即凝结过程。

6. 北阙：指天上的宫门。九霞：九天云霞，此处借指天庭。丹士修

---

① 注释综合参考了王沐撰写的《〈悟真篇〉校注》第22页的注释（刊登于《道协会刊》1984年第15期）以及陈全林《〈悟真篇〉注译》（中国社会科学出版社2004年版）第181—182页的注释内容。

出真神之后，出神之际，周身发光，有如霞光，乃五气朝元之后的彩光。鸾：传说中的灵鸟。驾翔鸾：喻出神远游，神入虚空。

[译文]

Poem 3[1]

If you study immortality,
you should study celestial immortality;
only the Golden Elixir
is the highest principle.[2]
When the two things meet,
emotions and nature join one another;[3]
where the five agents are whole,
Dragon and Tiger coil.[4]

Rely in the first place on wu and ji
that act as go-betweens,
then let husband and wife
join together and rejoice.[5]
Just wait until your work is achieved
to have audience at the Northern Portal,[6]
and in the radiance of a ninefold mist
you will ride a soaring phoenix. （Pregadio, 2009: 27）

[解析]

1. 译者玄英在逐句注释之前先对全诗的主题进行题解。译者解释道，张伯端说只有天仙能给予完全的超越，即消除先天与后天的界限。炼金丹可类比为修天仙，即飞升成仙拜见最高神①。译者的这一题解深得王沐

---

① 原文：In this poem, Zhang Boduan uses traditional images to describe the main features and benefits of the Golden Elixir. There are several grades of transcendence, but for the very fact of being graded, they pertain to the realm of relativity in which we live. Only "celestial immortality", says Zhang Boduan, grants complete transcendence, the removal of distinctions between the precelestial and postcelestial domains. Fulfilling the Way of the Golden Elixir is analogous to ascending to Heaven as an immortal and having audience with the highest deities. （Pregadio, 2009: 28）

《悟真篇浅解》的要旨。通过题解，读者可了解该诗的主题为金丹的主要成效和特征，知道道教神仙有品级之分。

2. 原文"学仙须是学天仙，惟有金丹最的端"传达给原文读者的信息：天仙是仙品中的最高等级，为修仙者力图达到的最高境地，只有修炼金丹才是修仙者达到这一最高境地的上乘之法。译文"If you study immortality, you should study celestial immortality; only the Golden Elixir is the highest principle"虽兼顾了原文的形意，但也只能是文字表面之形和意，至于诗句背后的内涵需借助注释才能完备。虽然这里把"仙"对应为英文中的"immortality"，但译者依然觉得"仙"译为"transcendence"更精确，因此在注释部分补充了自己的看法，并提供了载于《钟吕传道记》中的道教五级仙品之说及其对应翻译（"鬼仙"译为the demon immortals，"人仙"译为the human immortals，"地仙"译为the earthly immortals，"神仙"译为the spirit immortals，"天仙"译为the celestial immortals），用注释补充背景知识的目的旨在使读者明理，也是对"惟有金丹最的端"译为only the Golden Elixir is the highest principle的恰当解读。此外，译本后面所附的刘一明《悟真直指》选译中也有针对该诗句的解读，感兴趣的读者可以多渠道了解到道教"金丹"的内涵。

3. "二物"为人体内呈一阴一阳两种对应属性的金丹药物（陈全林，2004：181）。玄英直译为"two things"，并在该句的注释中标明其具体指代为真阴和真阳，以明示"二物"在内丹学中的意义。将"性"译为"inner nature"，"情"译为"emotions"（也可译为"feelings""sentiments""passions"），这样的双语转换也只是停留在字面解读上。这里译者针对"情性合"提供注释内容：本质纯正之"性"不受任何外物影响，而本质不纯之"情"常想挣脱"性"的羁绊，因而常有失控发生。这样的注释内容向读者讲明了"二物会时情性合"在内丹文本中实指代表真阴真阳的元神元精相会合之时，也是生命中的真情真性相合之时。译者对中文"情"的复杂内涵作了相应的补充，即"情"并非只是被看作心理现象，还关涉个体在大千世界中的存在，因此总会与天性超然之"性"发生不和。"性""情"交合时，"情"会表现为一个人的品性、脾气、态度，表达个体生活之内在本性。①

4. "五行"通常的英译是 the five agents 或 the five elements。"五行"既可指阴阳演变过程的五种基本形态（the differentiation of the One into the many），也可指代表人的精神、精气的"元气"所呈现的五种特质（the diverse qualities taken on by Original Breath (yuanqi) in the conditioned state），而"五行全处"（The five agents are whole）强调整体概念（the undividedness of the five agents），可类比阴阳统一（is analogous to the joining of Yin and Yang），是炼就真神的条件。"五行全处"的内丹意义皆体现在译者的注释中。

作为坎、离两卦的象征物，虎（真阳）龙（真阴）蟠（Dragon and Tiger coil）即指坎、离融合。译者在注释中添加了较多的涉及"龙虎"象征意义以及"坎、离、乾、坤"四卦的指代关系，为译入语读者提供了必要的内丹学知识。其注释内容为：

The Dragon stands for True Yin within Yang, also symbolized by the inner line of the trigram Li ☲ and the Tiger stands for True Yang within Yin, also symbolized by the inner line of Kan ☵. They are the "two things" mentioned in the previous line. Kan ☵ and Li ☲ are born from the union of Qian ☰ and Kun ☷, the True Yang and True Yin of the precelestial state. To generate the world, Qian entrusts its creative essence to Kun, and becomes Li; Kun receives the essence of Qian to bring it to fulfillment, and becomes Kan. In Neidan, Kan and Li newly join together ("coil") and return their essences to one another.

---

① 原文：The "two things" are, foundamentally, True Yin and True Yang. Inner nature (xing) is essentially pure and unaffected by phenomena or events of any kind. Emotions (qing, a word also translated as feelings, sentiments, or passions), are often impure and tend to disjoin from one's nature, to the point that they may become uncontrolled. According to many Neidan texts, the separation of inner nature and emotions is a feature of the conditioned state in which we live. Only when True Yin and True Yang merge can one's inner nature and emotions be not independent of one another, but in agreement with one another. The Chinese view of "emotions" is more complex than it might at first seem. Emotions are not seen as merely psychological phenomena, but rather as pertaining to the sphere of existence, of one's being in the world as an individual entity. For this very reason, emotions are often at odds with one's inner nature, which is inherently transcendent. When emotions and inner nature join one another, emotions turn into qualities—personality, temperament, attitudes—that allow a person to express his or her inner nature in life, according to his or her individuality. (Pregadio, 2009: 28-29)

Symbolically this liberates True Yin and True Yang from their residences in the conditioned state, and reestablishes the original pair of trigrams, namely Qian and Kun. (Pregadio, 2009: 29)

5. 天干中的"戊己"属土,土分阴阳,内丹修炼中"戊己"指代"真意"(the True Intention),"戊己为媒娉"(wu and ji that act as go-betweens)指"真意"可以促使体内呈阴阳道性的元神、元精的凝合(In Neidan, the True Intention (zhenyi) brings about the union of Yin and Yang. This is possible because intention, just like Soil, embraces both Yin and Yang, or wu and ji)。

"夫妻"也是坎、离的代称,译者在注释中将其解读为"结成金丹的阴阳两物"(Husband and wife respectively stand for the Yang and Yin principles which join to generate the Elixir),基本抓住了该象征语的真实内涵。"遂使夫妻镇合欢"译为 Then let husband and wife join together and rejoice,表面上漏掉了"镇"(守住,指精神内守)这一信息,但"镇合欢"实指金丹凝结过程,用"join together and rejoice"道出了金丹修炼过程及其产生的欢愉境界,也算是形神皆妙。

6. "功成"既可指金丹修炼过程的完成,也可指功德圆满(The expression *gong cheng*, translated above as "your work is achieved" can also mean "your merit is complete"),"北阙"指天上的宫门,朝北阙指功成后受到天帝之召,因此原文"只候功成朝北阙"译为 Just wait until your work is achieved to have audience at the Northern Portal,并在注释中补充"北阙"的具体指代,即 The Northern Portal is the gate of the heaven, and an emblem of the Center: the symbolic center of Heaven is at due North,完整再现了原文的含义。

小　结

上海外国语大学谢天振教授曾借助译介学的视角审视中国文化"走出去"的问题,在他看来,中国文化"走出去"不是简单的翻译问题;在涉及中国文化"走出去"的议题上,不但要注意它与文化的跨国、跨民族、跨语言传播的方式、途径、接受心态等相关的因素,还要重视

"语言差"和"时间差"等具体问题。谢教授明确指出：在西方我们不可能指望有许多精通汉语并深刻理解中国文化的专家学者，他们更缺乏相当数量的能够轻松阅读和理解译自中国的文学作品与学术著述的读者（谢天振，2013）。作为一名严肃的研究道教文化的汉学家，玄英对道教丹道文献《周易参同契》《悟真篇》的翻译沿袭了西方传统汉学学术翻译方法论，通过旁征博引，解释典故，考释出处，说明类比语言的具体指代，突出译文的叙述价值和文化价值，虽然其针对的读者对象应是对道教丹道文化有一定了解的异域读者或研究人员，但译者将文本置于丰富的文化和语言环境的这种操作可在一定程度上将其读者群扩展到对道教文化感兴趣的异域读者，有助于提高道教文化在海外的传播广度和深度。

对普通读者而言，道教炼养文本虽然语言优美，意象丰富，但要真正探知原文本意，没有炼丹的理论知识是很难的。玄英翻译《周易参同契》这部道教丹道学经典，其中翻译文本只有 57 页，占全文篇幅的百分之十八。除序言、附录（原书作者魏伯阳自传 2 篇，中文原文，主题词索引）、词汇表、参考文献外，该成果还包括 63 页的引言和长达 115 页的注释内容，这些阐释性文本充分展示了译者的研究过程，作为译文的必要补充材料，较好地为译文读者理解和鉴赏道教丹道文化扫清了障碍，与正文翻译共同构成《周易参同契》整套译本体系。《悟真篇》译本采用的也是类似的翻译路径，同样是带有明显研究特质的深度语境化翻译手段。

翻译不仅仅是文字层面的转换，更是思想精神方面的沟通，单从这个意义上讲真正的翻译应是有研究的翻译，它既要让读者看懂，又要显示出原文的思想和艺术价值。美国翻译学者克瓦米·安东尼·阿皮亚（Kwame Anthony Appiah）1993 年在 Callaloo 上撰文 "Thick Translation"（通常译为"深度翻译"、"厚翻译"、"丰厚翻译"或"厚重翻译"），并将其定义为"通过注释和伴随的注解，将文本置于一个丰富的文化和语言的语境中"（Appiah，1993：817）。"Thick Translation"这一概念源自美国人类学家克利福德·格尔茨（Clifford Geertz，1926—2006 年）的"深描"学说，强调文化的关联性和场景性，对异文化的描述与书写就是运用深描的方式去阐释，其核心是"阐释他人的阐释"（雷勇，2012：81）。把文化界定为一种符号体系和意义体系，所以人类学对文化的研究事实上是对这套符号体系的解码和对赋予文化以意义的行为之阐释。将"深描"学说应用于翻译研究，就是通过大量的脚注、译注、说明等阐释性文本材料为译文读者提供背景知识信息，从而引起译文读者对源语文化的关注和兴趣，以实现更佳的接受效果。虽然阿皮亚具体谈论的是翻译非洲谚语的问题，不少学者从跨文化翻译研究视角把这一概念提升为一种对抗文化侵略意识的翻译手法。如，西奥·赫曼斯（Theo Hermans）在文章"Cross-cultural Studies as Thick Translation"中的评价如下。

> 作为跨文化翻译研究的工具，深度翻译可以避免术语翻译研究的平淡无趣和刻板简化，能促使更加丰富多彩的多元化词汇的产生。此外，通过自下而上而不是自上而下的达成模式，深度翻译力图避免某一特定范式或传统范畴的强行介入。其固有的人类文化学特质决定了它不可能演变为类似阐释学"视域融合"概念使人联想到的那种善意却让人窒息的操控。可以略微夸张地说，深度翻译一方面承认充分翻译是不可能的，同时也肯定挪用他者文化的翻译是不妥的。（Hermans，2003：388）

文化之间的交流，并非单纯的语际沟通。作为翻译方法和策略的"Thick Translation"，重视文化的特殊之处。"Thick Translation"指的是阐释性文本材料，如序言、脚注、尾注、文内释义、文外说明、案语、附笔等，其目的是为译文读者提供背景知识，便于理解和鉴赏（李红霞、张政，2015：34）。这种翻译方法和策略被广泛地运用到中国典籍翻译的各个研究方面，从不同的角度阐释了译作的特点，为解释翻译现象提供了有力的理论依据。通过这种语境化翻译手段，读者能够获得译本产生的社会文化语境，由此产生对他者文化的尊重，并抵制英语文化的优越感（孙宁宁，2010：16）。玄英翻译道教丹道著作所采取的深度语境化翻译手段，并没有强烈的对抗文化侵略意识，更多的是通过各种注释和评注，重构出源文文本产生的历史语境，以帮助译入语读者更深入地理解源语文化，从而促进多元主体间的对话，加强跨文化交流与理解。这样的汉学翻译沿袭了西方传统汉学的研究模式，可深化西方学界对道教领域的研究效度。

自 20 世纪下半叶，海外译者开始更多地注意中国文化典籍的学术价值，研究与翻译并重逐渐成为中国文化典籍英译的主要特点，也构成了 20 世纪中国文化典籍英译海外译者的大概面貌。他们研究中国文化典籍，将研究结果运用到翻译中，来验证其研究结果的合理与有效，形成研究与翻译互补（赵长江，2014：207）。翻译在汉学研究中所起的作用经历了由隐形到显化的过程。在国际汉学的发展历程中，逐渐形成"翻译＋汉学"的研究模式（陈吉荣，2018：6）。从效果论，这种类型的翻译将翻译同严谨的学术研究结合起来，实际上属于学术翻译的范畴，适合涵纳丰富文化信息的文化典籍、学术作品和少数文学作品，其接受对象也是对原文及其背后的文化感兴趣的异域读者和研究人员（王雪明、杨子，2012：103）。玄英以传译源文本文化价值和文化事实为主导，兼顾其文学特征，希望把自己所认识到的中国道教丹道文化显现在其翻译作品里，向译入语读者讲述真正的中国道教。这一带有研究特质的翻译文本能有效促进道教文化典籍的海外传播，让不懂源语的英语读者知道、了解甚至欣赏道教典籍的思想内容及其文体风格，读到与典籍意义相当、文体相仿、风格相称的英译本，为当今语境下翻译工作者"复兴中国文化，讲好中国故事"提供了有益参考。

第七章

道教综合类文本
《抱朴子内篇》翻译研究

引　语

　　《抱朴子内篇》乃东晋著名道士、道教学者、医学家、炼丹术家葛洪的成名作之一，成书于晋元帝建武元年（317 年），全书 20 卷，每卷 1 篇。"抱朴子"为葛洪的号，意思是"坚守淳朴天性的人"，在施舟人、傅飞岚编撰的《道藏通考》（*The Taoist Canon*）三卷本中该典籍的英文标题就是 *Book of the Master Who Keeps to Simplicity*（Schipper, Verellen, 2004：70）。葛洪在《自序》中说："《内篇》言神仙方药、鬼怪变化、养生延年、禳邪却祸之事，属道家。"该书是集魏晋以来道教方术、神仙思想之大成的学术专著，素有"小《道藏》"之称，涉及现代宗教学、哲学、历史学、化学、医药学、养生学、民俗学、社会政治学、心理学、人体科学等多种学科（胡孚琛，1989：315）。中国台湾学者周绍贤也曾说过，"总览《抱朴子内篇》，凡玄理、仙道、修炼、诵经、服食、吐纳、画符、念咒、招神、驱鬼、镇邪种种法术，无不备述，此书可谓全部《道藏》之缩影"（周绍贤，1974：61）。这是一部集神仙理论、养生思想、医学贡献、化学史料等为一体的道教综合类典籍，在道教发展史上享有很高的地位，当然也吸引了国外汉学家、道教学者和科技史学家等学者的高度关注。因此，本章将该部典籍的翻译研究单列出来，探讨其在海外的传播和影响，并以美国学者魏鲁男完成的迄今为止英语世界的首个也是唯一一个全译本为分析对象，选取其中两篇内容（《畅玄》和

《微旨》）的英译文进行案例解析，探讨《抱朴子内篇》英译中存在的问题和可资借鉴之处。

第一节 《抱朴子内篇》在海外的传播与反响

葛洪在《抱朴子内篇》中不仅对先秦以来的神仙思想进行了系统总结，首次建立了一套颇具义理性和思辨性的道教神仙理论体系，还在宗教信仰的框架之内，借炼丹、养生等成仙手段的记录和探索，为中国科技史留下了宝贵的研究材料。王明先生曾在《抱朴子内篇校释》序言中写道，"《抱朴子内篇》是一部富有宗教哲学和科学技术内容的书。它的史料价值主要有二：一是有关道教的史料价值，二是有关化学技术的史料价值"（王明，1985：3）。如此重要的一部道教典籍在海外的译介从未间断过，从20世纪20年代到21世纪初，不断被译为英、法、德、意、日等国语言（俞森林，2020：155）。后文将简要介绍该书在海外的传播情况及其反响。

一 《抱朴子内篇》在海外的传播简况

早在1898年法国出版的《道教研究文献目录》中就写进了葛洪《抱朴子》的名字，美国学者约翰生（Obed S. Johnson）1928年所著的《中国炼丹术考》（*A Study of Chinese Alchemy*），则是第一部将《抱朴子内篇》引入西方国家的作品，该书第三、第四章摘译了《抱朴子内篇》的部分内容，涉及《论仙》、《金丹》、《释滞》、《仙药》和《黄白》这几卷的翻译。在此之后，英国汉学家韦利1930年对照研究了魏伯阳的《参同契》与葛洪的《抱朴子内篇》，并以"中国炼丹术纪略"（"Notes on Chinese Alchemy: Supplementary to Johnson's *A Study of Chinese Alchemy*"）为题再次探讨中国炼丹术这一话题，该文指出了约翰生在翻译理解《抱朴子内篇》上的一些偏差。此后，越来越多来自法国、日本、英国、德国、荷兰、意大利、美国、澳大利亚、俄罗斯等国家的汉学家从事中国道教史和科技史的研究，撰写了不少基于《抱朴子内篇》研究的学术论文和专著。这方面最有代表性的学者应是英国科学技术史专家李约瑟（Joseph Needham），他的鸿篇巨制《中国的科学和文明》（*Science and Civilisation in China*）多卷本中包含《科学思想史》《炼丹术与化学》等专题研究，涉及葛洪《抱朴子内篇》中多篇内容的翻译引用，法国学者索安高度评价了李约瑟对中国道教所展开的研究，认为"李约瑟赋予了葛洪的《抱朴子》在炼丹史上的重要地位"（Needham accords Ko Hung's *Pao-p'u tzu* an important place in the history of alchemy）（Seidel，1989：263）。另一位对道教内丹和当代道教炼养活动著述较多的学者是美国科技史专家席文（Nathan Sivin），相关系列成果有专著《中国炼丹术初探》（*Chinese Alchemy: Preliminary Studies*），论文《中国炼丹术对火候的把握》（"Chinese Alchemy and the Manipulation of the Time"），论文《炼丹术的理论基础》（"The Theoretical Background of Elixir Alchemy"）等；此外，德国道教学者法尔琴·巴德里安—胡赛因（Farzeen Baldrian-Hussein）撰写论文《内丹名称的由来及使用》（"Inner Alchemy: Notes on the Origin and Use of the Term Neidan"）；等等，这些成果都离不开对《抱朴子内篇》的理解和翻译。

目前已有《抱朴子内篇》的英译文本、意大利语文本、德译文本和日译文本等，但多数为节译。学者们依据自己的研究需求选择其中的部分内容进行翻译解读，就英译文本来看，代表性译作如下。

（1）美国化学家戴维斯（Tenney L. Davis）在其对中国炼丹史和古化学史的研究中探究了该书对化学、药学等领域的贡献，与他的学生中国学者吴鲁强于1935年合作翻译了《抱朴子内篇》中的《金丹》和《黄白》篇，之后又于1941年与陈国符合作完成《释滞》和《仙药》篇的完整翻译以及其余十八卷的节译。

（2）法国汉学家尤金·菲弗尔（Eugene Feifel）在20世纪40年代完整翻译了《畅玄》《论仙》《对俗》三卷内容，选译了《金丹》和《仙药》部分内容，分期刊载在辅仁大学主办的汉学期刊《华裔学志》（*Monumenta Serica*）上。

（3）李约瑟在1956年《科学思想史》研究中摘译了《论仙》《对俗》《黄白》卷的部分内容，又在1974年《炼丹术和化学》专题研究中摘译了其中《论仙》《对俗》《金丹》《微旨》《黄白》的部分内容，这些译文很大程度上参考了菲弗尔、戴维斯和吴鲁强、魏鲁男的翻译。

（4）美国道教学者孔丽维1993年节译了《金丹》《地真》两卷内

容，译文收录于她的研究专著《道教体验文萃》(The Taoist Experience: An Anthology) 中。

（5）法国汉学家傅飞岚（Franciscus Verellen）1999 年节译了其中的《论仙》，译文收录于狄百瑞（William Theodore De Bary）和艾琳·布鲁姆（Irene Bloom）编辑的华夏文明著作《中国传统资料编选》(Sources of Chinese Tradition) 丛书中。

（6）2005 年意大利汉学家玄英在其专著《太清：中古时期中国的道教与金丹》中节译了《微旨》《勤求》《地真》卷的部分内容。

迄今为止，英语世界的首个也是唯一一个《抱朴子内篇》全译本由美国汉学家魏鲁男于 1966 年完成，其书名为《公元 320 年的中国炼丹术、医学和宗教：葛洪的〈抱朴子内篇〉》(Alchemy, Medicine, Religion in the China of A.D. 320: The Nei P'ien of Ko Hung (Pao-p'u tzu)。该译本以清孙星衍平津馆校勘本《抱朴子内篇》为底本，主体采用归化策略，完整翻译了《内篇》的二十卷和《外篇》的卷五十《自叙》，自问世以来一直是欧洲学术界研究中国道教文化的重要参考资料。《抱朴子内篇》在英语世界的译介历时近一个世纪，从最初的节译引用，到单一的炼丹术章节翻译，再到魏鲁男集"炼丹术、医学、宗教"于一体的全译本的出现，体现着西方学者对中国传统文化认识的不断深入（俞森林，2020：160）。

二 魏鲁男《抱朴子内篇》英译本在海外的接受与反响

作为道教集大成之作，《抱朴子内篇》涵盖内容较广，涉及道教教义、修仙、内丹、外丹、药学等领域，研究中国道教文化的海外学者多会谈及葛洪的这部著作，魏鲁男的《抱朴子内篇》全译本为这些海外学者的研究提供了极大的便利。不过学者们对其译文评价褒贬不一，尤其是因为该书缺乏必要的注释这一点从一开始就受到汉学家们的诟病，导致学界对魏鲁男译本的评价几乎是贬多于褒。最初针对该译作的书评就有不少批判性意见，如美国汉学家康达维（David R. Knechtges）评价该译本"不符合严肃翻译的要求"（Mr. Ware's book falls short of the requirements of a serious translation）(Knechtges，1968：228)。美国道教学者薛爱华（Edward H. Schafer）的高徒柯慕白（Paul W. Kroll）曾撰写了一篇书评，虽然评价对象是汉学家孔立哲（Jay Sailey）1978 年译介的葛洪

《抱朴子外篇》作品《抱朴子——哲学家葛洪（公元283—343年）研究》（*The Master Who Embraces Simplicity：A Study of The Philosopher Ko Hung, A. D. 283 - 343*），但该书评也提到魏鲁男英译的《抱朴子内篇》文本，认为该译本"有时带有误导性"（at times misguided）（Kroll，1982：139）。法国学者索安在《西方道教编年史：1950—1990》（"Chronicle of Taoist Studies in the West：1950 - 1990"）中明确指出该译本"基本不做注释"（the absence of scholarly note）（Seidel, 1989：305）这一遗憾。此外，海外学者在进行实际道教学研究时，若需引用葛洪《抱朴子内篇》内容作佐证，有学者会直接引用魏鲁男译本中的内容，但也有一些学者选择重新翻译。如美国汉学家康儒博的专著《与天地同寿：葛洪〈神仙传〉翻译与研究》（*To Live as Long as Heaven and Earth：A Translation and Study of Ge Hong's Traditions of Divine Transcendents*）虽然研究的是道教神仙系统，但书中屡屡提及《抱朴子内篇》中有关神仙实有的记述，但凡该著作中需引证《抱朴子内篇》相关章节的内容，作者都进行了重新翻译，只标明魏鲁男译本中对应的具体页码，其理由是"这是一本迫切需要重译的版本"（a text in dire need of retranslation）（Company, 2002：XXVI）。汉学家玄英撰写的专著《太清：中国中古早期的道教和炼丹术》探讨中国炼丹术的起源以及炼丹术和存思在道教自我修炼实践中的相互作用，作者引用了大量的道教炼丹文献，《抱朴子内篇》也在其列，和康儒博同出一辙，玄英引用该书的内容时也只在注释中注明魏鲁男译本的相应页码，译文内容全是自己新译的。可见，当今海外道教界对魏鲁南的这部译作认同度不是很高。

当然，学术界也并非完全否定魏鲁南的这一译本。中国科学技术史专家何丙郁（Ho Peng-Yoke）也曾在《亚洲研究学刊》上撰文评价魏鲁南《抱朴子内篇》译本，虽然他对魏鲁男将"道"译成"God"、将"仙"译为"Genii"等颇有微词，但也不乏一些赞美之词。书评中这样写道：

Professor Ware is to be congratulated for bringing out the translation of a most difficult Chinese Daoist text in a very readable form. One cannot find another text that gives so useful and authoritative information on alchemy and Daoism in fourth century China. （Ho, 1967：145）

何丙郁教授充分肯定了该译本的可读性，认为这本书对中国 4 世纪的炼丹术和道教研究提供了颇有价值的权威信息。此外，虽然索安对该译本没有提供必要的学术注解颇为失望，但她并非完全否认魏鲁男这部译本的价值，在她看来：魏鲁男将"玄"、"玄道"、"微妙"和"天道"译为"上帝"（God），且将"真人"译为"上帝的子民"（God's Men）等，我们大可不必为该译本没有提供必要的学术注解而过分烦恼。新的详注译本，配上现有的索引，就可以成为有价值的参考著作（Seidel，1989：305）。这样的评价既肯定了魏鲁男译本的价值，同时也指出该译本的不足，需做进一步的补充完善。

第二节　基于魏鲁男《抱朴子内篇》英译本的翻译批评

尽管魏鲁男《抱朴子内篇》英译本从一开始起就因为没有注释而受到汉学家们的诟病，再加上秉持民族中心主义文化观的译者解读道教核心概念时缺失典籍翻译工作者须具备的文化自觉意识，导致他翻译时参照基督教信仰创设了各种不同属性的"上帝"形象，这种广泛利用西方的文化资源，如基督教文化、西方神话传说等诠释中国文化的杂合手法，体现了一位典型的民族中心主义译者的文化观，在文化多元并存的当今时代已变得不合时宜。然而，单从语言层面的翻译来说，魏鲁男在《抱朴子内篇》首译中为弥补中西文化差异搭建中西文化桥梁所做出的种种努力是值得肯定的（何立芳、李丝贝，2017a：82）。本节选取该译本中的《畅玄》和《微旨》两篇译文作为解析对象，对其展开翻译批评。因魏鲁男译本以清孙星衍平津馆校勘本《抱朴子内篇》为底本，原文和注释主要源自张松辉以孙星衍平津馆校勘本为底本的译注内容，注释部分还综合参考了邱风侠先生的《抱朴子内篇注译》和顾久先生的《抱朴子内篇全译》的内容。此外，本书作者在解析魏鲁男译本的合理翻译和问题翻译的同时，综合考察了其他译者的相关译文，在此基础之上尝试了这两篇内容的完整新译（详见附录Ⅰ和附录Ⅱ），因此本章在进行魏译本译文解析时，有时会附上本书作者的新译，供感兴趣的读者对照阅读。

一　魏鲁男《抱朴子内篇·畅玄》译文解析

《畅玄》是《抱朴子内篇》第一章，为该书的开宗明义篇。葛洪先寻出天地万物的本原、本体、规律来立本建基，称之曰"玄"（顾久，1995：1）。"玄"是由"道"推演出来的范畴，被看成是产生世界万物的总根源，是一个神秘莫测的精神实体，其哲学内涵与"道"相同，因此葛洪有时也将两者并列，合称"玄道"。"玄"不仅具备"道"的特征，而且也被赋予明显的宗教特征，被夸张神化了。

该篇从三个方面论证"玄"至高无上的地位，以此勉励人们立志修仙求道。这三个方面的内容分别为：（1）"玄"的基本特性；（2）世俗荣华之危害；（3）得道者和知足者的思想境界及外部表现。作者兼用比喻、对比的手法说明失道之俗人和得道之至人最后的结局完全不同，凡俗之人拥有的不过是渺小且得不到保障的荣华权势，只有玄道才是真正值得修习的大道。

葛洪借《畅玄》篇为他的神仙信仰寻求哲学理据。该篇最显著的语言特征是巧用典故、比喻、排比、夸张等修辞手法，将"道"的同义异名词"玄"这一抽象的哲学概念形象化，为推崇他的"玄道"之说，作者夸大地描述了"玄"的人格形象和神奇效能，翻译时需注意这些修辞用法所蕴涵的真实含义，不能只做字面解读。

[原文]

抱朴子曰："玄者，自然之始祖，而万殊之大宗也。[1]眇昧乎其深也，故称'微'焉。绵邈乎其远也，故称'妙'焉。[2]其高则冠盖乎九霄，其旷则笼罩乎八隅。[3]光乎日月，迅乎电驰。或倏烁而景逝，或飘滭而星流。或混漾于渊澄，或雰霏而云浮。[4]因兆类而为'有'，托潜寂而为'无'。[5]沦大幽而下沉，凌辰极而上游。[6]金石不能比其刚，湛露不能等其柔。[7]方而不矩，圆而不规。[8]来焉莫见，往焉莫追。乾以之高，坤以之卑。云以之行，雨以之施。[9]胞胎元一，范铸两仪。[10]吐纳大始，鼓冶亿类。[11]佪旋四七，匠成草昧。[12]辔策灵机，吹嘘四气。[13]幽括冲默，舒阐粲尉。[14]抑浊扬清，斟酌河渭。[15]增之不溢，挹之不匮。与之不荣，夺之不瘁。[16]故玄之所在，其乐不穷；玄之所去，器弊神逝。[17]

夫五声八音，清商流徵，损聪者也；[18]鲜华艳采，或丽炳烂，伤明者也;[19]宴安逸豫，清醪芳醴，乱性者也;[20]冶容媚姿，铅华素质，伐命者也。[21]其唯玄道，可与为永。[22]不知玄道者，虽顾眄为生杀之神器，唇吻为兴亡之关键;[23]绮榭俯临乎云雨，藻室华绿以参差;[24]组帐雾合，罗帱云离;[25]西、毛陈于闲房，金觞华以交驰;[26]清弦嘈囋以齐唱，郑舞纷绕以蛩蚝;[27]哀箫鸣以凌霞，羽盖浮于涟漪;[28]掇芳华于兰林之圃，弄红葩于积珠之池;[29]登峻则望远以忘百忧，临深则俯挚以遗朝饥;[30]入宴千门之焜煌，出骖朱轮之华仪。[31]然乐极则哀集，至盈必有亏;[32]故曲终则叹发，燕罢则心悲也。[33]寔理势之攸召，犹影响之相归也;[34]彼假借而非真，故物往若有遗也。[35]

夫玄道者，得之乎内，守之者外；用之者神，忘之者器，此思玄道之要言也。[36]得之者贵，不待黄钺之威;体之者富，不须难得之货。[37]高不可登，深不可测。乘流光，策飞景，凌六虚，贯涵溶。[38]出乎无上，入乎无下;经乎汗漫之门，游乎窈眇之野;[39]逍遥恍惚之中，倘佯仿佛之表。[40]咽九华于云端，咀六气于丹霞。[41]徘徊茫昧，翱翔希微；履略蜿虹，践跚旋玑。[42]此得之者也。

其次则真知足。知足者则能肥遁勿用，颐光山林。[43]纡鸾龙之翼于细介之伍，养浩然之气于蓬荜之中。[44]褴缕带索，不以贸龙章之晔晔也;[45]负步杖策，不以易结驷之骆驿也。[46]藏夜光于嵩岫，不受他山之攻;[47]沉灵甲于玄渊，以违钻灼之灾。[48]动息知止，无往不足。弃赫奕之朝华，避僨车之险路。[49]吟啸苍崖之间，而万物化为尘氛;怡颜丰柯之下，而朱户变为绳枢。[50]握耒甫田，而麾节忽若执鞭;[51]啜菽漱泉，而太牢同乎藜藿。[52]泰尔有余欢于无为之场，忻然齐贵贱于不争之地。[53]含醇守朴，无欲无忧，全真虚器，居平味淡。[54]恢恢荡荡，与浑成等其自然;浩浩茫茫，与造化钧其符契。[55]如暗如明，如浊如清;似迟而疾，似亏而盈。岂肯委尸祝之坐，释大匠之位，越樽俎以代无知之庖，舍绳墨而助伤手之工?[56]不以臭鼠之细琐，[57]而为庸夫之忧乐。藐然不喜流俗之誉，坦尔不惧雷同之毁。[58]不以外物汩其至精，不以利害污其纯粹也。[59]故穷富极贵，不足以诱之焉，其余何足以悦之乎?[60]直刃沸镬，不足以劫之焉，谤讟何足以戚之乎?[61]常无心于众烦，而未始与物杂也。[62]

若夫操隋珠以弹雀，舐秦痔以属车，[63]登朽缗以探巢，泳吕梁以求鱼，[64]旦为称孤之客，夕为狐鸟之余;[65]栋挠㯶覆，倾溺不振。盖世人之所为载驰企及，而达者之所为寒心而凄怆者也。[66] 故至人嘿《韶》、《夏》而韬藻梲；奋其六羽于五城之墟，而不烦衔芦之卫；[67] 翳其鳞角乎勿用之地，而不恃曲穴之备。[68] 俯无倨鹥之呼，仰无亢极之悔，[69] 人莫之识，邈矣，辽哉！"

[注释]①

1. 玄：道家术语，指玄妙之道。万殊：万般不同，多种多样。大宗：事物的本原。

2. 眇昧：高远而看不清。眇，通"渺"，深远。昧，不清楚。微：幽深微妙。绵邈：高远的样子。妙：意思与"微"近似。

3. 冠盖：像帽子一样盖在。九霄：九天云霄，指天的极高处。旷：空阔远大。八隅：八方。

4. 光：明亮。乎：介词，表比较，有"胜于"之义。倏烁：光线闪动的样子。景：日光。飘㵽：飘动。滉漾：水深广的样子。渊澄：清澈的深潭。雾霏：纷飞的样子。雾，同"氛"，雾气。

5. 因：附著。兆类：万物。兆，古代以"百万"或"亿万"为兆，极言其多。潜寂：深寂幽暗。有、无：均为哲学概念。有，指事物的存在，有"有形，有名，实有"等义；无，指事物的不存在，有"无形，无名，虚无"等义。《道德经》第四十章提出"天下万物生于有，有生于无"的观点，把"无"看作产生"有"的本原。

6. 沦：淹没，没落。大幽：北海。大幽本是传说中的国名，《山海经·海内经》："北海之内，有大幽之国。"辰极：指北极星。《尔雅·释天》："北极谓之北辰。"

7. 湛露：浓重的露水。

8. 矩、规：分别为画方、画圆的用具。

9. 乾：卦象名，象征天。坤：卦象名，象征地。卑：低下。

10. 胞胎元一：即"孕育元气"之义。胞胎，这里用作动词，当"孕育"讲。元一，教义名词，犹言元气，是产生和构成天地万物的原始

---

① 本节注释综合参考了邱凤侠《抱朴子内篇注译》（中国科学社会出版社2004年版）、顾久《抱朴子内篇全译》（贵州人民出版社1995年版）和张松辉《抱朴子内篇译注》（中华书局2011年版）的内容。

物质。范铸两仪：铸造天地。范，浇铸器物的模子。这里用作动词，与"铸"同义连用。两仪，指天地。《周易·系辞上》："易有太极，是生两仪。"

11. 吐纳：呼吸，这里比喻化育。大始：也作"太始"，即原始，元气开始形成万物的状态。《列子·天瑞》："太始者，形之始也。"鼓冶亿类：创造万物。鼓，为冶炼而鼓风。冶，冶炼。亿类，万物。

12. 佪旋四七：指天上星宿环绕天体运转。佪旋，环绕。四七，指二十八宿，这里泛指天上的星宿。匠成：培养造就。草昧：天地初开时的混沌状态。

13. 辔策：驾驭，驱使。辔，马缰绳。策，马鞭。这里都用作动词。灵机：指神妙的天地造化之机。吹嘘四气：吹动着春夏秋冬四季之气。四气，春夏秋冬四时之气。

14. 幽括：囊括，蕴涵。冲默：清静谦和的品性。舒阐：抒发，表现。粲尉：鲜明浓盛的风格。

15. 抑浊扬清：使浊重的事物下降，使清轻的事物上扬。斟酌河渭：安排好了黄河和渭水。斟酌，安排。河渭，指黄河和渭水，黄河水浊，渭河水清。

16. 挹：舀，把水盛出来。匮：缺乏，引申为干涸。荣：兴盛。瘁：憔悴，毁坏。

17. 器：指有形的具体事物，如人的肉体。《周易·系辞上》："形而上者谓之道，形而下者谓之器。"神：指无形的抽象精神，如人的灵魂。《荀子·天论》："形具而神生。"

18. 五声：古代分音阶为宫、商、角、徵、羽五类，称为"五声"或"五音"。八音：指金、石、土、革、丝、木、匏、竹八种乐器。金指钟，石指磬，土指埙，革指鼓，丝指琴瑟，木指柷敔，匏指竽笙，竹指箫管。清商流徵：清商和流徵都是我国古代汉族民间音乐，这里泛指动听的音乐。聪：听力。

19. 彧丽：文采繁盛的样子。炳烂：明亮光明的样子。明：视力。

20. 宴安：安逸。逸豫：安乐。清醪芳醴：泛指酒。醪，本指汁滓混合的酒，即酒酿，引申为浊酒。醴，甜酒。

21. 冶容媚姿：艳丽的容貌，妩媚的身姿。铅华素质：精心装扮和不加修饰的天生丽质。铅华，抹脸的粉。素质，白色的皮肤。伐命：伤害生命。

22. 玄道：谓玄妙之道，即道，指玄一之道。可与为永：可以与大道永远相处。

23. 顾眄：看一眼。顾，回头看。眄，斜视。神器：出自《道德经》第二十九章："将欲取天下而为之，吾见其不得已。天下神器，不可为也，不可执也。"指帝位和政权。唇吻：指嘴唇。这里指代言语。关键：指重要的权位。

24. 绮榭：华美的台榭。藻室：修饰华丽的屋舍。华绿：红花绿叶。指各种华美的图案。华，花。参差：高低错落。

25. 组：用丝织成的带子，用来系东西。罗，丝织物类名。帱，同"裯"，帐子。组帐、罗帱为同义词组，皆指丝织的帷帐。离：通"丽"，附着，笼罩。

26. 西、毛：西施、毛嫱，古代著名美女，这里泛指美女。金觯：金制的酒器。觯，古代喝酒用的酒器。交驰：指手握酒杯你来我往，相互劝酒。

27. 清弦：清亮的琴声。嘈囋：嘈杂，喧闹。郑舞：古代郑国仕女的舞蹈。这里泛指舞蹈。纷緌：纷纭杂沓。蜲蛇：舞步委婉的样子。

28. 羽盖：用羽毛装饰的车盖，这里应该指船篷。涟漪：水面上的波纹。

29. 掇：采摘，拾取。芳华：芳香的花朵。囿：蓄养鸟兽的园子。兰林：古代宫苑名。积珠：可能为古代殿阁名。

30. 擥：同"览"，观赏。遗：遗忘。

31. 千门：指皇宫。焜煌：光耀夺目。駈：同"驱"。朱轮：古时达官贵人所乘之车。

32. 集：会聚，会和。亏：衰落，亏损。

33. 燕：通"宴"，宴会。

34. 寔：此，这。理势：事物发展的自然趋势。攸：相当于代词"所"。影响：影子和回响。相归：指身影与身体、回响与呼声相互追随。

35. 彼：指上文提到的荣华富贵。假借：虚假的短暂存在。物：指所谈的真正事物。遗：怅然若失。

36. 守之者外：与"得之乎内"结构相同，当为"守之乎外"；内：内里，这里是指人的内心。外：外部，这里是指外部行为。神：指有神妙的作用。忘：同"亡"。器：这里是指人的肉体。

37. 黄钺：以黄金为饰之钺。最初为天子所用，后世作为帝王之仪仗。有时遣大臣出师，亦假以黄钺以示威重。体：体会。难得之货：这里是指奇异的珍宝。

38. 乘：追逐。流光：指月光。策：驾驭。飞景：这里指飞驰的日光。六虚：上下四方，指整个宇宙空间。贯涵溶：贯穿宇宙。涵溶，原意为包容，引申为包容万类的宇宙。

39. 无上：至高。无下：最深。汗漫：无边无际。窈眇：美妙。引申为幽暗玄妙。

40. 逍遥：自由自在的样子。恍惚：隐约不清。倘佯：同"徜徉"，自由往来的样子。仿佛：迷茫恍惚的样子。表：……之外。

41. 咽：吞咽。九华：日月之精华。六气：天地四时之气。

42. 茫昧：幽暗不清。希微：空虚寂静。《道德经》第十四章："听之不闻，名曰希，搏之不得，名曰微。"河上公注："无声曰希，无形曰微。"履略：脚踏，巡游。蜿虹：弯曲的彩虹。践蹦：脚踏。旋玑：旋，通"璇"，璇玑，即魁星，北斗七星中形成斗形的四颗星。这里代指北斗星。

43. 肥遁：亦作"飞遁"，隐居。后因称退隐为肥遁。勿用：不为世俗所用，即"不出仕"。颐光：和"韬光"的意思相近，指韬光养晦以修身养性。颐，养，保养。

44. 纡：绾系，收敛。鸾：传说中的凤凰一样的神鸟。细介：细小。介，指微不足道的鸟兽。浩然之气：原为孟子用语，《孟子·公孙丑上章》："我善养浩然之气。"这种"气"是一种主观的精神状态，后世把"浩然之气"理解为一种最高的正气和节操，即正大刚直之气。蓬荜："蓬门荜户"的略语，比喻穷人住的房子。蓬，蓬草。荜，同"筚"，用荆棘树枝编成的门、篱笆等。

45. 带索：以绳索为带，形容贫穷。贸：交换。龙章：带龙形图案的衣服，古代用于帝王诸侯的礼服，也称龙衮。昈晔：光彩鲜明的样子。

46. 负步杖策：背着重物拄着竹杖走路。策，这里指竹杖。驷：古代一车套四马。骆驿：同"络绎"，往来不绝。

47. 夜光：即夜光璧，宝玉名。这里泛指宝玉。嵩岫：高山峻岭。他山之攻：《诗经·小雅·鹤鸣》："他山之石，可以攻玉。"意思是说别的山上的石头用来作琢磨玉器的砺石。攻，制造，加工，引申为琢磨。

48. 灵甲：龟甲。古代人认为乌龟是灵异的动物，并用它的甲占卜，所以称"灵甲"。玄渊：深渊。讳：回避，脱离。钻灼：钻凿，炙烧。这里是指古代占卜把龟甲钻孔烧烤后，观其裂纹，以断恶吉。

49. 赫奕：显耀盛大。朝华：早晨片刻间盛开的鲜花。比喻短暂的荣华富贵。华，花。偾：倾覆。

50. 尘氛：即尘土。怡颜：和悦的容颜。丰柯：茂盛的枝条。代指茂密的森林。柯，树枝。朱户：漆成红色的门，指王侯贵族的住宅，比喻富贵。绳枢：用绳子系门代替门枢，比喻贫穷。

51. 耒：一种农具。甫田：大田。麾节：将帅用来指挥、调动军队的旌旗和符节。忽若：就好像。

52. 啜荈漱泉：啜，饮。荈，晚采的茶。漱，喝。太牢：本指古代祭祀时盛放牛羊猪三牲的器皿，后来多用"太牢"指丰盛的食物。藜藿：两种野菜名，多用以指穷困者的食物。

53. 泰尔：泰然。余欢：很多的快乐。忻然：即欣然，高兴的样子，忻，同"欣"。齐：等。不争：指顺应时变以静待，不是超然实际地去强求。

54. 含醇守朴：坚守淳朴的天性。醇，淳朴。全真：保全真性。真，本原，自身。《庄子·秋水》："谨守而勿失，是谓反其真。"虚器：看轻身外之物。器，指外在的东西。

55. 恢恢荡荡、浩浩茫茫：两者为同义词，均有宽阔宏大之义。浑成：浑然而成，这里代指大道。《道德经》第二十五章："有物混成，先天地生。"这个浑然而成的"物"就指大道。造化：创造化育，也指天地自然。钧：通"均"。符契：符节。古人朝廷用作凭证的信物。这里代指诚信。

56. 委：抛弃。尸祝：古人祭祀时任尸和祝的人。尸，代表鬼神受享祭的人。祝，传告鬼神言辞的人。坐：座位。释：放弃。大匠：技艺高超的工匠。樽俎：同"尊俎"，古代用以祭祀的酒器和盛肉的器皿。庖：

厨师。《庄子·逍遥游》:"庖人虽不治庖,尸祝不越樽俎而代之矣。"意思是:厨师即使不去做厨房的事情,尸祝也不会越过樽俎而去代替他做。绳墨:木匠画直线用的工具。《孟子·尽心上》:"大匠不为拙工改废绳墨"。

57. 臭鼠:腐烂的老鼠,比喻世人追逐的功名利禄。细琐:细小琐碎的事物。

58. 藐然:藐视的样子。流俗:世俗。坦尔:坦荡,坦然。雷同之毁:众口一致的毁谤。

59. 汩:扰乱。至精:至高无上的精神境界。纯粹:纯正不杂。引申指德行完美无缺。

60. 穷富:极其富有。悦之:使他感到高兴。

61. 直刃:利刃。沸镬:装满沸腾开水的大锅。镬,古代的一种大锅。古代有一种酷刑是把人放在煮沸的镬里煮死,叫作"烹"。劫:胁迫。谤讟:非议,诽谤。

62. 无心:无成心,事出自然,初本无意。众烦:众多的烦恼。与物杂:与外界事物混杂在一起。

63. 操隋珠以弹雀:出自《庄子·让王》:"今且有人于此,以隋侯之珠弹千仞之雀,世必笑之。是何也?则以其所用者重而所要者轻也。"比喻做事不知衡量轻重,因而得不偿失。本句用"隋侯珠"(古代传说中的明珠)比喻宝贵的生命,用"雀"比喻不值得追求的富贵名利。

舐秦痔以属车:出自《庄子·列御寇》:"秦王有病召医,破痈溃痤者得车一乘;舐痔者得车五乘,所治愈下,得车愈多。"后以舐痔比喻谄媚之徒趋炎附势的卑劣行为。舐,舔。属车,古代皇帝出行时跟从的车队。

64. 朽缗:朽烂的绳子。缗,穿线的绳子。敦煌本作"朽条"。探巢:掏鸟窝。吕梁:地名,位于今山西省中部西南侧,该地水势汹涌,为鱼不可游之处。《庄子·达生》这样记述这里的水流:"县水三十仞,流沫四十里,鼋鼍鱼鳖之所不能游也。"

65. 称孤:指帝王。中国历代帝王都自称"孤"或"寡人"。《道德经》第三十九章:"故贵以贱为本,高以下为基。是以侯王自称孤、寡、不谷。"狐鸟:这里泛指鸟兽。余:末流。

第七章　道教综合类文本《抱朴子内篇》翻译研究　　237

66. 栋挠悚覆：栋梁折断，鼎中之物倒出来，比喻社稷灭亡。倾溺：倾覆淹没。比喻国家灭亡。载驰，驾车奔趋，形容急切的样子。企及：努力达到。指努力追逐荣华富贵。达者：贤明通达之人。也即得道之人。凄怆：伤心悲痛。

67. 至人：古代用以指思想道德等某方面达到最高境界的人。嘿：通"默"，沉默不语。《韶》《夏》：都是古代优美的音乐名。这里用来比喻卓越的才能。韬：掩藏，掩盖。藻棁：画有彩饰的短柱，是天子的庙饰。六羽：鸟羽上的健翅，这里即指翅膀。五城：昆仑山的五座城池。指天上神仙所居住的地方。墟：地方。烦：烦劳。

68. 翳：掩盖。鳞角：代指龙。曲：深隐之处。

69. 倨鸱之呼：蹲坐在地上的猫头鹰发出的惊呼声。比喻人们担心失去富贵时发出的恐吓声。倨，通"踞"，蹲坐。鸱，通"鸥"，即猫头鹰。亢极之悔：物盛必衰的懊悔。

［译文］

God（the Mystery）Defined[1]

God IS THE FIRST ancestor to nature, the grandsire of all the different empiricals. God's depth being such as to make us squint and see obscurely, the epithet subtle may be used. God's length being so great, we may well speak of marvelousness. God is so high that even the ninth heaven is topped; so broad that all space is encompassed.[2] God is brighter than the sun or moon; speedier than lightning or the fleet steed. Sometimes God passes by as a flash of light; or blows and spouts in a show of stars. God is vaster and deeper than the deepest pool of pure water; and then again, God is the mist or snow, and the floating clouds.[3] In the million various things, God is empirical existence; in the secret and the silent, God is perfect freedom.[4] Plunged into the abyss "Big Obscure," God sinks to the bottom of the universe; rising to the celestial pole, God soars at its top.[5] Metal and stone are no analogy for God's hardness; nor are the wet and the dew any comparison for God's softness. God is square, but no carpenter's square has been applied; God is round, but there has been no compass.[6] Nobody sees whence God comes, and nobody follows where God goes. Through

God heaven is lofty and earth low. Through God the clouds move and rain is dispensed.[7]

God enwombed Primal Unity and cast in their mold the two symbols (the straight line, either whole or broken at the middle, = *yang* and *yin*). God breathed forth Grand Beginning and forged the thousands of genera. God turns the cycle of the 28 celestial mansions and fashions the beginning of things.[8] God is the reins and the whip for the whole complex of spiritual powers and blows the breaths characterizing the four seasons. God holds in subtle embrace all vast, silent space; enfolds in relaxed embrace all that is brilliant. Suppressing the turbid and promoting the clear, God distinguishes between the muddy Yellow River and its limpid affluent, the Wei.[9] Additions do not make God overflow, nor do withdrawals exhaust God. What is given does not glorify God. Depredations do God no harm. Therefore, where God is present, joy is inexhaustible; whomever God abandons finds his body declining and his inner gods departing.[10]

Distinguishing of the five notes, the eight instruments, and the various musical modes wears away our hearing.[11] Ornamentation with all its variety and beauty with its brilliance harm our eyesight. Festive gatherings, leisure, indulgence, and drinking throw our very natures into disorder. Lovely faces, fair skins artfully painted, erode our very lives. It is only with the Mystery that is God that there can be permanence. For those who do not grasp this Mystery, a mere glance may become the potent instrument of life or death; lips can become the key to rise or fall.[12]

Our pavilions of catalpa loom like the Milky Way; our decorated rooms are as beautiful as Orion and Scorpio. Sheathings are woven as light as mists; coverings, fluffy as clouds. Beauties like His-shih and Mao Ch'iang are displayed in our living rooms. Our metal goblets are adorned with intertwined, prancing steeds. The strings of our lutes reverberate clearly to the songs of Ch'i; Cheng dancers twist and turn in profusion. Flutes sound mournfully to high heaven; feather canopies float and ripple in the breezes. We pluck fragrant blossoms from gardens abounding in fragrances; toy with a red flower in pools of pearl.

We scale cliffs to gaze into the distance and forget our worries; search the valley depths for things that will allay our morning hunger. At home, banquets are served in resplendent abodes of a thousand doors; abroad, we race vehicles elegant with their red wheels. [13]

When joy has attained culmination, however, grief ensues; perfect fullness is bound to be followed by deficiency. When the song is ended, sighs are heard; when the feasting is over, hearts turn sad. Truly the evocations of logical situations are as closely knitted to their sources as shadows and echoes. Being artifice and unreal, all these activities, when ended, leave a void. [14] The Mystery that is God is attained within, but lost through externals. God's users become veritable gods; God's forgettors, instrumentalities. Thus I feel that God has been put to you succinctly. [15]

God's possessor will be honored even without the prestige of the gilt ax as badge of office. Who embodies God is rich, he needs no rarities. The eminence of such a man is not to be scaled; his depth is not to be plumbed. Borne on streams of light and plying the whip to flying rays, he traverses all space and pierces the floods. He exits through the zenith and enters through the nadir. He passes through the gateway of the Boundless and travels in fields of peace and beauty. He takes diversion in God (the Vague and Confused); he comes and goes far beyond all normal coming and going. He enthroats all the beautiful things at the very edge of the clouds; he tastes the six breaths of the universe at the red cloud accompanying the sun. He sojourns in God (the Obscure); he soars in God (the Infinitesimal). He travels the rainbow; he treads the celestial sphere. Such is the man who has found God. [16]

Second to him stands the man who really knows how to be satisfied. Such a man can find happiness in uselessness and cultivate his affairs in the mountains and forests. He deploys his phoenix-dragon wings in the company of simple folk and nourishes his overwhelming vitality in a humble cottage. [17] His garments may be patched and his belt a rope, but he would not exchange them for all the glory of the imperial robes. He may walk with a load on his back and use a branch for his staff, but he would not change this for the social cachet of four-horse teams. [18] He lets gems remain in Mount Sung's peak so that they will not be worked on the grindstone. He lets tortoise shells sink into the dark depths so that they will not suffer the drillings and scorching of diviners. [19] Whether active or resting, he knows when to stop; he is satisfied wherever he goes. [20] He casts aside the brief bloom of radiant beauty; he shuns the dangerous routes where vehicles overturn. As he hums and whistles among the verdant cliffs, all creation becomes for him but dust and evil air. [21]

He relaxes under thick branches, and the red doors of palatial homes are then seen to pivot on rope. He grasps the plow to help in the tillage, and immediately the banners of the military and the diplomas of office become no more than the whip in his grasp. He drinks tea and rinses his mouth from the spring, whereupon the suovetaurilia become as mere herb soups. [22] Grandly, in the seasons of leisure, he finds pleasure in the arena of action that is perfect freedom. Joyfully, he equates honors and low estate where there is no rivalry. As he partakes of pure drink and maintains simplicity, he is free from covetousness and worry. Maintaining God (Truth) intact and staying uncommitted, he leads the simple life. Partaking of its immensity and movement, he makes his naturalness one with the whirl of all nature. [23] Despite its vastness and confusion, he comes to terms with creation, whether dark, bright, murky, or pure. While seeming dilatory, he is quick; he looks empty, but he is really full. [24] He refuse to quit his post of master craftsman for the worldly tasks of corpse-representative or cantor; he refuses to disregard the cauldrons and other vessels of religious ceremony and take the place of the ignorant cook, and to reject the guidelines and help with work that could hurt his hands. [25] He does not engage in the sorrows and joys of an employee for a putrid pittance of a salary. Uninvolved, he finds no joy in the approval of the crowds; in his tranquility, he does not fear being criticized for plagiarism. [26] It is not for externals that he would dissipate the best of himself; it is not for profits and losses that he would soil his native purity. Therefore, since he cannot be lured from his chosen path by great riches or the highest honors, how can other things beguile him? Since he is not to be coerced by naked blades or boiling cauldrons, how can slander affect him? With never a thought for life's vexations, he is never one with created things.

To use Marquis Sui's gem to shoot a bird, lick the Lord of Ch'in's piles to amass vehicles, climb a rotten rope to view a nest, ford the weir of Lü to fish, be a prince at dawn but one with the foxes and birds by nightfall—these are instances of irretrievable loss, where the beams have warped and the soup has been spilled.[27] One might say that men of the world act with precipitation and are eager to arrive, but the wise man acts with coolness and melancholy.[28] Therefore, man in his highest form plays no official role in the state religious services and eliminates luxuries. Like a prince, he employs his own six rows of dancers in his religious services at that distant city of the mind Wu-ch'eng; therefore he need not take precautions against critics. Dragons that he is among men, he conceals his scales and horns at Useless where there is no need to trust to paltry lairs. When he looks down, it is not with a hoot of disdain; when he looks up, it is not with ambition which he will have cause to repent. Nobody recognizes him. He is far, far removed and aloof![29] (Ware, 1966: 28 – 32)

[解析]

1. 魏鲁男将篇名译为 God (the Mystery) Defined, 虽在括号补充了"玄"所包含的诸多内涵之一, 即"幽远之道"(the Mystery), 但主观上仍是把"玄"等同于基督教的"上帝"。这种深受民族中心主义思想影响的典型作法导致他在翻译《抱朴子内篇》时把但凡涉及"玄""道""一"这些表达宇宙本原的道教哲学范畴对译为 God。

其实,"玄"本是用以描述"道""德"的形容词, 比如,"玄德"即玄秘深邃之德; 在"玄之又玄, 众妙之门"(《道德经》第一章) 这一句中,"玄"只是"道"的一个重要特征, 有"幽深冥远"的意思。道教产生后,"玄"被沿用作为其教义思想的重要内容。葛洪为建构道教理论体系, 将"玄"拟定为宇宙的本原实体,"玄""道"也就成了异名同义词, 所以有时他把"玄"与"道"连言, 称"玄道"。不过, 葛洪只是借用《易经》《道德经》《庄子》中的概念记述其神仙思想, 而这些概念在《抱朴子内篇》中的应用语境已发生了改变, 其内涵已有明显不同。结合《畅玄》正文中的内容,"玄"字至少有三层意思: 第一, 万物之本原也; 第二, 妙也; 第三, 幽远也。尽管中外译者在英译《道德经》中

"玄"字时多用"mystery"一词，但是单单一个"mystery"无法表达上述三层意思。

翻译中国文化典籍中的基本术语和关键词语一直都是一个复杂而棘手的问题，这些含义丰富的概念很难在一个上下文中给出完整而确切的印象，如英语世界对"道"的理解就各说不一，有译为"Reason""Way""Nature""Path""Road""Guide""Law"的，也有选择音译"Tao"或"Dao"的，甚而有别出心裁译为"Way-making"的，虽各自都陈述了这样那样的理由，但没有一个能保证是完备而确切地反映了"道"的丰富含义。汉学泰斗理雅各首次选择音译法翻译"道"，他的理由如下。

> The Tâo therefore is a phenomenon; not a positive being, but a mode of being. Lâo's idea of it may become plainer as we proceed to other points of his system. In the meantime, the best way of dealing with it in translating is to transfer it to the version, instead of trying to introduce an English equivalent for it. （Legge, 1891：15）

在理雅各看来，随着阅读的深入，老子有关"道"的思想会越来越清楚，既然在英语中难以找到一个合适的对等词，用音译移植即是最佳方案。当今英语世界普遍也接受"道"的音译词"Tao"或"Dao"。对"玄"的翻译不妨也借鉴海外学者对"道"的音译法，用括号补充"玄"的语用意义，因此标题《畅玄》可以改译为：Xuan（玄，the Mystery）Defined，相信读者通过阅读葛洪对"玄"的基本特征及功用的具体描述，能获得这一与"道"同义异名的术语概念的内涵意义。

2. 该句从宇宙生成的角度阐释"玄"的超越状态，"深""远""高""旷"皆为"玄"的显性特征，这里仍沿用《道德经》中关于玄道之"微""妙"的说法。译者保留了原文的句式，对这些特征描述词一一对应为"depth""length""high""broad"，形意兼顾，忠实传达原文之含义。同理，"九霄"即九天，为天之最高处，"八隅"指八方，包括四方、四隅，译者分别译为"the ninth heaven"和"all space"。只是直译"九天"而无必要的解释会让英语读者不得其解，不妨省去中国特有的数字文化概念，泛化为"heaven's high"。

3. 古汉语常利用名词进行重复，重复结构较多，英译时常将重复的名词转换为代词。依照汉语重复的特点，可考虑采用类似的结构。该句采用明喻的修辞手法描述"玄"之特征，意思为：（玄）有时如日光一样忽闪忽灭，有时如流星一样飘摇而过。有时深广如澄澈的深渊，有时纷飞如飘动的浮云。翻译时可以直接处理为明喻，也可译成暗喻。魏译本除了武断地将"玄"等同于基督教之上帝（God）之外，有些译文过分拘泥于汉语字词的词典意义，如将"飘渺"译为"blows and spouts"；将"滉漾于渊澄"译为"God is vaster and deeper than the deepest pool of pure water"；将"雾霏"（纷飞的意思）译为"God is the mist or snow"。可改译为：Xuan has many external yet physical forms and characters. Its glory may be brighter than the sun and the moon combined while its speed of shaping this world may be faster than lightening. It can be the flashing sunlight or the shooting stars. It can be the unfathomable sea. It can also be the drifting clouds。其中"Xuan has many external yet physical forms and characters"为增译内容，有提挈主旨之用。

4. 老子把"无"看作产生"有"的本原，指出"反者道之动，弱者道之用。天下万物生于有，有生于无"（《道德经》第四十章）。葛洪在该篇中提出的"玄"在义理架构上包括老子的哲学概念"有"和"无"。这里的"有"指事物的存在，有"有形，有名，实有"等义；"无"指事物的不存在，有"无形，无名，虚无"等义。《道德经》英译者倾向于采用西方哲学概念"Being"（存在）和"Non-being"（非存在，无）翻译"有""无"这对哲学概念。如汉学家梅维恒将"反者道之动，弱者道之用。天下万物生于有，有生于无"译为：Reversal is the movement of the Way; Weakness is the usage of the Way. All creatures under heaven are born from being; Being is born from non-being（Mair, 1990：7），同样也是借用西方哲学中的这一对概念。

原文"因兆类而为有，托潜寂而为无"谈论的是"玄"的显现模式，意思："玄"附着于宇宙万物之上便呈现为"有"（存在），托身于深寂幽暗中就转化为"无"（虚无），魏译本解读：In the million various things, God is empirical existence; in the secret and silent, God is perfect freedom，没有凸显"有""无"这对哲学概念应有的内涵。可参照上文中对"玄"的音译加注法,将该句改译为: The being (*You* 有, meaning existence) can be realized via all of those external characters that are physically perceivable by the mind of human beings. The non-being (*Wu* 无, meaning non-existence) is when *Xuan* presents itself in an internal way。

5. 大幽:传说中的国名,意即大冥,北方极阴之地。冥,深深的海。据此,魏译本译为 the abyss "Big Obscure",按部就班将"大幽"处理为专有名词,通过添加"abyss"(深渊)说明其地理特征,也算忠实传译了原文信息,但原文的真实意蕴没有说透,因此同样需要增译。可以添加"metaphysically intangible",以补充原文主旨。改译为:and is metaphysically intangible in that it plunges into the abyssal buttom or soars beyond the celestial stars。

6. 矩、规:分别为画方、画圆的用具。矩,曲尺。规,圆规。《孟子·离娄上》:"离娄之明,公输子之巧,不以规矩,不能成方圆。"汉学家理雅各将该句译为 Mencius said, "The power of vision of Lî Lâu, and skill of hand of Kung-shû, without the compass and the square, could not form squares and circles" (Legge, 1895),其中用直译的方法英译"矩"和"规"。

"规""矩"的指示意义是校正圆形、方形的两种工具,多被引申为"法则、标准"等意,本段的"方而不矩,圆而不规"依然说的是"玄"的特性,翻译为白话文:它有时呈现出方形,却不能用矩尺来丈量;它有时呈现出圆形,又不能用圆规来测定。魏译本采用直译,保留了原文的文体特征,但语用意义凸显不够。可改为:It may be round or square, but neither the compass nor the square can be applied to it. In this sense, *Xuan* has no rules。这里添加"*Xuan* has no rules"("玄"不受定规约束),显现其语用意义,并通过"In this sense"与上文形成关联。

7. 原文借用《易经》的乾(天)、坤(地)概念从宇宙生成和运行角度论说作为宇宙万物本原之"玄"的超越状态。天高、地卑、云行、雨施不过是"玄"生成宇宙和运行宇宙的四个具体表象。除了该句补充的施事者"玄"的译文"God"不妥之外,魏译本该句的选词遣句均值得借鉴,若改译为 Yet it gives the unshakable harmony to the world that heav-

en is lofty and earth low, that the clouds move and rain is dispensed，原文的语用意义就更凸显了。

8. 胞胎，这里用作动词，当"孕育"讲，译为"enwormbed"非常形象，也可译为"nurturing"。元一，教义名词，特指元气，是产生和构成天地万物的原始物质，仅直译为"Primal Unity"无法达其要旨，可改译为"the primordial beginning of universe"。同理，两仪，指天地，范铸两仪即铸造天地。大始，也作"太始"，即原始，指元气开始形成万物的状态。魏译本皆用直译，分别译为"two symbols"和"Grand Beginning"，虽然补充了"天地即阴阳"这样的信息，但未能理清"两仪""元一""大始"之间的关系。这里可采用合译的方法将"胞胎元一，范铸两仪。吐纳大始，鼓冶亿类"译为"By nurturing the primordial beginning of universe, *Xuan* turns the world into a being that sustains the thriving of the livings"。四七：指二十八宿，这里泛指天上的星宿，因此可译为"the constellations"。草昧，指天地初开时的混沌状态，译为"the chaotic existence of world"。"辔策灵机"本意为"驾驭天地造化之机"，"吹嘘四气"则指"吹动春夏秋冬四时之气"，采用点化的手段译为"It determines the dawn of time and seasons the weather"更能达意。

9. 王明认为"幽"为"函"之讹，"幽括"即为"囊括，蕴涵"之义（王明，1985：5）。冲默：襟怀淡泊，语言缄默。说的是"玄"的品质。舒阐：抒发，表现。粲尉：鲜明浓盛的风格。讲的是"玄"的功用。河渭，指黄河和渭水，渭水为黄河的支流，黄河浊，渭水清。"抑浊扬清"为"玄"之特质，"斟酌河渭"为"玄"之功能，两者暗含因果关系，意指它既蕴涵着清静谦和的品性，也能表现出鲜明浓盛的风格。它抑浊扬清，于是编排了黄河、渭水的产生。魏译文与原意有明显差异，将该译文回译，即上帝拥有整个广阔、静谧的空间，将一切辉煌之物随意揽入怀抱。它抑浊扬清，将浑浊的黄河和清澈的渭水区分开来。完全偏离了这里是在论说"玄"之"幽括冲默""抑浊扬清"之品性。因此改译为"It gives vent to its feelings brilliantly despite of the fact that it is aloof from the worldly affairs. As such, *Xuan* suppresses the turbid and promotes the clear, distinguishing the muddy Yellow River from its limpid affluent, the Wei River"。

10. 该句与下句"故玄之所在……器弊神逝"共同构成该篇第一部分的总结句。其中"增"与"挹"、"溢"与"匮"、"与"与"夺"、"荣"与"瘁"为反义项，魏译本分别对应为 additions, withdrawals, overflow, exhaust, what is given, depredations, glorify, harm, 均为绝妙的选词。既然是总结句，我们可以添加"The essence of *Xuan* forms the perfect equilibrium in the universe"，以凸显段落主题。还可用 neither, nor, or 这些连词使这些反义项之间的关系更紧凑，因此改译为 The essence of *Xuan* forms the perfect equilibrium in the universe. Not a bestowment or a depredation can glorify or harm this equilibrium, nor can any tithe of additions or withdrawals make it overflow or exhausted。

11. 葛洪反对人们在世上恣情纵欲，引导人们抛弃世俗的荣华富贵，净化自己的思想向神仙境界飞跃，这便是道士修仙思玄体道的过程，只有体得了玄道的人才能进入神仙世界。"夫"用在句首，为汉语发语词，常依此判断为另一段的开始，英译时不必译出。"五声八音，清商流徵"分别指代中国古代音阶、乐器和民间音乐，因其复杂的内涵这里只能变通浅化，魏译文"the five notes, the eight instruments, and the various musical modes"采用的也是这种策略，也可译为"the musical instruments that we create and the melodies that these instruments subsequently produce"。原文句式对仗，堆砌辞藻，翻译这样的骈文时不必拘泥于字面，可适当运用浅化法，译出基本意思即可。英文段落常有主题句，这里可添加"The dissipation that we lust for is destructive to our sensibility and ethics"作为该段的主题句，以开宗明义。

12. 据王明《抱朴子内篇校释》中注："句下刻本有'难与为之'四字"（王明，1985：57），"不知玄道者"后需补上这四个字，据此应增加"will be condemned by the nature"，以获得语义逻辑上的完整。"虽顾眄为生杀之神器，唇吻为兴亡之关键"意思是说，即便是掌握了生杀大权占有重要的权位。魏译本译为"For those who do not grasp this Mystery, a mere glance may become the potent instrument of life or death; lips can become the key to rise or fall"，回译过来就是：对于不懂玄道的人而言，一个眼神就可以决定人之生死，一动嘴唇便能主宰天之沉浮。与下文所指不符。这里需综合文意进行合译。可改译为"Those who cannot realize the way of

Xuan will be condemned by the nature even though they could be so powerful that a mere glance of them becomes a potent weapon to kill a person or a slight movement of their lips the key to decide the rise and fall of a nation"。

13. 该段文字充分利用骈俪文体的特点，把"不知玄道者"的奢靡生活描绘得淋漓尽致。葛洪用对比的手法，以点明凡俗之人无非占有富贵权势，这种状态是渺小的，同时也是没有保障的，因此英译时人称代词用第三人称更符合语境，魏译本中用第一人称是不准确的。葛洪沿用了一些文化典故，例如，"西、毛"本指中国古代著名的美女西施和毛嫱，这里泛指美女；"兰林""积珠"为古代宫苑、殿阁名，引申意义为名贵华丽之处，用以比喻极度的奢靡豪华。原文还有许多具体形象的意象描述，例如，"哀箫鸣以凌霞，羽盖浮于涟漪；掇芳华于兰林之囿，弄红葩于积珠之池"，等等，翻译时只需翻译出原文的所指。

尽管魏译本在遣词造句上不乏许多妙语，如"榭"对应译为"pavilions of catalpa"（梓亭），"云雨"（据考证应为"云汉"，指银河）译为"the Milky Way"，将高低错落的华丽屋舍比拟为黄道十二宫（即西方占星学的十二星座）中的"Orion and Scorpio"（猎户座和天蝎座），方便了目的语读者的理解，"组帐雾合，罗帱云离"的译文"Sheathings are woven as light as mists; coverings, fluffy as clouds"也传译出原文所想表达的"华美的帷帐如轻雾聚合，锦罗的绣幕像彩云相并"这样的气势，但将"西、毛陈于闲房，金觞华以交驰"翻译为"Beauties like Hsi-shih and Mao Ch'iang are displayed in our living rooms. Our metal goblets are adorned with intertwined, prancing steeds"（Ware，1966：29），译者的理解：我们的客厅里摆放着像西施和毛嫱这样的美人，我们的金属高脚杯上装饰着盘绕在一起的奔腾的骏马。这样的翻译就有点流于表面，而未达原文之意了。原文的意思：身旁有像西施和毛嫱这样的美人聚集闲房，每天拿着金光闪耀的金属酒杯与人交杯畅饮。至于"清弦嘈囋以齐唱，郑舞纷绥以蜲蛇"的译文"The strings of our lutes reverberate clearly to the songs of Ch'i; Cheng dancers twist and turn in profusion"中"齐唱"（齐声欢唱）理解为"the songs of Ch'i"（齐之歌），不光有流于字面意义的问题，同样还有误读误译的问题。该句西施、毛嫱都是中国古代著名的美女，用"beauty"一词足以让读者清楚明白，"郑舞"指古代郑国仕女的舞蹈，但如果只是译为"Cheng dancers"而不加任何注释，读者肯定无法理解其蕴含的意思，因这里泛指舞蹈，完全可以省译"郑国"这一概念，译为"dancers"即可。该段可改译如下。

  Materialistically, these people could be rich and prosperous. Their properties might be vast. They could own great mansions that tower into the sky. They could reside in majestic houses where beautiful drapes could be mistakenly seen as clouds and mists from a far distance. They could have their beauties inside the living rooms and drink to their hearts with golden goblets in the hands. They could feast on the clear and loud music. They could make merry with the accompaniment of dancers. They could pluck fragrant blossoms from gardens abounding in fragrances and toy with red flowers in pools of pearl. They could forget their worries and anxieties in mountain climbing and sightseeing. They could dine in the most glorified chambers and travel in the most luxurious coaches that are drawn by the purest breed of horses. In a word, they could permit themselves in dissipation and abandon the simple life that is the way of *Xuan*.

其中增译"In a word, they could permit themselves in dissipation and abandon the simple life that is the way of *Xuan*"是对前文叙述要点的总结，也为下文引出作者的观点做好铺垫。

  14. 据《淮南子·道应训》载："夫物盛而衰，乐极则悲。"原文"乐极则哀集，至盈必有亏"用"至盈必有亏"的常理说明"不知玄道者"如果快乐到了极点，就可能要发生悲伤之事。紧接其后则描述了曲终宴散之后这些人的感受，之间采用衔接词"故"以明示两句之间的因果关系，翻译时需理顺原文的逻辑。魏译文"When joy has attained culmination, however, grief ensues; perfect fullness is bound to be followed by deficiency. When the song is ended, signs are heard; when the feasting is over, hearts turns sad"（Ware，1966：30），虽然没有缺失原文的任何一点信息，但译者未能正确解读"乐极则哀集，至盈必有亏"之间的逻辑关系，也忽略了"故曲终则叹发，燕罢则心悲也"中的衔接词"故"，将该句视为上句的平行结构而非因果关系,因而该译文未能准确反映说话者的真实意图。

需指出的是,原文"寔理势之攸召,犹影响之相归也"运用比喻结构说明事物发展的自然趋势犹如影子和回响一样,是必然产生的结果,魏译文"Truly the evocations of logical situations are as closely knitted to their sources as shadows and echoes"(Ware,1966:30)不仅保留了原文的喻体"影"和"响",用"the evocations of logical situations"对应"理势之攸召",用"closely knitted to their sources"对应"相归",堪称形神皆似之妙译,值得我们学习。

15. 葛洪在上一段主要叙说"不知玄道者"的富贵权势不会永恒,而这一段则以"夫玄道者,得之乎内,守之者外,用之者神,忘之者器,此思玄道之要言也"开始叙述"得玄道"之妙用,意思:玄道,得到它在于内心领悟,而在身外守住它,善于运用它,就会神妙无穷,失掉它就剩下一个没有精神的躯壳,这就是思玄道的要点。葛洪所谓的"思玄道"就是用存思的方法体得玄道,那些体得玄道的人,同时也体得了超出人间世俗社会的富与贵(胡孚琛,1989:203)。魏译本错误地将本句作为上一段的总结,置于上一段段尾,其理解:"玄",也就是上帝,可从内心领悟,却从外面丢失。上帝的使用者变成了真正的神,上帝的遗忘者,则成为工具,这样描述已经很清楚了。译者理解的文意与原文作者意图完全不符,故将其放在下一段之首,译文可改为"While the way of *Xuan* is realized internally, its application is of external character. When applied skillfully, *Xuan* will exhibit its power directly into one's mind. But when such application fails, he will be trapped within his mortal yet fragile body. This is the fundamental logic that guides our interpretation of *Xuan*"。

16. 这段文字描述得玄道者的最高境界。原文"乘流光,策飞景,凌六虚,贯涵溶"指:(得玄道者)能乘坐流动的光线,驾驭飞扬的日光,凌越上下四方,贯穿宇宙万类。六虚,上下四方,指整个宇宙空间。涵溶,原意为包容,引申为包容万类的宇宙。英译时需翻译出"六虚""涵溶"的深层含义。魏译本该句的理解有误,将"涵溶"译为"the floods"(洪水),的确让人百思不得其解。无上:至高无上,喻指神仙所在的天外之天,为不可再高之处。无下:无比深,喻指地狱,为不能再深之处。

汗漫：无边无际的样子。魏译本选用英语词 zenith（最高点）、nadir（最低点）、boundless（无边无际的）与原文的"无上"、"无下"和"汗漫"虽然形成了概念意义上的绝对对等，但缺失了对这些词语伴随意义的挖掘。该段可改译为"Therefore, people who truly master the way of *Xuan* have the capability that is beyond our understanding. They could ride the streams of light and ply the whip to flying rays. They have so miraculous powers that the access to every part of universe is within their palms. They could travel to the zenith of gods' realm or the nadir of devils' underworld at will. They could pass through the grand gate of heaven and wander in the empty vastness"。

原文为了形成结构上的对仗，部分句子的意义是重合的，"逍遥恍惚之中，徜徉仿佛之表"即为这样的同义反复结构，翻译时可取其一端或综合文意。参阅汉学家理雅各英译《庄子·逍遥游》时对"逍遥游"的解读：We might render the title by "Sauntering or Rambling at Ease"; but it is the untroubled enjoyment of the mind which the author has in view. And this enjoyment is secured by the Tâo, though that character does not once occur in the Book（Legge, 1891: 127），这里不妨将"逍遥恍惚之中，徜徉仿佛之表"合并翻译为"They could saunter and ramble at ease, masking their traces with delusions and miracles"。六气，天地四时之气，可泛化译为"the energy of world"（宇宙之气）。

需指出的是，受译者前理解的影响，魏译本将"茫昧""希微"翻译为"God（the Obscure）"（模糊不清的上帝）和"God（the Infinitesimal）"（极其微小的上帝），大致是因为《道德经》中有关"道"的特征描述也曾引用了这样的词语，据此译者断定"茫昧""希微"为"道"的代称，也即是"玄"，于是有了这样的翻译。然则"茫昧"意为"幽暗不清"；"希微"指"空虚寂静"。这段文字描述的是"得玄道者"的最高境界，"徘徊茫昧，翱翔希微"意指"徘徊于幽暗不清之中，翱翔于无声无形之际"，不妨按其本意简化译为"They are ubiquitous and their presence cannot be detected"，这样可与"履略蜿虹，践跚旋玑"的译文"They could be found treading on the rainbow or traveling among the stars"形成照应。

此外，"履略"和"践跚"为同义词，皆有"脚踏，巡游"之意，可用合译，也可借用魏译本中的选词"travel"和"tread"分别译出。古代汉语中的骈文常因堆砌华丽辞藻，导致文本部分意思有所重复，可择其要点译出，不必拘泥于原文。

17. "真知足"指的是修仙者通过存思守一而产生的恬静无欲的精神状态。"其次则真知足"是仅次于上文所说的"得玄道者"而言，该段讲述的是"知足者"的人格境界。原文"肥遁勿用，颐光山林。纡鸾龙之翼于细介之伍，养浩然之气于蓬荜之中"意指知足的人能够退隐无为，到山林里颐养精神，能够收敛如龙凤一般的才华，与卑微的鸟兽为伍，在蓬门荜户中培养浩然正气。这里的"鸾龙""细介""蓬荜"皆为喻体，汉语读者既能理解原文作者的意图，又能获得一种视觉美的阅读体验。虽然这些喻体在英语中可以找到匹配的词语，如魏译本就直接翻译为"phoenix-dragon"，"simple folk"和"humble cottage"，但原作者的真实意图却无法在这样的直译中体现出来。此外，"纡"意为"系结、绾结"，指"收敛"，而无魏译本中的"deploy"（施展）之意；魏译本将"浩然之气"翻译为"压倒一切的生命力"（overwhelming vitality），过分局限于原文的形式意义，不能不说是一种遗憾。

翻译该部分内容时需避免直译一些容易导致理解障碍的喻体，并对意义进行重组。因此改译为"Second to them are the group of contented people who really have the intellectual recognition of *Xuan* and thus know ways of moderation and self-satisfaction. They will not surrender their rationality and dignity to this materialistic world. They will withdraw from the society by becoming hermits in the mountains and forests. They may be poor and humble, but they are righteous and respectable"。

18. 原文"褴缕带索，不以贸龙章之晔晔也；负步杖策，不以易结驷之骆驿也"。意思：（知足的人）宁肯衣衫褴褛，用草绳作衣带，也不愿意拿它去交换光鲜亮丽的龙袍；宁肯背着重物拄着竹杖走路，也不去更换那往来不绝的车辆。魏译本在保留原文形式的基础上较好地传译了原文的意思，其中以"the glory of the imperial robe"对译"龙章之晔晔"，以"the social cachet of four-horse teams"对译"结驷之骆驿"，这样的直译同样传递了原文所想表达的权贵之人的威风气势，堪称佳译。

19. 原文"藏夜光于嵩岫，不受他山之攻；沉灵甲于玄渊，以违钻灼之灾"若按字面解读，其意思为将宝玉藏于高山崖穴之中，不借他山之石来琢磨成器；把灵龟的甲壳沉匿于深渊之中，以逃脱钻凿炙烧的灾祸。然而，该段讲述的是"知足者"的人格品性，作者借"夜光（璧）"这一宝石名喻指"知足者"的天赋才华，借"灵甲"可用于占卜之说来喻指人们的聪明智慧。译者需依据语境理解原文的真实含义，而非断章取义，只按字面译出。按其要旨，该句可改译为"They will purposely hide their talents so that the cunning world will never be able to manipulate them. They will also deliberately retard their wisdom in order to find peace away from the conspiracy"。

尽管魏译本在选词造句上颇有考究，例如，他用"be worked on the grindstone"翻译"他山之攻"，用"suffer the drillings and scorchings of diviners"翻译"钻灼之灾"，但这样脱离语境的解读完全让读者迷惑不解，不得要领。即便是从字面解读来看，该句译文也有理解不准确之处，比如，"嵩岫"虽字面可以理解为"嵩山之峰"，但这里泛指高山峻岭，魏译"Mount Sung's peak"，缩小了原文的能指。

20. 原文"动息知止，无往不足"指的是"劳作与休息都能适可而止，无论何时何地都能知足常乐"。该句可改译为"Keeping a balance between activity and rest, they always stay happy and content"。魏译本太拘泥于原文字面，"无往不足"译为"he is satisfied wherever he goes"（Ware, 1966: 31）可以算是字对字的典型直译。

21. 因"朝华"可指代早晨开的花朵，又有"朝华之草，夕而零落；松柏之茂，隆寒不衰"（《三国志·魏志·王昶传》）之说，故魏译本将"赫奕之朝华"译为"brief bloom of radiant beauty"（短暂的美丽绽放）。依据语境，这里的"赫奕之朝华"隐射的是仕途生活的显赫荣耀，因此不能只做表面文章，需译出其实指含义，可将"弃赫奕之朝华，避偾车之险路"翻译为"Abandoning the glories of the official life, they will not adventure into the unknown path that may lead to failures"。

22. 透过"吟啸苍崖之间，而万物化为尘氛；怡颜丰柯之下，而朱户变为绳枢"的描述，原文读者俨然可以看到"知足者"的那种逍遥自在。该句的白话文：知足者在苍翠的山崖间悠然吟啸，静观万物慢慢化为尘土；他们在茂密的树林间开怀大笑，冷眼朱门富贵人家转眼变为绳枢穷

第七章　道教综合类文本《抱朴子内篇》翻译研究　　253

家。"万物化为尘氛"描述的是自然界的运行变化，"朱户变为绳枢"讲的是世间俗人的命运变迁，因此该句可改译为"They will leisurely compose and chant their poems in the mountain's steep as they observe the changes of the world without involvement. They will heartily laugh at the life vicissitude of the aristocrats in the forest's deep without interference"。

至于"握耒甫田，而麾节忽若执鞭；啜荈漱泉，而太牢同乎藜藿"描述的则是"知足者"的另一生活态度，意思是知足者手握农具在田里耕作，将那将帅手持的符节视为农夫的鞭子；他们啜苦茶、饮山泉，却把猪牛羊肉看成野菜般的粗食。可改译为"These people sustain themselves through laboring, for they despise the totality of strength that warlords could wield. These people also feed themselves with humble fare, for they have no wants for the lavish feasts of the suovetaurilia"。无论是"麾节""执鞭"，还是"太牢""藜藿"都很难用直译的手法体现这些意象的真实所指，只能舍弃意象。魏译本中的"suovetaurilia"（古罗马的一种祭品，祭祀猪、羊和牛）翻译"太牢"实为非常难得的佳译，既有"太牢"一词的内涵所指，又照顾了目标语读者的阅读体验，因此沿用了这一词语，添加"lavish feasts"作为范畴词，只为突出这一语境下"太牢"指代的奢华盛宴。需指出的是，魏译本把"啜荈漱泉"译为"drinks tea and rinses his mouth from the spring"（喝茶，用泉水漱口）也是一种太局限于单个汉字的意思而作的死译。

23. "含醇守朴"中的"醇"意思为"淳厚、淳朴"，这里形容质朴敦厚之人。将"含醇守朴，无欲无忧，全真虚器，居平味淡"翻译为白话文：他们涵含淳厚，持守朴素，不存欲望，没有忧虑，保全真性，漠视外物，甘居平常，淡泊生活。魏译将"醇"译为"pure drinks"（纯正美酒），其译文为"As he partakes of pure drinks and maintain simplicity"（Ware, 1966: 31），显然是误读了原作者的意思。可选用"honesty""simplicity""realness"翻译"醇""朴""真"这三大知足者的特质，基本实现对等。改译为"These people embrace honesty, simplicity and realness of heart. They lead the simple life and stay uncommitted. They are free from covetousness and worries"。

24. 这里描述了知足者的境界特征："知足者"胸怀宽广，沉浸在

"如暗如明，如浊如清；似迟而疾，似亏而盈"的至高境界，恬静无欲，不求于道，而道自归之，无为自得，体妙心玄。《庄子·逍遥游》也有类似的描述："若夫乘天地之正，而御六气之辩，以游无穷者，彼且恶乎待哉。"因此，以其最终境界而论，知足者不需要依靠任何的凭借，都可以使自己处于逍遥的状态中。若可依乎天地自然之理而动，则无所待。魏译本拆分了暗明、清浊、迟疾、亏盈这些描述词语，将"暗明""清浊"视为天地造化的特质，而视"迟疾""亏盈"为知足者的表象，尽管单单阅读译文本身，情理上也是讲得通的，但是典籍英译需研究原作者的思想，这里应是作者借庄子中的"无待"之状描述"知足者"所能达到的至高境界。

魏译本误读为"玄道"之特征，以"immensity"对"恢恢"，以"movement"对"荡荡"，以"vastness"对"浩浩"，以"confusion"对"茫茫"，并将下句"如暗如明，如浊如清"同视为"玄道"之特征。其解读：知足者参与玄道的浩渺和运动，与大自然的运转浑然一体。尽管玄道广袤而杂呈，无论明暗清浊，知足者均坦然接受天地之造化。这种理解与原文意思相去甚远。因此可改译为"Being magnanimous and perfect, they are as natural and honest as the immaterialized and unmanifested creation. Their physical appearance will not be determined by mortal's perception. Being simultaneously dark and bright, murky and pure, quick and dilatory, empty and full, they can be perceived in a contradictory way"。

25. 原文"岂肯委尸祝之坐，释大匠之位，越樽俎以代无知之庖，舍绳墨而助伤手之工"的正确理解顺序：岂肯委尸祝之坐，越樽俎以代无知之庖；释大匠之位，舍绳墨而助伤手之工。意思：他们哪肯放弃尸祝一样的身份，越过樽俎去代替无知的厨子备办祭品？他们岂能放弃大匠一样的地位，丢开绳墨去帮助总砍伤双手的小工呢？翻译该句时需调整原文的顺序，并对其中的尸祝、大匠、樽俎等这类名词作出较为达意的理解。"尸祝之坐"与"大匠之位"相对。"尸"为古人祭祀时代表鬼神受享祭的人，魏译本译为"corpse-representative"；祝，传告鬼神言辞的人，魏译本译为"cantor"；大匠，技艺高超的工匠，魏译本译为"master craftman"；樽俎，同"尊俎"，古代酒器和盛肉的器皿，魏译本译为"the cauldrons and other vessels of religious ceremony"；绳墨，木匠打直线用的工具，魏译本译为"guidelines"；单从字面来看这些翻译皆为不错的选择。但由于译者受原文词序的约束，导致译文逻辑错位，将其英文回译过来：他不会为了尸祝的世俗工作而辞去工匠大师之职；他不会忽略宗教仪式上盛物的坩埚及其他器皿而去取代无知的厨师。显然错配了尸祝、大匠、樽俎、无知之庖、绳墨之间的关系。基于减轻读者阅读障碍的考虑，可对"尸祝""大匠"等做泛化处理，省去"樽俎""绳墨"等这样具体的意象，并采用疑问句译出，以加强语气。可改译为"Hence, why would these people abandon the social status and power that could be brought to them by their wisdom and competency for the worldly tasks of the unskilled and the unlettered？"

26. 原文"不以臭鼠之细琐，而为庸夫之忧乐。藐然不喜流俗之誉，坦尔不惧雷同之毁。不以外物汩其至精，不以利害污其纯粹也"。既回答上句"岂肯委尸祝之坐……"的问题，也自然引出下句"故穷富极贵，不足以诱之焉，其余何足以悦之乎"。依据中文注释内容，"臭鼠"即"腐鼠"，比喻世人追逐的功名利禄。细琐：细小琐碎的事物。"不以臭鼠之细琐，而为庸夫之忧乐"意指知足的人不会为得到"腐鼠"这般世俗的功名利禄，而让自己陷入庸人的忧乐中。"庸夫"并非魏译本所理解"被雇佣之人"（employee），而是"平庸之人"，将"臭鼠之细琐"译为"腐烂的一点薪酬"（a putrid pittance of a salary）更是不得原文要旨。该句可改译为"People who are blessed by the intellectual recognition of *Xuan* refuse to be caught in the sorrows and joys of a mediocre for sake of any trivialities"。

藐然，藐视的样子。流俗，指世俗。坦尔，坦荡，坦然。雷同之毁，众口如一的毁谤，可译为social imputation。魏译本将"藐然不喜流俗之誉，坦尔不惧雷同之毁"翻译为"Uninvolved, he finds no joy in the approval of the crowds; in his tranquility, he does not fear being criticized for plagiarism"。虽然可以接受译者用"uninvolved"译"藐然"，用名词短语"the approval of the crowds"对译"流俗之誉"，但将"坦尔"翻译为"in his tranquility"，将"雷同之毁"翻译为"being criticized for plagiarism"，这样的译文显然是对原文的误读误译。

27. "操隋珠以弹雀""舐秦痔以属车""泳吕梁以求鱼"，皆为典故，分别出自《庄子·让王》《庄子·列御寇》《庄子·达生》，"登朽缮以探巢"来源不明。"操隋珠以弹雀"指用隋侯的宝珠来弹射鸟雀，比喻做事不知衡量轻重，因而得不偿失。"舐秦痔以属车"意思是用口舐秦王的痔疮来获得车马，后以舐痔比喻谄媚之徒趋炎附势的卑劣行为。"泳吕梁以求鱼"意指在吕梁这等水势汹涌之处打鱼，必致事与愿违。这些都是发生在失道俗人身上的怪诞行为。魏译本选择的是保留形象的直译模式，同时提供了非常简单的注释，虽无典故的具体内容，只指出这些典故的来源，但译者补充了一句引导性的解读，即"These are all references to stories of mean or futile desires"（这些都是一些徒劳无益或卑劣下作之事），帮助读者理解主旨。这种翻译典故的方法也有一定的参考价值，可以借鉴。

翻译典故时，虽然采用直译可以保留原文之形，但很难译出典故的内涵，译者通常需舍弃其形而只译其意，有时候还可以增补一些说明主旨的语句，例如，"且为称孤之客，夕为狐鸟之余；栋挠铼覆，倾溺不振"中"栋挠铼覆"出自《易经·大过》《易经·鼎》，意思：栋梁折断，鼎倾食撒。与"且为称孤之客，夕为狐鸟之余"一样都用以喻指发生在失道俗人身上的无法补救之后果。魏译本虽增译"these are instances of irretrievable losses"做点题之用，弥补了直译典故有时不能尽显原文内涵之遗憾，但却因过分受限于原文字面结构导致译文词不达意或逻辑含混不清。依原文之义该句可改译为"The absence of *Xuan* in these people will make them prone to detriments. They could fall from grace and power within a day. They could never recover from a personal crisis"，其中"The absence of *Xuan* in these people will make them prone to detriments"为增译内容。

28. 原文"盖世人之所为载驰企及，而达者之所为寒心而凄怆者也"意思：世俗人四处奔走、汲汲以求的那些荣华富贵，却正是通达者感到寒心和可悲之所在。"盖"，句首语气词，无实在意义，其作用只是引出下面的议论或说明。魏译本将"盖"作副词解，意为"大概"，用以连接上文，说明原因，其理解：有人可能会说，世俗之人行事沉稳，急于到达，而智者行事冷静，略带忧思。仅从英译文的上下文来看，这种解读虽有一定的逻辑性，但误读了原文作者之意，因此可改译为"These people are always chasing after wealth and power. But in the eyes of the *Xuan*-mas-

tering people, their behaviors are both tragic and pathetic"。

29. 该段涉及几个比喻修辞和典故的翻译。作者用乐曲名《韶》《夏》比喻卓越的才能,"嘿《韶》《夏》"意思是不显示才华。"藻梲"是天子的庙饰,即有彩画的短柱。"韬藻梲"比喻抛却富贵。"衔芦之卫"出自《淮南子·修务训》,指防备暗算和伤害。"倨鹤之呼"出自《庄子·秋水》,比喻人们担心失去富贵时的惊呼。"亢极之悔"出自《周易·乾卦》,指物盛必衰的懊悔。这一段的白话译文如下。

> 所以那些修养极高的至人不去显示自己的才华而抛却荣华富贵。他们奋起翅膀翱翔在昆仑五城的上空,而不需要像鸿雁那样口衔芦苇以自卫;他们像蛰龙那样把自己隐藏在无用之地,而没有必要依恃深深的洞穴去防备灾难。在下他们不会像蹲坐在地上的猫头鹰那样发出担心受损的惊呼,在上他们没有盛极必衰时的懊悔。世上没有人理解这些思想境界极高的至人,因为他们的境界实在是太高远了,他们的胸怀实在是太旷达了!(张松辉,2011:18)

对照魏译本对该段的翻译,不难看出译者在翻译这些负载特有中国文化的句子时有时也显得力不从心而导致一些误读和误译。若把这段英译文回译为中文,大致意思为:因此,修养极高之人不在国家宗教机构担任官职,不受奢靡华丽之困扰。他征用作为诸侯应有的六行舞者在遥远的五城之地举行宗教仪式,不需要防范别人的指责。他是人中之龙,却将鳞角隐藏在"无用"之地,不必仰仗微不足道的巢穴。俯视时没有一丝轻蔑,仰望时没有让人追悔的狂妄。没有人认识他。他是那么的超然脱俗!

很显然,译者对《韶》、《夏》、六羽、五城、衔芦之卫、倨鹤之呼、亢极之悔这些文化特色词缺乏必要的了解,这样的翻译与原文作者所表达的意图完全不符,故需重译。改译为 "That is why the *Xuan*-mastering people take to hide their talents and wisdom. Discarding the secular wealth and power, they soar freely in the paradise of the immortals and don't have to consciously defend themselves from schemes and intrigues. When they are lower-down inferiors, they fear no loss of properties. When they are higher-up superiors, they feel no remorse of decline. Such people can never be truly approachable, because they are both miraculous and subtle that exceeds our understanding".

虽然文化传真是翻译的主要任务之一，但有的时候如果采取直译会导致读者阅读困难时，可退而求其次采取意译法，以达到语言交际的目的。就像这句中《韶》、《夏》、六羽、五城、衔芦之卫、倨鸰之呼、亢极之悔等包含深厚文化意义，翻译时只能采取意译法。

二　魏鲁男《抱朴子内篇·微旨》译文解析

"微旨"即"微妙旨趣"。该篇为《抱朴子内篇》第六卷，进一步论证了养生修仙的可能，重点介绍炼制金丹之外的其他修仙方术。

葛洪首先批评了世俗人的浅薄与荒唐，认为同他们谈论成仙大道，就如同与"宛转果核之内"的小虫子谈论广阔的天地一样。接着，作者介绍炼制金丹之外的其他修仙方术，认为，虽然炼制金丹是成仙的正途，但鉴于炼制金丹"事大费重，不可卒办"，"宝精爱器""服小药""学近术"等"小术"可作为辅助性的修仙手段，特别强调修炼者需结合各种"小术"，要坚定信念，循序渐进，才能收到良好的效果。葛洪在本篇中分三个方面为学道者介绍修仙护身养生方法。

第一，从道德层面提出修仙的首要任务是行善，这是因为"天地有司过之神，随人所犯轻重，以夺其算，算减则人贫耗疾病，屡逢忧患，算尽则人死"。作者详细列举了恶事与善事的具体内容，还举出了历史上善有善果、恶有恶报的典型事例，以增强自己观点的说服力。这些劝善思想在后来涌现的道教劝善类书籍中得到了很好的继承和发扬。

第二，从护身防盗层面介绍了一些巫术。比如，为了防范强盗，就应该"常以执日，取六癸上土，以和百叶薰草，以泥门户，方一尺，则盗贼不来"，在门上涂抹掺有植物叶片的泥巴就能阻止强盗的侵入。这样的巫术不过是当时这些术士荒诞不经的臆想罢了。

第三，从养生层面介绍了内丹和房中术。作者用神秘而瑰丽的语言介绍了内丹修炼和房中术的奇妙境界。在介绍房中术这一古老方术时，葛洪既肯定了它的养生作用，也批判了一些人对其作用的夸大之词，明确指出：房中术虽然重要，但不足以成仙，只能治疗小病，防止伤身而已。

第七章　道教综合类文本《抱朴子内篇》翻译研究

采用设问的方式作为提出个人观念的契机是葛洪这部《抱朴子内篇》独特的写作风格。《微旨》篇一共回答了九个问题，作者希望借他的答复让想修习仙道的人能够知道并拥有正确而安全的修仙方术。魏鲁南《抱朴子内篇》英译本保留了原文的对话形式，采用"Interlocutor：..."和"Ko：..."分别呈现问题与答复。

在魏晋时期的神仙道教中，房中术和存思术被视为两种最神秘的仙术。葛洪在该篇中用极为优美却又极其神秘的文字描述了这两种仙术，其中有关"太元之山"和"长谷之山"的内容既涉及道教存思术，也谈到了房中术，另一段源自先师的口诀则是气功修炼的内容，即道教修仙方术中的行气法，皆使用了大量的隐语，作者借助一种浪漫主义的艺术意境烘托出了修道者的宗教体验，近代学者多以其难以索解避而不论（胡孚琛，1989：151）。中国当代学者在其注译本中虽提供了注释和译文，各自的解读也不尽相同。英译《抱朴子内篇》的海外学者处理该段文字时也都明显地感到力不从心，这已不是语言层面能解决的问题，非有实际体验者确实很难将如此神秘之术清晰呈现于文字之中。

[原文]

抱朴子曰："余闻归同契合者，则不言而信著；途殊别务者，虽忠告而见疑。[1]夫寻常咫尺之近理，人间取舍之细事，沉浮过于金羽，皂白分于粉墨，而抱惑之士，犹多不辨焉，岂况说之以世道之外，示之以至微之旨？[2]大而笑之，其来久矣，岂独今哉？夫明之所及，虽玄阴幽夜之地，豪厘芒发之物，不以为难见；[3]苟所不逮者，虽日月丽天之炤灼，嵩、岱干云之峻峭，犹不能察焉。[4]黄老玄圣，深识独见，开秘文于名山，受仙经于神人，蹴埃尘以遗累，凌大遐以高跻。金石不能与之齐坚，龟鹤不足与之等寿，念有志于将来，悯信者之无文，垂以方法，炳然著明，小修则小得，大为则大验。[5]然而浅见之徒，区区所守，甘于荼、蓼而不识粘蜜，酣于醨酪而不赏醇醪。[6]知好生而不知有养生之道，知畏死而不信有不死之法；知饮食过度之畜疾病，而不能节肥甘于其口也；知极情恣欲之致枯损，而不知割怀于所欲也。[7]余虽言神仙之可得，安能令其信乎？"

或人难曰："子体无参午达理、奇毛通骨，年非安期、彭祖多历之寿，目不接见神仙，耳不独闻异说，何以知长生之可获，养性之有征哉？[8]若觉玄妙于心得，运逸鉴于独见，所未敢许也。[9]夫衣无蔽肤之具，资无谋夕之储，而高谈陶朱之术，自同猗顿之策，取讥论者，其理必也。[10] 抱痼疾而言精和、鹊之技，屡奔北而称究孙、吴之算。人不信者，以无效也。"[11]

余答曰："夫寸鲔泛迹滥水之中，则谓天下无四海之广也；芒蝎宛转果核之内，则谓八极之界尽于兹也。[12] 虽告之以无涯之浩汗，语之以宇宙之恢阔，以为空言，必不肯信也。[13] 若令吾眼有方瞳，耳长出顶，亦将控飞龙而驾庆云，凌流电而造倒景，子又将安得而诘我？[14] 设令见我，又将呼为天神、地祇、异类之人，岂谓我为学之所致哉？[15] 姑聊以先觉挽引同志，岂强令吾子之徒皆信之哉？[16] 若令家户有仙人，属目比肩，吾子虽蔽，亦将不疑。[17] 但彼人之道成，则蹈青霄而游紫极，自非通灵，莫之见闻，吾子必为无耳。[18] 世人信其臆断，仗其短见，自谓所度，事无差错，习乎所致，怪乎所希，提耳指掌，终于不悟，其来尚矣，岂独今哉？"[19]

或曰："屡承嘉谈，足以不疑于有仙矣，但更自嫌于不能为耳。[20] 敢问更有要道，可得单行者否？"[21] 抱朴子曰："凡学道当阶浅以涉深，由易以及难。志诚坚果，无所不济，疑则无功，非一事也。[22] 夫根荄不洞地，而求柯条干云；渊源不泓窈，而求汤流万里者，未之有也。[23] 是故非积善阴德，不足以感神明；非诚心款契，不足以结师友；非功劳不足以论大试；又未遇明师而求要道，未可得也。[24] 九丹金液，最是仙主。[25] 然事大费重，不可卒办也。宝精爱炁，最其急也，并将服小药以延年命，学近术以辟邪恶，乃可渐阶精微矣。"

或曰："方术繁多，诚难精备，除置金丹，其余可修，何者为善？" 抱朴子曰："若未得其至要之大者，则其小者不可不广知也，盖藉众术之共成长生也。[26] 大而喻之，犹世主之治国焉，文、武、礼、律，无一不可也；小而喻之，犹工匠之为车焉，辕、辋、轴、辖，莫或应亏也。[27] 所为术者，内修形神，使延年愈疾；外攘邪恶，使祸害不干。[28] 比之琴瑟，不可以子弦求五音也；方之甲胄，不可以一札待锋刃也。[29] 何者？五音合用不可阙，而锋刃所集不可少也。[30] 凡养生者，欲令多闻而体要，博见而善择，偏修一事，不足必赖也。[31] 又患好事之徒，各仗其所长，知玄、素之术者，则曰：'唯房中之术，可以度世矣。'明吐纳之道者，则曰：'唯行气可以延年矣。'知屈伸之法者，则曰：'唯导引可以难老矣。'知草木之方者，则曰：'唯药饵可以无穷矣。'学道之不成就，由乎偏枯之若此也。[32] 浅见之家，偶知一事，便言已足。而不识真者，虽得善方，犹更求

第七章 道教综合类文本《抱朴子内篇》翻译研究 261

无已,以消工弃日,而所施用,意无一定,此皆两有所失者也。[33]或本性 戆钝,所知殊尚浅近,便强入名山,履冒毒螫,屡被中伤,耻复求还,或 为虎狼所食,或为魍魉所杀,或饿而无绝谷之方,寒而无自温之法,死 于崖谷,不亦愚哉?[34]夫务学不如择师,师所闻素狭,又不尽情以教之, 因告云:'为道不在多也。'夫为道不在多,自为已有金丹至要,可不用 余耳。然此事知之者甚希,宁可虚待不必之大事,而不修交益之小术 乎?[35]譬犹作家,云不事用他物者,盖谓有金银珠玉,在乎掌握怀抱之中, 足以供累世之费者耳。[36]苟其无此,何可不广播百谷,多储果疏乎?是以 断谷辟兵,厌劾鬼魅,禁御百毒,治救众疾,入山则使猛兽不犯,涉水 则令蛟龙不害,经瘟疫则不畏,遇急难则隐形,此皆小事,而不可不知, 况过此者,何可不闻乎?[37]

或曰:"敢问欲修长生之道,何所禁忌?"抱朴子曰:"禁忌之至急, 在不伤不损而已。按《易内戒》及《赤松子经》及《河图记命符》皆 云:'天地有司过之神,随人所犯轻重,以夺其算,算减则人贫耗疾病, 屡逢忧患,算尽则人死。[38]诸应夺算者有数百事,不可具论。'又言:'身 中有三尸。'三尸之为物,虽无形而实魂灵鬼神之属也。[39]欲使人早死,此 尸当得作鬼,自放纵游行,享人祭酹。[40]是以每到庚申之日,辄上天白司 命,道人所为过失。[41]又月晦之夜,灶神亦上天白人罪状。[42]大者夺纪,纪 者,三百日也。小者夺算,算者,三日也。吾亦未能审此事之有无也。 然天道邈远,鬼神难明。赵简子、秦穆公皆亲受金策于上帝,有土地之 明征。[43]山川草木,井灶污池,犹皆有精气;人身之中,亦有魂魄;况天 地为物之至大者,于理当有精神,有精神则宜赏善而罚恶。但其体大而 网疏,不必机发而响应耳。[44]然览诸道戒,无不云欲求长生者,必欲积善 立功,慈心于物,恕己及人,仁逮昆虫,乐人之吉,悯人之苦,赒人之 急,救人之穷,手不伤生,口不劝祸,见人之得如己之得,见人之失如 己之失,不自贵,不自誉,不嫉妒胜己,不佞谄阴贼,如此乃为有德, 受福于天,所作必成,求仙可冀也。[45]若乃憎善好杀,口是心非,背向异 辞,反戾直正,虐害其下,欺罔其上,叛其所事,受恩不感,弄法受赂, 纵曲枉直,[46]废公为私,刑加无辜,破人之家,收人之宝,害人之身,取 人之位,侵克贤者,诛戮降伏,谤讪仙圣,伤残道士,弹射飞鸟,刳胎 破卵,春夏燎猎,骂詈神灵,[47]教人为恶,蔽人之善,危人自安,佻人自功,坏人佳事,夺人所爱,离人骨肉,辱人求胜,取人长钱,还人短陌,[48]决放水火,以术害人,迫胁尪弱,以恶易好,强取强求,掳掠致富,不公不平,淫佚倾邪,凌孤暴寡,拾遗取施,欺绐诳诈,好说人私,持人短长,牵天援地,咒诅求直,[49]假借不还,换贷不偿,求欲无已,憎拒忠信,不顺上命,不敬所师,笑人作善,败人苗稼,损人器物,以穷人用,以不清洁饮饲他人,轻秤小斗,狭幅短度,[50]以伪杂真,采取奸利,诱人取物,越井跨灶,晦歌朔哭[51]。凡有一事,辄是一罪,随事轻重,司命夺其算、纪,算尽则死。但有恶心而无恶迹者夺算,若恶事而损于人者夺纪,若算、纪未尽而自死者,皆殃及子孙也。[52]诸横夺人财物者,或计其妻子家口以当填之,以致死丧,但不即至耳。[53]其恶行若不足以煞其家人者,久久终遭水火劫盗,及遗失器物,或遇县官疾病,自营医药,烹牲祭祀所用之费,要当令足以尽其所取之直也。[54]故道家言,枉煞人者,是以兵刃而更相杀。[55]其取非义之财,不避怨恨,譬若以漏脯救饥,鸩酒解渴,非不暂饱,而死亦及之矣。[56]其有曾行诸恶事,后自改悔者,若曾枉煞人,则当思救济应死之人以解之。若妄取人财物,则当思施与贫困以解之。若以罪加人,则当思荐达贤人以解之。皆一倍于所为,则可便受吉利,转祸为福之道也。[57]能尽不犯之,则必延年益寿,学道速成也。夫天高而听卑,物无不鉴,行善不息,必得吉报。[58]羊公积德布施,诣乎皓首,乃受天坠之金。[59]蔡顺至孝,感神应之。[60]郭巨煞子为亲,而获铁券之重赐。[61]然善事难为,恶事易作,而愚人复以项托、伯牛辈,谓天地之不能辨臧否,而不知彼有外名者,未必有内行;有阳誉者不能解阴罪。[62]若以荠、麦之生死,而疑阴、阳之大气,亦不足以致远也。[63]盖上士所以密勿而仅免,凡庸所以不得其欲矣。[64]"

或曰:"道德未成,又未得绝迹名山,而世不同古,盗贼甚多,将何以却朝夕之患、防无妄之灾乎?"[65]抱朴子曰:"常以执日,取六癸上土,以和百叶薰草,以泥门户,方一尺,则盗贼不来。[66]亦可取市南门土,及岁破土、月建土,合和为人,以著朱鸟地,亦压盗也。[67]有急则入生地而止,无患也。天下有生地,一州有生地,一郡有生地,一县有生地,一乡有生地,一里有生地,一宅有生地,一房有生地。[68]"

或曰:"一房有生地,不亦逼[69]乎?"抱朴子曰:"经云:'大急之极,隐于车轼。'如此,一车之中,亦有生地,况一房乎?"[70]

或曰:"窃闻求生之道,当知二山,不审此山,为何所在,愿垂告悟,以祛其惑。"[71]抱朴子曰:"有之。非华、霍也,非嵩、岱也。夫太元之山,难知易求,不天不地,不沉不浮,绝险绵邈,峯嵬崎岖。[72]和气氤氲,神意并游。[73]玉井泓邃,灌溉匪休。[74]百二十官,曹府相由。[75]离、坎列位,玄芝万株,绛树特生,其宝皆殊,金玉嵯峨,醴泉出隅。[76]还年之士,挹其清流,子能修之,乔、松可俦。[77]此一山也。长谷之山,杳杳巍巍,玄气飘飘,玉液霏霏,金池紫房,在乎其隈。[78]愚人妄往,至皆死归。有道之士,登之不衰,采服黄精,以致天飞。[79]此二山也。皆古贤之所秘,子精思之。"

或曰:"愿闻真人守身炼形之术。"抱朴子曰:"深哉问也!夫'始青之下月与日,两半同升合成一。[80]出彼玉池入金室,大如弹丸黄如橘。[81]中有嘉味甘如蜜,子能得之谨勿失。既往不追身将灭,纯白之气至微密。[82]升于幽关三曲折,中丹煌煌独无匹。[83]立之命门形不卒,渊乎妙矣难致诘。'[84]此先师之口诀,知之者不畏万鬼五兵也。[85]"

或曰:"闻房中之事,能尽其道者,可单行致神仙,并可以移灾解罪,转祸为福,居官高迁,商贾倍利,信乎?"[86]抱朴子曰:"此皆巫书妖妄过差之言,由于好事增加润色,至令失实。[87]亦奸伪造作虚妄,以欺诳世人,隐藏端绪,以求奉事,招集弟子,以规世利耳。[88]夫阴阳之术,高可以治小疾,次可以免虚耗而已。其理自有极,安能致神仙而却祸致福乎?人不可以阴阳不交,坐致疾患;若欲纵情恣欲,不能节宣,则伐年命。[89]善其术者,则能却走马以补脑,还阴丹以朱肠。[90]采玉液于金池,引三五于华梁,令人老有美色,终其所禀之天年。[91]而俗人闻黄帝以千二百女升天,便谓黄帝单以此事致长生,而不知黄帝于荆山之下、鼎湖之上,飞九丹成,乃乘龙登天也。[92]黄帝自可有千二百女耳,而非单行之所由也。[93]凡服药千种,三牲之养,而不知房中之术,亦无所益也。[94]是以古人恐人轻恣情性,故美为之说,亦不可尽信也。玄、素谕之水火,水火煞人,而又生人,在于能用与不能耳。大都知其要法,御女多多益善;如不知其道而用之,一两人足以速死耳。彭祖之法,最其要者,其他经多烦劳难行,而其为益不必如其书。人少有能为之者,口诀亦有数千言耳。不知之者,虽服百药,犹不能得长生也。"

[**注释**]①

1. 归同契合：志同道合。归，归宿，引申为目标、志向。契，符合。信：信任、信赖。见：被。

2. 寻常：长度单位。古代八尺为一寻，十六尺为一常。咫：长度单位。古代八寸为一咫。这里都是用来形容短小的距离。皂白：黑白，常比喻是非。粉：化妆用的白色粉末。

3. 玄阴：阴暗。豪：通"毫"，长度单位。十丝为一毫，十毫为一厘。芒：谷类植物种子壳上或草木上的针状物。这里都是用来比喻非常细小的东西。发：古长度名。《新书·六术》"十毫为发，十发为厘，十厘为分，十分为寸。"引申形容细微。

4. 丽：附着，依附。焰灼：灿烂明亮。嵩：即嵩山。在今河南境内。岱：即泰山。在今山东境内。干云：直冲云霄。干，冲。

5. 蹶：蹶然，疾起的样子。埃尘：即尘埃，这里比喻尘世。遣累：排遣各种拖累。大遐：高远的太空。跻：登，升。有志：指有志于修道成仙的人。文：文字，即记载仙道的书籍。垂：流传。炳然：清楚明白的样子。

6. 区区：拘泥，局限。荼、蓼：草名。荼，苦菜，为陆上的秽草；蓼，辛辣的野菜，为水中的秽草。粘蜜：蜜糖。醨：薄酒。酢：醋。醇：味道醇厚的酒。醪：浊酒，这里代指味美的酒。

7. 畜：作"速"，招致。

8. 参午达理：十五条长长的纹理。参午，又写作"参五"，即"三五"。参，通"三"。一说"参午"义为错杂纵横。达，通达，长长的。通骨：流畅的骨相。通，流畅，无阻碍。这里指骨节纤细而不明显。征：验证，效验。

9. 逸鉴：超人的见解。逸，通"轶"，超越。许：同意，赞成。

10. 无谋夕之储：不能保证晚上有饭吃。即朝不保夕。陶朱：即范蠡。春秋时人。曾帮助越王勾践灭吴，后隐居于陶，改名为朱公，经商

---

① 本节中文注释综合参考了邱凤侠的《抱朴子内篇注译》（中国科学社会出版社 2004 年版）、顾久的《抱朴子内篇全译》（贵州人民出版社 1995 年版）和张松辉的《抱朴子内篇译注》（中华书局 2011 年版）的内容。

成为巨富。猗顿：春秋人。以经营畜牧及盐业而致富。

11. 痼疾：积久不易治疗的病。和、鹊：即医和、扁鹊。古代名医。北：败北，失败。孙、吴：即孙子和吴起。古代著名军事家。

12. 鲭：鱼名。王明认为当作"蜎"，井中的一种小虫（王明，1985：130）。芒蝎：很小的木中蠹虫。芒，形容细小。八极：八方最远处。代指整个天地之间。兹：这里，指果核之内。

13. 浩汗：即"浩瀚"。辽阔的样子。

14. 方瞳：两个瞳孔呈正方形。《抱朴子内篇·祛惑》记载："仙人目瞳皆方。"耳长出顶：耳朵从头顶长出。《抱朴子内篇·论仙》说神仙"邛疏之双耳，出乎头巅"。庆云：五色的祥云。造：到达。倒景：道教指天上最高之处。景，通"影"。《汉书·郊祀志》："登遐倒景。"注："如淳曰：在日月之上，反从下照，故其景倒。"

15. 呼：称呼，认为。地祇：地神。

16. 姑聊：姑且。先觉：先知先觉。指自己。

17. 蔽：受蒙蔽，愚昧。

18. 紫极：星座名。

19. 度：推测，思量。所致：所得到的东西。代指身边的事物。提耳指掌：犹言"耳提面命"，形容教导之恳切。提耳，提着耳朵教导。指掌，指着手掌教育。尚：久远。

20. 承：承受，接受。这里是聆听的意思。是一种客气用语。自嫌：自己怀疑。嫌，疑惑，怀疑。

21. 单行：专行。这里指某一方面的简单方法。

22. 阶浅：通过浅近的阶段。阶，台阶。用作动词。通过。济：成功。

23. 根荄：根部。荄，根。洞地：穿入大地。泓窈：洪大深邃。泓，水大的样子。窈，深。汤：水大的样子。一般"汤汤"连用。

24. 阴德：暗中施德于人。款契：诚挚亲密。大试：大用，重任。

25. 仙主：成仙的关键。主，主要，关键。

26. 藉：凭借。世主：国君。

27. 辕：车前驾牲畜的直木。辋：车轮的外圈。辖：安在车轴末端的挡铁，用以防止车轮脱落。莫或：没有一个。或，有的。

28. 干：干犯，侵害。

29. 子弦：单独的一根琴弦。子，孤单。甲胄：甲衣和头盔。札：铠甲上用皮革或金属制成的叶片。

30. 阙：通"缺"，缺乏。

31. 体要：体会、使用其中的要点。

32. 玄、素：玄女和素女。是传说中向黄帝传授房中术的两名神仙。偏枯：偏狭，偏执。

33. 两有所失：两方面都有所失。既失去了好的方术，又浪费了宝贵的时间。

34. 戆钝：愚钝。殊：非常。魍魉：传说中的山川精怪。

35. 素狭：向来知识面就很狭窄。交：共同，结合。

36. 作家：治理家务。事用：使用，从事。疏：通"蔬"，蔬菜。

37. 厌劾：镇压。厌，镇压。劾，弹劾，审判。闻：听到，学习。

38. 算：时间单位。三天。

39. 三尸：道教认为人身内有三种作祟的神，分别居于上、中、下三丹田内，称上尸、中尸、下尸。每逢庚申的日子，就向天帝报告人们罪过。学仙之士必须除去三尸，才能升仙。

40. 祭酹：祭祀。酹，把酒洒在地上以示祭奠。

41. 司命：神名，掌管人的生死。

42. 晦：旧历每月的最后一天。

43. 赵简子：春秋末期晋国贵族。《史记·赵世家》记载：赵简子生病，五天不省人事，醒来后说自己在天帝的宫廷里过得很快乐，天帝还赐给他两个竹器，预示他的后代会成为诸侯。秦穆公：春秋时期秦国君主。《史记·封禅书》记载：秦穆公病卧五日而不醒，醒后说梦见了上帝，上帝命令他平定晋国动乱。金策：黄金制成的简策。

44. 机发：扳动机关而发射。响应：像回音那样回应。形容速度极快。响，回声。

45. 恕：用自己的心去推想别人的心。逮：及，达到。赒：周济，赈救。佞谄：巧言谄媚。阴贼：阴险狡诈的人。

46. 背向异辞：背后当面说法不一。戾：违反，反对。纵曲枉直：纵容邪恶，冤枉好人。曲，不正直的人。

47. 燎猎：用放火烧山的方式去打猎。詈：骂。

48. 佻：窃取。长钱：很多钱。陌：通"佰"，古代计量钱的单位，一百钱。这里代指钱。

49. 尪：孱弱。绐：欺骗。牵天援地：指天画地。形容发誓的样子。一说指人短长时乱扯一通。求直：求得理直气壮以掩饰自己的理亏。

50. 假：借。换贷：换东西和借钱。穷：穷尽，消耗完。狭幅短度：窄幅面、短尺子，指卖布匹时不给足应有的数量。

51. 晦歌朔哭：每月的最后一天唱歌，每月的最初一天哭泣。朔，旧历的每月初一。

52. 恶心：做坏事的动机。恶迹：坏事。

53. 以当填之：用来抵偿别人的损失。

54. 县官：代指官府。这里指吃官司。

55. 更相杀：反过来杀自己。

56. 漏脯：隔宿之肉。古人认为这种肉为漏水所沾，有毒，食之会致死。鸩酒：用鸩鸟羽毛浸泡的毒酒。鸩，一种有毒的鸟。

57. 所为：指过去所做的坏事。

58. 听卑：监察着人间。听，指监察、观察。卑，低。指人间。鉴：监察。

59. 羊公：即羊祜。晋代人。《抱朴子外篇·广譬》："羊公积行，黄发不倦，而乃坠金雨集。"但《晋书·羊祜列传》记载，羊祜去世后，"襄阳百姓于岘山祜平生游憩之所建碑立庙，岁时飨祭焉。望其碑者，莫不流涕，杜预因名为'坠泪碑'"。史书只有百姓为他坠泪之说，未见上天为他坠金的记载。诣：到，至。

60. 蔡顺：东汉人。《后汉书·周磐列传》："蔡顺，字君仲，亦以至孝称。……母年九十，以寿终。未及得葬，里中灾，火将逼其舍，顺抱伏棺枢，号哭叫天，火遂越烧它室，顺独得免。"

61. 郭巨：西汉人。《太平御览》卷四百一十一："刘向《孝子图》曰：郭巨，河内温人。……妻产男，虑养之则妨供养，乃令妻抱儿欲掘地埋之，于土中得金一釜，上有铁券云：'赐孝子郭巨。'"铁券：铁制券契。帝王颁赐功臣，授以世代享受特权的凭证。这里指上天赐给郭巨的铁券。

62. 项托：据说他七岁时就当了孔子的老师，十岁夭折。伯牛：孔子弟子冉耕，因德行高尚而著称，但却生病早死。臧否：善恶。臧，善。否，恶。

63. 荠、麦：荠菜和小麦。而疑阴、阳之大气：怀疑阴、阳大气的运行规律。春夏阳气盛，是万物生长的季节，而荠、麦却在夏季枯萎。致远：实现远大的志向。

64. 密勿：勤勉努力。

65. 却：打通，清除。无妄之灾：不是由于自己的过错而引起的灾难。这里泛指意外的灾难。妄，行为不正，不法。

66. 执日：即未日。古人用天干地支纪日，"执日"即地支中的"未日"。《淮南子·天文训》："寅为建，卯为除，辰为满，巳为平，主生；午为定，未为执，主陷。"六癸：指甲寅这一天。古人认为天干中的"甲"是最尊贵的，一般隐而不露，所以甲子称"六戊"，甲寅称"六癸"。上土：指六癸日取回的土。百叶：即"柏叶"。柏树叶。薰草：香草名。又叫蕙草。

67. 岁破：古代术士所说的凶日名。岁，指太岁。古代天文学中假设的星辰名。古代术士认为太岁所在之日为凶日，与太岁相背之日也是凶日，叫"岁破"。王充《论衡·难岁》："抵太岁名曰'岁下'，负太岁名曰'岁破'，故皆凶也。"月建：农历每月所置之日为"月建"。如正月建寅，二月建卯等。朱鸟：即朱雀。这里代指南方。朱鸟本是南方七星宿的总名，其形状似鸟，故名朱鸟。与青龙、白虎、玄武合称"四灵"，分别代指南、东、西、北四方，故朱鸟指南方。压：压制，抵御。

68. 生地：可以安全地保护生命的地方。里：一种居民组织。古代二十五家为一里。

69. 逼：狭窄。

70. 轼：古代车厢前用作扶手的横木。

71. 窃闻：听说。垂：敬辞。表示对方高于自己。祛：除去。

72. 太元之山：指人的头颅。太元，头发。道教称头发神为太元。嵬嵬：山高峻的样子。

73. 氤氲：云气很盛的样子。

74. 玉井：即玉泉。内丹术术语。指口中津液。泓邃：水深而清澈的样子。匪休：无休止。匪，不。

75. 百二十官：泛指体内各种器官的神灵。曹府：官府。曹，分职治事的官署。相由：相互帮助。由，帮助。

76. 离：卦名，代表火。坎，卦名，代表水。"玄芝"二句：这里用玄芝、绛树的茂盛比喻生命力的旺盛，玄芝，黑色的灵芝。绛树，红色的树木。特，耸起，挺立。金玉：代指炼成的内丹。嵯峨：高大的样子。醴泉：内丹术术语。指口中津液。隅：一角，一边。

77. 挹：舀。这里指饮用。乔、松：两位神仙名。王子乔和赤松子。俦：伴侣，同辈。

78. 长谷：长谷在古代的含义很多。根据下文，这里当暗指女性的阴部。杳杳：深远幽静的样子。巍巍：高大的样子。玄气：内丹术术语。即肾间之气。玉液：这里指肾液，即阴液。霏霏：盛多的样子。金池紫房：性器官的隐语。指女性的阴部。隈：山或水的弯曲之处。暗指两股之间。

79. 黄精：指女性的精气。房中术的目的之一就是男性采阴补阳，即采女性的精气以达到强身的作用。

80. 始青之下月与日：刚开始修炼内丹时要让两只眼睛内视丹田。始青，刚开始修炼内丹的时候。《云笈七签》卷十二："三玄出始青，言万物生而青色也。"月与日，指两只眼睛。左目为日，右目为月。两半同升合成一：让口中的津液与体内的神气共同出现并合二为一。两半，指口中的津液与体内的神气。《云笈七签》卷五十六："口中舌上所出之液，液与神气一合，谓两半合一也。"升，出现。合成一，二者合为一体，目的是要把它们结合起来炼成内丹。

81. 出彼玉池入金室：内丹就是这样从口中进入心室。玉池，指口中出津液处。《云笈七签》卷五十六："玉池者，口中舌上所出之液。"金室，指心室。《云笈七签》卷五十六对"入金室"解释说："在于心室。心室者，神之舍，气之宅，精之主，魂之魄。"大如弹丸黄如橘：内丹如弹丸大小，颜色黄如橘子。

82. 纯白之气至微密：还要让这颗内丹化为纯白的细微之气。

83. 升于幽关三曲折：这股纯白之气出现在两肾之间时多次委婉辗转。幽关，指两肾之间。《云笈七签》卷十一："两肾间为幽关。"三，泛指多次。中丹煌煌独无匹：中丹光彩夺目无可比拟。中丹，处于中等水平的内丹。《丘祖全书》："一尘不染，绵绵固守精气神，如此三年不漏下丹结，六年不漏中丹结，九年不漏上丹结。"煌煌，光彩夺目的样子。

84. 立之命门形不卒：内丹处于丹田之内而人就不会死亡。命门，这里指脐下丹田穴。有时也指脾、鼻、肾等处。卒，死亡。渊乎妙矣难致诘：这种境界深邃微妙很难探讨清楚。渊，深渊。比喻深邃难识。诘，追究，探讨。

85. 五兵：五种兵器。这里泛指兵器。

86. 尽其道：完全懂得房中术。

87. 好事：指好事的人。

88. 隐藏端绪：隐藏自己的动机。端绪，开端。这里指动机。奉事：指让别人来侍奉自己。规：图谋。

89. 节宣：对性欲进行节制和疏导。

90. 却：节制，阻止。走马：指漏泄精液。阴丹：还精之术。即把精液转化为有利于健康的丹药。朱肠：使肠胃更加红润、健康。朱，红。

91. 玉液：指实施房中术时所采到的精华之液。金池：比喻女性的阴部。三五：内丹术术语。说法不一。这里指精、气、神的结合体。华：华美的大梁。暗喻男阴。天年：自然的寿命。

92. 荆山：有许多山叫荆山，这里指河南灵宝南的覆釜山。鼎湖：地名。古代传说黄帝曾铸鼎于荆山下，鼎成，有龙垂胡须迎黄帝上天。后人因名其处为鼎湖。飞：炼制。因为金丹在炼制过程中，变化非常大，所以用"飞"来形容。

93. 所由：所得，结果。

94. 三牲：古人一般以牛、羊、猪为三牲。道教则以獐、鹿、麂为三牲。这里泛指美食。

[译文]

The Meaning of "Subtle"[1]

I HAVE BEEN taught that those who accept common opinions and conform to established patterns are trusted without a word, whereas those who travel a different path or pursue different interests are doubted despite their protestations of loyalty. Among the little townsfolk who have never been beyond the confines of their own village, petty matters vying for their acceptance or rejection sink or swim more readily than metals or feathers. For such people, things are either black or white, as rice flour and ink; but doubters are far more undecided than that. This is particularly true when you wish to persuade them about things transcending normal worldly experience or to instruct them about the infinitesimal. They just guffaw. [2] This has been going on for a long time; it is not a new problem.

So long as vision can be applied, though it be on dark and obscure places or on tiny and barren things, it is felt that it is not difficult to see. However, in the case of things which are unattainable, though it be the brilliance of sun and moon and magnificent heaven, or the heights of Mounts Sung, T'ai, Kan or Yün, people still find it impossible to examine them! [3] The profound knowledge and unique views of those Saints of God, Yellow Emperor and Lao Tan, have been revealed in secret texts from the famous mountains or in genii classics handed down by the gods. [4] Removed from the impediments and dust of our human world, these texts contain no shackles; mounting the greatest heights, they carry us to the empyrean itself. (The reading of such texts brings nothing but elation.) Metal and stone cannot equal them in hardness; they enjoy longer lives than do turtles and cranes.

Mindful of the future and anxious lest believers in these things lack texts, those Saints transmitted prescriptions which are brilliantly clear. [5] The minor ones produce lesser effects; the important ones will produce strong effects. Shallow-minded persons, however, observe only the most paltry things. Thinking only of infusions of sow thistle or smartweed as sweet, they remain ignorant of sugar and honey; preferring the poorer wines, they disdain the excellent. [6] They know how to cherish life, but they are ignorant of the divine process that nurtures it. They know enough to fear death, but they will not believe that there are methods that can produce immortality. They know the many illnesses that result from excesses of eating and drinking, but they are unable to moderate the fats and sweets entering their mouths. They know that overwork and covetousness produce desiccation, but they are ignorant of methods to curb their desires.[7] In the same way, I may declare that divinity and geniehood are obtainable, but how can I command credence?

Interlocutor: Your own person bears none of the lineaments of superiority, nor do strange hairs cover your frame. You have not reached the age of either An-ch'i or Old P'eng. Your eyes have never set upon a god or genie, nor have your ears enjoyed a unique hearing of strange tales. How do you know that Fullness of Life is achievable or that there is any evidence of life being nurtured?[8] You will not yet admit that you feel God (the Mystery and the Marvelous) in your heart and mind or that you enjoy a unique view of extraordinary sights.[9] Your clothes are not sufficient to cover your hide, and your general resources are not enough to last from one day to the next, yet you talk mightily of arts that only a millionaire like Fan Li could practice; you associate yourself with schemes appropriate to a wealthy man like I-tun. It is only logical that you bring criticism upon yourself. You are sickly, yet claim to have the essence of the arts of Doctors Ho and Ch'in Yüeh-jen. You have frequently run away, but claim to understand thoroughly the calculations of the strategists Sun Wu and Wu Ch'i. If people do not believe you, it is because you do not show any effects of your own claims.[10]

Ko: Floating in its well, the tiny grub declares there is no such expanse in the world as the four seas; twisting within a kernel, the worm believes that the six extremities of the universe are restricted to his one fruit. If you were to tell these insects about the boundlessness of great expanses of water or the vastness of the universe, they would find your words meaningless and utterly incredible.[11]

When my eyes have square pupils and my ears grow from the top of my head; when, driving a flying dragon and riding a cloud of good fortune, I shall mount above the darting lightning and reach Lighted-from-below, how will you be able to interrogate me?[12] If you see me, you will then cry out that it is a heaven or an earth deity, or a strange sort of man. It will never occur to you to say that I am something produced by mere study![13] Meanwhile, being the first one to be awakened to these truths I can draw along those who are like-minded, but how can I compel people like you to believe me?[14] If there were a genie in your own household, right under your eyes and standing at your very side, you would never suspect it even if you consulted the lots. [15] But once his course was completed, he would do his walking in the blue yonder and sojourn on Purple Summit. Then, unless you were attuned to such things, you would neither see nor hear him. You must be an earless fellow![16]

People of the world have faith only in their own opinions and rely upon their own shortsighted views. They claim that nothing differs from what they personally have experienced. They accept all the everyday things, but are amazed at the unusual ones. They prick their ears and point fingers at everything they do not understand. [17] This attitude has been around for a long time; there is nothing new about it.

Another person: Having frequently listened to what you had to say, I cannot doubt the existence of genii. Nevertheless, I personally feel that I simply could never become one. Are there any other significant divine processes that could be pursued more simply?

Ko: Any pursuit of the divine process begins in the shallows before attaining the depths; facility is acquired only after difficulties. [18] If your will is firmly formed, you can reach any shore; if you are hesitant, nothing is achieved. It is a complex matter. You cannot expect a tree's branchings to tower high into the clouds unless its roots go deep into the soil, nor can a stream flow mightily for thousands of miles if its springs do not run deep. Therefore, unless effective secret action is accumulated ahead of time there can be no influencing of the gods; without a meeting of sincere hearts and minds there can be no winning of a teacher's friendship. Unless there is hard preparatory work there can be no question of the Grand Attempt. [19] If you search for the important divine process before consulting an intelligent teacher, you will not succeed. The Nine-crucible cinnabars and the Potable Gold are by far the chief of the divine processes leading to geniehood, but they are so elaborate and the expense is so heavy it has not been possible to carry them through to the end. [20] There is the greatest urgency that sperm be valued and breath preserved. In addition, by taking the lesser medicines to protract one's life and studying the lower recipes to avoid evils, progress is gradually made into the subtleties.

Still another person: There are so many prescriptions that it is very difficult to carry them out fully. Aside from the gold and cinnabar processes, which are the best of the others?

Ko: Before acquiring those of the highest importance a man has no choice but to become widely acquainted with the lesser ones. It might be said that one must rely upon the whole mass of recipes jointly to produce Fullness of Life. [21] To compare the situation with a similar one of significance, it is similar to a king's governing of his domain. Not a single one of the many civil or military rites and standards can be dispensed with. Or to compare it with some lesser undertaking—it is like the cartwright's work, where neither the shafts nor the rims nor the axles nor the hub-locks may be missing. The recipes we follow stimulate gods within our bodies so that a prolongation of life may be acquired more quickly, and externally they exorcize evils so that no misfortunes interfere. [22] One might compare all this with a lute, from which we must not expect the Five Notes if there is only one string left. Or we might take for comparison the lorica and helmet, which require more than a single plaque to withstand a point or blade. [23] Why? There must be nothing missing if you would have a harmonic use of the Five Notes, and the place where points and blades strike must have all its parts.

In everything pertaining to the nurturing of life one must learn much and make the essentials one's own; look widely and know how to select. There can be no reliance upon one particular specialty, for there is always the danger that breadwinners will emphasize their personal specialties. That is why those who know recipes for sexual intercourse say that only these recipes can lead to geniehood. Those who know breathing procedures claim that only circulation of the breaths can prolong our years; those knowing methods for bending and stretching say that only calisthenics can exorcize old age; those knowing herbal prescriptions say that only through the nibbling of medicines can one be free from exhaustion. Failures in the study of the divine process are due to such specializations.[24] People with shallow experience who happen to know one particular thing well will immediately declare it a panacea. But those ignorant of the true divine process, though possessing potent prescriptions, continue to do more and more searching, without end. Their days are lost in wasted effort, and they lack certainty about their labors. All of this type are suffering double loss.[25] Sometimes, since they are naturally stupid, what they know is extremely superficial, and, feeling compelled to enter a famous mountain, they tread upon or are struck by the bite of some poisonous animal and suffer a wound from it. Then they are ashamed to try a second time. Or they may be devoured by a tiger or a wolf; slain by a *wang-liang* demon (in the form of a brown child with red eyes, long ears, and a fine head of hair); or become hungry and remain without a method for dispensing with starchy foods; or become cold and lack a method for warming themselves. Wouldn't it be stupid to die in a mountain valley?[26]

Selection of the right teacher is more important than hard study. If the teacher is not widely schooled, he will not teach his subject exhaustively, and will go on to claim that pursuit of the divine process does not reside in quantity.[27] This declaration merely signifies that, given the possession of all the essentials pertaining to gold and cinnabar, no use will be made of the rest. Very few people, however, know these matters. How can you stand around waiting for instruction in what is not necessarily the big thing, without meanwhile practicing the lesser recipes which are also quite beneficial? This would be as though a householder said that he would not use other things, for he had been told that the handling and preservation of gold, silver, pearls, and jade could of themselves provide for generation upon generation. Yet, if he lacked such things, how could he help but sow the various grains and provide by accumulating abundant stores of fruits and vegetables?[28]

Therefore, by giving up starches one can become immune to weapons, exorcize demons, neutralize poisons, and cure illnesses. On entering a mountain, he can render savage beasts harmless. When he crosses streams, no harm will be done to him by dragons. There will be no fear when plague strikes, and when a crisis or difficulty suddenly arises, you will know how to cope with it. All these are minor matters, but one must not fail to be aware of them. How can you then fail to learn things that are more important than these?[29]

Interlocutor: Would you mind listing the taboos for one wishing to carry out the divine process leading to Fullness of Life?

Ko: Taboos are most urgent for avoiding harm and losses. *Inner Commands of the Book of Changes*, *Ch'ih-sung tzu's Classics*, and *The Life-dealing Amulets of the Ho-t'u-chi* are unanimous in saying that the gods of heaven and earth who are in charge of misdeeds make deductions from people's three-day reckonings according to the degree of their wrongdoing. As these reckonings decrease, a man becomes poorer and falls ill; frequently he suffers anxiety. When no more are left, he dies. Since there are hundreds of things that may give rise to deductions, I cannot give a complete account.

It is also said that there are Three Corpses in our bodies, which, though not corporeal, actually are of a type with our inner, ethereal breaths, the powers, the ghosts, and the gods. They want us to die prematurely. (After death they become a man's ghost and move about at will to where sacrifices and libations are being offered.) Therefore, every fifty-seventh day of the sixty-day cycle they mount to heaven and personally report our misdeeds to the Director of Fates. Further, during the night of the last day of the month the hearth god also ascend to heaven and makes an oral report of a man's wrongs. For the more important misdeeds a whole period of three hundred days is deducted. For the minor ones they deduct one reckoning, a reckoning being three days. Personally, I have not yet been able to determine whether this is really so or not, but that is because the ways of heaven are obscure, and ghosts and gods are hard to understand.[30]

We do know that both Viscount Chien of Chao and Duke Mu of Ch'in received a gold plaque from Emperor-up-there; the site god himself was witness.[31] We know that there are spirits in mountains, rivers, plants, trees, wells, hearths, water holes, and also pools. Even within the bodies of us human beings there are gods. Therefore, since heaven and earth are the biggest things in creation, it is logical that they should also have spirits. And if they do have gods, it is also logical that they reward good and punish evil. Yet, given their physical size and the looseness of their organization, they simply must not be expected to respond mechanically. [32]

Accordingly, when we examine the moral injunctions of the various teachings, we find all of them agreeing that those desiring Fullness of Life must strive to accumulate goodness, win merit, be kind and affectionate to others, practice the Golden Rule, love even the creeping things, rejoice in the good fortune of others and commiserate with their sufferings, help those in distress, aid the poor, harm no living thing, utter no curses, look upon the successes and failures of others as their own, not be proud, not vaunt themselves, not envy their betters, and conceal no evil intentions with flattery. In this way they become men of exalted character and receive good fortune from heaven. Their undertakings are sure to be successful, and they can seek geniehood with hope of success. [33]

On the other hand, when goodness is disliked and slayings preferred, lips approve while the heart disapproves, things are said behind a back that would not be said to a face, the upright are opposed, subordinates oppressed, superiors deceived, those being served are rebelled against; when there is no gratitude shown for favors, bribes are accepted when the law is applied, crooked dealing is acquiesced in and honesty corrupted, private interest is given precedence over the public, the innocent are punished, the homes of others destroyed and their valuables taken, harm is done to others and their positions usurped, those of high caliber are plundered, those who have surrendered are put to death, genii and sages are maligned, harm is inflicted on processors, flying birds are shot with pellets, the pregnant disemboweled and eggs broken; when there is hunting by fire during spring and summer, gods and powers are cursed, people are taught to do evil, the virtues of others are concealed, others are jeopardized in order to bring security to oneself, the credits of others are seized, the good deeds of others are destroyed and the things they love taken from them; when one separates others from their families, one's victory is pressed to the point of disgracing others, one borrows full strings of cash and repays with deficient strings, floods are caused and fires set, spells are cast on others, the weak are oppressed, evil is returned for good, one takes or requests forcibly, plunders for enrichment, is not objective and fair, is licentious and base; when orphans and widows are oppressed, bequests are amassed and gifts extracted, deception and falsehood are practiced, the secrets of others are betrayed and their vices abetted, Heaven and Earth are invoked, justification is sought through the help of the gods, things are borrowed but not returned, exchanges and loans are not repaid, one's demands and desires are insatiable, loyalty and honesty are repulsed, a superior's orders are not obeyed, the teacher is not respected, another's good deeds are mocked and his crops destroyed, the things of others are damaged, those with no ability are given employment, the impure is considered clean and given to others to drink and eat, light weight is given and short measure, the bolt of cloth is short in width and length, truth is interspersed with falsehood, dishonest profits are amassed, goods are taken under false pretenses, associates are surpassed, even including one's father—then there will be singing on the last of the month but weeping on the first. [34] Every one of these constitutes one fault, and according to its severity the Director of Fates deducts a reckoning or a period; when no more reckonings remain, death ensues. When there is only evil intention but no overt act, only one reckoning is deducted, but if another suffers as the result of your wrongdoing, a whole period is deducted. In all cases where suicide is committed before the allotment is exhausted, misfortune will befall the sons and grandsons.

  Whenever you interfere with or appropriate another's property, your wife, children, and other members of your household may be reckoned in as compensation even if this requires their deaths, which however may not occur immediately. And if your wrongdoing does not bring death upon the members of your household, floods, fires, burglaries, and other losses will continuously occur among your belongings. Or you may be obliged to provide personally the medication for the district magistrate's illnesses and meet the costs of the animals for the sacrificial services until you have compensated for the wrongs you have committed. Therefore, the Taoists say that whenever a person has been wrongfully slain, there will follow mutual slayings with weapons; wealth acquired through improper acts will create resentments. It is like satisfying hunger with putrid corned meats or slaking thirst with poisoned wine; death ensues despite your momentary satiation. [35]

These are the rules governing atonement for wrongdoings of the past: if there have been wrongful slayings on your part, thought must be given to rescuing those deserving death in order to absolve one's own fault; if the property of others has been wrongfully seized, thought must be given to donations for the poor and needy; if others have been inculpated in your wrongs, thought must be given to recommending those of high caliber for office. All these propitiatory actions being diametric opposites of the wrongs done, they will promptly bring enjoyment of good luck and profit; this is the way to turn misfortune into good. [36]

If one violates none of the prohibitions, one's years are sure to be protracted, one's longevity increased, and one's study of the divine process quickly concluded. Heaven is high, but its hearing reaches low, and every creature is under its observation. If good is done unremittingly, one is sure to be rewarded with good fortune. Yang Hsü accumulated good works and was charitable, therefore in his old age he received gold dropped from heaven. Ts'ai Shen was so highly filial that all the gods reacted favorably to him. Kuo Chü was willing to kill his son for the sake of his own mother and got as rich reward an iron token inscribed in gold. [37] However, goodness being difficult and evil easy, the unthinking among us hold that heaven and earth cannot distinguish good from evil because of the misfortunes suffered by such persons as Hsiang T'o and Jan Keng. They do not realize that one with a good reputation is not necessarily deserving of it internally; that the man praiseworthy for one thing need not be absolved of guilt for the very opposite. It is like observing the life-and-death cycle of shepherd's purse and wheat and then not believing that the grand breaths of yin and yang have effect from great distances. It is probably for similar reasons that superior officers barely escape punishments despite earnest efforts, and ordinary men do not get their wishes fulfilled. [38]

Interlocutor: Before God and the natural life have been achieved, or before all trace of oneself has been obliterated in a famous mountain—the present being different from antiquity and bandits being very numerous—how are we to banish sudden anxiety and obviate sure disaster?[39]

Ko: Always gather Six-kuei superior earth on a friendly day, and after mixing it with a hundred leaves of fragrant plants paint a square foot of your door with it. No bandits will then come. A human form may also be fashioned of a mixture of Market-south-entrance earth, Sui-p'o earth, and Yüeh-chien earth, and then placed to the south to check robbers. In an emergency, place yourself in a nucleus (life site); then there will be nothing to fear. There is a nucleus to the world, a province, a prefecture, a subprefecture, a town, a neighborhood, a house, and even a room.[40]

Interlocutor: Isn't that getting quite small—a room?

Ko: The classics tell us that in the greatest of emergencies one can hide in the crossbar of a vehicle, so you see that there is a nucleus even in a vehicle. Why shouldn't there be one in a room?

Interlocutor: I have been taught that when carrying out the divine process in search of life one should know the two mountains, but I have never been clear as to where they are located. I should like you to enlighten me and allay my doubts.

Ko: They exist, but they are neither Mount Hua and Mount Huo, nor Mount Sung and Mount Tai.

> *Tai-yüan's mountain, hard to know but easy to seek.*
> *It is neither in heaven nor on earth; it is not sunk under water, nor does it float.*
> *It is exceedingly steep and long-lasting; rocky and rough-pathed.*
> *Pleasant and wholesome; our inner gods and thoughts like it there.*
> *Jade-like wells run deep there with clear water, irrigating the mountain without cease.*
> *There is an administrative force of one hundred twenty, well coordina-*

第七章　道教综合类文本《抱朴子内篇》翻译研究　　281

ted.

Since it is situated on a line with east and west, there are black growths by the thousands.

Particularly, the peach grows there, all the fruit exceptional.

There are rocks of gold and jade, and springs of new wine flowing from the corners.

Officers of the past have quaffed from its pure streams.

If you can find it, you will join the company of Wang Ch'iao and Ch'ih-sung tzu.

This is one of them.

Ch'ang-ku's mountain, filled with fragrances and looming ever larger and larger.

The breath of God blows in breeze after breeze there; exudates of jade continuously fall in flakes.

Golden pools and crimson rooms in its crevices.

Any ignorant person accidentally straying there will surely die.

The officer in possession of the divine process who climbs it will not weaken.

Having gathered and taken knotgrass, he acquires ability to fly heavenward. [41]

This is the second of them. Give careful thought to them, for they are the places which the Ancients of high caliber kept secret.

Interlocutor: I should like to learn the recipe of God's Men for protecting one's person and refining one's well-being.

Ko: Your question probes to the very depths. Here are the oral directions I received from my late teacher:

At the foot of Shih-ching (Beginnings-Azure) are the moon and sun.

Like two halves, they mount jointly to become one.

An emission from the Jade Pool (mouth) enters the Golden Room (lungs).

Large as an arbalest's pellet, yellow as an orange;

Within it has an excellent taste, sweet as honey.

When you have been able to secure it, be careful not to lose it.

One does not pursue that which has already passed, otherwise the body would perish.

The pure, white breath becomes thoroughly sublimated.

Proceeding to the Somber Gateway (kidneys), it bends and twists thrice.

The Cinnabar Field of the center portion of the body sparkles as never before.

When the emission comes to a halt at the Gateway to Life (belly), the physique will not perish.

Profound is this marvel, and hard to call in question. [42]

As I say, these are the oral directions I had from my late teacher. He who knows them will fear no ghosts at any time, nor weapons.

Interlocutor: I have been taught that he who can fully carry out the correct sexual procedures can travel alone and summon gods and genii. Further, he can shift disaster from himself and absolve his misdeeds; turn misfortune into good; rise high if in office; double his profits if in business. Is it true?[43]

Ko: This is all deceptive, exaggerated talk found in the writings of mediums and shamans; it derives from the enlargements and colorings of dilettantes. It utterly belies the facts. Some of it is the work of base liars creating meaningless claims to deceive the masses. Their concealed purpose is to seek service from others; to gather about themselves pupils solely with a view to obtaining advantages for themselves in their own time.

The best of the sexual recipes can cure the lesser illnesses, and those of a lower quality can prevent us from becoming empty; but that is all. There are very natural limits to what such recipes can accomplish. How could they ever be expected to confer the ability to summon gods and genii and to dispel misfortune or bring good?[44]

It is inadmissible that man should sit and bring illness and anxieties upon himself by not engaging in sexual intercourse. But then again, if he wishes to indulge his lusts and cannot moderate his dispersals, he hacks away at his very life. Those knowing how to operate the sexual recipes can check ejaculation, thereby repairing the brain; revert their sperm to the Vermilion Intestine (? for small or large). They can gather saliva into the Pool of Gold (? gall bladder); conduct the three southern and the five northern breaths to their Flowered Rafters (? lungs). They can thus cause a man, even in old age, to have an excellent complexion, and terminate the full number of his allotted years.[45]

The crowds, however, learning that Yellow Emperor mounted to heaven after having a harem of 1200, proceeds to claim that this is the sole reason he attained Fullness of Life. They do not know that Yellow Emperor mounted to heaven on a dragon only after having successfully sublimed the Nine-crucibles cinnabars on the shores of Tripod Lake at the foot of the Ching Mountains. Yellow Emperor could naturally have a harem of 1200, but his success was not due to that sole fact.[46]

In sum, there is no benefit from taking all sorts of medicines and eating beef, mutton, and pork, if one does know the arts of sexual intercourse. The Ancients, therefore, fearing that people might treat existence itself lightly or arbitrarily, purposely lauded these arts beyond complete credibility.[47] Sexual intercourse may be compared with water and fire, either of which can slay man or bring him life, depending solely upon his ability to deal with them. On the whole, if the important rules are known, the benefits will be proportionate to the number of one's successive copulations. If, however, the procedure is employed in ignorance, sudden death could ensue after only one or two copulations.[48] Old P'eng's methods contain all the essentials. Other books on the subject teach only many troublesome methods difficult to carry out, and the resulting benefits are not necessarily as claimed. Man is scarcely able to follow the directions, and there are thousands of words of oral directions. Whoever does not know them would still be unable to attain Fullness of Life, even though he took many medicines. (Ware, 1966: 109 – 123)

[解析]

1. 标题"微旨"意指对仙道的"微妙旨趣"的说明。该篇葛洪针对如何修习并实践仙道意趣的重要观点提出他个人的意见。因此,魏鲁男翻译为 the Meaning of "Subtle",译者将"微"对应英文"Subtle",并采用双引号标识,将其视为一个名词概念。参照这一翻译,标题可改译为 The Meaning of Subtlety,去掉引号,改用名词,更能显化"微妙旨趣"的意义。

2. 这里葛洪批评了连"沉浮过于金羽,皂白分于粉墨"这样如此分明的是是非非都不能辨别的"抱惑之士",认为不可能同他们谈论成仙大道。该句涉及"寻常咫尺之近理"的理解问题,魏鲁男译本对应为"那些从来没有走出过自己村子的普通市民"(the little townsfolk who have never been beyond the confines of their own village),大概是没能了解"寻常"作为古代的一种计量单位,与"咫尺"同义,都是形容距离很近,用以形容"近理"之浅显。魏鲁南将其等同于今日所谓的"平常",进而引申为"普通市民"(the little townsfolk)。此外,"沉浮过于金羽,皂白分于粉墨"皆是比喻,作者将"人间取舍之细事"比拟为沉浮明显的金属羽毛,黑白分明的白粉黑墨,为复义叠句,翻译时取其一端即可。该段可改译为"The social principles that consolidate the functioning of secular world are insignificant matters which can be competently perceived with ease, for the underlying principles are as apparent as the unmistakable difference between the black and the white, or between the heavy and the light. However, people who are in the state of mental confusion are viewing this world with bewilderment. Therefore, if we wish to instruct them about things of immortal beings that are beyond these people's intellectual capacity, naturally they will falsely react by mocking it as superstitious exaggeration. Their reactions are not new"。

汉语为意合型语言,其意义的连贯是隐性的,其语法关系也是隐性的,用文言文撰写的典籍内容尤其如此。要翻译这样的文字,译者需将隐性的内容显性化,也就是作大量的补充,只有这样,才能足意成章,否则读者会不知所云。比如，该段的"大而笑之"不是指"大笑"，而是指"（俗人认为这是）夸大之辞因而加以讥笑"，因此仅译为 They just guffaw 是不够的，需采用明晰化翻译。

3. 原文"夫明之所及，虽玄阴幽夜之地，豪厘芒发之物，不以为难见。苟所不逮者，虽日月丽天之炤灼，嵩、岱干云之峻峭，犹不能察焉"意思：视力能看见的人，即使是在黑暗如夜的地方，一毫一厘细小得如同麦芒、头发那样的事物，也不难看见；如果是看不见的人，即使是天上日月的光芒，嵩山、泰山直冲云霄的峻峭，他们也无法看到。魏鲁男译本的理解：只要视力能企及，即是在幽暗之地，或附于细小荒芜之物，也不难看见；但如果是无法企及的事物，即便是日月昊天之光芒，或是嵩山、泰山、干山、云山之高耸，人们依然难以察觉。其中最为严重的误读是将"干云"（意思是"直冲云霄"）理解为与嵩山、泰山同类的山脉，名其为"干山""云山"，译文为"the heights of Mounts Sung, T'ai, Kan or Yün"（Ware，1966：109），故需修正。

4. 原文"黄老玄圣，深识独见，开秘文于名山，受仙经于神人，蹑埃尘以遣累，凌大遐以高跻"意思：黄帝、老子是思想玄远的圣人，见识深远独到，他们在名山之中写出神秘的文章，从神仙那里接受修仙的经书，急速地离开尘世以排除各种拖累，飞越高远的天空以得道成仙。魏译本对该句的理解：圣人黄老的深识独见或揭示于名山秘文，或载于神人仙经，这些秘本脱离了人世的妨碍与尘埃，没有束缚；这些秘本使我们登上最高顶峰，把我们带到最高天界。强调的是黄老深邃思想的来源，以及阅读这些秘本带来的体验。非常有意思的是，译者选用 the empyrean（意思为"最高天界"，早期基督教认为该处是上帝的家园）一词翻译"大遐"（意思为"高远的太空"）。此外，担心目标语读者难以理解这样的阅读体验，还添加括号内容加以说明。这样的理解无疑带有译者的主观性。故可改为"Yellow Emperor（Huangdi，黄帝）and Lao Tzu（老子）were two of the wisest sages whose capability and intellects were of infinity. They gained their wisdom from the immortals and produced their miraculous works in the misty mountain's deep. As such, they removed themselves from this mortal world, ascending to the the empyrean for achieving immortality"。

5. 原文"念有志于将来，愍信者之无文，垂以方法，炳然著明"意思："考虑到将来那些有志于修仙的人，同情这些修仙信道的人没有文字典籍可读，于是就把修仙的方法流传下来，这些典籍把修仙的方法说得清清楚楚"，魏鲁男译为"Mindful of the future and anxious lest believers in these things lack texts, those Saints transmitted prescriptions which are brilliantly clear"（Ware，1966：110），回译为中文：念及将来，担心信仰者无文本，这些圣人将炼养方法非常清楚地流传下来，译者略去了"有志"（指有志于修道成仙的人）这一信息，原文意群逻辑衔接不畅，故改译为"Being sympathized with the fact that people of later ages desiring to seek the enlightenment of transcendence would require guidance, they produced classics clearly demonstrating the methods for realizing immortality"。

6. 原文"然而浅见之徒，区区所守，甘于荼蓼而不识粘蜜，酣于醨酪而不赏醇醪"意思：那些见识短浅的人，守着自己浅陋无知，只知道吃苦不堪言的荼蓼而不识粘蜜，沉醉于薄酒酸醋而不去品尝甜美醇醪。"区区"的辞典意义之一为"数量小或不重要"，因此魏译本翻译为"the most paltry things"。依据该语境，此处应理解为"拘泥，受限"。作者借用"荼蓼"与"粘蜜"、"醨酪"与"醇醪"这两对反义项凸显浅见之徒的无知狭隘，所以可以增译"Their way of thinking has no room for openness, innovation and comprehensiveness"，以凸显这一主题。

7. 原文"知极情恣欲之致枯损，而不知割怀于所欲也"的意思：明知放纵情欲会招致身体衰败，却不知道割舍心中的欲望。魏译本把"极情恣欲"译为"overwork and covetousness"意思上也说得过去，但不符合道教护身养生思想，不如译为"dissipation and excessive pleasures"。而"枯损"也不是其辞典意义上的"干燥受损"，译为"desiccation"（干燥，使失水）不如译为"health detriments"更符合原文意思，吻合道教反对纵欲、提倡节制的养生思想。

8. 中国古代经籍常使用"三五"这一名词，语境不同解释也就有异，可为数字"十五"的另一指称，也可指代"三皇五帝""三辰五星""三才五常""三元五行"等，葛洪《神仙传》中有一段老子的肖像描写，原文：老子黄白色，美眉，广颡长耳，大目疏齿，方口厚唇；额有参午达理，日角月悬。其中"额有参午（通'三五'）达理"意思

"额头有错杂的纹理",英译《神仙传》的汉学家康儒博将该句翻译为 "On his forehead there were patterns [symbolizing] the three [powers] and the five [phases]"(Campany,2002:199),将"参午达理"理解为额头上有象征"三才""五行"的皱纹图案,魏鲁南英译本中该句的翻译为"Your own person bears none of the lineaments of superiority"(Ware,1966:110),将"参午达理"浅化译为"the lineaments of superiority",意指"超凡脱俗的面部特征",这种处理为传意法,基本达意,但似乎少了一些原文对神仙形象的刻画。单从文字表面来看,康儒博的解读似乎有点牵强,但若从原文所发生的语境来看,康儒博的译文似乎更符合古籍对老子的神化,因此这里可以借用康译,改译为"You have neither the physical signs of divinities nor the powers of performing miracles. Your forehead bears no intertwining patterns symbolizing the three powers and the five phases, nor do strange hairs and fine bones cover your frame. You have not reached the age of the longeval Anqi(安期)or Pengzu(彭祖). Your eyes have never set upon a transcendent, nor have your ears heard of strange tales. How do you know that immortality can be achieved? Are there any evidences?"

安期和彭祖都是善于养生因而以长寿闻名的道教神仙,考虑到译入语读者缺乏这样的认知,因此在直译之外增译 the longeval。此外,段首增加"You have neither the physical signs of divinities nor the powers of performing miracles",更清楚地解释文意。

9. 语序一般体现信息的排列和接受的心理顺序。英译古文,虽有结构之变易和词语之更替,但在可能时仍以保持原文的语序为要,间或照顾原文的行文节奏和风格语气。原文"若觉玄妙于心得,运逸鉴于独见,所未敢许也"的意思:如果只是您自己领悟到的玄妙道理,独自得到的过人见解,那么我不敢苟同。该句指的是以提问者为代表的世俗之人对抱朴子的观点表示怀疑,魏译本的理解:您(抱朴子)不敢承认您只是内心领悟到了玄妙之道,或是您自己有过人的独特见解。显然与原文意指有异,故需改译为"If you claim that you have realized the miracle of immortality internally, or that you obtain a unique view of extraordinary sights, I'm afraid I can't readily accept your view"。古籍常有省略或隐含主语的现象,英译时需根据语境进行正确的补充。

10. 该部分涉及一些历史人物的翻译。这里的陶朱即春秋时代的巨富范蠡的别称，猗顿为同时期因经营畜牧和盐业而致富的商人，在音译的基础上添加人物身份范畴词为英译人名的常用手法。魏译本对这些人名的处理值得借鉴，因此可将"陶朱之术""猗顿之策"合译为 the money-making schemes of the millionaire Fanli（范蠡）and the wealthy Yidun（猗顿）。和、鹊指医和、扁鹊两位古代名医，扁鹊的真名叫秦越人，译为 doctors Yihe（医和）and Qin Yue-ren（秦越人），孙、吴指古代著名的军事家孙武和吴起，译为 the strategists Sunwu（孙武）and Wuqi（吴起）。英译中国文化中的历史人物名称时，通常需查证其真实姓名，需结合原文的详略并针对译文读者的知识背景，作或详或略的译文处理。

11. "泛迹滥水"当作"泛滥迹水"，指游荡于足迹坑的水中。"八极"意为八方最远处，代指整个天地之间。《庄子·田子方》中有这样的记载："夫至人者，上窥青天，下潜黄泉，挥斥八极，神气不变。"海外译者通常会直译"八极"为"the end of the eight directions"，例如，美国汉学家华兹生 1968 年出版的全译本《庄子》（*The Complete Works of Chuang Tzu*）将该句译为"The Perfect Man may stare at the blue heavens above, dive into the Yellow Springs below, ramble to the end of the eight directions, yet his spirit and bearing undergo no change"（Watson, 1968: 184），魏译本把"八极"译为"the six extremities of the universe"（宇宙的六极），这是因为中国在春秋战国时代用"六极"或"六合"指代宇宙，即指东南西北上下，秦汉以后始用"八方"。可选择只译其所指意义，译为"the infinite universe"。

12. 倒景：道教指天上最高之处。景，通"影"。"造倒景"指的是"到达天庭的最高处"。魏译本将"倒景"译为"Lighted-from-below"，大概是因为译者参考了《汉书·郊祀志》"登遐倒景"的注解："如淳曰：在日月之上，反从下照，故其景倒。"但因没有提供注解，让读者无法领悟。倒不如译为"the transcendent world"清楚明白。

13. "设令见我，又将呼为天神地祇异类之人，岂谓我为学之所致哉？"的意思：假如见到我，也会把我称为天神地祇般的异人，哪里会认识到我是学仙道而致呢？魏译本将天神、地祇、异类之人视为并列关系，不够准确，故改译为"a heavenly or an earthly deity, something not of the

same clan"。这里可增添"If I was as inapproachable as the immortals, there would be no practical way that the secrets to achieve immortality could be shared among the transcendence-seekers",将原文的隐性意义显性化。

14. "姑聊以先觉挽引同志"的意思：姑且凭着自己的先知先觉来提携志同道合的人。魏译本过于依赖原文的字面意义，将该句译文回译为汉语：作为第一个意识到这些真理的人，我可以拉上志同道合的人。显然没有译出原文的真实意义，故改译为"Moreover, I merely provide guidance to the people sharing the same belief"。

15. 魏译本中将"属目比肩"翻译为"right under your eyes and standing at your very side"（Ware, 1966：111），形象生动，意义精准，堪称佳译。但"吾子虽蔽"的"蔽"指的是"受蒙蔽"，有"愚昧"之意，魏鲁男转译为"even if you consulted the lots"（即使你多方咨询），不够准确，故改为"even if you were slow-witted"。

16. "通灵"指"与神灵沟通之人"，魏译本将"自非通灵"翻译为"unless you were attuned to such things"（除非你顺应了这些东西），可改译为"have psychic powers"。"耳"的古汉语含义除了指耳朵之外，可作助词表示肯定，还可作语气词，相当于"而已"，译作"罢了"。依据上下文，这里应为助词之用，因此"吾子必为无耳"的意思：你们一定会认为没有这样的事儿。魏译"You must be an earless fellow"（你一定是个没耳朵的家伙）确实有点让人啼笑皆非。全句可改为"Then, unless you had psychic powers, you would never obtain the chance to observe immortal beings in person. In this case you will inevitably question the stance that I take in connection with achieving immortality"。

17. "提耳指掌"，也称"耳提面命"，形容教导之恳切。提耳，提着耳朵教导。指掌，指着手掌教育。"提耳指掌，终于不悟"的意思：即便是提着他们的耳朵讲解，用手指在他们的手掌上指点，也始终不会觉悟。依据上文"世人总是相信自己的主观臆断，仗着自己的短浅见识，自认为所揣度的事，肯定没有差错，习惯于已经达到的，惊叹于世所罕见的"。魏译本同样犯了囿于字面意义之错，译为他们竖起耳朵，用手指着他们不懂的东西（They prick their ears and point fingers at everything they do not understand），这种翻译为典型的误读误译，与原文意思相去甚远。该句回应上文所强调的内容，即"世人"既无知又固执，因此可省去"提耳指掌"字面意象，依其真实意义翻译为"They refuse to be lectured and will never be enlightened"。

18. "凡学道当阶浅以涉深，由易以及难，志诚坚果，无所不济，疑则无功，非一事也"的意思：凡是学习仙道，都应当由浅入深，由易及难，心志虔诚，坚定果敢，就能无所不成；心存疑惑就会劳而无功，没有一件事可以做成。魏译本"由易及难"英译为"facility is acquired only after difficulties"，虽然该句放在整段译文中毫无违和感，但与原文意思正好相反，更适合表达"风雨之后见彩虹"的含义，故需修正。

19. "夫根荄不洞地，而求柯条干云，渊源不泓窈，而求汤流万里者，未之有也。是故非积善阴德，不足以感神明；非诚心款契，不足以结师友；非功劳不足以论大试；又未遇明师而求要道，未可得也"的意思：根不深入大地，而求枝条高入云霄；渊源不宏大深邃，而求疾流横荡万里，这种事是不会有的。所以，不行善事积阴德，不足以感动神明；不诚心真挚地投合，不足以结交师友；没有功劳不足以论以大用；未遇明师，却想求大道，是不可能得到的。中文采用对偶式的骈俪文体论述了仙道可学但修仙者必须具备"积善阴德""诚心款契""（做足）功劳""（巧）遇明师"这些前提条件，英文采用"unless… there can be no…"句式译出，对应了原文对偶句式的明快节奏与紧凑感。"大试"意指"大用""重任"。若只按字面译为"the Grand Attempt"，即便是首字母大写，表示特指意义，但也会因没有添加进一步解释始终无法让目的语读者明白。翻译是一种再创造，译者需根据原文提供的信息进行再创造，可将"大试"译为"offcial position"。

20. "九丹金液，最是仙主。然事大费重，不可卒办也"的意思：服食九丹金液是最为重要的成仙途径。然而炼制工程巨大、费用昂贵，不可能在短期内操办成功。九丹金液为古代方士炼制而成的神丹妙药，谓服之可以成仙。魏译本直译了这一道教术语，译为"The Nine-crucible Cinnabars and the Portal Gold"，但因缺乏必要的注释，很难让读者懂得其所指意义。因此改译为"Jiudan Jinye（九丹金液），the elixir of immortality, is the key to one's transcending. However, the elixir is so costly that its availability is greatly limited"。这里采用音译加意译的手法翻译这一道教专有术语，既能向目的语读者植入道教元素，也能帮助他们理解该术语的所指含义。

21. 汉语遵循结述性原则，常把结论性、印象性、表态性的话语放在句尾，而把表示细节的信息放在前面。英语却与此相反，遵循焦点信息靠前的原则，往往是观点性、意见性的话语在前。依据上下文，"盖藉众术之共成长生也"为结论性话语，可翻译为"All of the practices for achieving immortality listed here are mutually complimentary"，置于该段之首，以遵循英语的表达习惯。

22. "所为术者，内修形神，使延年愈疾，外攘邪恶，使祸害不干"的意思：所修炼的方术，能够内修形神，使自己延年益寿，除病化疾；外除邪恶，使祸害不来犯。魏译本理解为：我们所遵循的方法激发了我们体内的神，这样可以更快地延长寿命，并且在外部可以驱除邪恶，免受灾祸干扰。魏译把"延年愈疾"理解为"可更快捷地延长寿命"（so that a prolongation of life may be acquired more quickly），孤立且错误地理解了"愈疾"的含义。因此改译为"Therefore, people who pursue the secrets of immortality are expected to develop themselves physically and spiritually that they can safeguard their health from diseases and prolong their lifespans. They are also required to have a firm grasp of the divine capability that they will not be prone to the external threats"。若要"外攘邪恶"定是需要掌握一些特殊技能的，因此可增译"They are also required to have a firm grasp of the divine capability"。

23. 原文"比之琴瑟，不可以子弦求五音也；方之甲胄，不可以一札待锋刃也"为两句比喻，意思：好比是琴瑟，琴瑟不能用一根弦弹出五音；又好比是甲胄，甲胄不能用一片甲抵御住锋刃。"琴瑟"、"五音"和"甲胄"这些意象都是英语文化中的缺失项。魏译本翻译该句的两处比喻时颇得要旨，选用目的语读者所熟悉的意象"lute"和"the lorica and helmet"翻译原文中的喻体"琴瑟"和"甲胄"，方便了读者理解，但由于将"五音"直译为"the Five Notes"，又没有其他解释性内容，削减了该句的达意程度。因此可改译为"An example which illustrates the logic of this argument will be that one cannot play a full musical composition with the last string of a lute. In a similar instance, one also cannot arm himself with a

single piece of metal taken from the lorica and helmet"。此处采纳了魏鲁南对"琴瑟"和"甲胄"的换译法。

24. 古文极为精练，内涵却极为丰富，加之缺乏必要的衔接或断句提示，译文需深入挖掘原文的结构和信息安排，有时需重组信息结构，方能达旨。原文"凡养生者，欲令多闻而体要，博见而善择，偏修一事，不足必赖也。又患好事之徒，各仗其所长，知玄素之术者，则曰唯房中之术，可以度世矣；……"的意思：凡是养生的人，都想让自己多见识，多体会要旨，博见而善于抉择，这是因为单单只修炼一种方术，不足以完全依赖。此外还要担心好事之徒，各自仗恃自己的长处：懂得玄素之道的，就说只有房中术可以离开世俗而成仙；……。魏译本译这段译文基本传达了原文的旨意，其中将"偏修一事，不足必赖也"与"又患好事之徒，各仗其所长"合译，采用连词"for"引导第二分句，对前面的话进行解释，以补充说明理由。接下来再添加"That is why"引出由此而产生的现象。通过这些衔接手段，让主旨更明确，也顺应英语的表达习惯。不过该段依然有值得商榷之处，比如，将"好事之徒"译为"bread-winners"（养家糊口的人），似乎太过牵强。

汉学家玄英在其著作《太清：中国中古早期的道教和炼丹术》（*Great Clarity: Daoism and Alchemy in Early Medieval China*）中曾引用葛洪这段讨论养生术和长生术差异的文字，其中的"好事之徒"对应译为"those who devote themselves to one of these practices"，指"热衷修行任何一种方术的人"，应该更符合该语境。玄英的译文和魏译本也有较大差异，现摘录如下。

In everything pertaining to Nourishing Life, one should listen much but incorporate the essential, look wide but choose the best. One cannot rely on one's bias to a single practice. Moreover, the danger is that those who devote themselves to one of these practices trust only their discipline of choice. Those who know the arts of the Mysterious Woman and the Pure Woman say that one can transcend the world only through the arts of the bedchamber. Those who are expert in breathing (*tuna*) say that one can extend the number of years only through circulation of breath (*xingqi*).

Those who know the methods for bending and stretching [their body] say that one can avoid aging only through *daoyin*. Those who know the methods based on herbs and plants say that one can surpass any limit only through medicines and pills. When the study of the Dao does not bear fruit, it is because of biases like these. (Pregadio, 2005: 135)

该部分涉及几个具体道术的翻译。翻译"玄素之术""房中之术""吐纳之道""行气""导引"这些修炼术语时，魏译本基本采用意译的方法，而玄英则采用直译加拼音的模式，基本保留道教文化特征。

25. "浅见之家，偶知一事，便言已足"的意思：见识短浅的人偶然懂得了一种方法，就认为已经足够了。魏译本用"declare it a panacea"（称其为灵丹妙药）对应"便言已足"，这一翻译较之原文语义更足，表达意蕴胜过原文本身的文笔。此外，"消工弃日"意为"耗费功夫荒弃时日"，魏译本翻译为"Their days are lost in wasted effort"，非常巧妙地传译了原文的意旨。同样，"两有所失"译为"suffer double loss"，措词简练且有文采。所有这些妙译均有很好的借鉴价值。

26. 古文今译，需首先对原文语句作一语义和语法分析，区分主谓，判明定状，然后依英文句法规则转译而出。原文"或本性戇钝，所知殊尚浅近，便强入名山，履冒毒螫，屡被中伤，耻复求还，或为虎狼所食，或为魍魉所杀，或饿而无绝谷之方，寒而无自温之法，死于崖谷，不亦愚哉？"的意思：有的人本性愚钝，所懂得的尚很浅薄，就勉强进入名山修炼，践踏和冒犯毒虫，屡被咬伤又耻于回去。有的被虎狼吞食，有的被山中精怪所害，有的挨饿却不知道辟谷的方术，受冻却不懂得自求温暖的方法，死于深山崖谷中，不也是很愚蠢了吗？因"本性戇钝"才有"强入名山，履冒毒螫，屡被中伤，耻复求还"这样的鲁莽行为，因"所知殊尚浅近"才会有"或为虎狼所食，或为魍魉所杀，或饿而无绝谷之方，寒而无自温之法，死于崖谷"这样的后果。魏译本对该段内容的逻辑关系判别过细，将"本性戇钝"视为导致"所知殊尚浅近"之原因，对"履冒毒螫，屡被中伤，耻复求还，或为虎狼所食，或为魍魉所杀，或饿而无绝谷之方，寒而无自温之法"进行语义分析时又受原文信息排列顺序的影响，比如，译者将"履冒毒螫，屡被中伤，耻复求还"翻译为"they tread upon or are struck by the bite of some poisonous animal and suffer a wound from it. Then they are ashamed to try a second time"（他们踩踏一些有毒动物，或被一些有毒动物攻击咬伤，又耻于再度尝试），显然误读了原作意思，故需改译。

此外，"魍魉"为古代传说中的山川精怪，魏译本采用拼音加范畴词，并附加描述文字做进一步解释的方法，译为"a *wang-liang* demon in the form of a brown child with red eyes, long ears, and a fine head of hair"，姑且不去讨论译者把魍魉详细描述为"外形为小孩，棕色皮肤，红眼睛，长耳朵，有一头漂亮的头发"是否准确，这种过于冗长的语言在这一语境中毫无必要。因此淡化翻译为"evil spirit"即可。

27. "如"在古汉语中有多重意思，可作动词，也可作副词或连词。作动词时可解释为"比得上"，这样看来魏鲁男用比较级译出似乎无可厚非，其译文为"选取一位明师比努力学习仙道更重要"。然而，葛洪一贯主张修道者需勤学多练，这样的翻译从逻辑上讲不通。其实，"如"做副词时与"不"字连用，可解释为"应该"。因此，"夫务学不如择师"可理解为学习仙道之人务必要选择明师。"师所闻素狭"与"不尽情以教之"中间用"又"字连接，应是并列关系，共同构成"因告云"的条件状语。不过魏译本选用"not widely schooled"翻译"所闻素狭"，用"teach his subject exhaustively"翻译"尽情以教之"，皆为不可多得的妙译，尤其是"subject"一词的选用，该词可表达"弟子"之意，也可指"主题，学科"，一语双关，比单纯译为"pupils"或是"disciples"更有文采。

28. 该句涉及"作家"一词的理解。学界大体有两种解读：（1）治理家务，治家（邱风侠，2004：89）；（2）炼制金丹的人（陈飞龙，2011：231）。基于这里是一种比喻，将"自为已有金丹至要，可不用余而"（自以为已经懂得了金丹这种最重要的方术，才可以不用其他的方法）比拟为"作家，云不事用他物者，盖谓有金银珠宝，在乎掌握怀抱之中，足以累世之费者耳"（自以为手中拥有的金银珠宝足够供几代人的消费而声称不需要用其他东西的"作家"），再加下文又有"广播五谷，多储蔬果"这样的文字，理解为"治家"更合理一些。改译为"This is comparable to the fact that the necessity for the daily industrious labouring de-

pends on the amount of wealth and fortune in any household. If there is no sufficient amount of wealth for sustaining a decent life, people will have to participate industriously in various types of farming to accumulate abundant stores of fruits and vegetables"。

改译中省去"金银珠宝""五谷"这类意象,只点化其意,且将"作家"之意转化体现在短语"in any household"中。

29. 原文"断谷辟兵,厌劾鬼魅,禁御百毒,治救众疾……"为平行结构,指的是除金丹修仙术之外的其他道教方术可达成的效用。葛洪认为,"此皆小事,而不可不知"。其中"断谷"即辟谷,既可指道教的一种养生方术,也可指其达成的结果。魏译本将"断谷"理解为可以达成"辟兵,厌劾鬼魅,禁御百毒,治救众疾"的手段,句法逻辑上虽然说得通,但是道教有祛邪术,有御毒术,有治病神术,还有隐形法术,等等,众多法术各自具有不同功能,魏译本将"断谷"与其他道教小术的功能混淆一起的解读不符合道教的这一实情,容易误导读者。此外,"遇急难则隐形"谈的是道教的隐身术,被魏鲁南解读为遇到急难的事知道如何处理。该句可改译为"The basics of comprehensive learning may include: abstaining from grains, dodging of weapons, exorcism of demons, practices of detoxication and medication. As such, people who recognize the extensiveness of immortality and learn the basics comprehensively will consequently be invincible. They could subjugate beasts in mountains or dragons in water. They feel no fear when plague strikes. They turn invisible when an emergency or a danger occurs. These basics ought to be mastered, though they may be minor matters. How can we then fail to learn things that are more important than them?"翻译该句需理清这些道教方术及其效用之间的关系,因此增译"As such, people who recognize the extensiveness of immortality and learn the basics comprehensively will consequently be invincible",将隐性的内容显性化,以免误读误译。

30. 尽管《抱朴子内篇》主要论及的是道教成仙了道的思想,但葛洪把道教修炼和儒家的纲常名教结合起来,认为只重道术修炼而不重道德修养是成不了仙的,这一思想在后来的道教劝善书中得到很好的继承与发扬。例如,该段关于善行、恶行的具体论述在宋代道人李昌龄作的

《太上感应篇》一书中就有大量引用，文字内容基本雷同。本书第二章第一节已对英国汉学家理雅各的《太上感应篇》英译本、日本禅学大师铃木大拙和美国学者保罗·凯拉斯合作完成的《太上感应篇》英译本进行过解析，这里仅摘录两部译作中该段的翻译供读者对照阅读。

原文：是以天地有司过之神，依人所犯轻重，以夺人算。算减则贫耗，多逢忧患。人皆恶之，刑祸随之，吉庆避之，恶星灾之，算尽则死。又有三台北斗神君，在人头上，录人罪恶，夺其纪算。又有三尸神，在人身中，每到庚申日，辄上诣天曹，言人罪过。月晦之日，灶神亦然。凡人有过，大则夺纪，小则夺算。其过大小，有数百事，欲求长生者，先须避之。

理雅各译本：Accordingly, in heaven and earth there are spirits that take account of men's transgressions, and, according to the lightness or gravity of their offences, take away from their term of life. When that term is curtailed, men become poor and reduced, and meet with many sorrows and afflictions. All (other) men hate them; punishments and calamities attend them; good luck and occasions for felicitation shun them; evil stars send down misfortunes on them. When their term of life is exhausted they die.

There also are the Spirit-rulers in the three pairs of the Thâi stars of the Northern Bushel over men's heads, which record their acts of guilt and wickedness, and take away (from their term of life) periods of twelve years or of a hundred days.

There also are the three Spirits of the recumbent body which reside within a man's person. As each kang-shän day comes round, they forthwith ascend to the court of Heaven, and report men's deeds of guilt and transgression. On the last day of the moon, the spirit of the Hearth does the same.

In the case of every man's transgressions, when they are great, twelve years are taken from his term of life; when they are small, a hundred days.

Transgressions, great and small, are seen in several hundred things. He who wishes to seek for long life must first avoid these. (Legge, 1891: 236 – 237)

铃木大拙译本：It is apparent that heaven and earth are possessed of crime-recording spirits. According to the lightness or gravity of his transgressions, the sinner's term of life is reduced. Not only is his term of life reduced, but poverty also strikes him. Often he meets with calamity and misery. His neighbors hate him. Punishments and curses pursue him. Good luck shuns him. Evil stars threaten him; and when his term of life comes to an end, he perishes.

Further, there are the three councilor, spirit-lords of the northern constellation, residing above the heads of the people, recorders of men's crimes and sins, cutting off terms of life from twelve years to a hundred days.

Further, there are the three body-spirits that live within man's person. Whenever Kêng Shên day comes, they ascend to the heavenly master and inform him of men's crimes and trespasses.

On the last day of the month the Hearth Spirit, too, does the same.

Of all the offences which men commit, the greater ones cause a loss of twelve years, the smaller ones of a hundred days. These their offences, great as well as small, constitute some hundred affairs, and those who are anxious for life everlasting, should above all avoid them. （Suzuki, Carus, 1906a：52 – 53）

葛洪认为行善是修仙的首要任务，因为如果人作恶多端，修仙养生必定无果。作者详细列举了善事和恶事的具体内容，还举出历史上的善有善报、恶有恶报的典型事例，以增强自己观点的说服力。这里涉及道教文化专属词语"纪""算""三尸""庚申日""司命""司过之神"的翻译，综合参照上述译者《太上感应篇》译本中类似内容的译文，本书对这些专属词语的翻译作出如下解读。

（1）该段多次出现的古代时间单位词语"纪"和"算"的翻译，根据语境的不同或泛化为"lifespan""term of life"，或明晰为具体的天数。因人们对"纪""算"的具体天数说法不一，可根据相应文献中的解读具体译出，该篇明确说明了一纪为300天，一算为3天。

（2）"三尸"可直译为"Three Corpses"，"庚申日"用拼音加直译的方法译为"Geng-shen Day"，"灶神"直译为"the Kitchen god"，但都需提供相应的注释内容，为目标语读者补充相关背景知识。

（3）"司命"为神名，可采用直译法，译为"the Director of Fates

（simin 司命）"，在括号内添加拼音与汉字，以示严谨。"司过之神"指"掌管人间过错的神仙"，而非神名，因此按意思译出即可，译为"crime-recording gods"。

31. 原文"赵简子、秦穆公皆亲受金策于上帝，有土地之明征"意思：赵简子、秦穆公都从天帝那儿亲自接受了黄金简策，作为他们后来拓展疆域拥有土地的明确证据。魏译本译为"We do know that both Viscount Chien of Chao and Duke Mu of Ch'in received a gold plaque from Emperor-up-there; the site god himself was witness"。据《史记》记载，赵简子、秦穆公皆为春秋时期的显贵人物，前者是晋国贵族，后者是秦国君主，两人都曾获得天帝的恩赐或授意，成为一方诸侯或霸主。如果说魏译本用归化翻译法将历史人物赵简子、秦穆公对应翻译为目的语读者所熟悉的享有爵位的人物姑且可以接受，基于中国的上帝与西方的上帝指代完全不同，魏译本将原文的"上帝"翻译为"Emperor-up-there"，也有他的道理，但将"有土地之明征"翻译为"the site god himself was witness"（土地神可以为证）就值得商榷了，故改译为"However, the historical facts that Zhao Jianzi（赵简子）and Qin Mugong（秦穆公），two of the formidable figures during the Spring and Autumn period（770 – 476 B. C.），successfully managed to obtain lordship are the crucial evidences for showing the Heavenly Emperor's power in this mortal world"。

32. 原文"山川草木，井灶污池，犹皆有精气；人身之中，亦有魂魄；况天地为物之至大者，于理当有精神，有精神则宜赏善而罚恶，但其体大而网疏，不必机发而响应耳"的意思：山川草木，井灶污池，都有精灵之气，人身上也有魂魄，何况天地作为万物中最大的，按理也应当有精灵神怪。有精灵神怪，就应该赏善罚恶。但是，天地的形体庞大而法网疏漏，不一定能像触动机关那样立即就有响应罢了。原文采用"精气""魂魄""精神"这三种不同的表达来描述魂灵鬼神之属，魏译用"spirits"和"gods"指代精灵鬼怪之类，顺应西方读者的认知习惯。"但其体大而网疏，不必机发而响应耳"译为"Yet, given their physical size and the looseness of their organization, they simply must not be expected to respond mechanically"固然很好，但也可译出作者意图，译为"Yet in reality, this vast world is essentially loose in organization that it may damn the evil

in long term, not necessarily eradicating all the evilness immediately with the touch of a trigger"。

33. 该段的意思：然而浏览各类修道的戒律，都告诫那些想追求长生不死的人，一定要积善行德，爱护万物，推己及人，仁爱施及昆虫，为别人的喜事而感到快乐，为别人的痛苦而感到伤心，赈济别人于急难之时，解救别人于困境之中，手不伤害生灵，口不劝勉惹祸，看见别人的成功有如自己获得成功，看到别人的错误如同自己犯了错误，不把自己看得很尊贵，不自我称赞，不嫉妒胜过自己的人，也不讨好阴险狡诈的人，如此才算是有了美好的德行，将会得到上天的赐福，所做的事情一定能够成功，而求仙的事情也就有了希望。《太上感应篇》也有类似表述，虽然部分内容有所不同，但主题大意区别不大。下文摘录理雅各、铃木大拙《太上感应篇》英译本中该段文字的译文，读者可对照学习不同译者遣词造句之异同。

原文：是道则进，非道则退；不履邪径，不欺暗室；积德累功，慈心于物；忠孝友悌，正己化人；矜孤恤寡，敬老怀幼；昆虫草木犹不可伤。宜悯人之凶，乐人之善；济人之急，救人之危。见人之得如己之得，见人之失，如己之失；不彰人短，不炫己长；遏恶扬善，推多取少；受辱不怨，受宠若惊；施恩不求报，与人不追悔。所谓善人，人皆敬之，天道佑之，福禄随之，众邪远之，神灵卫之，所作必成，神仙可冀。

理雅各译文：Is his way right, he should go forward in it; is it wrong, he should withdraw from it. He will not tread in devious by-ways; he will not impose on himself in any secret apartment. He will amass virtue and accumulate deeds of merit. He will feel kindly towards (all) creatures. He will be loyal, filial, loving to his younger brothers, and submissive to his elder. He will make himself correct and (so) transform others. He will pity orphans, and compassionate widows; he will respect the old and cherish the young. Even the insect tribes, grass, and trees he should not hurt.

He ought to pity the malignant tendencies of others; to rejoice over their excellences; to help them in their straits; to rescue them from their perils; to regard their gains as if they were his own, and their losses in the same way; not to publish their shortcomings; not to vaunt his own superiorities; to put a stop to what is evil, and exalt and display what is good; to yield much, and take little for himself; to receive insult without resenting it, and honour with an appearance of apprehension; to bestow favours without seeking for a return, and give to others without any subsequent regret:—this is what is called a good man. All other men respect him; Heaven in its course protects him; happiness and emolument follow him; all evil things keep far from him; the spiritual Intelligences defend him; what he does is sure to succeed. He may hope to become Immaterial and Immortal. (Legge, 1891: 238)

铃木大拙译文:

The right way leads forward; the wrong way backward. Do not proceed on an evil path. Do not sin in secret. Accumulate virtue, increase merit. With a compassionate heart turn toward all creatures. Be faithful, filial, friendly, and brotherly. First rectify thyself and then convert others. Take pity on orphans, assist widows; respect the old, be kind to children. Even the multifarious insects, herbs, and trees should not be injured. Be grieved at the misfortune of others and rejoice at their good luck. Assist those in need, and rescue those in danger. Regard your neighbor's gain as your own gain, and regard your neighbor's loss as your own loss. Do not call attention to the faults of others, nor boast of your own excellence. Stay evil and promote goodness. Renounce much, accept little. Show endurance in humiliation and bear no grudge. Receive favors as if surprised. Extend your help without seeking reward. Give to others and do not regret or begrudge your liberality.

Those who are thus, are good: people honor them; Heaven's Reason gives them grace; blessings and abundance follow them; all ill luck keeps away; angel spirits guard them. Whatever they undertake will surely succeed, and even to spiritual saintliness they may aspire. (Suzuki, Carus, 1906a: 53 - 54)

魏译本将"恕己及人"翻译为"practice the Golden Rule",用的是西方读者熟知的黄金法则"你愿意别人怎么待你,你就应该怎么待人"(Therefore all things whatsoever ye would that men should do to you, do ye even so to them: for this is the law and the prophets),为基督教《马太福音》

中涉及伦理的规定，顺应的是西方基督文化，也可直译为"to treat others the way they would like to be treated"。"不忌妒胜己，不佞谄阴贼"，魏翻译为"not envy their betters, and conceal no evil intentions with flattery"（不可嫉妒比自己强的人，也不可用谄媚的话遮掩自己的恶意）与原文"不忌妒胜过自己的人，不谄媚讨好阴险贼子"不尽相符，故修改为"nor envy their betters, nor flatter the crafty and evil"。

34. 原文"若乃憎恶好杀……，晦歌朔哭"为一长句，葛洪列举了恶事的具体内容，所有恶行多为并列关系，也有一些属于互为关联由此及彼之类的关系。魏译本运用英文的外位语结构，依照原文顺序构成英文长句，其间译者调动英文的语法手段，即以从属连词 when 引导的状语从句表时间或条件，将该长句分成几个分句逐一译出，以分号为标记，其目的是想让各条恶行的呈现既杂然相陈又秩序井然。尽管这种处理手法完全符合译入语读者的阅读习惯，给阅读者带来浑然一体的意境体验，但其对所列恶行之间的逻辑推断有些是错误的。比如，"弄法受贿"本意为"玩弄法律收受贿赂"，魏译为"bribes are accepted when the law is applied"（利用法律受贿），所以改译为"accept bribes unlawfully"。又如，"晦歌朔哭"和"越井跨灶"一样，皆是不被修道之人认可之恶行，魏译本将此作为外位语，用破折号与前面所列恶行分开，译为"then there will be singing on the last of the month but weeping on the first"（结果便是在月初哭泣月末唱歌），将此恶行解读为前面所列恶行带来的后果。此外，该部分还有一些因误读而导致的误译，例如，"损人器物，以穷人用"意思是"破坏他人用以谋生的器物，造成别人要使用时无处设法"，魏译本译为"the things of others are damaged, those with no ability are given employment"，理解为"破坏他人器物，雇佣无用之人"，显然与原文旨意相违，故改译为"spoil others' implements, deprive them of the things they require to use"。道教认为，井有井神，灶有灶神，从井灶上跨过，是对神极端无礼的亵渎行为。"晦"为农历每月的最末一天，是天神考察人善恶的时候，人们应端洁正行，不能歌舞以亵渎神灵。"朔"指每月的初一，是总结自己功过的时候，应当倍加虚心静气，仔细检查自己的行为得失，在这个时候哭泣，是对神灵不恭。"越井跨灶"（跨越别人的水井和灶台）在魏译本中被解读为"associates are surpassed, even including one's father"，译者将"越井跨灶"理解为"跨越包括父亲在内的人伦等级",盖是因为译者不了解这样的道教文化背景,过度解读导致的误译,故可改译为"if they stride over the well or the hearth, sing on the last of the month but weep on the first, thus profaning their gods and spirits",增加"profaning their gods and spirits"以表明这些都是亵渎神灵、不被道教所认可和容许的行为。原文均采用四字词语,历数各种恶行的具体内容,翻译该段时可依据对原文的理解进行意群划分,尽量显现它们之间的逻辑关系。

中西方文化都蕴含着丰富的美德资源,人类对善恶的认知判断有很大的共同性。葛洪在该段列举了道教积善成仙思想所规定的诸多善行和恶行,多数都是人类共有的道德追求,完全可以通过直译的方法逐条翻译。当然,有些"恶事"的说法在西方读者看来无法理喻,如"晦歌朔哭""越井跨灶"等,均需添加补充性解释。

35. 原文"故道家言,枉煞人者,是以兵刃而更相杀。其取非义之财,不避怨恨,譬若以漏脯救饥,鸩酒解渴,非不暂饱,而死亦及之矣"意思是:所以道家说,枉杀好人的,就等于是拿着兵器反过来杀害自己。那些获取不义之财、不怕别人怨恨的人,就好比用漏脯充饥、用毒酒解渴一样,虽然暂时吃饱了,然而死亡也随即而来。葛洪采用明喻暗喻的手法来描述"枉煞人者"和"取非义之财者"应该受到的惩罚。《太上感应篇》有几乎一致的说法,其原文如下。

又枉杀人者,是易刀兵而相杀也。取非义之财者,譬如漏脯救饥,鸩酒解渴,非不暂饱,死亦及之。

理雅各译文:Those who wrongfully kill men are (only) putting their weapons into the hands of others who will in their turn kill them. To take to one's self unrighteous wealth is like satisfying one's hunger with putrid food, or one's thirst with poisoned wine. It gives a temporary relief, indeed, but death also follows it. (Legge, 1891: 245)

铃木大拙译文:Those who unlawfully kill men will in turn have their weapons and arms turned on them; yea, they will kill each other. Those who seize properties, are, to use an illustration, like those who relieve their hunger by eating tainted meat, or quench their thirst by drinking poisoned liquor. Though they are not without temporary gratification, death will anon overcome them. (Suzuki, Carus, 1906a: 65)

西方基督教《圣经·新约》"启示录"第 13 章中有类似的规定：用刀杀人的，必被刀杀（he that killeth with the sword must be killed with the sword），所以不难理解上述两位汉学家对"枉煞人者，是以兵刃而更相杀"的翻译。原文"其取非义之财，不避怨恨"应指同一桩罪过，即"不顾别人怨恨获取不义之财"，魏译本这段话回译为汉语：道家说，一旦有人被误杀，接下来就会有相互残杀；用不当行为获得的财富将会引起怨恨，这就像用腐烂的腌肉充饥，或用毒酒解渴；尽管你有片刻的饱足，死亡还是接踵而来。尽管这种理解逻辑也算合情合理，但与原文旨意有出入。故改译为"Therefore, Daoism dictates that whoever has wrongly committed killing is bound to be killed by that weapon he had used. If one acquired wealth through improper acts with no fear of creating resentments, it is like eating rotten meat for hunger and drinking poisoned beverage for thirst. It would be true that his hunger and thirst ought to be satisfied, but it would also be obvious that rotten meat and poisoned beverage would eventually claim his life"。

此外，"道家"既可对应为 Daoists，指信仰道家道教思想的人；也可用 Daoism，指先秦之前的哲学流派"道家"或后来的宗教派别"道教"。

36. 这里葛洪为那些曾犯下恶行但有悔改之意的人，即原文所说的"其有曾行诸恶事，后自改悔者"，提供了一些改过自新的建议。魏译本该段译文的第一句"These are the rules governing atonement for wrongdoings of the past"为译者增译，以说明以下内容是一些为过去所犯错误赎罪的条例，这是原文暗含却没明确表述的内容，译者将其增译出，并作为该段的总说，符合英语前述结构的表达习惯，能更清楚地表达文意。译者用冒号与后面所列举的每一恶行可实施的补救法隔开，采用"if"引导的条件从句翻译所犯恶行，用"thought must be given to …"翻译"则当思……"（那就应当设法……），通过视点转换［从原文的"行诸恶事，后自改悔者"转换为"atonement for wrongdoings of the past"（为过往恶行赎罪）］，条理更清楚，结构更紧凑。只是"皆一倍于所为，则可便受吉利"应为"需加倍补偿过去的恶行，才可能获得吉祥福佑"，魏译本强调的是这些赎罪补救措施能带来的效果，理解为所有这些补救行为都与所犯的错误正好相反,它们会立即带来好运和利益。尽管这样的解读于情于理也都行得通,但与原文的信息不符,故改译为"Double efforts are required to compensate for the wrongdoings, which will possibly bring blessings of good luck and profit"。

37. 这里葛洪举出历史上善有善报恶有恶报的典型事例,以增强自己观点的说服力。翻译历史典故时,译者需明示典故的基本内涵,若这些典故提供的信息完整,只需照原文译出即可,如魏译"羊公积德布施,诣乎皓首,乃受天坠之金"便是采用这一方法,译文为"Yang Hsü accumulated good works and was charitable; therefore in his old age he reveived gold dropped from heaven"。但如果原文有所遗漏,翻译时需补全,以避免主旨不明所带来的理解障碍。"蔡顺至孝,感神应之"讲的是"蔡顺有至孝之心,感动了天神,避免了火灾的肆虐"的事迹,"郭巨煞子为亲,而获铁券之重赐"讲的则是"郭巨至孝,想牺牲儿子以侍奉母亲,而获得了铁券的重赐"的故事。铁券,本为帝王颁赐给功臣,赐其世代享有特权的信物。后多用丹粉书在铁板上,又称丹书铁券。上天赐予孝子郭巨一釜黄金时就附有这样的丹书,上面写道:"孝子郭巨,黄金一釜,以用赐汝。"因此,翻译这些典故时需采用增译法,旨在完善典故内容或补充文化背景信息。可改译为"Speaking from a historical angle, there have been countless examples that demonstrate the ethical stance which Heaven takes. For example, Yanghu(羊祜)was a Samaritan that in the last years of his life he was richly rewarded with gold by the divine deity for his selfless charity. Likewise, Caishun(蔡顺), a filial son, was protected by the miraculous power of the divine during a catastrophic fire. Additionally, when poverty beset, Guoju(郭巨) decided to kill his own son to save food for his elderly parents, which was considered by the divine as an act of filial piety so that he was also awarded with gold"。因西方读者熟知的"Samaritan"是一位助人为乐之善人,因此可用于翻译"羊公积德布施"这一典故。

38. 原文"而愚人复以项托、伯牛辈,谓天地之不能辨臧否,而不知彼有外名者,未必有内行;有阳誉者不能解阴罪,若以荠、麦之生死,而疑阴、阳之大气,亦不足以致远也"意思:愚笨的人又拿项托、伯牛这些人的早死为例,说天地不能分辨好坏,却不知道那些具有外在美名的人，未必有内在的品行，表面受到赞誉的人并不能消除暗里所犯的罪行，如果以荠、麦的冬生夏死，而怀疑阴阳大气的运行规律，那也就不足以完成远大的修仙大业了。该句中的"项托、伯牛辈"指代"以才智或德行著称的项托、伯牛夭折"之事，同上述典故的翻译一样，需增译内涵，而不是仅仅提供让西方读者陌生的人名，可改译为"premature deaths of gifted Xiangtuo（项托）and moral Boniu（伯牛）"，补充了两人的身份以及他们虽德行优良却不幸夭折的背景。葛洪认为，荠菜和小麦在夏季枯萎，违背了夏季通常为万物生长最好季节的自然规律，但不能因为这样的特例就怀疑阴阳大气的运行规律。借用自然界荠麦冬生夏死这样的特例比拟项托、伯牛辈夭折之事，翻译时无须直译这一自然现象，只译出原作者的真实意图。

39. "道德未成"与"未得绝迹名山"可视为并列结构，作为后半句"将何以却朝夕之患、防无妄之灾"的原因，原文意思：仙道还未修成，又不能遁迹在名山之中，而当今的世道也不同于古代了，盗贼很多，那么拿什么来躲避朝夕之患，预防那些无妄之灾呢？魏译本除了依其先入之见将"道德"译为"God and the natural life"，又受限于"绝迹名山"的概念意义，译为"be obliterated in a famous mountain"，忽略了"遁迹名山"之联想意义是"隐居修行"。"道德未成"和"又未得绝迹名山"都是指（学道者）尚处于修仙道的过程中，因此可泛化合译为"during the learning of immortality"。

40. 由于作者所处的社会是一个动乱的社会，护身防盗就特别为世人所关心，于是葛洪介绍了一些近乎荒唐的护身防盗的巫术，比如，在门上涂一片掺有植物叶片的泥巴，强盗就不敢光顾。这里涉及几个中国文化特色词的翻译。例如，中国古代计时方法中的"执日""六癸""岁破""月建"，因这种天干地支计时法在英语中无对应说法，只能采用音译加注释的方法，读者可通过注释大致了解这些词语的内涵。魏译本采用直译的方法翻译"六癸上土"为"Six-kuei superior earth"，"南门土""岁破""月建"分别对应直译为"Market-south-entrance earth""Sui-p'o earth""Yueh-chien earth"，由于没有添加任何注释，实质上没有达到文化传播的功能，故需增加简要的注释内容。另有表达方位概念的"朱鸟"以及表达社团组织的"州、郡、县、乡、里"等文化特色词，均可采用意译法大致译出其含义。该句中的"生地"指"可以保护生命安全的地方",并非魏译本理解的"nucleus"(中心),因此可改为"safe site"。

41. 葛洪的神仙道教认为金丹大药、行气和房中术是长生成仙的三个主要方术。其中服金丹大药是长生之本,行气能加速服药的效果,而房中术则又能配合行气,三者缺一不可(胡孚琛,1989:300)。因道教认为这些修仙方术不可轻易示人,几乎所有的道教文献在记述神仙修炼术时都喜欢使用隐语,通过形象化的类比修辞于优美的文字中描述修道者的宗教体验。葛洪介绍内丹修炼时也是如此,这段文字实际是道教行气术和房中术的内容,通过近乎夸张的瑰丽语言,葛洪向读者描述了"太元""长谷"两山的玄妙。葛洪笔下的太元之山,险峻幽邃,高耸崎岖,雾气浓厚,神气飘游,那里的玉井深邃而清澈,灌溉永不干涸,那里设有一百二十个仙官,曹府官署幢幢相连,水火并存,山中遍布仙芝万株,仙树高大无比。珍珠宝物都很特别,金玉犹如高山,甘美的泉水流出山湾,返老还童的人,悠闲地取饮清澈的流水。这是多么让人神往的仙道体验。而另一座山叫长谷之山,它深暗幽远高大,玄气飘飘,玉液纷飞,金池紫房坐落在山水的弯曲之处。愚笨的人胡乱闯去,都会死亡而归,而有道之士常登这座山,采食那里的精华之气,还可以升天成仙。尽管许多中文注释本都提供了这段文字的内丹学解读,如,张松辉《抱朴子内篇译注》和邱凤侠《抱朴子内篇注译》皆在注释中指明其中采用的内丹术隐语的确切指代,但各自解读却不尽相同。比如,"太元之山"在邱凤侠译注中为"丹田"的隐喻,"玉井"的注释内容为"人体关窍名,可能是喉部的隐喻"(邱凤侠,2004:98),张松辉译注本中"太元之山"则指"人的头颅","玉井"是"口中津液"的隐语(张松辉,2011:216),等等。但两位学者在释义时选择遵循原作的风格,保留原文神秘隐晦的内修意蕴。魏鲁男的处理手法与此相似,只不过用诗歌体裁翻译了这段优美的骈文,并通过改变排版的模式来凸显这部分内涵与其他段落有所不同。保留了原文不直接且迂回的叙述方式,尽力在译文中重现原文的美感,舍弃其在内丹学意义上的解读实属不得已之举。一些过于晦涩的提法,如,"和气氤氲""坎离列位""采服黄精"等也可省译。

42. 葛洪引用先师的一段口诀介绍一种以存思和服炼口中津液相配合的行气法(胡孚琛,1989:294),引文"始青之下月与日,两半同升合成一。出彼玉池入金室，大如弹丸黄如橘。中有嘉味甘如蜜，子能得之谨勿失"谈论的是具体的修炼方法，指导修炼者把津液与神气结合起来，炼成大如弹丸、黄如橘子的内丹，以保证自己的长生。如上文所言，针对内丹修炼术的隐语基本采用直译法或直译加注法，魏译本如此，其他汉学家也是如此。但这种译法始终无法传递出原文隐藏的内丹旨意，所以必要的注释还是需要的。

汉学家玄英在其著作《太清：中国中古早期的道教和炼丹术》（*Great Clarity：Daoism and Alchemy in Early Medieval China*）中谈论道教文献中涉及冥想修行的一些线索时，提到《抱朴子内篇》留有此类踪迹，并引用该段描述内丹修炼的文字为证，现摘录其译文如下。

> Under Initial Green (*shiqing*) the Moon is with the Sun：
> the two halves ascend together and combine to become one.
> Exiting from the Jade Pond (*yuchi*), it enters the Golden Chambers (*jinshi*)；
> it is as large as a pellet, as yellow as an orange,
> and has a delicious taste within, as sweet as honey.
> If you are able to obtain it, be careful not to lose it：
> once gone you cannot chase it, and it will be extinguished.
> The pure and white pneuma, utterly subtle and rarefied,
> ascends to the Obscure Barrier (*youguan*) by bending and twisting three times,
> and the middle Cinnabar [Field] (*zhongdan*) shines incomparably；
> when it is established in the Gate of Life (*mingmen*), your bodily form will know no end.
> Profound! Wondrous! And difficult to investigate. （Pregadio, 2005：206）

玄英引用该段文字只是为了论证道教文献《抱朴子内篇》中也有一些涉及冥想修行的线索，其中的内丹术语皆是直译，并在其后用括号的形式附加汉语拼音，这是一种学术翻译的典型做法，以增强翻译的严肃性,但作者在接下来的文字叙述中指明了该段引文所包含的内丹文化的深层内涵,对其中的术语说了专门说明,诸如,"明堂"隐喻内丹学意义中的"上丹田","紫宫"指"中丹田","华盖"暗指"眉毛"或"上丹田","玉池"为"口"的类比,"金室"指"肺","幽关"指居于两肾之间的中间地带,"命门"或为下丹田,或为该区域的某一焦点。具体内容如下:

These two poems contain several terms that appear in contemporary texts related to meditation, and in later texts related to *neidan*: Hall of Light (the upper Cinnabar Field, or one of its "chambers"), Crimson Palace (the middle Cinnabar Field), Flowery Canopy (the eyebrows and, again, the upper Cinnabar Field), Jade Pond (the mouth), Golden Chambers (the lungs), Obscure Barrier (the central space between the kidneys), and Gate of Life (the lower Cinnabar Field, or a locus in its region). These analogies show that a set of cognate meditation practices existed by the third century, and that a common codified terminology was used to describe them. (Pregadio, 2005: 206)

此外,译者玄英还对原文"始青"这一概念作了脚注: Initial Green is the first stage of life after the joining of Original Yin and Yang。因此,尽管译文只是直译加汉语拼音,读者可以通过注释和上下文的解读了解隐含在美妙文字后的内丹修炼方法。

魏鲁南翻译该段文字时也有类似考虑,采用直译加注的方法译出这些内丹术语,直译是为保留原文的意象,括号里的注解为这些术语的具体所指。只是对"始青"这一概念用拼音加直译的方法译为: Shih-ching (Beginnings-Azure),由于缺乏必要的注释内容,读者依然无法理解该部分的具体含义所在。究其原因,应是译者本人对此概念意义缺乏清楚的认识,只能做一大概的猜测。译者在该段译文后添加了这样的文字说明:秘传口诀充满了各种隐微术,其真实内涵也许终有一天在更深入的研究得到揭示(Further search may someday reveal precisely what this means, but oral traditions abound in esotericisms) (Ware, 1966: 121)。

考虑到这里谈论的是具体的修炼方法,因此可以采用直译与意译相结合的方法,括号内用意译法指明其内丹意义。比如,"始青"意指"刚开始修炼内丹的时候",《云笈七签》卷十二:"三玄出始青,言万物生而青色也。"所以可意译为"the beginning of time"。

43. "闻房中之事,能尽其道者,可单行致神仙,……"的意思:听说如果能够穷究房中术,就可以单独的施行而成就神仙的境界。魏译本理解:我听说,如果一个人能完全实施正确的性交步骤,就可以独自旅行,召唤神和精灵(I have been taught that he who can fully carry out the correct sexual procedures can travel alone and summon gods and genii)。显然是没有吃透原文的意思,故可修订为"I have been taught that the correct application of the Daoist practice of sexual health is the sole means for achieving immortality"。

44. 该句的"阴阳之术"与上文的"房中之事"皆指"房中术",是中国十分古老的一种养生术,即古代方士房中节欲、养生保精之道。道家认为阴阳交合乃自然之理,故又称"阴阳之术"。葛洪在介绍这一方术时,既肯定了它的养生作用,也批判了一些人对此术作用的夸大,明确指出:房中术虽然重要,但不足以成仙,只能治疗小病,防止伤身而已。葛洪并非在评判房中术本身的价值问题,而是明确表明不能将其作为唯一修行方式的态度。魏鲁男直接将其翻译为"the sexual recipes"(两性秘诀),大体传译正确。关于"房中术"不同说法的翻译,可统一译为 the Daoist practice of sexual health,以免导致译入语读者理解上的混乱。汉学家玄英在其论著《太清:中国中古早期的道教和炼丹术》中引用该句时推出了自己不同于魏译本的翻译,译文为"Among the arts of Yin and Yang (i. e., the sexual practices), the best ones can heal the lesser illnesses, and the next ones can prevent one from becoming depleted. Since their principles have inherent bounds, how could they confer divine immortality, ward off calamities, and lead one to happiness?"(Pregadio, 2005:135)

45. 原文"人不可以阴阳不交,坐致疾患"中的"坐致疾患"不是指"坐着等待疾病的到来",而是表达"容易导致疾病"之意,这里的"坐"用以比喻容易,不费力。《孟子·离娄下》:"天之高也,星辰之远也,苟求其故,千岁之日至,可坐而致也。"魏译为"man should sit and bring illness and anxiety upon himself by not engaging in sexual intercourse",意思:人应该通过不进行阴阳交合给自己带来疾病忧患。这一理解与原意"人不能不进行阴阳交合,不然会因此带来疾病"正好相反。该句是在回应上文"高可以治小疾"的说法，肯定合理采用"阴阳之术"可以防病治病，因此依此改译为"It is true that appropriate practice of sexual health can provide us with reasonable degree of immunity against diseases"。

原文"善其术者，则能却走马以补脑，还阴丹以朱肠。采玉液于金池，引三五于华梁，令人老有美色，终其所禀之天年"描述了擅长"房中术"所能带来的短期效应和长远效应，该句的意思：擅长这种方术的人，能够阻止泄精以补益大脑，把精液收回而使肠胃更加红润。到金池中采回玉液，把精、气、神引向华梁，能够使老人具有美好的面容，可以享尽自己应有的天命。其中"阴丹""朱肠""玉液""金池""三五""华梁"都有其内丹学的特殊含义。魏译本对这些内丹术语的翻译基本采用直译法，试图用括号的模式解读其具体指代，但因这些暗喻的神秘性，译者无法确认每一个喻体的真实指代，所以只得按字面含义直译，即便括号内提供了一个解读，但也因不敢确定而在解释之前添加了问号。如"朱肠"译为"the Vermilion Intestine（? for small or large）"，"金池"译为"the Pool of Gold（? gall bladder）"，"华梁"译为"Flowered Rafters（? lungs）"，充分反映了道教典籍翻译中译者的无奈。遇到这种情况也只能打破句本位的翻译常规，可省译"却走马以补脑，还阴丹以朱肠。采玉液于金池，引三五于华梁"这些具体细节，采用阐释法将这些内容简略为"People who have mastered appropriately the Daoist practice of sexual health will be able to harvest bodily well-being from the intimate contact with the opposite gender"，以此总结善用"房中术"可带来的终极效应，基本能够维护原文所提供的信息。

46. 葛洪为了进一步说明他对房中术的态度，选取与炼丹术和房中术都有关系的黄帝为例，说明黄帝最终能修炼成仙应归功于"鼎湖之上飞九丹成"。玄英也曾引用该段文字，下附他的译文。

The common people hear that the Yellow Emperor rose to heaven with 1200 women, and say that he obtained longevity only thanks to this. They do not know that the Yellow Emperor compounded the Nine Elixirs on Lake Ding at the foot of Mount Jing, and then rose to heaven by riding a dragon. He might have had 1200 women, but it was not for this reason that he was able to do it. （Pregadio，2005：136）

47. 这里葛洪评价了服食草药美食与实施房中术这些修行小术的优劣。其中"是以古人恐人轻恣情性,故美为之说,亦不可尽信也"的意思:古人担心人们轻易地放纵情欲,于是就将这种方术的效果讲得很美,他们的话也不可完全相信。魏译本的理解:古人担心人们可能会轻视这些方术的存在,因此,他们故意大肆称赞,超出了令人信服的程度。译者错误地理解了"轻恣情性"的含义,故改译:To prevent us from being lustful, the ancient had sugarcoated the miraculous effects of Daoist practice of sexual health. Therefore, their descriptions are also doubtful after close examination。

48. 房中术在道书中亦隐名为"玄素"(由玄女、素女之名而来),葛洪认为,房中术非常隐秘而难以掌握,只有善于此术者才能达到益寿延年的效果。原文"玄、素谕之水火,水火煞人,而又生人,在于能用与不能耳"的意思:可将房中术比喻为水火,水火既能杀人,也能救人,关键在于是否能够正确使用。魏译本该段的译文颇得要旨,尤其该段中谕玄、素为水火的比喻以及水火之用"煞"和"生"的翻译,译者的处理堪称形神兼顾,译文:Sexual intercourse may be compared with water and fire, either of which can slay man or bring him life, depending solely upon his ability to deal with them, 既译出了原文的所指,也传达了原文的能指。

小　结

作为一门研究中国道教的学问,汉学家英译道教典籍时通常会参阅包括辞典在内的各种参考资料,这种现象一方面说明他们严谨的翻译态度,但同时也成了他们可能误读原作者意图的主要原因,有时候他们孤立地理解单个汉字的词典释义,尤其是翻译那些带有丰富文化内涵的词句时,容易做出有违原作本意的理解,这种现象在魏鲁男的这部英译本中也不难发现。虽然在一定程度上我们可以把这种现象解释为译者忠实再现原文表达形式的结果,但如果因为这样的直译会曲解原作者的意图,从而误导译入语读者,那就不该是翻译的文化传真功能的应有之用。再加上译者没有提供足够合适的注解内容,这样的直译也不能很好地传达原文的本真内容。

葛洪在序言中曾谈到创作《抱朴子内篇》的动机，他说："考览奇书，既不少矣，率多隐语，难可卒解。……今为此书，粗举长生之理，其至妙者，不得宣之翰墨。"可见，葛洪写作该书的初衷是用简易通俗的语言完成一部全面论述长生之道的书籍，因此，相较于《周易参同契》《悟真篇》等其他道书，《抱朴子内篇》整部作品的语言已是直率显明了许多，但因作者参阅和征引了前代流传下来的数以千计的仙经符书，隐语的使用也是难免的。单从语言层面来看，《畅玄》和《微旨》均为"骈赋"文体，讲求对仗，用词华丽，大量使用叠音词和同义词，句子中多含有韵脚，且借用许多隐语和典故，这些都是翻译的难点。王宏印教授在谈中国文化典籍翻译的理论与技巧时曾明确指出，"古文今译首先要解决典故的问题。……翻译时要准确地说明原文的所指，而不能只做表面文章"（王宏印，2009：15）。要将这样的道教文献翻译为英文，不仅要解决典故的问题，还要做好诸多隐语的处理。

《抱朴子内篇》围绕修道成仙的核心展开论述，涵盖丰富而驳杂的内容，在道教发展史上占有很高的地位。为寻求修道成仙的理论支撑，葛洪借用了《易经》《道德经》《庄子》等道家经典中的语句阐述了以"玄""一""玄一""真一"为代表的道教哲学思想，在论证神仙实有和仙道可学时又援引了《列仙传》《神仙传》《仙经》中的内容。此外，书中各种养生学仙的具体方法在后世道经中均得到较好的传承和发挥。例如，他在《微旨》中所举道戒不仅适用于修仙的道士，也适用于社会各阶层的俗人，包括官吏、商人、军人、猎户在内，为道教开辟了劝善度人的发展道路之同时，也为后世劝善书《太上感应篇》《阴骘文》《功过格》提供了原型。托名宋代李昌龄所著说的《太上感应篇》有很多内容直接照搬了《微旨》中的道戒。这些道教典籍在海外均得到了不同程度的关注，有些已被翻译为英文，这些道教典籍的英文翻译均可为我国学者开展道教典籍的海外译介提供很好的参考。

笔者认为，通过各种手段挖掘原文的意义是翻译的重点。参照海外学者翻译道教典籍的策略方法，为保留原文语言特色所折射的特殊情调，在不影响目的语读者理解的前提下可首选直译法，但如果因保留形象导致读者无法理解其真实含义时，需通过加注的模式，或是舍弃形象进行意译。原文频繁使用典故，有时候接连出现多个典故，涉及一些神秘的修仙方术时又有诸多隐语，若采用直译保留原文形象会导致词不达意，甚至误解原文的含义，须增译补全，但如果添加注释又会因过于冗长而影响读者阅读的流畅性，遇到这种情况时只能采用意译，以求最大限度地传达原文之意。这种手法也常用于原文中的一些比喻修辞的翻译。涉及一些基本的道教概念时通常采用音译的方法，括号内提供汉字和意译，这也是许多汉学家的惯常做法，目的是增强道教典籍翻译的严肃性。这些都是海外译介道教典籍的有效经验。

结　语

　　道教是中国文化的重要组成部分，道教典籍蕴含着丰富的中国传统文化与思想的精华，自东学西渐以来一直得到海外学者的持续阐释和译介。这些对道教文化有着浓厚热情的海外学者通常融翻译与研究为一体，为中国道教文化的海外传播做出了巨大的贡献，他们的研究成果是国内道教学研究可资借鉴的宝贵资料，而他们研究道教文化所必须借助的道教典籍翻译文本也是国内翻译学研究不可或缺的研究素材。本书分哲学、善书、戒律、仙传、炼养、综合类六个专题对海外学者完成的部分道教典籍英译文本进行了翻译批评解析，分析他们翻译道教典籍中的成败得失，总结规律和方法，考察他们进行道教文本翻译的方法论，旨在获得历史的智慧，归纳提炼可供国内学者借鉴的从事道教典籍英译的启示。

　　就道教哲学文本的海外传播来看，这类文本在海外的译介相对较多，部分原因应归结于这类文本通常兼具哲学内涵丰富、文学韵味浓厚之特点。虽然侧重挖掘原文哲学内涵的译本与看重再现原文文学风韵的译本在翻译体例及副文本的使用上表现出一定的差异，但添加导论、评注，提供注释、词语表仍是这些译作最大的共性，只不过详略程度不同而已，充分说明海外学者解读这类文本时普遍认同文本本身固有的认知难点，并力图借助副文本来扫清这些障碍。显然，无论是侧重哲学内涵挖掘还是着力文学形式再现，仅从语言层面翻译道教哲学文本是远远不够的，除翻译和文字注解本身之外，为减少非母语读者的阅读障碍，需要利用导论、评注等有效手段深挖道教哲学文本的思想价值，尽量补充完善仅靠译文本身不足以表达的内涵。

　　道教善书文本集中呈现道教的伦理道德思想。这类文本常被视作方内方外人士的道德教材，即能规范约束教内人士的思想行为，又能教化普通大众趋善从善，其教化对象涉及社会各个阶层，尤其以民间大众为主，因此最明显的文本特征就是语言通俗易懂、方法简便易行，具有很强的可读性和较高的普及度。既然崇善行善是世界各大宗教共有的伦理准则，选择这类文本进行翻译研究的海外学者，尤其是有着传教士翻译家双重身份的学者，重点关注的也是这类典籍的社会教化功能。英译者们通常采用以达意为前提的直译法，以保留原文平易直白的文体特征。此外，译者们还倾向于添加原文没有的小标题，提炼原文各部分所蕴含的微言大义，以凸显道教劝善书作为官方推行的社会教育基本教材的功能，最大限度保持译文和原文之间的功能对等。与道教劝善书同样具有社会教化功能的道教戒律文本句法简约，论述条理清晰，英译这类文本的学者与英译道教劝善书的学者选择的路径大同小异，首选直译策略，最典型作法就是按条目逐条译出戒律内容，分主题细分段落，区分层次，合理使用祈使句和英语情态动词等，以凸显道教戒律文本简单凝练、逻辑分明等语言特征，既能做到大意不爽，又能实现小处有别的语义迁移。

  道教仙传文本属于一种特殊的传记文学体裁，记录道教诸多神仙的生平事迹，是道教典籍中不可或缺的一部分。这些文本既有宗教典籍的私密性，又有传记文学的通俗性和艺术性，不失为神仙思想的生动教材，流传版本众多，流传形式多样，具体到神仙个体的传记内容时存在详略差异或措词有别的情况。英译道教神仙传记文本的海外学者充分认识到这一显著的行文特征，普遍重视与原文本相关的各种注、疏内容的研究，翻译时倾向于选择更加贴近文本真相的"互文性"研究方法，以保障最大限度传译原作全貌。美国汉学家康儒博基于互文资源的互文解读模式对神仙传记文本的翻译做了有益的尝试，具有很好的借鉴价值。

  本书探讨的道教炼养类文本特指那些记述仙丹炼制和身心修养方术的文献。这类文献多数为诗词体裁，记述中夹杂大量的隐语，文意晦涩、佶屈聱牙是这类文本留给读者的最深刻印象。如果不具备相应的炼丹基本知识，即便是学贯中西的汉学家也很难真正探知原文的含义。因此，海外学者英译这类文献的主流策略为带有明显研究特质的深度语境化翻译手段，通常会借助序言、引言、图表、注释（随文逐句注释或文后主题注释）、术语解释等阐释性文本重构源文文本产生的历史语境，为译文读者理解和鉴赏道教丹道文化扫清障碍。这些补充材料与正文翻译互为表里，共同构成道教炼养类文献翻译的译本体系。该研究模式实则沿袭了西方传统汉学"实证的、求实的学术态度和科学的精神"（张西平、郭景红，2019：6）。

虽然国内不少学者都主张中华文化文学典籍的对外翻译工作主要应该由外国汉学家完成（张西平，2018；曹明伦，2019），但也认同由中国人自己翻译的必要性，只是不主张"闭门造车"，而需"借船出海"（罗选民，2012），或是"借帆出海"（曹明伦，2019），最好选择国人和外国人的"合作翻译"（王宏印，2015），可以彼此取长补短。显然，学习借鉴海外学者成功译介道教文化典籍的经验，吸取他们失败的教训，可为推进中华优秀传统文化传承发展，实施中国文化"走出去"战略提供有益的历史经验和现实参考。海外汉学家或翻译家积累了相对丰富的道教典籍翻译经验，向他们学习能够帮助本土译者高质量展开译介活动。本书附录Ⅰ和附录Ⅱ内容即为笔者遵循"取长补短、择善而从，既不简单拿来，也不盲目排外"的原则，在学习借鉴海外学者魏鲁男等译者相关译文基础之上完成的《抱朴子内篇》中《畅玄》和《微旨》两篇的完整新译，是从实践层面探讨道教典籍的翻译机制，以助推中华优秀传统文化的国际传播。

本书首次成体系地对海外道教典籍翻译文本展开语言层面的翻译批评，不仅有助于国内学者深层次了解海外学者的道教学研究成果，其中对这些海外学者道教典籍翻译个案的分析和总结，以及将这些历史经验应用于道教典籍的对外翻译实践可有效拓展翻译学研究领域，最终对建立一套科学合理的道教典籍翻译机制大有裨益。

本书具体形成五点基本认识。

第一，作为中华文化典籍的重要组成部分，道教典籍翻译理应是中国文化"走出去"的重要内容。翻译以古代汉语为载体的中国道教典籍作品，最大的困难莫过于对原文的正确理解，译者须充分认知道教典籍语言的模糊性特征，通假字、省略用法、隐语、典故等语言学问题均须译者小心应对，应尽量避免因疏忽而可能导致的误读误译。

第二，语言流畅和可读性强是英美出版界和评论界长期使用的译作品评标准。道教典籍所蕴含的传统文化精髓既是中国的，也是世界的，要让道教文化"走进"西方主流文化市场和阅读圈，宜采用以译语读者为导向的归化翻译策略,照顾读者的审美诉求和阅读体验。这既是海外道教典籍翻译的历史经验,也是现实需求。原文语言洗练简约,讲究"字字珠玑",翻译时须做必要的引申,以求达意;原文骈散结合,结构严密紧凑,长短相间,运用了不少对偶句、排比句等,全文有着均衡和谐的旋律之美,同时也有因堆砌辞藻导致语义反复之赘述,翻译时须尽量跳出原文句法结构的束缚,参照原文的意义结构重新构思句子和语段关系,以符合译入语的表达习惯和思维逻辑,从而达到准确传译原文思想的效果。

第三,道教的跨文化传播关乎中国的软实力建设,道教典籍翻译肩负着传播中国文化的使命,翻译中我们要有足够自信采用"中国英语"传播原汁原味的中国文化核心概念,在不影响语义晓畅的前提下可尽量向原文风格、形式等方面倾斜,努力在译文中保留源文本中看似奇特的叙述。若借助上下文语境译本内容能不言自明的地方可尽量采用直译法,但如果直译会引起误解或难以接受的话,需辅以释义和背景描述,以保障接受效果。

第四,道教典籍的注、疏、今译有很多,对原文的理解起着至关重要的作用,是典籍翻译研究必须关注的内容。译者须反复对比和参考与原作有关的各种古文注、疏以及今译,尽量全面地理解原作的思想内涵,基于各种资料的互文解读是保障全面理解原作的有效模式,适用于译介因历史变迁版本差异明显的道教典籍文本。

第五,道教文化的国际交流与互鉴并非单纯的语际沟通。深度语境化翻译策略重视原文文本产生的历史语境,通过各种注释和评注帮助译入语读者深入了解原语文化,从而促进多元主体间的对话,加强跨文化交流与沟通,可作为当今语境下道教文化典籍对外译介的主流方法和策略。

本研究既有对道教典籍海外翻译的方法论研究,也有对从事道教典籍翻译实践新问题的探索性研究,难度远远超出了预期,导致该研究仍存在一些不尽如人意之处。

第一,研究对象局限于道教典籍的英语译本,广度和深度尚需进一步延展。尽管很多国家尚未形成专门道教学学科,但目前已开展道教学研究且有一定影响规模的国家囊括了法国、日本、德国、英国、荷兰、加拿大、美国、俄罗斯和韩国,因此道教典籍在海外的译介,除了以英语为媒介,涉及的语种还包括法语、日语、德语、俄语、韩语等。这些翻译成果都值得学界下一步展开更深入的研究。

第二,国人对道教典籍的训诂解释尚且见仁见智,见解不一,何况是文化背景迥异的外国专家学者站在译入语读者一方对道教典籍的解读译介,通俗易懂是这些译本的优势,但误读误译也是他们最大的遗憾。本书虽然指出了译本中的一些不准确解读,并提出了修改建议,但囿于笔者的学识积累,对道教典籍语言及其宗教内涵的把握也一定存在不够准确乃至错误之处。

道教典籍特色鲜明,其内容和形式皆具有独特的个性特征,翻译时需选取适合的变通策略,切实有效地提高翻译质量。一方面,译者需努力跨越语言与文化层面的局限与障碍,让译语文本适应西方读者的认知能力和审美习惯,让译语读者享有自然、流畅、通达的阅读体验;另一方面,译者要肩负起传播道教原生态文化的职责,要注意保留道教典籍中的陌生感、民族性及其背后所蕴含的道教文化基因和审美方式。尽管笔者在尝试《抱朴子内篇》中《畅玄》和《微旨》两章内容的新译时试图努力消解原文作者与译文读者、原文文本与译文文本、译文的陌生化与可读性之间的角力,然而在实际翻译过程中发现要做到这一点绝非易事。借力魏鲁男译本为搭建东西方文化桥梁所作的种种努力,吸取海外汉学家译介道教典籍的成功经验,笔者才得以忐忑完成该部分的翻译实践。毋庸置疑,道教典籍的翻译之路充满了各种艰辛和困难,本书基于海外学者翻译道教典籍经验教训之上的翻译实践还只是初步尝试,不过是一抛砖引玉之举,希望借此引发更多学者关注道教典籍的对外译介,让更多的翻译爱好者加入道教典籍对外译介的研究队伍,助力道教文化的国际交流和互鉴。

参考文献

中文文献

［美］柏夷，2014，《道教研究论集》，孙齐、田禾译，上海中西书局。

曹明伦，2019，《关于对外文化传播与对外翻译的思考——兼论"自扬其声"需要"借帆出海"》，《外语研究》第 5 期。

常青，2015，《安乐哲、郝大维英译〈道德经〉的哲学释义与翻译》，载《鞍山师范学院学报》第 5 期。

常青、安乐哲，2016，《安乐哲中国古代哲学典籍英译观——从〈道德经〉的翻译谈起》，《中国翻译》第 4 期。

陈飞龙，2011，《抱朴子内篇今注今译》，台湾商务印书馆。

陈鼓应，2016，《庄子今注今译》，商务印书馆。

陈吉荣，2018，《论"翻译 + 汉学"研究格局的渊源、内涵与影响因素》，载《上海翻译》第 5 期。

陈开科，2007，《巴拉第的汉学研究》，学苑出版社。

陈全林，2004，《〈周易参同契〉注译〈悟真篇〉注译》，中国社会科学出版社。

陈全新，2006，《道教文化中的类比思维》，《宗教学研究》第 4 期。

陈霞，1999，《道教劝善书研究》，巴蜀书社。

陈耀庭，2000，《道教在海外》，福建人民出版社。

丁培仁，2006，《道教戒律书考要》，《宗教学研究》第 2 期。

范祥涛，2006，《科学翻译影响下的文化变迁》，上海译文出版社。

冯友兰，1985，《中国哲学简史》，涂又光译，北京大学出版社。

高深，2016，《国外〈庄子〉版本概述》，《出版发行研究》第 8 期。

顾久，1995，《〈抱朴子内篇〉全译》，贵州人民出版社。

郭晨，2019，《比较哲学视域下古典汉语特征及对典籍英译的思考——美国汉学家任博克教授访谈录》，《燕山大学学报》（哲学社会科学版）第 6 期。

郭建洲，2005，《张伯端道教思想研究》，博士学位论文，山东大学。

何立芳，2010，《试析理雅各〈太上感应篇〉英译》，《内蒙古农业大学学报》（社会科学版）第 5 期。

何立芳，2011，《铃木大拙〈文昌帝君阴骘文〉英译本解析》，《当代外语研究》第 10 期。

何立芳、陈霞，2014，《道教术语汉英双解词典》，四川人民出版社。

何立芳、李丝贝，2017a，《论魏鲁男〈抱朴子内篇〉英译的宗教阐释与文化观》，《宗教学研究》第 3 期。

何立芳、李丝贝，2017b，《道教典籍语言隐喻认知特征解析与翻译》，《外语学刊》第 4 期。

何立芳、李丝贝，2020，《康儒博英译道教典籍〈神仙传〉的互文解读模式》，《国际汉学》第 1 期。

胡孚琛，1989，《魏晋神仙道教〈抱朴子内篇〉研究》，人民出版社。

胡孚琛，1995，《中华道教大辞典》，中国社会科学出版社。

胡孚琛、吕锡琛，2004，《道学通论》，社会科学文献出版社。

黄鸣奋，1995，《英语世界先秦散文著译通论》，《厦门大学学报》（哲学社会科学版）第 2 期。

黄中习，2009，《典籍英译标准的整体论研究——以〈庄子〉英译为例》，博士学位论文，苏州大学。

霍克功，2006，《道教性命之学——内丹》，《中国宗教》第 12 期。

季光茂，2002，《隐喻理论与文学传统》，北京师范大学出版社。

姜莉，2018，《近年来〈庄子〉研究英文期刊成果述评》，《国际汉学》第 4 期。

姜莉，2018，《孔丽维的〈庄子〉译释思考：语境重构与宗教之维》，《上海翻译》第 6 期。

雷勇，2012，《"深描"的指向与路径——以格尔茨〈文化的解释〉为中心》，《贵州民族学院学报》（哲学社会科学版）第 3 期。

李刚，1995，《汉代道教哲学》，巴蜀书社。

李国来，2015，《柳存仁〈周易参同契〉三期衍变说述评》，《世界宗教文化》第 3 期。

李明，2003，《文本间的对话与互涉——浅谈互文性与翻译之关系》，《广东外语外贸大学学报》第 2 期。

李红霞、张政，2015，《"Thick Translation"研究 20 年：回顾与展望》，《上海翻译》第 2 期。

李开荣，2002，《文化认知与汉英文化专有词目等值释义》，《南京大学学报》（哲学社会科学版）第 6 期。

刘宓庆，2005，《中西翻译思想比较研究》，中国对外翻译出版公司。

刘绍云，2006，《道教戒律与传统社会秩序研究》，博士学位论文，山东大学。

刘湘兰，2017，《〈周易参同契〉的文本形态与隐喻手法》，《文学遗产》第 6 期。

刘妍，2011，《梅维恒及其英译〈庄子〉研究》，《当代外语研究》第 9 期。

刘妍，2015，《倾听译者的心声：〈庄子〉英译本序跋研究》，《外语学刊》第 3 期。

刘永明，2016，《敦煌本道教〈十戒经〉考论》，《历史研究》第 1 期。

卢红梅，2006，《华夏文化与汉英翻译》，武汉大学出版社。

罗选民、杨文地，2012，《文化自觉与典籍英译》，《外语与外语教学》第 5 期。

马丽涛，2001，《〈赤松子中诫经〉的教育思想》，《中国道教》第 2 期。

蒙文通，1987，《古学甄微》，巴蜀书社。

［英］麦克斯·缪勒，1989，《宗教学导论》，陈观胜、李培茱译，上海人民出版社。

卿希泰，1996，《中国道教史》（第 3 卷），四川人民出版社。

邱凤侠，2004，《〈抱朴子内篇〉注译》，中国社会科学出版社。

邱鹤亭，2004，《〈列仙传〉注译〈神仙传〉注译》，中国社会科学出版社。

苏宁，2018，《张陵创教的神格化传说谱系内涵研究》，《宗教学研究》第 2 期。

孙宁宁，2010，《翻译研究的文化人类学纬度：深度翻译》，《上海翻译》第 1 期。

孙清海，2012，《语言中的"上帝"：经验指称与情感赋义——近代西方基督教背景下的宗教语言研究》，博士学位论文，山东大学。

[美] 邰谧侠，2019，《〈老子〉译本总目》，《国际汉学》第 S1 期。

唐大潮等，2004，《劝善书注译》，中国社会科学出版社。

唐雄山，2005，《老庄人性思想的现代诠释与重构》，中山大学出版社。

唐怡，2006，《道教戒律研究》，博士学位论文，四川大学。

王秉钦，2004，《20 世纪中国翻译思想史》，南开大学出版社。

王宏印，2009，《中国文化典籍英译》，外语教学与研究出版社。

王宏印，2015，《关于中国文化典籍翻译的若干问题与思考》，《中国文化研究》第 2 期。

王克非，1994，《关于翻译批评的思考——兼谈〈文学翻译批评研究〉》，《外语教学与研究》第 3 期。

王明，1960，《〈太平经〉合校》，中华书局。

王明，1985，《〈抱朴子内篇〉校释》，中华书局。

王沐，1981，《〈悟真篇〉丹法源流》，《道协会刊》第 1 期。

王沐，1982，《〈悟真篇〉丹法要旨》（上），《道协会刊》第 1 期。

王沐，1984，《〈悟真篇〉校注》，《道协会刊》第 15 期。

王沐，1990，《〈悟真篇〉浅解》（外三种），中华书局。

王沐，2011，《内丹养生功法指要》，东方出版社。

王晓俊，2013，《中国本土文化背景下的隐喻认知观研究——Lakoff 概念隐喻理论再思考》，博士学位论文，上海外国语大学。

王晓俊，2014，《论庄子之言说与隐喻的关系》，载《海南师范大学学报》（社会科学版）2014 年第 10 期。

王兴平，1996，《文昌文化在国外》，《中华文化论坛》第 1 期。

王兴平，2000，《文昌文化在日本的传播和影响》，《中国道教》第 2 期。

王雪明、杨子，2012，《典籍英译中深度翻译的类型与功能——以〈中国翻译话语英译选集〉（上）为例》，《中国翻译》第 3 期。

王寅，2013，《认知翻译学与识解机制》，《语言教育》第 1 期。

王宗昱，2016，《国际道教研究的问题与视野——评美国学者柏夷〈道教研究论集〉》,《宗教学研究》第 1 期。

汪榕培,1991,《中国英语是客观存在》,《解放军外国语学院学报》第 1 期。

汪榕培英译,秦旭卿、孙雍长今译,1999,《庄子》(汉英对照),湖南人民出版社。

向群,2015,《葛洪〈神仙传〉研究——以文本流变为中心的考察》,博士学位论文,山东大学。

肖坤学,2005a,《论词汇层面翻译的认知取向》,《外语与外语教育》第 1 期。

肖坤学,2005b,《论隐喻的认知性质与隐喻翻译的认知取向》,《外语学刊》第 5 期。

谢青云,2017,《〈神仙传〉译注》,中华书局。

谢天振,2013,《中国文化走出去不是简单的翻译问题》,《社会科学报》12 月 5 日第 6 版。

辛红娟,2019,《〈道德经〉思想意涵的世界性意义》,《湖南科技大学学报》(社会科学版) 第 6 期。

辛罗滨,2011,《洞玄灵宝天尊说十戒经》,10 月 1 日,道教之音,http://www.daoisms.org/article/sort026。

徐克谦,2000,《论作为道路与方法的庄子之"道"》,《中国哲学史》第 4 期。

徐来,2008,《庄子英译研究》,复旦大学出版社。

阎国栋,2005,《汉学大国俄罗斯》,《环球时报》12 月 28 日第 22 版。

于辉、宋学智,2014,《翻译经典的互文性解读》,《外国语文》第 5 期。

俞森林,2020,《道经英译史》,上海三联书店。

曾文雄,2010,《翻译的文化参与——认知语境的互文顺应视角》,博士学位论文,华东师范大学。

詹石窗,2003,《道教文化十讲》,北京大学出版社。

詹石窗、李怀宗,2018,《张天师与云台山治考论》,《世界宗教文化》第 1 期。

章伟文,2014,《〈周易参同契〉译注》,中华书局。

张继禹,2008,《尊道溯源于真　立教导人达善——祖天师张道陵开立道教历史意义探溯》，《宗教学研究》第 3 期。

张景华，2015，《论"翻译暴力"的学理依据及其研究价值——兼与曹明伦教授商榷》，《中国翻译》第 6 期。

张思齐，2007，《德国道教学的历史发展及其特点》，《西南民族大学学报》（人文社会科学版）第 12 期。

张思齐，2010a，《英国道教学成长时期的历史和特点》，《西南民族大学学报》（人文社会科学版）第 1 期。

张思齐，2010b，《英国道教学在初创时期的历史和特点》，《中国道教》第 6 期。

张松辉，2011，《〈抱朴子内篇〉译注》，中华书局。

张西平，2017，《中国儒学经典跨文化传播的学术大师理雅各》，《文化软实力研究》第 5 期。

张西平，2018，《20 世纪中国古代文化经典在域外的传播与影响研究导论》（上），大象出版社。

张西平、郭景红，2019，《海外汉学（中国学）研究模式探究》，《国际汉学》第 1 期。

张泽洪，1999，《道教斋醮科仪中的存想》，《中国道教》第 4 期。

赵长江，2014，《19 赵世纪中国文化典籍英译研究》，博士学位论文，南开大学。

赵艳芳，2001，《认知语言学概念》，上海外语教育出版社。

仲伟合、朱琳，2015，《具身认知视角下的翻译认知心理特征与过程》，《外国语》第 6 期。

中共中央办公厅、国务院办公厅，2017，《关于实施中华优秀传统文化传承发展工程的意见》，《中国博物馆通讯》第 2 期。

中国社会科学院语言研究所词典编辑室，2002，《汉英双语现代汉语词典》，外语教学与研究出版社。

钟书能，2016，《话题链在汉英篇章翻译中的统摄作用》，《外语教学理论与实践》第 1 期。

钟书能、徐晶晶，2018，《中华文化典籍翻译中的篇章建构机制研究—中华典籍英译探微之五》，《外语教育研究》第 1 期。

钟肇鹏，2010，《道教小辞典》，上海辞书出版社。

周文晟，2012，《〈神仙传〉版本及其流传情况》，《语文知识》第 2 期。

周绍贤，1974，《道家与神仙》，台湾中华书局。

朱大星，2007，《敦煌本〈十戒经〉的形成及流传》，《浙江大学学报》（人文社会科学版）第 3 期。

朱舒然，2019，《论〈庄子〉的哲学翻译》，博士学位论文，中央党校。

朱越利，2012，《海外道教学研究任重道远——〈理论·视角·方法〉前言》，《宗教学研究》第 1 期。

朱越利，2013，《理论·视角·方法——海外道教学研究》，齐鲁书社。

外文文献

Ames, Roger T. and David L. Hall trans., 2003, *Dao De Jing "Making This Life Significant": A Philosophical Translation*, New York: Ballantine Books.

Appiah, Anthony K., 1993, "Thick Translation", *Callaloo*, No. 4.

Bokenkamp, Stephen R., 1997, *Early Daoist Scriptures*, Berkeley: University of California Press.

Campany, Robert F., 2002, *To Live as Long as Heaven and Earth, A Translation and Study of Ge Hong's Traditions of Divine Transcendents*, Berkeley and Los Angeles: University of Canlifornia Press.

Correa, Nina trans., 2006, *Zhuangzi: Being Boundless*, http://www.daoisopen.com/Zhuangzi.

Girardot, Norman J., 2002, *The Victorian Translation of China: James Legge's Oriental Pilgrimage*, Berkeley, Calif.: University of California Press.

Hermans, Theo, 2003, "Cross-Cultural Translation Studies as Thick Translation", *Bulletin of the School of Oriental and African Studies*, No. 3.

Ho, Peng Yoke, 1967, "Review of James R. Ware [1966]", *The Journal of Asian Studies*, No. 1.

Kirkland, Russell, 2011, "The *Huainanzi* Translated by John S. Major, Sarah A. Queen, Andrew Seth Meyer and Harold D. Roth", *Religious Studies Review*, Vol. 37, No. 2.

Knechtges, David R., 1968, "Review of James R. Ware [1966]", *Philoso-*

phy East and West, No. 3.

Kohn, Livia, 2004, *Cosmos and Community*: *The Ethical Dimension of Daoism*, Cambridge: Three Pines Press.

Kroll, Paul W., 1982, "Review of Jay Sailey [1978]", *Chinese Literature*: *Essays, Articles, Reviews*, No. 1.

Legge, Helen E., 1905, *James Legge*: *Missionary and Scholar*, London: The Religious Tract Society.

Legge, James trans., 1895, "Mencius", in F. Max Müller, ed. *The Sacred Books of the East*, London: Oxford University Press.

Legge, James trans., 1876, *The Book of Poetry*, London: Trubner & Co., Ludgate Hill.

Legge, James trans., 1891, "The Texts of Taoism", in F. Max Müller, ed. *The Sacred Books of the East*, London: Oxford University Press.

Mair, Victor H. trans., 1990, *Tao Te Ching*: *The Classic Book of Integrity and the Way*, New York: Bantam Books.

Mair, Victor H. trans., 1994, *Wandering on the Way*: *Early Taoist Tales and Parables of Chuang Tzu*, New York: Bantam Books.

Major, John S. et al. trans., 2010, *The Huainanzi*: *A Guide to the Theory and Practice of Government in Early Han China*, New York: Columbia University Press.

Newmark, Peter, 2001, *Approaches to Translation*, Shanghai: Shanghai Foreign Language Education Press.

Newmark, Peter, 1988, *A Textbook of Translation*, New York: Prentice Hall.

Nylan, Michael, 2011, "The *Huainanzi*: A Guide to the Theory and Practice of Government in Early Han China", *The Journal of Asian Studies*, Vol. 70, No. 2.

Palmer, Martin et al. trans., 1996, *The Book of Chuang Tzu*, Arkana: Penguin Books.

Pregadio, Fabrizio, 2005, *Great Clarity*: *Daoism and Alchemy in Early Medieval China*, Stanford: Stanford University Press.

Pregadio, Fabrizio trans., 2009, *Awakening to Reality——The Regulated Verses* of *Wuzhen Pian*, *A Taoist Classic of Internal Alchemy*, Mountain View CA: Golden Elixir Press.

Pregadio, Fabrizio trans. , 2011, *The Seal of the Unity of the Three*, Mountain View CA: Golden Elixir Press.

Roberts, Moss, 2010, "The *Huainanzi*: A Guide to the Theory and Practice of Government in Early Han China", *Journal of the American Oriental Society*, No. 2.

Robson, James, 2016, "Distorted Reflections: Cutural Exchange and Mutual Misunderstanding in the Western Appropriation and Translation of the Daode Jing", *The Harmony of Civilizations and Prosperity for All*, Beijing Forum.

Schipper, Kristofer and Franciscus Verellen eds. , 2004, *The Taoist Canon: A Historical Companion to the Daozang*, Chicago: The University of Chicago Press.

Seidel, Anna, 1989, "Chronicle of Taoist Studies in the West: 1950 – 1990", *Cahiers d'Extrême-Asie*, Vol. 5.

Sellmann, James D. , 2013, "The *Huainanzi* and the Essential *Huainanzi* of Liu An, King of Huannan", *Dao*, Vol. 12, No. 4.

Sivin, Nathan, 2011, "A New View of The *Huainanzi*", *China Review International*, No. 4.

Stenudd, Stefan, 2011, *Tao Te Ching: The Taoism of Lao Tzu Explained*, Sweden: Arriba.

Suzuki, Teitaro and Paul Carus trans. , 1906a, *T'ai-Shang Kan-Ying P'ien: Treatise of the Exalted One on Response and Retribution*, Chicago: The Open Court Publishing Co. .

Suzuki, Teitaro and Paul Carus trans. , 1906b, *Yin Chih Wen: The Tract of the Quiet Way*, Chicago: The Open Court Publishing Company Co. .

Venuti, Lawrence, 1995, *The Translator's Invisibility: A History of Translation*, London & New York: Routledge.

Waley, Arthur trans. , 1996, *The Book of Songs*, New York: Grove Press.

Wallacker, Benjamin E. , 2011, "The *Huainanzi*: A Guide to the Theory and

Practice of Government in Early Han China", *Journal of Asian History*, Vol. 45, No. 1/2.

Ware, James trans., 1966, *Alchemy, Medicine, Religion in the China of A. D. 320: The Nei P'ien of Ko Hung*, Massachusetts: the M. I. T. Press.

Watson, Burton trans., 1968, *The Complete Works of Chuang Tzu*, New York: Columbia University Press.

附 录 Ⅰ

《抱朴子内篇·畅玄》新译*

Xuan（玄, the Mystery）Defined

Ge Hong：*Xuan*, the miraculous way of nature, is the origin manifesting the universe and the law determining the presence of this world. It is both intangible and metaphysical. Rooted in nature's deep, the intangible *Xuan* is subtle for us to perceive. Expressed in heaven's high, the metaphysical *Xuan* is miraculous for us to understand. Its power is exhibited in every part of this universe that exceeds our recognition.

Xuan has many external yet physical forms and characters. Its glory may be brighter than the sun and the moon combined while its speed of shaping this world may be faster than lightening. It can be the flashing sunlight or the shooting stars. It can be the unfathomable sea. It can also be the drifting clouds. The being（*You* 有, meaning existence）can be realized via all of those external characters that are physically perceivable by the mind of human beings. The Non-being（*Wu* 无, meaning non-existence）is when *Xuan* presents itself in an internal way and is metaphysically intangible in that it plunges into the abyssal

---

* 鉴于学界对魏鲁男《抱朴子内篇》英译本总体评价不高的缘故，本书作者不揣浅陋尝试新译了其中的《畅玄》《微旨》两篇。为了尽可能多地向西方读者显示中国道教文化的深层内涵，助力读者了解葛洪的修仙思想，英译时译者遵循"语义明晰且行文晓畅"的翻译原则，力求尽可能挖掘原文的应有之义，修正魏鲁男翻译中因过分拘泥于字面理解而导致的一些误译，以及译者在翻译道教核心概念时直接套用基督教文化概念而导致的文化误解，努力实现翻译的文化传真功能。当然，魏鲁男译本行文流畅，遣词造句有许多精妙之处，这些都是新译的"可借之船"，或是得到保留，或是有所借鉴。

bottom or soars beyond the celestial stars. *Xuan* can neither be observed nor defined. It may be the firmest stone. It may also be the softest droplet of morning's dew. It may be round or square, but neither the compass nor the square can be applied to it. In this sense, *Xuan* has no rules, coming and going with no traces left behind, yet it gives the unshakable harmony to the world that heaven is lofty and earth low, that the clouds move and rain is dispensed.

By nurturing the primordial beginning of universe, *Xuan* turns the world into "a being" that sustains the thriving of the livings. It makes the constellations orbit in the universe. It creates the chaotic existence of world. It determines the dawn of time and seasons the weather. It gives vent to its feelings brilliantly despite of the fact that it is aloof from the worldly affairs. As such, *Xuan* suppresses the turbid and promotes the clear, distinguishing the muddy Yellow River from its limpid affluent, the Wei River. The essence of *Xuan* forms the perfect equilibrium in the universe. Not a bestowment or a depredation can glorify or harm this equilibrium, nor can any tithe of additions or withdrawals make it overflow or exhausted. Therefore, the presence of *Xuan* is the foundation for humanity to exist. When such presence is gone, humanity is lost both spiritually and physically.

The dissipation that we lust for is destructive to our sensibility and ethics. For example, the musical instruments that we create and the melodies that these instruments subsequently produce are detrimental to our hearing. The colorful yet majestic robes that we wear and the glorified ornaments that we use are harmful to our eyesight. Festivals and feasts are disruptive to the formations of our appropriate manners and ethics and thus throw our very natures into disorder. And erotic desires will be a gentleman's Achilles heel. Hence only through the realization of *Xuan* can we appreciate the eternal and harmony.

Those who cannot realize the way of *Xuan* will be condemned by the nature even though they could be so powerful that a mere glance of them becomes a potent weapon to kill a person or a slight movement of their lips the key to decide the rise and fall of a nation. Materialistically, these people could be rich and prosperous. Their properties might be vast. They could own great mansions that tower into the sky. They could reside in majestic houses where beautiful drapes could be mistakenly seen as clouds and mists from a far distance. They could have their beauties inside the living rooms and drink to their hearts with golden goblets in the hands. They could feast on the clear and loud music. They could make merry with the accompaniment of dancers. They could pluck fragrant blossoms from gardens abounding in fragrances and toy with red flowers in pools of pearl. They could forget their worries and anxieties in mountain climbing and sightseeing. They could dine in the most glorified chambers and travel in the most luxurious coaches that are drawn by the purest breed of horses. In a word, they could permit themselves in dissipation and abandon the simple life that is the way of *Xuan*. However, things always change under the extreme situation. In this case, a drowning sense of sadness awaits these people once they could not feel the stimulation of materialistic pleasures. So when no music is heard, they could do nothing but sigh, and when a banquet is over, they could sense nothing but sorrow. This is the inevitable end of the law of nature just like shadows and echoes are closely knitted to their sources. The delusional pleasure that materialistic properties can provide will always degrade into an eternal sense of emptiness and sorrowfulness.

While the way of *Xuan* is realized internally, its application is of external character. When applied skillfully, *Xuan* will exhibit its power directly into one's mind. But when such application fails, he will be trapped within his mortal yet fragile body. This is the fundamental logic that guides our interpretation of *Xuan*. When he becomes one with *Xuan*, he will naturally be able to ascend himself to a higher status within society. He will command authority without the courtly prerogative. He will gain unimaginable amount of prosperity. He will no longer be required to present his wealth by attaining priceless assets. Therefore, people who truly master the way of *Xuan* have the capability that is beyond our understanding. They could ride the streams of light and ply the whip to flying rays. They have so miraculous powers that the access to every part of universe is within their palms. They could travel to the zenith of gods' realm or the nadir of devils' underworld at will. They could pass through the grand gate of heaven and wander in the empty vastness. They could saunter and ramble at ease, masking their traces with delusions and miracles. They could ingest the energy of world in flowing clouds. They could be found treading on the rainbow or traveling among the stars. They are ubiquitous and their presence cannot be detected. Such are the people who master *Xuan* internally.

Second to them are the group of contented people who really have the intellectual recognition of *Xuan* and thus know ways of moderation and self-satisfaction. They will not surrender their rationality and dignity to this materialistic world. They will withdraw from the society by becoming hermits in the mountains and forests. They may be poor and humble, but they are righteous and respectable. Their garments may be patched and their belts ropes, but they would not exchange them for all the glory of the imperial robes. They may walk with loads on their backs and use branches for their staffs, but they would not change these for the social cachets of four-horse teams. They will purposely hide their talents so that the cunning world will never be able to manipulate them. They will also deliberately retard their wisdom in order to find peace away from the conspiracy. Keeping a balance between activity and rest, they will always stay happy and content. Abandoning the glories of the official life, they will not adventure into the unknown path that may lead to failures. They will leisurely compose and chant their poems in the mountain's steep as they observe the changes of the world without involvement. They will heartily laugh at the life vicissitude of the aristocrats in the forest's deep without interference. These people sustain themselves through laboring, for they despise the totality of strength that warlords could wield. These people also feed themselves with humble fare, for they have no wants for the lavish feasts of the suovetaurilia. Such an attitude towards the life and world makes them confident and self-assured. Hence, they require no external stimulation for happiness and they see no difference between the powerful and the humble.

These people embrace honesty, simplicity and realness of heart. They lead the simple life and stay uncommitted. They are free from covetousness and worries. Being magnanimous and perfect, they are as natural and honest as the immaterialized and unmanifested creation. Their physical appearance will not be determined by mortal's perception. Being simultaneously dark and bright, murky and pure, quick and dilatory, empty and full, they can be perceived in a contradictory way. Hence, why would these people abandon the social status and power that could be brought to them by their wisdom and competency for the worldly tasks of the unskilled and the unlettered? The answer to this question lies in their characters. People who are blessed by the intellectual recognition of *Xuan* refuse to be caught in the sorrows and joys of a mediocre for sake of any trivialities. They reject the idea of degrading themselves in this way. They are withdrawn from the secular world that they treat earthly matters with a sense of contempt. Their way of life is not influenced by the social reputation. The external environment cannot bend their spirit for seeking honesty and simplicity. They will not be troubled by human relations when embracing the purity of life principles. Nothing in the materialistic sphere of world can loosen the ethics of these people. The temptations of wealth and absolute power will never be able to corrupt them. They will never be intimidated by the violence and brutality of the secular authority. They also will never be triggered by the spread of malicious rumors. Having no thought for life's vexations, they transcend themselves from this troublesome world of treachery and deception.

People who forsake the way of *Xuan* will have absurd standard for appropriate behaviour. They will act without rationality and decency. They might use precious stones to hunt birds for entertainment. They might mouth servile flattery for personal favors. They might climb rotten tree branches for destroying bird's nests. They might also fish in a swift river for food. All of these behaviors could be observed in people who do not appreciate the way of *Xuan*. The absence of *Xuan* in these people will make them prone to detriments. They could fall from grace and power within a day. They could never recover from a personal crisis. These people are always chasing after wealth and power. But in the eyes of the *Xuan*-mastering people, their behaviors are both tragic and pathetic.

That is why the *Xuan*-mastering people choose to hide their talents and wisdom. Discarding the secular wealth and power, they soar freely in the paradise of the immortals and don't have to consciously defend themselves from schemes and intrigues. When they are lower-down inferiors, they fear no loss of properties. When they are higher-up superiors, they feel no remorse of decline. Such people can never be truly approachable, because they are both miraculous and subtle that exceeds our understanding.

附录 Ⅱ

《抱朴子内篇·微旨》新译

The Meaning of Subtlety

Ge Hong: I have been taught that people who share the same value and vision will naturally develop a sense of mutual trust even without communications. In contrast, people who have fundamentally different pursuits will always be suspicious of each other regardless of their sincerity. The social principles that consolidate the functioning of secular world are insignificant matters which can be competently perceived with ease, for the underlying principles are as apparent as the unmistakable difference between the black and the white, or between the heavy and the light. However, people who are in the state of mental confusion are viewing this world with bewilderment. Therefore, if we wish to instruct them about things of immortal beings that are beyond these people's intellectual capacity for recognition, naturally they will falsely react by mocking it as superstitious exaggeration. Their reactions are not new.

People with an adequate vision will be able to see tiniest objects in the dark. However, those who have any impairments to their eyes will fail to grasp the most wonderful sight, though it be the brilliance of the sun and the moon or the towering height of Mount Song or Mount Tai. Yellow Emperor (Huangdi, 黄帝) and Lao Tzu (老子) were two of the wisest sages whose capability and intellects were of infinity. They gained their wisdom from the immortals and produced their miraculous works in the misty mountain's deep. As such, they removed themselves from this mortal world, ascending to the the empyrean for achieving immortality. They were blessed by the divine. Their bodies could be firmer than the metal and stone. Their life span could be much longer than that of the legendary turtles and cranes. Being sympathized with the fact that people of later ages desiring to seek the enlightenment of transcendence would require guidance, they produced classics clearly demonstrating the methods for realizing immortality. People who pursue the divine way of immortality will be rewarded with satisfactory results with their corresponding amounts of dedications and cultivations.

Meanwhile, shallow-minded people have their thoughts and behaviors restricted by the rigid interpretation of traditional values. Thinking infusions of sow thistle or smart weed as sweet, they have no idea of honey and sugar. Preferring the poor wines, they spurn the mellow nectar. Their way of thinking has no room for openness, innovation and comprehensiveness. They know how to value their life but fail to appreciate the concept of maintaining health. They also comprehend the desperation of death but refuse to accept the idea of being immortal. Such paradox is the result of ignorance and arrogance. Hence, they will not control their desire for greasy flesh although they know very well that over-eating will bring them nothing but diseases. They also will not eliminate their lustful characters despite the fact that they understand that dissipation and excessive pleasures will bring them nothing but health detriments. Given that I continuously emphasizes the possibility of achieving immortality, still I could not lend credence to them.

Interlocutor: You have neither the physical signs of divinities nor the powers of performing miracles. Your forehead bears no intertwining patterns symbolizing the three powers and the five phases, nor do strange hairs and fine bones cover your frame. You have not reached the age of the longeval Anqi (安期) or Pengzu (彭祖). Your eyes have never set upon a transcendent, nor have your ears heard of strange tales. How do you know that immortality can be achieved? Are there any evidences? If you claim that you have realized the miracle of immortality internally, or that you obtain a unique view of extraordinary sights, I'm afraid I can't readily accept your view. There is no ground for sound reasoning, just like a person who boasts of the money-making schemes of the millionaire Fanli（范蠡）and the wealthy Yidun（猗顿）when he has insufficient clothes to cover his hide and bare resources to last one day to the next. Naturally it is too inconceivable to receive any praises. The same is true for a sickly person who claims to know much of the medical arts of doctors Yihe（医和）and Qin Yueren（秦越人）, or a defeated general who claims that he understands thoroughly the calculations of the strategists Sunwu（孙武）and Wuqi（吴起）. People do not trust you purely because you have no creditable capacity that can prove the practical existence of the secrets to achieve immortality.

Ge Hong: The ultimate truth of transcendence is beyond the imagination of the mortals. For such truth is infinitely complex that an ignorant mind of the mortal will never be able to handle. Will the insignificant fish in a small pond know the boundless oceans? Will the tiny worm inside a fruit comprehend the infinit universe? Therefore, the mortals, like the creatures of insignificance, have no ability that can facilitate their understanding of a much bigger world. Although I aim to demonstrate the miracle of immortality, these demonstrations will nevertheless be regarded as lies and hearsay by the narrow-minded mortals.

If I was as inapproachable as the immortals, there would be no practical way that the secrets to achieve immortality could be shared among the transcendence-seekers. Supposing my eyes had square pupils and my ears grew from the top of my head, I should mount the clouds and steer a chariot pulled by dragons, and then I should rise above the darting lightning and reach the transcendent world. How would you be able to see me and interrogate me? Even if you could see me, you would then regard me as a heavenly or an earthly deity, something not of the same clan. It will never occur to you that the status of immortality is a learned process!

I merely provide guidance to people sharing the same view and desire no coercive efforts to enforce on people the belief that achieving immortality through learning is of practical reality. Moreover, people tend to believe what they see. If immortals could be found in every household, right under your eyes and standing at your very side, you would never suspect it even if you were slow-witted. Immortals, however, would do their walking in the heavenly palaces once they completed their practices. Then, unless you had psychic powers, you would never obtain the chance to observe immortal beings in person. In this case you will inevitably question the stance that I take in connection with achieving immortality.

People in this mortal world are in accordance with their subjective judgements. They are blindly confident and arrogantly believe that nothing differs from what they personally have experienced. They are parochial that their intelligence is sheathed in a thick scabbard of ignorance. Hence, they can either be stubborn or easily surprised. They refuse to be lectured and will never be enlightened. There is nothing new about it, for this is the norms of mortal beings since the dawn of time.

Interlocutor: Having listened to your instructions frequently, I'm convinced and do not doubt the existence of immortals. Nevertheless, I personally have queries about my competency in training for immortality. Are there any simplified ways?

Ge Hong: The learning of immortality has to be undertaken by a gradual process. With the determined spirit comes the formidable success. Hesitation will always be the grave of any great undertakings. One cannot expect a tree to grow without divelloping its roots. One also cannot expect a stream to flow mightily for thousands of miles if its springs do not run deep. Therefore, a steady progress forms the basis of any great achievements. As such, no affection of the gods will be obtained without accumulating secret virtues; no friendship of the teachers will be won without showing sincerity and loyalty; no official position will be entrusted without making the best endeavors. Likewise, when seeking the essential truth of immortality, there won't be success without the instructions of the bright teachers.

Jiudan Jinye (九丹金液), the elixir of immortality, is the key to one's transcending. However, the elixir is so costly that its availability is greatly limited. Therefore, the first step to the gradual learning of immortality will be cultivating the natural energy internally. Meanwhile, one will be expected to take medicines that are inferior in effects when compared with the elixir of immortality to prolong the life continuance. Concurrently, one can also learn to practice some basic exorcisms, which may be gradually built upon in future for understanding the subtlety of immortality.

Interlocutor: Although there exist various practices for achieving immortality, it is impossible for a person to master all of them. Apart from the elixir, is there an ultimate way, among this variety, that can produce optimal outcomes when learning the subtlety of immortality?

Ge Hong: All of the practices for achieving immortality listed here are mutually complimentary. If you can't learn those of the highest importance, you have no choice but to become widely acquainted with the minor ones, for the effects of these practices cannot be guaranteed when comprehensive adherence is absent. Speaking from a macro-perspective, on the one hand, the learning of immortality is like governing a nation, where not a single one of the many civil or military rites and standards can be dispensed with. On the other hand, the learning of immortality, speaking from the micro-perspective, can also be compared to the artisan's making of a horse carriage, where neither the shafts nor the rims nor the axles nor the hub-locks may be missing. Therefore, people who pursue the secrets of immortality are expected to develop themselves both physically and spiritually so as to safeguard their health from diseases and prolong their lifespans. They are also required to have a firm grasp of the divine capabilities that they will not be prone to the external threats. Being comprehensive is the key to the learning of immortality. An example which illustrates the logic of this argument will be that one cannot play a full musical composition with the last string of a lute. In a similar instance, one also cannot arm himself with a single piece of metal taken from the lorica and helmet. In other words, for either the playing of a composition or the arming of a man, extensiveness and comprehensiveness are fundamental. This is the same for cultivating immortality.

People who have begun the training for immortality need to learn much and experience the essentials in everything pertaining to the nurturing of life. They are required to broaden their horizon and be of polymath to become intellectually well informed, for the study of immortality cannot simply be relied upon a single practice. Moreover, there is always the danger that those who devote themselves to one of these practices would emphasize their personal specialties. Those who are fond of the legendary art introduced by the Daoist goddesses Xuan（玄）and Su（素）[1] may suggest that the Fangzhong Shu（房中术）, a Daoist practice of sexual health, is sufficient for achieving immortality. Those who indulge in the breathing exercise Tuna（吐纳）may also propose that only through expiration and inspiration can their lifespan be extended. In addition, those who know the ancient methods of body bending and stretching Daoyin（导引）may believe that such a kind of calisthenics can prevent them from aging. Likewise, those who have partiality toward herbalism may make the claim that only the nibbling of medicines can free them from exhaustion. Failures in the acquisition of immortality are actually caused by their ignorance and shallowness.

Less experienced people who happen to know one particular thing well will immediately declare it a panacea, whereas those ignorant of the true divine process will continuously pursue other techniques regardless of the potent methods at hand. Their days are lost in wasted effort and they lack certainty about their labors. Consequently the outcomes will never outmatch their devoted efforts. They suffer a double loss.

Ignorance and shallowness always nurture moronic behaviour. People who are only able to acquire the intellects superficially may still arrogantly insist on entering the famous mountains. Some of them may get bitten and wounded by

---

[1] Xuan（玄）and Su（素）are two Daoist goddesses who are said to know much of the Daoist practice of sexual health called *Fangzhong Shu*（房中术）, literally translated as the Art of the Bedchamber).

poisonous insects; others devoured by a tiger or a wolf, or slain by evil spirits. Some may die from hunger for knowing nothing about abstaining from grains (Juegu 绝谷), and the others may die from cold for lacking a method for warming themselves. Wouldn't it be stupid for them to die in the mountains?

It is vital for a learner to choose an adequate master. If a master is not widely-schooled, he would not teach his subject exhaustively. And in the worst case scenario, the said master may even mislead him by lecturing that there is a sole means to reach the state of being immortal. The only occasion that truth is reflected in such lecturing is when the elixir of immortality is freely available to the learner so that he needs no use of the other minor methods. However, the elixir is difficult, if not impossible, to attain. Therefore, why would we give up the opportunity of practicing the minor but beneficial ways for the uncertain access to the elixir? This is comparable to the fact that the necessity for the daily industrious labouring depends on the amount of wealth and fortune in any household. If there is no sufficient amount of wealth for sustaining a decent life, people will have to participate industriously in various types of farming to accumulate abundant stores of fruits and vegetables.

Therefore, people who are determined to appreciate the way of immortality will have to master all of the basic learning so that they will be immune to external dangers. The basics of comprehensive learning may include: abstaining from grains, dodging of weapons, exorcism of demons, practices of detoxication and medication. As such, people who recognize the extensiveness of immortality and learn the basics comprehensively will consequently be invincible. They could subjugate beasts in mountains or dragons in water. They feel no fear when plague strikes and turn invisible when an emergency or a danger occurs. These basics ought to be mastered, though they may be minor matters. How can we then fail to learn things that are more important than them?

Interlocutor: Would you mind listing the taboos for those who wish to attain immortality?

Ge Hong: Essentially, people are prohibited to undertake any practices that can lead to harm and damages. It is unanimously stated in many of the Daoist classics, including *The Inner Commands of the Book of Changes* (*Yi-nei Jie* 《易内戒》), *The Scriptures of Master Redpine* (*Cisongzi Jing* 《赤松子经》), *the Life-Dealing Amulets of the River Chart* (*Hetu Jiming Fu* 《河图记命符》), that crime-recording gods in heaven and earth deprive the sinful of their lifespans in accordance with the extent to which the crimes are committed. As their terms of life decrease, they become poorer and frequently harassed by diseases and disasters. Eventually they will die when no more lifespans are left. Since hundreds of things may give rise to the deprival of their lifespans, it is difficult to make a complete account here.

It is also stated that our bodies are presided over by the Three Corpses (Sanshi 三尸)①. The Three Corpses have no physical forms. They are of supernatural deities. For their own sake, they want us to die prematurely so that they could become the ghosts and move about at will to where sacrifices and libations are being offered. Subsequently, they will ascend to the divine realms on every Geng-Shen Day② (Gengshen Ri 庚申日) to report the sins committed by their hosts to the Director of Fates (Simin 司命) for judgement. In addition, on the last night of every month the Kitchen god (Zaoshen 灶神)③ will also come forth to delate the transgressions of the mortals. The divine deities will then carry out their judgemental duty by having the sinful deprived of their pros-

---

① The Three Corpses (*Sanshi* 三尸) are said to be spirits that preside over the vital functions of a man's body, living respectively in the upper, middle and lower part of the abdomen. They may leave their habitation to bring the Heavenly Master information concerning the sins which they have witnessed at the time of judgment, specifically on the Geng-shen days (Gengshen Ri 庚申日).

② The Gengshen day, a day of judgment in the heavenly courts, is the fifty-seventh of the sixty pairs in the Sexagesimal Almanac, a system paired up by combining alternatively each of the ten Heavenly Stems (Tiangan 天干) of jia 甲, yi 乙, bing 丙, ding 丁, wu 戊, ji 己, geng 庚, xin 辛, ren 壬, gui 癸 with that of the twelve Earthly Branches (Dizhi 地支) of zi 子, chou 丑, yin 寅, mao 卯, chen 辰, si 巳, wu 午, wei 未, shen 申, you 酉, xu 戌, hai 亥 in the Chinese lunar calendar.

③ The Kitchen God watches the events in the house, and his day of reckoning is the last day of every month, called Hui (晦) in Chinese, which can be translated in verbatim translation by "ultimo" in the sense in which the word is used in continental Europe.

perity. If the sins committed were deemed to be severe, the lifespan of the mortals would be significantly shortened by 300 days. In comparison, the punishment that descends on the mortals would be a three-day deduction if the violations are in a minor way. But it is to be noted that all of the things mentioned above are of mystical nature. I cannot provide a thorough elucidation as to the existence of such things because the ways of the supernatural are too obscure to perceive. However, the historical facts that Zhao Jianzi（赵简子）and Qin Mugong（秦穆公）, two of the formidable figures during the Spring and Autumn period（770–476 B.C.）, successfully managed to obtain lordship are the crucial evidences for showing the Heavenly Emperor's power in this mortal world.

All things in the universe have their own spirits and gods. This includes Heaven and Earth（Tiandi 天地）, the biggest things in the universe. Spirits and gods also dwell in mountains, rivers, plants, trees, wells, hearths, water holes, and pools. Even within the human bodies there are some. As such, the spirits of Heaven and Earth, speaking from a theoretical perspective, should recognize the explicit difference between good and evil. Consequently, they should promote goodness within the world by punishing the evilness. Yet in reality, this vast world is essentially loose in organization that it may damn the evil in the long term, not necessarily eradicating all the evilness immediately with the touch of a trigger.

All the moral injunctions of various teachings agree that those desiring immortality must strive to accumulate merits and virtues via the practices of charity. They are expected to be kind and affectionate to everything in the universe, to treat others the way they would like to be treated, to be benevolent even to the multifarious insects, to rejoice in the good fortune of others but commiserate with their sufferings, to help those in distress and those in poverty, not to harm living things, to utter no words that might bring trouble, to look upon the successes and failures of others as their own, not to be proud, nor vaunt themselves, nor envy their betters, nor flatter the crafty and evil. Only in this way can they be of virtue and receive blessings from heaven. Their undertakings are bound to be successful. Consequently they will hopefully ascend to the state of immortality.

Nevertheless, the corresponding punishments are in place in accordance with the judgement of the Director of Fates, and each violation mentioned below constitutes one crime: if they are blood thirsty and prefer slayings; if they are double-faced and say things behind a back that would not be said to a face; if they oppose the upright, oppress the subordinates, deceive their superiors and abandon their obligations; if they show no gratitude for favors received, accept bribes unlawfully; if they hold the right to be wrong and the wrong to be right, sacrifice the public interest for their private advantage; if they inflict punishments on the innocent, destroy others' homes and take their valuables, harm them and usurp their positions; if they bully the sagacious, slay the surrendered, revile the transcendent, harm the practitioners; if they shoot flying birds with pellets, disembowel the pregnant and break eggs, hunt by burning the thickets in spring and summer; if they curse gods and spirits, lure people to do evil, conceal others' virtues, endanger others in order to secure themselves; if they seize the credits of others, destroy their good things and usurp their beloved; if they separate others from their families, disgrace others in seeking victory for themselves; if they borrow full strings of cash but repays with deficient strings; if they cause floods, set fires, cast spells to hurt others; if they oppress the weak, exchange shoddy products for good ones, take or request forcibly, make themselves rich by rapine; if they are impartial, licentious and base; if they bully orphans and widows; if they pick up lost properties but do not return to their owners, or accept charity unreasonably; if they practice deception and falsehood, gossip and betray the secrets of others; if they seek justification through curses and vows; if they borrow and barter but do not return and repay; if they are lustful, disloyal, dishonest, disobedient or disrespectful; if they mock at others' good deeds, destroy others' crops, spoil others' implements, deprive them of the things they require to use; if they provide others with filthy water and food; if they use short cubit, narrow measure, light weight, or small pint in doing their business, or mix the fake with the genuine, and thus take others' wealth by fraud and amass illicit profits; if they stride over the well or the hearth, sing on the last of the month but weep on the first, thus profaning their gods and spirits. If the sins committed were of severity, one's continuance of life would then be permanently terminated.

When the malicious as yet confine his ill will to a thought, the damnation that will descend upon him is as minor as a three days' deduction from his life span. By contrast, any actions that have brought harm to others will cost three hundred days of life continuance for the sinful. Premature deaths of the sinful, caused by suicide, will have disastrous consequences on his offsprings. For the bully and tyrannical, the damnation alone may sometimes not be serious enough so that his family will also have to face the punishments. This would occasionally, although not immediately, lead to the chronic death of the whole family. If the sins committed were not that severe, still they would be continuously haunted by flood, fires, burglaries, and losses of their belongings in the long run, or they would be obliged to provide personally the medication for the district magistrate's illness and meet the costs of the animals for the sacrificial services that will expend all of their filthy lucre. Therefore, Daoism dictates that whoever has wrongly committed killing is bound to be killed by that weapon he had used. If one acquired wealth through improper acts with no fear of creating resentments, it is like eating rotten meat for hunger and drinking poisoned beverage for thirst. It would be true that his hunger and thirst ought to be satisfied, but it would also be obvious that rotten meat and poisoned beverage would eventually claim his life.

What follows are the rules governing atonement for wrongdoings of the past: for people who had wrongly slayed others, thought must be given to rescuing those deserving death in order to absolve the fault; for those who had acquired the filthy lucre, thought must be given to donations for the poor and needy; for those who had wrongly inculpated others, thought must be given to recommending those of high caliber for office. Double efforts are required to compensate for the wrongdoings, which will possibly bring blessings of good luck and profit. This is the way to turn misfortune into good.

If one managed to avoid all the taboos in the process of learning immortality, then he would be awarded with prolonged life expectancy and maximized achievement for Daoist practices. The miraculous character of Heaven（tian 天）makes it omniscient that the duty of judgement will be performed with fairness and righteousness. If one practices goodness unremittingly, he is sure to be rewarded with good fortune. Speaking from a historical angle, there have been countless examples that demonstrate the ethical stance which Heaven takes. For example, Yanghu（羊祜）was a Samaritan that in the last years of his life he was richly rewarded with gold by the divine deity for his selfless charity. Likewise, Caishun（蔡顺）, a filial son, was protected by the miraculous power of the divine during a catastrophic fire. Additionally, when poverty beset, Guoju（郭巨）decided to kill his own son to save food for his elderly parents, which was considered by the divine as an act of filial piety so that he was also awarded with gold. However, it is easier to wrong than to right. Moreover, the fatuous will falsely employ the premature deaths of gifted Xiangtuo（项托）and moral Boniu（伯牛）as examples to show that Heaven is incapable of distinguishing the difference between good and evil. They do not realize that the respectable reputation of a man is not necessarily the sole evidence that he is indeed living up to that reputation; that a reputable man could be hiding dark secrets deep in his closet. Similarly, superficial details cannot be the basis for questioning the miraculous way of nature, which also cannot be taken seriously if one is to learn transcendence. For this reason, people who are not distracted by the ostensible are far more achieving than those who are distracted.

Interlocutor: Unlike in ancient times, we are living in a time that is filled with violent highwaymen and blood-craving bandits. Given the chaos currently experienced by this world, is there a way to ensure the personal safety of secular mortals during the learning of immortality?

Ge Hong: For defending against the raids by highwaymen and bandits one must utilize a certain Daoist practice. This practice involves three steps. Firstly, one must acquire seraphic soil on the Jiayin days (Jiayin Ri 甲寅日)①. Subsequently, the seraphic soil must be mixed with the cedar leaves and sweet grass on the Wei days (Wei Ri 未日)②. And finally, one will need to apply the mixture on the front door so that one's household will be free from the highwaymen and bandits. An alternative that will have the same effect is also available. This alternative requires one to obtain mud from the mountain located in the south of the town's market. Then, on either Suipo days (Suipo Ri 岁破日) or Yuejian days (Yuejian Ri 月建日)③, one will have to make clay from the obtained mud that a statue can be sculptured. Once the sculpturing is completed, one needs to place the statue in the south of one's house that one can cease to be harassed by the highwaymen and bandits. Under emergent circumstances, one will have to remove himself from the danger by taking refuge in safe sites. These safe sites are ubiquitous. They can be found in nations, provinces, shires, counties, towns, neighborhoods, households and even rooms.

Interlocutor: If safe sites are to be found in a room, would it be too small?

Ge Hong: According to the Daoist classics, one can even hide under the carriage when facing extreme danger. In this sense, if a carriage was to be recognized as the safe site, why not a room?

Interlocutor: I've been taught that people seeking immortality should know the locations of two mountains that are vital for the divine enlightenment. Would you school me the secrets of these two mountains?

Ge Hong: There indeed exist two mountains which serve to be the prerequisite of immortality. They are, however, neither observable nor perceivable.

---

① According to the Chinese lunar calendar, Jia-yin days (甲寅日) is the 51th pair of the Sexagesimal Almanac, a system paired up by combining alternatively each of the ten Heavenly Stems (Tiangan 天干) with that of the twelve Earthly Branches (dizhi 地支).

② Wei days (未日), the eighth of the twelve Earthly Branches.

③ Both the Suipo days (岁破日) and Yuejian days (月建日) are considered unlucky days in Chinese lunar calendar.

The only information about the existence of the mountains accessible to the mortals is that they are neither Mountain Hua and Mountain Huo, nor Mountain Song and Mountain Tai①. One is named as Taiyuan (太元, literally translated as Great Beginning), which is beyond our recognition for it is neither in heaven nor on earth. However, it is not so difficult to seek. It is exceedingly steep, rocky and roughly-pathed. It is a place where jade-like wells run deep with clear water that irrigates the mountain without cease, where an administrative force of one hundred twenty celestial guardians coordinate their duties, and trees of life grow luxuriantly and fountains of youth flow from the corners. If one had the enviable opportunity to learn immorality there, then one would personally be an immortal like Wang Ziqiao (王子乔) or Chi Songzi (赤松子).

The second mountain is called Changgu (长谷, literally translated as Long Valley). Looming ever larger and larger, it is filled with fragrances of natural energies. There mysterious breaths blow breeze after breeze while exudates of jade continuously fall. One will find golden pools and crimson rooms in its crevices. However, this is the realm that can only bring death to the ignorant mortals. For the enlightened, however, it is the place for them to gather and take essential emergies, thus acquiring longevity and the ability to fly heavenward.

The secrets are only shared among the ancient sages. Therefore, they deserve your attention greatly.

Interlocutor: I should like to learn the practices that Zhenren (真人, meaning Perfect Man) employ for bodily protection and spiritual refinement.

Ge Hong: It is a quite profound question. Here are the oral directions I received from my late teacher:

"The Sun and the Moon at the beginning of time,
Will combine to nurture the origin of great prime.
From the Jade Pond one will enter the Golden Shrine,

---

① All of them are great mountains of China.

There exists the elixir of immortality that one shall find.

The elixir tastes deliciously fine,

And the loss of it will be a serious crime.

For such crime will undermine

One's learning of bodily refine.

The bending of natural energy one shall fetch,

To the Sombre Gateway one will reach.

The aid of elixir is needed for the glorious flashes,

As it will safeguard our Life Gate against demise.

Alas for the glory of divinity!

How profound is this for the immortal prime!"[①]

The above is the ancient spell that I have learned from my late master. The full comprehension of the spell will make one invincible in the face of external danger.

Interlocutor: I have been taught that the correct application of the Daoist practice of sexual health is the sole means for achieving immortality. Furthermore, it can remove disasters and absolve misdeeds, turn misfortune into good, rise high if in office, double profits if in business. Do the claims made above merit any truth?

Ge Hong: These claims which falsely exaggerate the effects of the Daoist sexual health practice are the products of witchcraft and superstition. The popularity of such deceptive claims among the learners of immortality is caused by manipulations of the ill-intended. What is more, there are the cunning that disguise their crafty lies as "orthodoxy" of the Daoist sexual health practice for profiting their personal gains. This practice has only two observable benefits.

---

① The poem contains several terms that appear in texts related to inner alchemy (neidan 内丹). They are analogies illustrated as follows: the Moon (the right eye), the Sun (the left eye), Jade Pond (the mouth), Golden Shrine (the lungs), Sombre Gateway (the central space between the kidneys), and Life Gate (the lower Cinnabar Field, or a locus in its region), etc.

Firstly, it provides us with immunity against minor ailments. Secondly, it can restore health for the weak and the depressed. In other words, the limitations found within the Daoist sexual health practice make it impossible to dispel misfortune and bring vast wealth and grand status to the mortals, let alone to attain immortality.

It is true that appropriate practice of sexual health can provide us with reasonable degree of immunity against diseases. However, if one unleashed all of his lust, he would gain nothing but health detriments. People who have mastered appropriately the Daoist practice of sexual health will be able to harvest bodily well-being from the intimate contact with the opposite gender. In this way they can have an excellent complexion even in old age and terminate the full number of their allotted years.

People hear the story that Yellow Emperor (Huangdi, 黄帝) achieved immortality by forming sexual intimacy with 1200 women. And hence, they assume that this is the sole reason he attained immortality. Yet what they fail to realize is that he had practiced the ways comprehensively for achieving the transcendence. He had successfully fabricated the elixir of immortality Jiudan (九丹) on Dinghu (鼎湖) at the foot of Jingshan (荆山, in He'nan Province nowadays) before he rose to heaven riding a dragon. Although Yellow Emperor formed intercourse with 1200 women, it is to be pointed out that Daoist practice of sexual health is not the determining factor for his immortality.

Conversely, if one had no knowledge of the Daoist practice of sexual health, he still would not be able to find enlightenment for immortality despite the fact that he might have taken all sorts of medicines and eaten beef, mutton, and pork for nourishment. To prevent us from being lustful, the ancient had sugarcoated the miraculous effects of Daoist practice of sexual health. Therefore, their descriptions are also doubtful after close examination. The appropriate attitude toward this Daoist practice is to metaphorically compare it to fire and water, which is like a double-edged sword. Depending on different ways of application, fire and water can either be life-saving or lethal. In general, one could form as many intimate sexual relationships as he wishes if he has competently mastered this Daoist practice. But if he has not appreciated its wisdom, one or two sexual activity would bring upon him damage and death. The practices introduced by the long-living Pengzu（彭祖）are very important for achieving immortality. Additional practices mentioned in other classics are most likely to be impractical. Anyway, few people can find the effective practice from the redundant narrations. Those who fail to comprehend this will never be able to achieve immortality even when they have access to various medicines of immortality.